WASN'T THAT A TIME

The Weavers,
the Blacklist,
and the
Battle for the
Soul of America

WASN'T THAT A TIME

The Weavers, the Blacklist,

and the

Battle for the Soul of America

JESSE JARNOW

DA CAPO PRESS

Da Capo Press
Hachette Book Group
1290 Avenue of the Americas, New York, NY 10104
dacapopress.com
@DaCapoPress, @DaCapoPR

Printed in the United States of America

First Edition: November 2018

Published by Da Capo Press, an imprint of Perseus Books, LLC, a subsidiary of Hachette Book
Group, Inc. The Da Capo Press name and logo are trademarks of the Hachette Book Group.

The Hachette Speakers Bureau provides a wide range of authors for speaking events.
To find out more, go to www.hachettespeakersbureau.com or call (866) 376-6591.

The publisher is not responsible for websites (or their content) that are not owned by the publisher.

Illustration and print book interior design by Cynthia Young at Sagecraft

Library of Congress Cataloging-in-Publication Data
Names: Jarnow, Jesse, author.
Title: Wasn't that a time: the Weavers, the blacklist, and the battle for
the soul of America / Jesse Jarnow.
Description: First edition. | New York, NY: Da Capo Press, 2018. |
Includes index.
Identifiers: LCCN 2018021085| ISBN 9780306902079 (hardcover) | ISBN
9780306902055 (ebook)
Subjects: LCSH: Weavers (Musical group) | Folk singers—United
States—Biography. | Folk singers—United States—Political activity. |
Folk music—Political aspects—United States—History—20th century. |
Blacklisting of entertainers.
Classification: LCC ML421.W415 J37 2018 | DDC 782.42162/1300922 [B]—dc23

LC record available at https://lccn.loc.gov/2018021085

ISBNs: 978-0-306-90207-9 (hardcover), 978-0-306-90205-5 (ebook)
LSC-C

10 9 8 7 6 5 4 3 2 1

To those who came before,
to those who came after,
and to Jill & Lois

CONTENTS

Prologue

The Loathsome Traveler

February 1952

It was front-page news in Akron, the five men who arrived at the nightclub and sat at the table in the first row, center stage, and silently glowered at the headline act. They were "just ordinary customers," one of the men told a reporter, "with no intentions of starting anything." In the *Beacon Journal*'s photograph, they stare at the stage, beers and ashtrays in front of them, occupied by their appointed roles.

Arraying themselves around the single microphone—three men in tuxedos and a sole woman in a gown—the Weavers certainly didn't *look* dangerous. Nor did the group acknowledge the stone-faced American Legion delegation from the stage, though the folk quartet was surely aware of its presence. In Cleveland, where the chart-topping musicians had performed earlier that week, they were under "constant surveillance by Legion members, police subversive squad members and F.B.I.," the ranking American Legion representative said.

For weeks, the Legion commander and his friends had lobbied the club owner to cancel the band's Akron appearance. The Weavers' manager had flown from New York to discuss the situation, but the Legion members hadn't shown up for a scheduled meeting. The Yankee Inn was nearly sold out.

Looking down on the glum squad from the American Legion as they performed, one or all of the Weavers almost surely—at some point during the performance—closed their eyes and saw flashing, deeply burned images of one of their previous run-ins with members of the veterans' organization: *a gorgeous summer day, a long corridor of trees, late-afternoon sunlight casting through the branches, people screaming, rocks shattering windows, uniformed police officers standing by passively.*

In Akron, the American Legion members almost certainly did not join the singing when the band encouraged the audience to do so. Unable to find anything subversive about their performance, Louis Mancini, the 14th District Legion commander for Summit and Portage Counties, allowed that the Weavers were in fact "good entertainment."

While the military veterans from the Legion didn't start anything that night in Akron, what had been started had been started long ago, not by them, and not by the Weavers. What had reestablished itself in the years after World War II was a long and intricate fissure down the center of American culture, becoming visible in the fog when certain issues illuminated it, a fissure that might be seen throughout the country's history.

The Yankee Inn was merely the latest battlefield in an unceasing clash between deeply set forces locked in philosophical and political and even spiritual combat, manifesting to face off on the physical plane only on occasion. Each side held its own values, its own sense of history, and its own hopes for the American future. With great determination and intention, the Weavers had fought and sung their way to the front lines. In Akron in 1952, the battle raged at its peak, the results seeming to hang in the balance, with the Weavers at the lead of a powerful cultural battalion.

For the previous two years, the quartet had been not only among the most dependable hit-makers on the pop scene but perhaps the most eclectic, filling out an astonishing array of songs with their ebullient four-part harmonies. Their first hit, "Tzena Tzena Tzena," was an English-language arrangement of an Israeli folk dance. Their second and even bigger smash they'd learned from Lead Belly, a former convict and underground folk-music hero. The mournful waltz "Goodnight Irene" became an instant American standard. They'd been in the upper reaches of the hit parade constantly since mid-1950 and their recent Christmas album, an early concept collection, had earned unexpectedly high sales too.

Their newest 78 rpm record at the time of the Akron performance was a typically wide-ranging Weavers pairing. "The quartet comes through in fine style" on the A-side, *The Billboard* noted, an arrangement of an old cowboy song. But the editors raised their eyebrows at the song that backed it, a "strange foreign-sounding folk-tune, with a one-word lyric."

Like Weavers songs before it, "Wimoweh" especially would begin its path to global ubiquity with their version, a shifting chant capped by a soaring and mysterious falsetto melody, not an English word within it. And like the other songs the Weavers brought into the pop and folk canons, few of the arrangements that followed would sound much like the Weavers themselves. As selectors of songs, the Weavers were nearly unparalleled, drawing music from across continents and centuries, then transforming—regularizing—them into standards, from "Goodnight Irene" to the Bahamian sailor song "The Wreck of the John B."

While the multicultural novelty of their choices surely fed their chart success, so did their performances. Backed by pop orchestras, and sometimes fighting their way through strings and horns and choirs foisted upon them by their record company, the Weavers' inventive vocal harmonies cut through—as often did the peculiar ringing sound of a banjo, itself almost as novel in pop music as the songs they performed.

But if they didn't look dangerous, when the Weavers stepped together to sing at Akron's Yankee Inn, the spotlight turned on, their voices joined, one might hear a nearly militant unity in the quartet. This too would be underscored if one attended their recent holiday shows in New York, where the woman in the gown stepped to the front and sang an untranslated Spanish Civil War song in a jolting electric contralto that barely needed a microphone to fill a concert hall. In Akron, the Weavers most likely didn't do "Venga Jaleo," but one might imagine the American Legion clearly receiving the signal even if it couldn't quite decode the message.

"Good entertainment" though they might be, the Weavers' deeper sense of mission was threaded through their music and nearly every intake of breath, a vision of cultural equity and global harmony. To the local newspaper, their banjo player declined to deny any charges that the band were Communists. "When people have asked us, we've said, 'Look, do you like our music?'" he told the reporter. "We're musicians, not politicians. The only platform we can stand on is our songs. Let the people judge."

The American Legion delegation got their news from *Counterattack*, a newsletter that printed the names of alleged Communists in the entertainment field. Often, news traveled slowly in the 1950s, but across right-wing anti-Communist networks it could move with lightning speed.

That same week in Washington, DC, a former employee of People's Songs, the organization that birthed the Weavers, was preparing to testify at a congressional hearing on the topic of Communist Activities Among Youth Groups. He'd sung with them at hootenannies, a fellow harmonizing traveler. The Weavers would be only a small part of his testimony. He hit the circuit of right-wing newspapers, providing a sensationalistic five-day, five-part tell-all.

The day after the Weavers appeared on the front page of the *Akron Beacon Journal*, the hyperactive bow-tied human named Harvey Matusow took the stand in a Washington, DC, hearing room and—amid a torrent of names named—identified the Weavers one by one for the permanent record of the House Un-American Activities Committee. For Matusow, it was the beginning of a storied career as a professional ex-Communist that would land him in the national news constantly for the next half-decade.

"There was Pete Seeger," Matusow said. To the American Legion members in Ohio, he was the banjo player, the skinny, kinetic Weaver who tilted his head back and sang in a soaring voice capable of reaching ecstatic high notes.

"Will you spell the last name?" the Committee asked.

"S-e-e-g-e-r," Matusow told them. "He was a member of the Weavers, and he had also been a member of the Almanac Singers, People's Songs, and the Progressive Party and the Communist Party."

He named Freddie Hellerman, too, the guitarist in the Weavers, the younger male of the group, with a high forehead and a sharp jawline.

"H-e-l-l-e-r-m-a-n," Matusow told the committee. "He had been a member of the Communist Party in Brooklyn College in New York, was very active in the American Folksay Group of the [American Youth for Democracy], and later very active in People's Songs, People's Artists, and in the Communist Party."

The woman, whose crystal voice had shot over the heads over the American Legion two days earlier, was "Ronnie Gilbert," Matusow informed the committee. "She was the only feminine member of the Weavers group and was very active in People's Songs, People's Artists, and she had done a lot of volunteer work, as I recall it, at the defense of the 11 Communist leaders during that trial in New York and had attended Communist Party meetings."

"The last is Lee Hays," Matusow said. "H-a-y-s." The large Arkansas man who acted as the group's rumbling bass singer seemed older than his thirty-seven years. "He had dropped out of the Communist Party at the time I had known him, but was still in the good graces of the

Communists," Matusow told the congresspeople. "For some reason, they said, 'He just isn't the kind of person we can discipline in party discipline, but he is very helpful to us.'"

The Weavers provided entertainment at Communist "hootenannies" and "whing-dings" in Washington Square Park, Matusow asserted with stunning inaccuracy, attracting impressionable youth by singing their future hits like "Goodnight Irene" and "On Top of Old Smoky." The names of the organizations he spouted were accurate, the invisible lines between them leading directly to the formation of the Weavers. But aside from that, the information the twenty-five-year-old Matusow passed to the committee was either utterly bogus or distorted beyond reason, sometimes comically so, a yarn tailored to the demands of the white men asking the questions.

As with everything to do with the Red Scare of the 1950s, the truth was far more complicated than either side presented. Both cloaked their language in the nuances and colors of the ongoing battle occurring almost always just off-screen, in the imagination of American citizens, each a miniature battlefield in the evolving shape of American democracy.

The day after Harvey Matusow testified against the Weavers in Washington, the Yankee Inn canceled the final four nights of the band's scheduled appearance. "They played to a full house for the first time on Wednesday," the club owner told the paper, as if he didn't fully understand what had happened. "The public seems to be completely unpredictable in this affair."

The unofficial but very real blacklist lurched downward on the Weavers. In fact, the band had been served their own committee subpoenas before Harvey Matusow had even testified. Indistinguishable from a torrent of harassment they'd already received, they were unsure if the legal documents were even real. Their manager was looking into it.

What the loathsome traveler Harvey Matusow told the committee wasn't anything new. Their files on the Weavers ran deep, provided by the Federal Bureau of Investigation, a paper trail connecting back to the beginning of the previous decade, long before there was a Weavers. The committee knew all about them. But the House Un-American Activities Committee hadn't started this either.

The battle's infinite fronts twisted into the past and projected into the future. But even the coordinated info war that conflated progressive left-wingers with dangerous subversives was only one manifestation, the various government divisions having no more agency than the American Legion representatives in the front row at the Yankee Inn. Down the fissure, the two sides faced off as if against a mirrored window, seeing as much of themselves as their opposites, and looking for the hidden passageway across, a quest of exploration that continues into the twenty-first century.

In many regards, it was clear the government's interdepartmental understanding was still no better than that of the first agents they'd sent into the field. But it was also clear that, when the Weavers opened their mouths and their voices combined, something was added to the air forever. And while maybe the committee couldn't tell where or how, the Weavers had found a way across the divide.

If one is to take the committee at their word, both they and the Weavers shared a common interest and belief in the power of song. Even if the committee never understood its own inquiry as a technological question about how the world might *actually* be changed through music, it would still behoove what remains of them, their associated agencies, and their ignoble ghosts to understand exactly how—despite the committee—the Weavers came to arm their music and transform the world anyway.

CHAPTER ONE

The New Situations

May 1943

Agent Harwood E. Ryan left the base and crossed the harbor through a panoramic view of lower Manhattan and Ellis Island and the Statue of Liberty, and stepped into Greenwich Village's side streets, pursuing information about the Subject. At a West Village walk-up, Ryan ascended the narrow stairs to the fourth floor and found himself face-to-face with a short, wiry man with wiry hair. Ryan had every reason to believe this man had useful background information.

The United States was a year and a half into its involvement in World War II and, down in Mississippi, the rest of the Subject's company had already shipped out. But the army had lingering questions about whether the recent inductee might rightly be considered *subversive*, if he could be entrusted to repair battle-ready airplanes, and so he was kept on American soil, doing menial work in the Southern heat.

The man with the wiry hair was the recipient of correspondence with the Subject, and one of many leads the Counterintelligence Corps was pursuing, paperwork and agents fanning out from field offices and through inter-bureau channels. They read the Subject's mail and invented a pretext under which to interview the Subject's father, an eminent scholar in the nation's capital.

The week before, Agent Laubscher had crisscrossed New England, inter-viewing the Subject's high school teachers. Other agents were on the case in other jurisdictions, but Agent Ryan's lead on Charles Street was the best so far, having worked with the Subject most recently.

At Keesler Field in Mississippi, it hadn't taken long for Pvt. Peter Seeger to be reported as a potential subversive. On the base, his fellow soldiers had quickly nicknamed the young musician "New York," and it was easy to see why. At age twenty-three, Seeger plunged into the world as he thought it should be. It came partly from privilege, but also the ability to see the injustice of its opposite. He spoke as if he'd attended a prestigious university, which he had. That he'd dropped out after his freshman year made little difference.

"Badly pimpled face and rather prominent red nose," the confidential War Department memo said of the six-foot-four-inch Seeger. Officially, he was under investigation for "disaffection," but that hardly described Pete Seeger. Several interview subjects mentioned Seeger's prodigious banjo skills, and that much was true.

A few months after Seeger arrived, his superiors received notice from the FBI office in San Francisco about a particular letter Seeger had sent. The American Legion had announced their support of a motion to deport all Jap-anese citizens following the presumed defeat of Japan.

"I felt shocked, outraged, and disgusted," Seeger wrote to the organiza-tion of veterans. "We, who may have to give our lives in this great struggle— we're fighting precisely to free the world of such Hitlerism, such narrow jingoism . . . America is great and strong as she is <u>because</u> we have so far been a haven to all oppressed." The American Legion forwarded the letter to the FBI, and the FBI forwarded it back to the base in Mississippi.

Concern for racial equality was precisely the kind of danger sign that set antennae a-twitch. The year before, Martin Dies, then chairman of the House Un-American Activities Committee, had observed that "throughout the South today subversive elements are attempting to convince the Negro that he should be placed on social equality with white people, that now is the time for him to assert his rights." These subversive elements were connected to foreign powers, Dies and others suggested.

If that weren't enough for Seeger to be suspected of enemy sympathies, he had received correspondence on stationery belonging to the Japanese-Amer-ican Committee for Democracy, from his half-Japanese girlfriend, Toshi Ohta. Never mind that her father was working for the army as an unofficial diplomat.

Now, in New York, Agent Ryan pieced together the mystery of Seeger. None seemed to think he was any kind of imminent threat. The latest was the wiry-haired man Ryan interviewed. "The Subject is not an overthrower, but he is out to win the war," Ryan summarized in his report.

The wiry-haired interviewee was a musician too, Ryan noted, employed with Seeger in a group called the Almanac Singers. According to this man, these Almanac Singers (as Agent Ryan duly recorded) "slept on freight trains, under bridges, in churches, and so forth" and wrote and sang "hillbilly songs and ballads" in union halls. In the interviewed man's estimation, Seeger was the most original lyricist of the bunch.

A picture of the Subject was starting to emerge: well organized, motivated, a bit awkward, but possessing an always-moving mind. "Brilliant," Ryan's interviewee stressed.

And also perhaps almost completely guileless. When Seeger had been called in for his own interview he'd asked in his high-spoken manner why *hadn't* he been deployed? He'd explained firmly that the Japanese-American Committee for Democracy *opposed* the Japanese government. Albert Einstein was one of their sponsors.

The initial report concluded, "From all indications, Subject has no idea that anything he has done or any associations he might have had in the past or might have at the present time would be cause to hold him on this field or keep him under surveillance at any time."

But under surveillance he was. In New York, Ryan had more subjects to interview. The wiry-haired man on Charles Street provided some good leads. Agent Ryan didn't think the man was misleading him, but during the interview observed something amiss and noted it in his report.

Hanging on the wall of the apartment was what Ryan described as a "large guitar" containing the inscription THIS MACHINE KILLS FASCISTS. To Ryan, this confirmed beyond doubt that the Almanac Singers—both Seeger and perhaps this wiry-haired man—were Communists. If there was one thing Communists hated, it was Fascists.

This W. W. Guthrie had been truthful "as far as he went," Ryan noted, but the agent suspected "he knew a great deal more about the Subject's politics and activities than he admitted." Certainly, thirty-one-year-old Woody Guthrie also knew the drill, and what he should or shouldn't say when someone came 'round askin' questions 'bout his good buddy Pete.

Seeger's former landlord, on the other hand, was ready to grumble. They were a "noisy and troublesome crowd," Bernie Schultz said. A woman named

Bessie Lomax had appeared, signed a lease, and they'd taken over the two-room apartment at the back of the disused office building across from the Jefferson Market Courthouse on Sixth Avenue. "Disreputable, no account type of individual[s]," Schultz called them. He suspected two of them of being Oklahomans.

Schultz told the agent that Seeger was the group's leader. But really, he was "just as erratic as the other members," the landlord concluded. "He stood out only because he had more education."

Over at the Village Vanguard, the basement club on Seventh Avenue, Special Agent Harwood E. Ryan interviewed impresario Max Gordon. One of the two integrated nightspots in Manhattan, along with Café Society (where Billie Holiday had debuted "Strange Fruit"), the Vanguard was an eclectic home for bohemian culture beginning in 1935, including a six-month residency by the black folk-singing duo of Josh White and Lead Belly.

Sure, the club owner told Ryan, he'd hired the Almanac Singers a few times. But they were too left-wing for the club. "Gordon considered [Seeger] to be the most interesting person of the aggregation," Ryan recorded, and one can just about hear the club owner sigh through decades of bureau paperwork about how it was too bad that Seeger was so committed to political music, and if only he could hire him for some other purpose. But Gordon liked the Almanacs. They were harmless.

Gordon pointed out to Agent Ryan, as well, that the Almanac whom he had previously interviewed—Woody Guthrie—was likewise the author of the recent memoir *Bound for Glory*, at that very moment en route up the best-seller list. "Woody is just Woody," novelist John Steinbeck said in praise of the book, part fiction but all Guthrie.

Back at the base on Governors Island, Ryan finally received the files pertaining to the Almanac Singers, provided by G-2, the army intelligence division, and it seemed to confirm what he suspected. Clippings abounded from the *Daily Worker*, the Manhattan-based Communist newspaper. They'd sung songs of *peace*, another topic that only Communists made a cause in the early 1940s. According to the report, one song was called "Get Out and Stay Out of the War." Another was titled "Jim Crow." The Almanac Singers attempted to "stir up resentment for . . . the entry of the United States into the war."

It wasn't exactly an incorrect conclusion for Special Agent Harwood E. Ryan to draw, familiar and comfortable as he was with the American security apparatus. As it happened, only two days before Ryan began his Seeger assignment, FBI Chief J. Edgar Hoover himself had called an end to his own search for the Almanac Singers. Special Agent Ryan hadn't been the first to investigate Pete Seeger, either.

In his Washington office, Hoover still wasn't happy. The Almanac Singers' 78s were now collectors' items, Hoover's agents had been told when they finally tracked down the tiny independent label that had issued them from a record store just off Times Square. But the agency's copies broke somewhere along the line. "See to it that records are more carefully packed, in order that incidents of this type will not reoccur," Hoover harrumphed into the margins of the report.

With or without the remains of the 78, the FBI filed the group's music under "Gramophone Records of a Seditious Nature." But—as Woody Guthrie and Keynote Records' owner told the agents—by 1943, the Almanac Singers were defunct, diffused, defused. In the years to come, there would be plenty of mythologizing, not least of which would come from the many Almanac alumni. But perhaps even more mythologizing—and more testimony to the power of their music—came from the government agencies intent on tracking them down.

The 10-inch record and organization that J. Edgar Hoover sought information about began with a knock on the door in late 1940. Outside the New York apartment was Pete Seeger. Inside was the person Seeger sought: Lee Hays, a twenty-six-year-old Arkansas man as tall and round as the twenty-one-year-old Pete was tall and scrawny. When it opened, it marked the beginning of the path to the Weavers.

Had Seeger stayed at Harvard, he might have graduated in the spring of 1940, and on an alternate timeline would have been establishing his first postgraduate employment alongside classmates like John F. Kennedy. Having spent the intervening years traveling the country, playing and studying music while working occasionally at the Library of Congress, Seeger's latest project was to assemble and publish a collection of labor songs.

Hays had arrived in Manhattan only weeks before on exactly the same mission. The son of a Methodist minister, it would often be said—sometimes by Hays himself—that he'd spent time as a preacher, though it wasn't true, exactly. With a booming voice and genial Southern politesse, Hays could engage an audience with an authority that Seeger admired. A former protégé of radical Presbyterian minister Claude Williams, Hays had helped organize the wonderfully acronymed Southern Tenant Farmers Union and led songs at the experimental and progressive Commonwealth College in the Ozarks. He charmed Seeger with a deeply learned Southern wit delivered with impeccable quiet timing, each punch line seemingly coiled with shared secret knowledge.

Lee Hays had witnessed the worst of the Depression firsthand, an entwining of personal and economic circumstances. Alongside an "early religious brainwashing," it left Hays with wounds from which he'd spend his lifetime trying to recover. The scars of his upbringing would never fully heal.

After his father died in a grisly car crash when Hays was thirteen, his mother's mental health deteriorated almost instantly. Unable to attend college as his older siblings had, the sixteen-year-old Hays hitchhiked the country.

"If I didn't get a ride for a day or two going east, I'd go to the other side of the road and go west," he would recall. "It didn't make much of a difference so long as you kept moving, always hoping for work, for anything to happen. And some good things did happen."

The best of those was unquestionably when his older brother secured Lee a job as a page in the Cleveland Public Library. "The system faced such an imminent breakdown that it could have gone in any direction, depending on who came forward," Hays would recall of the darkest Depression years.

It was in the Cleveland Public Library that Hays radicalized himself. "Every book that was unfit for children to read was stamped [and] I'd go through the stacks looking for books that were stamped," Hays said. First he found saucy British novelist D. H. Lawrence, but soon made his way into more political writing, notably muckraking journalist Upton Sinclair. "It was like doors opening," he would remember, doors that led out of the fundamentalist South. Lee would spend a full four years absorbing books and small-circulation magazines.

He'd already been a contrarian before his father's death and the Depression cleaved his family. He could feel the uncomprehending anger around him as rival political ideologies duked it out on street corners, in bars, and workplaces. "Somewhere along in there I became some kind of Socialist," he would say. "Just what kind, I never have figured out."

As a Hays-ism, it inevitably made the more reserved Pete Seeger smile, a one-liner smoothed with writerly precision to communicate deeper beliefs. Like Seeger, Hays believed unequivocally in the power of music. *Art was a weapon*, Hays learned, after the library led him to Commonwealth College. But it was more than that, he found.

Over Christmas 1938, when Hays was twenty-four, he and friends from Commonwealth had road-tripped to Tulsa to entertain striking oil workers. They presented "zipper plays," ready for local causes to be zipped into the loose scripts. There was a large puppet dragon representing capitalism that breathed actual fire. And on the way home, they found themselves puttering through Arkansas in the middle of the night in the deepest, meanest, racist South in an unreliable and easily recognizable car with an integrated passenger load.

To soothe jangled nerves and get themselves home, they sang hymns. "As we drove along," Hays remembered "harmonies swelling and breaking . . . all the voices searching, working for harmonies unheard and unknown, perfect blends of tones and feelings and fears."

For Lee, already adept at leading groups in song, it was revelatory. "What mattered was that we were singing," he figured out, offering their voices to each other.

In New York, Hays made another discovery: someone he could almost effortlessly sing with. Not only that, but he and Pete could trade songs, and rewrite them themselves. Together, the two tapped a rich vein, enough to put aside the proposed songbook.

The history of radical songs stretched back as far as the invention of songwriting, as far as the two could see. Union songs had sent them on their quests, often old melodies set to new and varying words. But there was also the deeper wellspring of American music that lay behind the songs, to which both were likewise drawn. Lee had connected to it listening to Emma Dusenbury on her porch back in the Ozarks, and Pete had his ears opened at the Mountain Dance and Folk Festival in Asheville, North Carolina, in 1936, where he'd met the great banjo player Bascom Lamar Lunsford.

In exchanging repertoires, Pete and Lee began to construct an alternate history of the United States, a narrative of melodies linked like a river system, both of them equally interested in hunting for the source as riding the rivers to where they might run. There were the parodies of the Wobblies—the Industrial Workers of the World—collected in the *Little Red Songbook*, many designed to drown out Salvation Army street bands. Most notable among them were the songs of Joe Hill, the Swedish-born songwriter hanged in 1915 for a crime he most likely didn't commit. There was a small repertoire from the international Abraham Lincoln Brigade who fought the Fascists in the Spanish Civil War in the late '30s. From West Virginia came "We Shall Not Be Moved," an old hymn refit to new use by striking miners. And there were the songs of Sarah Ogan Gunning and Aunt Molly Jackson, half sisters and songwriters from Kentucky coal country.

Though Seeger and Hays would sing and work from their own complex ideologies and personalities, their shared recognition of an intangible and powerful musical mother lode would keep them connected through the next four decades. Actively looking for new songs and new causes, it was a history they would soon sing themselves into. Quickly, Seeger was crashing with Hays and his roommate most nights.

Hays was instantly astonished at Seeger's innate musicality and remained so for the rest of his life. "I could change and improvise and ad lib and Pete would be right behind me," he remembered decades later. "Take a song like 'State of Arkansas,' which you're never quite sure if it's major or minor and I could turn it into a major or minor feeling at any point knowing full well that Pete would be right there."

Even so, the two continued to find new ways to be opposites over the decades of their relationship. Whereas Pete was *all* music, Hays could talk endlessly. Lee's tumultuous existence had left him both vulnerable and capable of an emotional intimacy far beyond Pete's.

Seeger had been struggling to find gigs. Alan Lomax, his old boss at the Library of Congress, and sometimes a big-brother figure, had gotten him work as a banjo player on CBS radio. But Seeger hadn't cut it. Though Pete was getting less shy onstage, Hays made a perfect foil, as influenced by the fiery rhetoric of Claude Williams as the vaudeville routines of Doc Rockwell, alongside his minister father. Seeger got the duo their first booking, at the Jade Mountain Chinese restaurant in the East Village in December 1940, and gave the $2.50 payday to Hays in its entirety. "You need it more than I do," Seeger told him.

The new singing group made its big stage debut, still unnamed, at Turner Arena in Washington, DC, and premiered the song that would launch the FBI's subsequent investigation. Powered by the high-pitched silver-toned flash of Pete's banjo, a sonic and visual novelty also guaranteed to cut through crowd noise, the soon-dubbed Almanac Singers received a thunderous ovation at the American Youth Congress for one song, especially.

The origins of "Ballad of October 16th," its first performance, and its reception encapsulates the story of the Almanac Singers. The line that won the applause, and that would echo back to them in unpredictable and destructive ways, was penned by Lee's roommate and the expanding group's third member, Millard Lampell: "I hate war and so does Eleanor, but we won't be safe 'til everybody's dead."

The reasons for the rhyme's explosiveness in the context of 1941 were numerous, but the reasons for its effectiveness as a piece of music stemmed almost entirely from the songwriter Lampell was slavishly imitating. For Lampell, like perhaps millions to follow, discovering Woody Guthrie wasn't merely discovering the songs of the Oklahoma-born guitar slinger, but an attitude.

Pete's mentor on a cross-country hitchhiking adventure the previous summer, Woody had blown into town filled with songs and advice and inspiration just after Pete and Lee had started singing together with Lampell. Any song at all could be disassembled and rewritten at will, Woody impressed upon them, for whatever (or no) reason at all. Songs could be weapons, sure, or tools of reassurance and solidarity, but they could also be fleeting objects of play, made to be whatever the moment wanted. And within weeks, Guthrie was off to the West Coast again.

It was an irreverent songwriting strategy that perfectly appealed to the bubbling squad of young progressives. They would and could be useful up-to-date singers, ready to serve worthy causes on a moment's notice. They found inspiration in newspaper headlines, the newspaper of choice unquestionably the Communist Party organ the *Daily Worker*. But as Lee pointed out, the *Worker* was easily the best paper in New York, covering local and global news events from race and class angles that other dailies ignored. It was certainly the only paper in town to offer regular coverage of the Louisiana-born musician Huddie Ledbetter, known as Lead Belly. Plus, as Lee pointed out, the *Worker* had the best sports section too.

The Almanac Singers' early rent parties at their Union Square loft with friends like Lead Belly, Burl Ives, Josh White, and Aunt Molly Jackson often constituted the whole of the New York folk scene as it existed. Even if politicized folk music was a relatively new phenomenon in early 1941, the Almanac Singers came into existence as part of a fertile cultural scene that stretched far past music. The Popular Front had been so named by the Communist Party, but from a cultural perspective it had even deeper roots.

Positing a unified force against the fascism creeping over Europe, the Popular Front championed the importance and history of culture across race and class lines, celebrating the power of the worker. In the United States, the Congress of Industrial Organizations (CIO) became the center of American labor in the mid-1930s, anchoring a swirl of art and theater and literature and music deeply entwined with both Franklin D. Roosevelt's Works Progress Administration and the American Communist Party.

It was exactly the type of broad mission that might grab a teenager with a seemingly unlimited capacity for folk music. Shuffled off to boarding school at the young age of four after his parents divorced, Pete Seeger had a subscription to the Marxist literary journal *New Masses* by age fourteen. An aloof adolescent who would stay aloof into adulthood, Pete could often seem emotionally distant even to close friends despite his boundless enthusiasm and general warmth.

Being an Almanac Singer was a job that Pete Seeger was virtually born into. His father, the avant-garde composer Charles Seeger, had pioneered dissonant counterpoint and almost single-handedly invented musicology. A Communist in the utopian early days of American communism, even before the Russian Revolution, Charles was part of the elite Composers' Collective, attempting to write radical twelve-tone music for workers' choruses. Folk music would arrive like a controversial new technology.

"Communism Is Twentieth-Century Americanism," ran the American Communist Party's amorphous new slogan, and Pete joined the Young Communist League when he turned eighteen. At the same time as generation-destroying atrocities unfolded in the Soviet Union, the American Communist Party opened itself as a powerfully antiracist pro-labor entity, arguably the most visible and well-organized outlet for any American of a progressive political persuasion in the late 1930s, establishing social clubs in many communities.

Though the Popular Front was officially abandoned as a party policy in 1939, its influence was incalculable on a generation of American artists, writers, musicians, actors, filmmakers, and cultural workers of all varieties, whether Communist Party members or not. As it happened, the reason for the Popular Front's official abandonment is precisely what made the Almanac Singers' "Ballad of October 16th" so contentious: Joseph Stalin and Adolf Hitler's shocking nonaggression treaty. Party members were now to be "pro-peace," as the American Communists spun it, putting them in alignment with right-wing groups like the anti-Semitic America First isolationists.

Many, like Woody Guthrie, continued to view the Communists as the only political party with a committed working-class stance. As Hitler's forces ravaged Europe, the party line continued to push for peace, framing war as a Capitalist ruse. When Millard Lampell retrofit the cowboy ballad "Jesse James" with his new antiwar lyrics for its debut at the American Youth Congress, it was for an audience well versed in the nuances of contemporary politics.

"We are in the peace army," Lee Hays declared to the *Daily Worker* in March 1941, the beginning of the paper's long love affair with the group. "Remember that a singing army is a winning army." It was to be a ragtag army.

"Like roving reporters they are on the scene—wherever things are happening," the *Worker* enthused a few months later.

If Lee Hays and Pete Seeger often shared political stances and the dream of a singing labor movement, it wasn't because Hays was a Communist. It was less that he disagreed with Communists than that he disagreed with political parties, and oftentimes, it seemed, just about everybody else. Too much of a constant question-asker to stick to any rigid discipline, it was Lee's constant analysis that side-tracked many an Almanacking session as he disassembled arguments and song lyrics and life in his slow Arkansas drawl.

Hays found the whole notion of the Almanac Singers being a Communist front to be fairly laughable. "I can't remember that anybody ever issued any orders," he would say much later, "certainly not to the Almanacs, that independent bunch of stubborn people. They would not have been subject to orders from anybody. They couldn't even give themselves orders." Still, they were embedded deep inside the Popular Front and the machinations of the party. Novelist and *Daily Worker* columnist—and longtime Seeger hero—Mike Gold could sometimes be found jamming on recorder at the rent parties.

A folk rumble started around New York. On West Forty-Fourth Street, a tiny record store called the Music Room distributed hard-to-find 78s from around the world, almost certainly including Woody's new *Dust Bowl Ballads* on New Jersey's Victor Records. Sensing an emerging new market, Victor had started reissuing recordings of the Carter Family, Uncle Dave Macon, and the Monroe Brothers. That year, as well, Alan Lomax issued his first field recordings from the American South.

The Music Room's owner was well acquainted with left-wing music. A former treasurer for the Communist magazine *New Masses*, Eric Bernay had issued a world-famous-among-the-left collection of Spanish Civil War songs in 1940 and, later in 1941, would put out Josh White's *Southern Exposure: An Album of Jim Crow Blues*. Though Bernay released *Songs for John Doe*, the Almanac Singers' triple 78 debut, he could sense something even more dangerous about it, making the group finance themselves, and removing his own label's name from the packaging, each side receiving a sticker that simply read "Almanac Record."

"Within a few weeks, the Almanacs' record was known from coast to coast in this narrow circle of leftwingers, and peaceniks of one sort or another,"

Seeger would remember. The result was shocking, even to a longtime progressive like Eric Bernay. *Songs for John Doe* was a live wire, transubstantiating controversial political positions instantly into humor and catchy music.

The Almanac Singers had their calling card, and a budding career. In May, they sang at Madison Square Garden, delivering their pro-union, antiwar songs for 20,000 members of the Transport Workers Union and their families. "Talking Union," started by Hays and Lampell and finished up by Seeger on the fire escape of their loft one afternoon a few weeks earlier, was an instant crowd favorite.

Pretty soon, Woody Guthrie was back from the West Coast, and ready for life as an Almanac Singer. Told of imminent Almanac plans to head for California, Guthrie was more than happy to head back, if that's where the action was going. They recorded more music, less-controversial collections of union songs and sea chanteys, and bought a car with the proceeds.

One Sunday in late June, while a rent party was in full swing, a friend arrived with the news that the Nazis had invaded Russia. Stalin's pact was off. Peace was out, war was in.

A massive chunk of the Almanac Singers' repertoire expired in a flash. They'd written songs to serve a moment, and the moment was not only over but had changed far more drastically than any of them could have conceived. It wouldn't be for many years but Seeger, especially, would express deep regrets for his support of Stalin's Russia, though never the broader dreams of the age. He was a Popular Fronter for life, he would always say, the music carrying all the ideas he believed in.

Perhaps 78s were exactly the wrong medium for the Almanac Singers' headline songs. Out in the world, now, the records had their own lives, artifacts and by-products of the Almanacs' new method of songwriting. It was music not meant to be fixed, but they missed the moment to explain that. The 78s zigzagged across the country, eventually breaking free of left-wing circles in most unexpected ways. When the record made it to the White House, even folk-enjoying Franklin D. Roosevelt couldn't see the humor, wondering briefly if he could arrest the Almanacs somehow. Eric Bernay destroyed his remaining stock. The band needed new songs, of course. That wouldn't be a problem.

Woody Guthrie, who knew the ephemerality that went along with rewriting songs, devised his own commentary, a parody called "On Account of That New Situation." He would never record it. He might have known better, anyway, its only lyrics remembered in fragments by ex-housemates, and perhaps teaching them another lesson in the process. Just because a song needs to be made up, it doesn't always need to be set down.

A cross-section view of the first building known as Almanac House, at 130 West Tenth Street, in early autumn 1941, panning down from the roof toward the street. Two windows wide, there is a firehouse next door.

In a small third-floor bedroom, Pete Seeger, practices banjo relentlessly, perhaps waking up anyone who'd crashed in the guest bed across the hall the night before. "He would get up in the morning, and before he'd eat or anything, he'd reach for the banjo and begin to play, sitting on his bed in his underwear," Millard Lampell told writer David King Dunaway many years later.

In the second-floor bedroom, just below Seeger, is Woody Guthrie with his own portable turntable, setting the needle back to the beginning of a record, copping licks and vocal moves from blues 78s.

Just under Woody's room, in the kitchen at the back of the ground floor, Bess Lomax is glaring up at the ceiling, listening to Woody restart his Blind Lemon Jefferson records over and over and over again and a bit frustrated that she's more or less been expected to clean up after the men.

Out in the front room by the street is the office, where various Almanacs wander through to check the bulletin board operated by the studious Seeger. The group has expanded, and don't all live together, but meet nearly every night for performances on what they dub "the subway circuit," bouncing from union meeting to fund-raiser to house party, never quite getting paid as much as would be useful. The money is communal.

Life in the different corners of Almanac House blends together, most especially around the custom extra-long table and matching benches that seat fourteen. As at the old loft, Lee Hays is the cook, baking many loaves of bread at once, stewing stews, and overseeing the kitchen with a quietly overbearing Southern presence.

Arriving at the front door is the "nice young man" from the Communist Party's Bronx headquarters, showing up for what Seeger remembered as hapless weekly sessions where he "tried to guide us in learning a little bit more about dialectical materialism." While the Almanacs' utopian goals remained undiminished and Seeger's mission remained straight-ahead, the nice young man inevitably exited Almanac House somewhat disappointed.

Sure, the Almanacs promised to keep up with the latest in the *Daily Worker*. Other concerns would always be more pressing, though, like paying the rent and keeping the place heated. They weren't excelling at those either.

Different Almanacs had different strategies for dealing with bookings. Once, Woody beat Lee to the phone, and Lee overheard Guthrie's end of the conversation: "Lady, the Almanacs sing for nothing *but* worthy causes, and they pay."

Pete did almost all of the proper office work anyway. In fact, Pete Seeger had a secret. Officially becoming a member of the Communist Party earlier in the summer, Seeger had committed an act of defiance that Robert Cantwell would compare to burning a draft card in the '60s. Joining likely as a show of solidarity following Hitler's invasion of Russia, American communism had started moving itself underground, surrendering to the creeping paranoia of the landscape they saw coming. Pete Seeger, twenty-two and ready to sing down any comers, saw a very different horizon. He was happy he didn't have to reconcile the Party with Stalin's peace pact anymore.

Much as they would have liked to forget it, though, the Almanac Singers' *Songs for John Doe* twanged onto the national radar that summer, while they were on a shoestring cross-country tour of union halls. Even the *Daily Worker* had touted the collection as "pretty seditious stuff," though it did so almost admiringly. An article in the *Atlantic* titled "Poison in Our System" called the album "strictly subversive and illegal." It was "a matter for the Attorney General," the magazine wrote. It had only been a matter of time. Not for the last time, the members of the Almanac Singers kept on singing.

When they appeared at San Francisco's Longshoremen's Hall, an FBI agent filed a report, observing their insidious song-leading techniques. The audience "joined in not from their own desire, but were led into it through mass psychology and apathy toward the utter control of the meeting by Communist officers and members." Other offices were warned, and the Almanac Singers' name was officially in the spook network, accumulating cross-references. Their shadows grew deeper, as if coming alive.

It was Pete's relentless networking, in the Party and otherwise, that set their itinerary on the subway circuit. Between gigs, they moved as a pack of energy and conversations and songs and half-drunk giggles, Seeger bouncing among them with a teetotaler's adrenaline. Weekend appearances almost inevitably began with their usual repertoire of singing news, but the wee hours were for sing-alongs on the widening songbook of folk standards they and their audiences knew, like "On Top of Old Smoky," first gathered by folklorist Cecil Sharp in the Appalachian Mountains.

Panning down to the basement of Almanac House, one finds the site of their Sunday afternoon "hootenannies," the term Pete and Woody introduced into the wilds of Manhattan culture after they'd discovered it in Seattle. They lug the mattresses down the stairs, line the floor with newspapers, and present sing-alongs and performances nearly every week, Pete doing "The Golden Vanity" or Lead Belly singing "Rock Island Line," a song originating from a train company in Arkansas that mutated even further in Lead Belly's repertoire.

One basement frequenter is Elizabeth Gurley Flynn, the veteran organizer and subject of Joe Hill's "Rebel Girl." Now fifty-one, the year before, she'd been asked to resign from the board of the American Civil Liberties Union for being a Communist, a moment some would point to as the true beginning of the darker years to come. She would share some of Hill's papers with the Almanacs, and trade bawdy stories with Lee Hays. A charming drinking partner to many of the house's guests, Hays also made friends with mystery writer Dashiell Hammett, the Popular Front hero who'd pioneered the hard-boiled detective novel via his character Sam Spade.

Since the return from their cross-country tour, though, Lee had been an increasing problem, beyond his usual portentous declarations. While Woody was a punchy, fun-loving drinker, Hays could and would turn dark, sulking endlessly. What's more, he'd started to skip out on bookings.

Occasionally, he would try to rationalize his habits by telling them "the creative power comes from loafing and inviting the soul." For Pete Seeger, who sprang from bed every morning ready to save the unions, the Union, and whatever needed saving or unionizing, Hays's molasses-slow existence could be maddening.

"I had no doctor, no doctor's diagnosis," Hays would say much later. But since the tour, "I wasn't able to function. I was just physically beat and just unable to carry my share of the bookings and the day-to-day work. I remember spending day after day in bed and their having to rustle up money to go out and get grub for me."

It was up to Seeger to kick Hays out and Seeger kicked Hays out, bluntly and directly at a house meeting. Hays was brilliant, but impossible to work with, and so the Arkansas traveler traveled on from Almanac House, and—for a time—to the periphery.

There was a time for peace songs, and a time for war songs, and—filling a demand that they recognized early—they swiftly adapted their writing operations for wartime use. Never precious about his own material, Woody happily reconfigured his standards like "So Long, It's Been Good to Know Yuh" with new verses about departing soldiers.

The Almanacs had been expanding and contracting since Woody's arrival the previous year, with the occasional inclusion of the theatrical Almanac Players troupe and guests like Josh White. But following Lee's departure, the Almanac Singers transcended from band to collective. Pete remained the (almost) unflappable organizer, trying hopelessly to schedule early-morning meetings, a lost cause even without Lee. New members arrived, most notably Sis Cunningham and Gordon Friesen, who took over Lee's old room.

A former organizer of the Red Dust Players in her native Oklahoma, Sis played accordion and wrote and gathered songs, a natural-born Almanac. Gordon was a journalist and couldn't carry a tune, only appearing onstage when a booking required an extra member to mouth vocal parts. At Alan Lomax's suggestion, the group wrote to blues guitarist Son House in Mississippi, an influence on Robert Johnson, offering him a bus ticket and a room in Almanac House, if he'd like to join them. He politely declined.

Downstairs, the extra-long Almanac dinner table continued to host a revolving door of guests. One day, Pete had run into Charles Olson, the modernist poet he'd met while working as a cook at Harvard. Visiting Almanac House for dinner, Olson fell under Woody Guthrie's spell, like many before, and encouraged him to contribute to his magazine, *Common Ground*, an article that led directly to a book contract.

The long table downstairs soon became Woody's office, where he warmed himself by the oven, brewing pot after pot of what Gordon Friesen called "Oklahoma-style" coffee, generating more diluted coffee out of used grounds.

"When morning came he would either fall asleep beside his typewriter or stumble to his feet and disappear into one of the Almanac House rooms, leaving as many as twenty-five or thirty pages of new manuscript on yellow-pad paper, single-spaced with no measurable margins," Friesen wrote.

As winter set in and Woody bundled up even more during his late-night writing sessions, after-dinner jams powered the Almanacs' last sustained songwriting burst. Finally, as 1941 turned into 1942 and the United States officially entered the war, the most recent of the New Situations seemed to actually align the Almanacs with the world around them for the first time.

The hoots got popular. Lampell had noticed a new crowd, "a smattering of Junior League debutantes who thought it was so colorful to go down to Greenwich Village and see these folk singers." In the accelerated time of a few weeks, the Almanac singularity rushed in and out of existence. *LIFE* magazine showed up, publishing images of the Almanacs mid-hoot.

There were radio appearances. "Round and Round Hitler's Grave" led off *This Is War*, a thirteen-week series broadcast coast-to-coast over all four major networks, when an estimated 30 million listeners heard the Almanac Singers. They were on the Navy Department's Treasury Hour billed as *comedy*—which may've been accurate too—and the US Office of War Information's broadcast. Timely songs were timely songs.

An agent from William Morris promised them a spot on NBC radio, singing headlines on the quarter-hour. An audition at Rockefeller Center's Rainbow Room ended with Woody improvising rude verses and a gig offer, *if* they wore hayseed costumes. Decca suggested they might put out their next record. Finally having some union gigs, the Almanac Singers joined the Local 802 of the American Federation of Musicians.

And then, zip, three days later, another new situation. "Singers on New Morale Show Also Warbled for Communists" blared one version of the headline in the *New York World-Telegram*. The "Ballad of October 16th" echoed back to haunt them.

"The program's backers were much upset today to learn that the Almanac Singers have long been the favorite balladeers of the Communists and their official publications, the *Daily Worker* and *New Masses*," the *World-Telegram* reported.

So it was with new situations, always changing. Though a viable political movement for left-wing intellectuals in the years before the Second World War, for many, communism also undoubtedly still brought to mind the Red Scare of twenty years previous. After a series of anarchist bombings in 1919, Attorney General A. Mitchell Palmer linked the bombers to both the Russian Revolution and a growing anti-immigration movement, less a political critique than a manifestation of American paranoia. Like radicalism, it was a thread that stretched back in American history,

Launched only a few months after Pete Seeger's birth, the so-called Palmer Raids gathered suspected Russian-born radicals, with nearly two hundred detained and deported, mostly on the vaguest suspicions of wrongdoing. Overseen by twenty-four-year-old J. Edgar Hoover, young assistant to the attorney general, the raids built political capital that Palmer squandered the following year, championing a conspiracy that Anarchists, Socialists, and Communists were planning to overthrow the American government on May Day 1920.

But the raids also launched the career of J. Edgar Hoover, responsible for accumulating secret dossiers on those arrested. Magazine subscriptions and other tenuous connections were marked down as violent threats, character notes in files secreted in Washington, where Hoover's occult forensic magick conjured doppelgängers of those the bureau suspected of being Communists. That very season in early 1942, his agents began to pad out folders pertaining to Seeger-comma-Peter, Guthrie-comma-Woodrow-double-U, and others, all just waiting for the right spark.

In New York, Woodrow Wilson Guthrie experienced an escalating series of new situations as the Almanac Singers spiraled toward their destiny, some of which required songs, and all at least some bemusement. Once, as the war was heating up, after they'd wearily tossed aside the union and labor songs they'd started with—*no strikes during wartime!*—Woody and Pete and Sis Cunningham got a well-paying gig at the Waldorf Astoria for a well-paying audience, and came loaded with their freshest anti-Fascist sing-alongs.

"Bring on the girls!" someone in the very rich and extremely sauced crowd shouted a few songs into their set, and Pete Seeger flipped.

"What are you, human beings or a bunch of pigs?" Pete snarled into the microphone. "Don't you care that American boys are dying tonight to save your country for you, and many more thousands will die before this is over? Great God Almighty, haven't you got any shame?"

From one of the tables, someone shouted for "She'll Be Comin' Around the Mountain."

And they played it, and when Woody took a verse, he took it loud, clear, and direct into the microphone: "*She'll be wearin' a union button when she comes. She'll be wearin' a union button when she comes. . . .*" When they finished there was a hush in the room. The Almanac Singers showed themselves out.

By midsummer, Pete was drafted, headed for Mississippi. Woody and others kept up the cause in New York. THIS MACHINE KILLS FASCISTS appeared in blue paint on Guthrie's guitar. A Detroit branch of the Almanacs sprouted too. The Almanac Singers were ever-shifting. One cadre was even led by the deposed Lee Hays. Almanac *life* was ever-shifting, new situations left and right. The Almanac House itself changed behind Woody as he worked at his typewriter.

Early in the harried sequence, he typed away at the long dinner table while the junior Almanacs disassembled the house behind him. Working overnight to move the communal possessions a few blocks away to the newest Almanac quarters, they left the door propped open. When they took the long table, Woody went to sleep on the floor in the kitchen, waiting to see what new situations the morning might bring.

S ailing away from the United States on a troop ship, Pete Seeger carried his new custom extra-long banjo, three extra frets added by luthier John D'Angelico. In New York, Agent Harwood E. Ryan had concluded his investigation. The Subject would never be allowed near the planes he was trained to repair. Headed for Saipan and a job coordinating entertainment at a hospital, Pete Seeger departed the United States that had been saved from the Depression by Franklin Roosevelt, the country where the Popular Front found some of its most magnificent expression, channeling America's noble and open-hearted past to point toward a bold future.

On the ship, Pete played a half-hour set every night for his fellow soldiers. As a challenge, he tried not to repeat himself, making it a solid two weeks. He ran through his entire repertoire, all three hundred songs he could remember, presumably minus the early Almanac peace numbers. Forming his sense of self in the years between the two world wars, the years when communism came close to being twentieth-century Americanism, and the power of the people seemed limitless, Pete Seeger knew that it was the United States that needed liberation too.

CHAPTER TWO

People's Songs

In her new bedroom at the rooming house, Ronnie Gilbert heard singing. She was sixteen and far from Brighton Beach. Not as far as her mother fretted about, though, just a train ride from Union Station to Grand Central and then back onto the Brooklyn subways, if she needed to get home. But her mother was sick, there was a war on, and government jobs were plentiful, so here she was in an unfamiliar house in Washington, DC, a quick walk to her new position in the Federal Housing Authority typing pool.

She followed the singing down the stairs to the half-open door of the basement apartment. When the song finished, a woman inside noticed the teenager standing tentatively outside the entryway, and waved her in. There were three acoustic guitars among the four people singing, two men and two women, and they started another song without talking, as if they'd been waiting for her.

Not that it was hard to get Ronnie Gilbert to sing. She'd been doing that all her life, at home and at school, picking up songs from musicals, and even in the Rainbow House Children's Radio Choir. And not that this particular song about dancing around Hitler's grave was hard to learn. Woody Guthrie and Millard Lampell and Pete Seeger had seen to that, attaching it to "Old Joe Clark" as they had. But when Ronnie Gilbert joined the chorus of singers in the Washington, DC, basement, she plugged her voice into a swelling nationwide chorus, and perhaps the chorus even noticed a jolt of electricity, a guitar string popping at a hootenanny in some far-off city.

The Priority Ramblers, a wartime configuration of folk-singing government workers, were linked quite directly to the Almanac Singers. Organized by Alan Lomax himself, absent the night Ronnie Gilbert wandered in, they'd had a brief and storied career, performing on the White House lawn for Eleanor Roosevelt. Much of their repertoire came from the Almanacs' *Talking Union* and its 1942 pro-war follow-up, *Dear Mr. President*, featuring "Round and Round Hitler's Grave."

While Ronnie hadn't heard of the Almanac Singers before, it was probable the name rang a bell with her mother and her *Daily Worker*–reading friends. A dressmaker and active member of the International Workers Order and the Communist Party, Sarah Gilbert had been singing labor songs since before she emigrated to the United States from Poland. But they were meant to be sung at work or at rallies or with the Jewish Bund Chorus. *Music* was something else, though, operettas and high art. Even in the darkest Depression, with both Ronnie's parents working trade jobs, Sarah Gilbert made sure there were piano lessons to be had.

But it was through the union itself that Ronnie had first been electrified by singing. Sarah had dragged Ronnie all the way into the city on a Saturday morning for an outdoor rally in the Garment District, her eyes glazing over at the rambling speeches in Yiddish from the back of a truck, "when this man comes in front of the microphone, a big, huge black man, and starts to speak to the crowd in a very deep voice."

"It was as if someone had sprayed the crowd with a can of happiness," she recalled another time.

"Comrades," the man said, and Ronnie felt it in her chest as he spoke to a street full of Jewish garment workers of "my people and your people." Her mother was crying. "Your people and mine are forever connected by our slave heritage," he said, and Ronnie's eyes and ears and heart popped open.

And then Paul Robeson began to sing "Go Down, Moses," with its immortal "let my people go" refrain.

"It was incredible," Ronnie would say. "I'd never heard sounds like that; never heard a vocal sound like that. And that man had such a bearing, such a magnificent bearing."

A former lawyer and college athlete who'd gone on to international success as an actor and a concert singer, Paul Robeson would remain a hero to Ronnie Gilbert and many others.

"The artist must take sides," Robeson declared in 1937. "He must elect to fight for freedom or slavery. I have made my choice." Radicalized by the Spanish Civil War, it wasn't long before Robeson was using his operatic tenor to sing for civil rights and trade unionism. In the Gilbert household, Sarah simply called him "Paul."

Ronnie would remember that day as the beginning of a decades-long conversation with her mother about "politics, power, and songs." It was a world she'd inhabited before she fully understood it, playing field drum in the May Day parade as an eleven-year-old member of the IWO's Brighton Beach Drum and Bugle Corps. Stretched across the street was a yellow silk banner with striking red letters that read REMEMBER THE HAYMARKET MARTYRS, commemorating those who died in an 1886 demonstration in Chicago. Robeson concerts became a regular activity for the Gilbert women, taking the elevated train as it turned into a subway, and up into "the old Madison Square Garden of toe pinching cold in the winter and back tickling summer sweat," Ronnie would remember, "the old Garden of waving banners, workers' anthems, speaker following speaker." Ronnie heard the headlines of her mother's *Daily Worker* reading transformed into chants.

"When I was about 10 years old, I tried to explain to the kids on Sterling Place about how the little candy store on the corner would be transformed under Socialism," she would say. "It would be like a new gymnasium with soda water and syrup we could mix ourselves." And though Ronnie would likewise remember her vision of utopia blurring from there, it was a childhood deep inside the worker's culture of outer Brooklyn and the Popular Front.

During summers she attended Camp Wo-Chi-Ca, its typically midcentury faux–Native American name a meaningful abbreviation for a different subculture: the Workers' Children's Camp. Located a bus ride away in New Jersey, "there's not another camp like mine" the camp's cheer went, and Ronnie understood that instantly. There, she sang Wobbly songs, the anti-Fascist ballads of the Spanish Civil War and, as part of a chorus, performed Earl Robinson's Popular Front epic "Ballad for Americans" for Paul Robeson himself.

Singing was "an integral part of every activity in the camp," Ronnie said. "We learned to sing with great verve and deep feeling for the material." *Singing is a form of battle*, they were told. The camp was filled with what Ronnie called "dangerous ideas," like to "respect the dignity of the kitchen worker and the kitchen worker's work."

Born Ruth Alice Gilbert in 1926, it was at Camp Wo-Chi-Ca that she became Ronnie after the residents of the Marie Curie Bunk adopted boys' names for the summer. Hers stuck. She would return to Brooklyn enthralled by the long-lost Spanish Civil War.

"It was a very organic part of our lives," Ronnie would say of the entwined relationship between politics and music.

So when Ronnie Gilbert wandered into a Priority Ramblers mini-hoot in Washington, DC, she was primed for folk music as it existed in wartime, a collision of progressive priorities and youthful energy, and she jumped in fully. Her supervisor at the Federal Housing Authority invited Ronnie for dinner and DJed from her extensive collection of blues 78s, starting to connect Ronnie to the lineage of the music, and strong female voices like Bessie Smith and Ma Rainey.

Singing remained the "only stereotypical female thing" she associated with her movie-going youth. "I envied and dreamt of being the girl singer in front of a band," she would say. "That seemed so romantic to me."

She began singing duets with Jackie Gibson, too, one of the Priorities she'd met at the rooming house, an instant mentor and confidant. A Brooklyn-born folkie insider from the get-go, Gibson had even been privy to a test pressing of the Almanac Singers' *Talking Union*. As Alan Lomax's secretary at the Office of War Information in Washington, she pulled Ronnie into the close-knit folkie network.

"Jackie and friends of hers had this huge apartment, this big old apartment in an old ramshackle Victorian," Ronnie recalled. "They always had room for people from out of town to sleep and so on." She and what she would later call her "girl gang" obsessed over Billie Holiday records and dispatches from another friend, off working in Paris, who sent back long, convoluted letters about European politics.

It was at Jackie's apartment that Ronnie received her send-off from the Priority Ramblers. Her mother was better and had moved to DC herself. It was time for Ronnie to finish high school. "The singing started early and never stopped," Ronnie remembered. Crammed wall-to-wall with friends and strangers, plus a bathtub brimming with a sloe gin–infused punch, Ronnie gently spun herself to sleep in the guest bed to the sound of the party at full hoot.

In the morning, she woke by rolling over and finding her hand entwined in the wiry hair of a short man lying next to her. She rolled off the bed, startled and hungover. Woody Guthrie, having arrived late and crashed out next to her in the guest room, greeted her groggily, "Good mornin', purty girl."

Moving with her mother to a DC suburb, Ronnie didn't readjust easily to life in high school after her time as a Priority Rambler, let alone Camp Wo-Chi-Ca. When the high school music teacher drafted Ronnie into what Ronnie called a "minstrel show," the future Weaver's refusal to participate nearly cost her a diploma. Like a popular vaudeville song might go if subjected to the folk process: How you gonna keep 'em down on the farm after they've seen a Woody Guthrie?

Floating in a small room in the North Atlantic, eighteen-year-old Freddie Hellerman considered the object in his hands. The room was his secret place. The captain didn't even know about it. By some definitions, the object in his hand was a guitar. "You couldn't really call it a guitar. It was a [fret board], it had some strings on it. Nobody onboard could help me with it," he said. It had no back, and no sides.

Joining the Coast Guard near the end of the war, the skinny Brooklyn teen worked as a radio operator. As his ship traversed the hemisphere on month-long missions that took him from Brazil to the Arctic Circle, Fred retired to the closet-sized space and, through trial and error, figured out how to tune the former guitar, make a few chords, and play something that sounded like "Oh, Susanna." He'd played a little ukulele in high school. It went from there.

Born to Latvian immigrant parents in Gravesend in 1927, just before the Depression, the Hellermans' corner of Brooklyn echoed with music and politics long before the war, schoolyard chants about Herbert Hoover, rallies against Hitler, collections for the anti-Fascist brigades in the Spanish Civil War. Freddie Hellerman grew up among the left, a member of the Young Communist League in high school.

"When I was about 12 or 13, I had a friend who one night was babysitting in a very nice apartment filled with records and from the phonograph, I'm hearing strange songs about Jim Crow and about the union movement," Hellerman would recall of his first encounter with the Almanac Singers and their epochal *Talking Union*. "These became another great influence, politically as well as musically."

Not long after, Fred and his older brother Ray escaped to Greenwich Village while their parents were out of town. Ray had heard about one of the Almanacs' Sunday hootenannies, and the two climbed the stairs to what was probably the final iteration of the Almanac House and a motley later version of the collective. But for a fourteen-year-old, it was decidedly mind bending, writing about it a few years later in a college term paper.

A sign on the door said WALK RIGHT IN, and as they did, "the full impact of the noise hit us and I could see about thirty or forty people seated and draped on the furniture in this smoke-filled, cider-jug-strewn, paper-cup-littered room." Sitting with his legs crossed on the floor, Freddie watched and listened transfixed as the group led sing-alongs and various singers tried solo songs, all music that was new and wildly exciting to him. "Time was a nonentity," he wrote.

But as naturally as Freddie would slide into the progressive musical scene a few years later, it wasn't the Almanac Singers he cut class to go see in high school, despite his foray into the West Village. Working summers at his father's woolen sweater business, he fell in love with the pop music on the office radio. Describing himself as a "chronic truant," Hellerman said, "I was down at the Paramount Theater, where all the good truants were in those days, standing in line, getting in to hear Benny Goodman, Glenn Miller and Tommy Dorsey." In the years to come, many acoustic guitar slingers would aim for a rawness that imitated Woody Guthrie's dust-blown Oklahoma yowl, but Woody wasn't yet the legend he would become, and Freddie's musical horizons were always leveled with a firmly aligned pop compass.

Having acted in a few plays, too, Fred returned from the Coast Guard for a stint as a dramatics counselor at Camp Wo-Chi-Ca—the Workers' Children's Camp—and found a new singing partner in a teenage Ronnie Gilbert, fresh from her time in the Priority Ramblers. The two spent the summer cycling through songs from the songbooks of Richard Dyer-Bennet and Almanac hoot regular Burl Ives, like "Jimmy Crack Corn," "Greensleeves," and "Blow the Candles Out."

They weren't very good counselors, Ronnie allowed, more interested in singing than looking after their charges. Like Freddie, Ronnie was pop-versed, among the first generation to grow up among a unifying national popular culture, connected by cross-country broadcasts like the Saturday-night *Your Hit Parade*, launched in 1935, the same year as the Communists' Popular Front. Freddie came with a knowledge of swinging big-band pop and Ronnie's pre-folk songbook included a lifetime of movie musicals. "I'd go to a movie and I'd come out knowing the songs," she would say.

Ronnie Gilbert and Freddie Hellerman returned to a postwar Manhattan in which folk music was one of many developing musical threads amid a tangle of dance music bands of all sizes, plus pop and mambo and swing and bebop and street-corner doo-wop, alongside the many dozens of styles imported to New York by immigrant communities from the Caribbean, eastern Europe, and the other forty-seven American states. Home to swelling ranks of experimental painters and writers, since the '20s, too, the city became the center of the new national media, home of radio networks and publishing companies and magazines, a self-assembling mega-machine driven by creative energies.

It was a city of boundless possibility, even at the microscopic scale of the folk scene. "If you're interested in ninth-century Chinese pottery from the province of Umblang, with only the left-handed handles on it, those people are gonna find each other," Hellerman would remember. "That's how the folk-music scene was then. People huddling together for warmth."

Enrolling in Brooklyn College on the GI Bill, Freddie was a founding member of American Folksay, a combination musical troupe and dance company that grew from Camp Wo-Chi-Ca. Their mission was almost painfully earnest: "to bring to working people a lesson in democracy by exhibiting to them a people's culture as opposed to a commercialized, Arthur Murray, Fifty-Second Street imitation," as Fred wrote in a term paper. Never mind that square dancing had been a regular attraction at the Village Barn, a West Village staple since 1929. Like the Almanac Singers, American Folksay precociously hoped to affix new messages to an old form.

Appropriated during the 1950s by both the left and right, square dancing *was* a people's culture, at least in the Dust Bowl. "They weren't rollicking affairs, where folks joked and laughed," Almanac Singer Sis Cunningham would remember. "They were serious." She remembered desperate, serious faces, looking for release. It wasn't the only folk culture to be transformed in the postwar years.

Freddie earned a reputation as a good musician. "A lot of kids [at Brooklyn College] were left wing or liberal," Freddie remembered. "They'd say, 'Hey, look. We're having this meeting. Why don't you come and sing us a song or two?'" After singing at the Popular Front–birthed Photo League, Freddie received a postcard from a man named Lee Hays, the executive secretary of a new organization called People's Songs. He'd heard Fred was a pretty good singer. They should meet.

Ronnie Gilbert heard about the organization through one of her Priority Rambler friends. She'd moved back to New York with her mother after the war, landing on the Upper West Side. Just as quickly as she got there, it seemed, she was plugged back into the folk network. Soon she was singing Christmas

carols with Pete Seeger and company, careening around snow-covered Greenwich Village. The new peace army was on the march.

W oody Guthrie was almost vibrating with excitement on the plane. Pete
Seeger studied the thirty-four-year-old Oklahoman from his seat. Lee
Hays sat napping. Pete was reading a magazine, thinking, pondering their
new venture, and "there was Woody, looking out the window and making up
verse after verse about the plane, the stewardess, the ground below, the union
folks we were bound for, and the beautiful country this could be."

People's Songs had sprouted a few months earlier at Pete and Toshi's place
on the cusp of 1946, nearly as soon as Pete Seeger arrived home, only hours
after Woody arrived back in Brooklyn after his own army discharge. Pete was
the director, Lee was the executive secretary. "The spirit has not died," *Daily
Worker* cultural critic Mike Gold declared. "It has only been unemployed."

The organization endeavored to do nothing less than facilitate a singing
labor movement and change the country through song. And this March 1946
semi-reunion of the Almanac Singers to rally 8,000 striking electrical workers
in Pittsburgh was exactly the type of gig Seeger had dreamed about when
People's Songs first appeared in an ever-expanding thought bubble above his
head late during his restless army service.

The bubble opened wider and wider the more he thought about it. There
would be a newsletter, of course, and a vast and ongoing collection of topical
songs, ready to be re-zipped and dispatched for the newest of the new situations. In another nook of the enlarging bubble, there were hootenannies,
and—*look over there!*—workers' choruses for every union. Also, a facilitation
of a national network of song sharers and performers. More thought bubbles
stretched from sea to shining sea as Pete Seeger finally returned to active duty.

Descending into Pittsburgh in early spring with fresh songs, it finally
seemed like just the right moment. The peace army couldn't fail this time.

As is the case for almost all wars, the previous half-decade had been a time
of plans put on hold. Unions had deferred all contract negotiations and strikes
until peacetime. And when peacetime came, the labor movement seemed to
bloom anew across the United States. The Westinghouse strike in Pittsburgh
where the ex-Almanac trio was headed was small beans compared to some of
what was occurring. In January, 750,000 steelworkers walked out. In April, it
would be more than 300,000 coal miners.

Standing on the marble steps of Pittsburgh's city hall during a long day of
speeches, the ex-Almanacs watched women from the union throw hundreds,

maybe thousands, of song leaflets into the crowd from the upper windows of office buildings. Pete and Woody and Lee began by leading the masses in "Solidarity Forever."

One of the Pittsburgh newspapers called it a "Communist song" and Woody was incensed. "Oh. Well," he wrote. "Any song that fights for the cause of the workhand is a communist song to the rich folks."

Back in New York, the new organization awaited. They'd taken out a two-room office a half block east of the New York Public Library. In one room was an upright piano and just enough space to lay out the monthly newsletter. In the other was Lee Hays.

Sitting behind an overflowing rolltop desk, the Arkansas-born bass singer looked far older than his thirty-two years. His half decade since being deposed from the Almanac Singers in late 1941 had been hard. Sewn together with a great sadness, a montage of his lost years includes a period working at the New York office of War Prisoners Aid, a summer trying to get in shape as a night watchman at the left-wing Camp Unity, time spent as a charming (and sometimes seriously uncharming) guest of various radical friends at country farmhouses and West Village apartments, and late nights with Lead Belly on the east side followed by a long crosstown trudge because the bus ran only once an hour.

There was drinking, beer, and whiskey, and a lifetime of wounds, from his father's death to his falling-out with the Almanac Singers, plus a confused inner life set in motion during Lee's youth as the son of a Methodist minister with whom he could never again reconcile anything. "I'm sure if I'd lived through the Civil War, I would've remembered it better than this one," he once said of World War II.

But at the People's Songs office, Lee was back in his element, and a positive whirlwind by his often sedate standards. Behind a desk was a good place for him, it seemed, zipping out letters to the folk network he'd been part of before the Almanac Singers (like Zilphia and Myles Horton at Highlander Folk School in Tennessee) soliciting them to write for the People's Songs bulletins, and zapping out postcards to musicians of whom he'd only heard tell.

"What I saw was a small, crowded room with three desks, a telephone on each," recounted Freddie Hellerman, who turned up a few days after receiving a card from Lee, recounting the experience in a term paper. "A sloppy, ink-stained mimeograph machine stood silently in the corner of the room, a large overstuffed filing cabinet occupied another corner, and the remainder of the floor space was taken up by a few scattered straight-backed wooden chairs and a large quantity of mimeo paper, leaflets, and other printed material piled against the wall in such a manner as to indicate an attempt at maintaining a semblance of order. . . ."

Freddie was shocked to identify the people in front of him. "Here were the old Almanac Singers, returned from the dead," Fred wrote. "Reading at one desk was massive, triple-chinned Lee Hays, the Arkansas preacher until he 'decided to make an honest living.'" Composer Earl Robinson was there, too, and "wearing dark maroon pants with a blue [work] shirt and Army boots, sat tall, skinny, cherry-nosed Pete Seeger . . . he was lazily plucking out a tune on a long-necked banjo as I introduced myself to Lee Hays."

The three men examined the Brooklyn teenager and "within a few short minutes, instruments came flying out of nowhere" and the playing and singing began. "I have always had the feeling that they were 'testing me out,'" Fred wrote, "for it was hard to believe that their regular business routine could be so disrupted by the slightest provocation."

But breaking into song was part of their jobs, and Fred Hellerman became the newest People's Singer, invited to join them for their next event at Town Hall. Fred jumped deep into the folk world, and there was plenty to absorb, both music and history.

From his rolltop, Lee cranked out the bulk of introductions for the songs that took up much of the publication. Beginning with "Solidarity Forever" in the February 1946 issue, with a handwritten #1 next to it, the newsletter would begin the conscious creation of a new canon, encouraging readers to punch holes in the issues and save their issues of the bulletin in loose-leaf binders.

Folk-music research stretched back nearly a century, to Francis Child, the American-born scholar of British balladry. But it was a conversation that largely limited itself to the pages of academic journals, the purview of gate-keepers like Seeger's old friend Alan Lomax, and those deep in the network, like Seeger himself. People's Songs aimed to do it in real time—miner songs, songs about union heroes, union dances, jailhouse songs, lumberjack songs, farming songs, old songs, new songs, any song that worked.

Former Priority Rambler Bernie Asbell was a new editor, and savored Lee's knowledge. Compared to the up-and-coming generation of folk enthusiasts on the scene, Lee was a well-traveled veteran, and what Asbell called a "genu-ine 'out-there' American." Bernie and his wife were among the first group of so-labeled "young people" to begin to create circles around Hays.

"He was the one who convinced us that the Left was the great continuum of the American tradition, or at least that it was part of the mainstream of the

American tradition," Asbell said. "Lee thought in terms of events, history; he saw large, and that rubbed off on the rest of us."

Lee made a bevy of new friends, growing close with Fred Hellerman too. Drinking together, Lee told Fred about the Almanac Singers and his own past, including a story he told a few of his friends through the years, but which seemed to have little basis in truth. Lee was once married, he told Fred. They'd had a child, about ten years ago now, and his wife had died shortly after giving birth, the child going to her family. But Lee's past, so far away now, in the Depression and earlier, was like a half-forgotten country from which he'd been exiled, someplace he only discussed in the starkest of terms. His family was the peace army now.

In coming to New York, Hays's mission hadn't been to preserve the Southern folk tradition as he'd found it on the porch of Emma Dusenbury, but to put it to use, acknowledging its history, appropriating as needed, and—most of all—spreading and popularizing. Building on a small but devoted subscriber list, starting with around 3,000 names, the *People's Songs* newsletter was responsible for beginning a new part of the conversation about American folk music.

A call for songs suggested that songwriters consult with their local unions about their needs, but rattled off a number of topics for which songs were required with the utmost urgency: "Gerald L. K. Smith, the Freeport murders, the high cost of living, picket lines, labor unity, housing for veterans, the fight against Rankin and Bilbo, Hearst and Pegler . . . the people's concern about atomic power, about labor's role in the peace, and our concern for minority peoples everywhere." They would receive many. After "Solidarity Forever," People's Song #2 was Lee and Walter Lowenfels's "The Rankin Tree," about the long-serving and notoriously anti-Semitic senator John Rankin.

From their Forty-Second Street offices, People's Songs sold song sheets, like Joe Hill's version of "Casey Jones" (People's Song #6) and they ambitiously made themselves distributors for a selection of a dozen 78 collections, including Josh White, *Hebrew and Palestinian Folk Songs*, a children's musical, and a reliable set of good ol' Woody Guthrie Dust Bowl ballads. They put out calls for workers' choruses, too, offering up new numbers and discount subscriptions, ready for *their* needs.

That was mostly Pete Seeger's department. He wanted "hundreds, thousands, tens of thousands of union choruses," and was ready to tap into the new postwar labor movement. A few days after People's Songs had started up, Pete headed off to meet with a cultural emissary from the Communist Party, offering the organization's services in the hopes that the party would employ them, connect them with gigs, and generally make them part of the Party's plans. But there was another new situation, and Pete Seeger could only sense the surface of it.

For starters, they weren't the Communist Party of the United States of America anymore. They were the Communist Political Association. There'd been a shifting in the ranks and a rearrangement of priorities. When Pete Seeger arrived at the CPA's Bronx headquarters with the latest ideas from the Popular Front that he'd scouted with his new peace army—*songbooks! workers' culture!*—the CPA all but dismissed him. The Popular Front was over. It had been for years. This enthusiastic man with the banjo must have seemed like he was returning from some distant region, raising funds for an obscure cause that didn't translate to the changed place in which he found himself.

The values that Pete and Lee and Woody and the rest had built into their new organization grew directly from the concerns set forth during the thick, dusty years of the Depression. The causes they reflected in their music promoted equality, championed the worker, and attempted to give strength to the disempowered. Woody, especially, remained a staunch anti-Fascist. That same year, he and Lee and Cisco Houston traveled to Washington, DC, on People's Songs business, where a security guard barred Woody from entering the Capitol grounds with his THIS MACHINE KILLS FASCISTS guitar. "I suppose it could be considered a little bit too lethal," Lee would say.

"They're determined to help organize America against fascism, finishing up the job that wasn't done in the war itself," the *Daily Worker* said of the new organization.

And though neither side expressed much awareness of the other, the years of the Almanac Singers and People's Songs coincided with a powerful flowering of anti-Fascist, non-authoritarian arts in the United States. There had long been socially aware culture outside the folk sphere, like Duke Ellington's *Jump for Joy* revue, a hit in Los Angeles around the same time the Almanacs hit the West Coast in 1941. But in the postwar years, it took on new shapes. Growing from the work of anthropologists like Gregory Bateson and Margaret Mead, and unconnected to the Popular Front, the systemic critique of propaganda and totalitarianism manifested in multimedia works like the expansive and well-attended museum exhibits of former Bauhaus designer Herbert Bayer as well as the radical poets of North Carolina's Black Mountain School. One new kind of art-weaponry were the widely misunderstood compositions of John

Cage, radical musical creations that attempted to force listeners into new modes of thinking and, by extension, new modes of freedom.

Woody Guthrie encountered John Cage's music and identified with it instantly. Seeing Cage perform directly on a piano's inner strings at several Village gatherings in 1946, Woody was reminded of his own instinctive rule-bending experiments on his grandmother's upright back in Oklahoma.

But as People's Songs climbed to its feet in the first year after the war, they worked to build themselves an infrastructure using their best Popular Front instincts, establishing field offices and finding causes, like an early iteration of the classic anti-Capitalist holiday, Buy Nothing Day, for which Pete and former Almanac Singer Sis Cunningham composed the new "Black Market Blues."

And of course there was the absolutely *urgent* issue of the Office of Price Administration. Established during the war to monitor the market in order to keep consumers from being gouged during various shortages, it was the first of many Republican-led repeals of New Deal–era policy, a world now quickly receding into the past.

In April, *People's Songs* issued a special *FIGHT TO SAVE OPA* supplement, brimming with new songs to protest the OPA's impending closure, like Tom Glazer's "Inflation Talking Blues" (People's Song #35) and the Almanacs' "Eighty Cent Butter!" (People's Song #38), itself a zipped-up version of the Depression standard "'Leven Cent Cotton."

The Office of Price Administration was closed soon thereafter, a small shift among a larger one, business interests superseding nearly all else. The future would be filled with causes, and good ones.

This time, Lee Hays was bitching about the hootenannies. For all of People's Songs' causes, the man that People's Songs advertised as a "substantial singer from Arkansas" sometimes seemed to have an equally substantial number of personal gripes.

The hoots had resumed where the Almanac Singers' house parties stopped, starting with eighty people crammed into Pete Seeger's in-laws' place, where he and Toshi lived near Washington Square Park. But the new events soon outgrew apartments and that's when Lee Hays found reason to fret. They *cost* too much, Lee declared, the giant man behind his rolltop desk in the tiny office, and the organization simply didn't have the *resources*, or the available space. Militantly ready to take the next step, Pete pushed the group to hire proper venues and sell proper tickets.

Lee did love a good crowd, though, missing it desperately during his years in the post-Almanac wilderness. With only rudimentary instrumental skills, he required at least musical collaborators to perform. And with a mighty Southern sigh, by the time People's Songs staged a hoot at the left-wing Little Red Schoolhouse in Greenwich Village, Lee was fully on board.

Woody went full Woody in recording it: "I saw these Peoples [*sic*] Songs raise up storms of stiff winds and wild howls of cheer from the people in their seats, and saw also, that almost every chronic headache was eased and made quieter."

As the hoots got bigger, they took on formal qualities as well, like a pair in May 1946 at Town Hall, one focused on Union Songs and one on Freedom Songs. Lee constructed scripts for the events, returning to the dramatic focus of his days at the Commonwealth Labor College in Arkansas, and transformed the freewheeling basement soirees to more polished productions worthy of the Broadway venues they were soon selling out.

"What has made the organization possible has been the arrival of the young soldiers from the demobilized Army and Navy," *Daily Worker* cultural columnist Mike Gold observed at an early hoot. "Dozens of them were singing and making music at the jam session. They are the art and song of America's proletarian future."

Freddie Hellerman, not yet twenty and fresh from the Coast Guard, certainly fell into this category, or at least the demobilized part. Desperately trying to avoid following his father into the family rags business on the Lower East Side, Hellerman was attending Brooklyn College on the GI Bill, doing "the all-purpose fuck-off thing, being an English major." While remaining committed to progressive causes, his political interests were unquestionably those of his own generation.

A member of the Young Communist League, Hellerman was only briefly a member of the party itself. "It struck me as a tremendous waste of a lot of energy and a lot of good will," he told Robbie Lieberman in 1989. "People got lost in long doctrinaire speeches." He found himself dozing off at meetings. For Hellerman and an increasing number of others, the music could easily carry its deeper concerns without formal connections to a political party.

American communism had begun its decline and the power of American unions would gradually follow, an intricate and entwined spiral. The years of American prosperity were beginning. With the disinterest of the Communist Party and their abandoned Popular Front, People's Songs charted its own course. They continued to promote folk music as something inherently good, naturally carrying the message of the People and support of the labor movement how they could.

"We recognize our affinity to the songs of all working people," Pete had written in an overview of People's Songs. Even still, Pete was called out by the leader of a Ukrainian chorus.

"The trouble with your People's Songs organization, it's not American enough," is how Pete recalled the complaint. "Where are the Italian songs, the Polish songs, the Greek songs? We're American, too." They expanded their reach. If the always-conflicted Communist Political Association had no interest in popular music, the Popular Fronters at People's Songs surely did.

But the points that Bess Lomax and others had made about the Almanac Singers still stood: folk music might provide good labor-organizing tactics in Kentucky mining country but it was hardly universal. If they were going to do real battle, and transform American consciousness in any way, they would have to grapple with the contradictions of playing banjo in an age of big-band jazz and hit-parade melodrama.

"Popular Song Writers Committee Formed," read the top headline in the second issue of People's Songs. There'd been discussion of how to write radio jingles and on "treatments of social problems which would be acceptable to the commercial market." They reported back in the second issue under the title "What Makes a Good Pop Song?" It was a conversation that would continue in the pages of People's Songs for the duration of its existence as they endeavored to use every new tool available to them, even while struggling to understand them. "Cliches [sic] put to a boogie beat still sound like cliches [sic]," the committee warned.

As the debate heated up, Lee Hays stepped in with his own typically contrarian refrain, reading many lifetimes later like an early clarion call for what later music critics dubbed "poptimism." "I like Stephen Foster; I like opera; yes, though I take my life in my hands, I like juke box music! I like music!" Hays wrote.

"Who am I, or who is anyone, to say that the music of the juke-box, the beetle organ, which the millions of Americans listen to, and drink their beer to, and dance to, and argue by, and make love by, and relax by, and make up their minds who to vote for by, is trash?" Lee continued.

Even in the broad-minded context of People's Songs, though, Lee's opinions could raise hackles. "You have to be a pretty subtle character to make folk music out of [opera] and you KNOW it," retorted one reader from Idaho. "It's part of the system AND IT MAKES ME SICK." And while Lee defended music "with a beat," it would never receive much coverage in the publication's pages.

Lee Hays had come north from Arkansas to popularize the songs and techniques he'd learned at Commonwealth Labor College, and—in fact—People's Songs was well situated to do exactly that, though he'd have to pick up a few new tricks, too, and learn the new pathways that music traveled in the United States. While their peace army may have been armed with banjos and human voices, their amassment began within a quick walk of some of the most pivotal movers in American popular music. Instigating politically charged hootenannies and crammed into a tiny office a few blocks east of Times Square, the squad of People's Songsters were also just another group of hustlers in a broad and independent music scene that clustered in midtown Manhattan.

Located ten blocks to the south was the neighborhood known as Tin Pan Alley, home to the network of writers and song pluggers that fed material into vaudeville and the hit parade beyond. From the perspective of the average People's Songster, Tin Pan Alley was the dream machine pumping musical opiates into the cultural bloodstream.

"We have set up a new technique and organization for getting people's songs spread, and circumventing the music monopoly of Broadway and Hollywood," Pete wrote optimistically. In that, People's Songs had more in common with the neighborhood's burgeoning indie music scene than perhaps either side thought, an emerging infrastructure to sustain the kind of music the Almanac Singers were making a half decade earlier. Independent jazz and R&B labels flourished in Manhattan, such as Atlantic Records, which was soon established a dozen blocks to the north.

One People's Songs–affiliated imprint getting on its feet alongside them and trying to get product into the new national market was Charter Records. Founded by Pete's army buddy and inveterate People's Songster Mario "Boots" Casetta, Charter's discography soon included topical calypso and progressive cabaret. Folk was neither the only the musical platform for social commentary, nor even the most visible. At Café Society Downtown, former Almanac collaborator Josh White was forging a new style of cabaret blues with his versions of "Strange Fruit" and radical chain-gang songs like "Timber (Jerry the Mule)."

But 78s were only one kind of technology through which to spread the message. The People's Radio Foundation was beginning a two-year losing fight for a license on "the new system of interference-free broadcasting" known as FM radio, still some twenty years from its actual countercultural and commercial rise. *People's Songs* encouraged the use of filmstrips ("instead of the audience fumbling with song sheets") and enthused over other hot new tech like wire recorders ("you can erase what you don't like and start over again"). But the songs were the products, the weapons themselves, and still the primary currency in which Lee Hays and Pete Seeger and their friends were concerned.

It was the *songs* that made everything happen, these simple formulations around which Lee and Pete and everybody constructed an elaborate apparatus. The song swapping never stopped. While the national tribulations of People's Songs generated an unceasing stream of tensions, the Manhattan-based scene of folk musicians clicked together like never before. There were regular sessions over at Lead Belly's apartment, a spotless sixth-floor walk-up on the Lower East Side, where bottles of whiskey flowed.

Freddie Hellerman was part of a Sunday-night gang for a while. One of the youngest members of a still-expanding circle, Fred was still learning his way around. The nights with the legendary Huddie Ledbetter (Lead Belly), his wife, Martha, and their friends were magical. By the end, when even Brownie McGhee and Sonny Terry had stopped singing, Huddie would play by himself on his twelve-string guitar. "Like with a Pied Piper, sleepy little kids from all across the building would sort of wander into the apartment, come on in," Freddie remembered.

Lee and Woody and Huddie and Cisco Houston came over other times and drank and sang and sang and drank while Pete Seeger would shake his head, at least at Lee and Woody. That Huddie dressed formally while patrician Pete wore blue jeans never failed to amuse Lee, which never failed to unamuse Pete. Somewhere along the line, Huddie assigned Lee his own verse in "Goodnight Irene," Huddie's signature number (People's Song #178).

But at the office, the arguments with Lee had grown tiresome. At these often grandiloquently dubbed "policy discussions," Lee talked and questioned and interrogated his way through a sea of logistics, from projector rentals to the mechanics of getting the monthly bulletin off to the printer's, weighing each option in his deliberate manner, all while Pete Seeger zipped in hyperspeed time-lapse around him, chairing meetings, leading sing-alongs, adapting songs, organizing jam sessions, gigging on the subway circuit, teaching nights at the Jefferson School of Social Sciences.

One of the blowups with Lee was over a folk singer who wanted to sing Confederate folk songs from the Civil War. Lee's People's Songs colleagues argued that the songs preserved a racist legacy and ran counter to everything that they were trying to accomplish. Lee argued that the songs were legitimate parts of history. He was outvoted and threatened to resign.

It was tedious. So barely a year into the People's Songs venture, at a national board meeting, on a day when Lee hadn't even threatened to resign, Pete asked him to resign. It was full speed ahead, and Lee was drag energy. He shuffled off to Philadelphia with a typewriter.

The newest situation was a pretty grim one, if the members of People's Songs were being honest. In the spring of 1946, just as the young organization was establishing itself, relations between the United States and the Soviet Union disintegrated. British prime minister Winston Churchill declared that an Iron Curtain had fallen across Europe, while Russian leader Joseph Stalin proclaimed communism and capitalism to be incompatible. Unions purged Communists across the United States, their use for song-leaders like People's Songs shrinking to a conspiratorial whisper.

With that, the Cold War began. The singing peace army was now in unfriendly territory. "A country needs to beware when such an outfit as People's Songs is constantly issuing so-called songs as a new form of propaganda to undermine national morale," cigar-chomping right-wing columnist George Sokolsky wrote under the headline "Stalin's Army."

The FBI, of course, had been checking out People's Songs from the start, opening a file in early 1946 and connecting the organization into the encompassing and ever-expanding meta-index that constituted their dark alternate reality. Over the course of the late 1940s, this world populated in the files of the bureau, growing cross-referenced like a labyrinthine network of identical corridors.

Soon the new files would connect up with the Army Counterintelligence Corps' report on Pete from 1943, including Agent Ryan's interview with Woody Guthrie, the hallways bringing together Pete's various doppelgängers. It was a vast place, one the real Pete couldn't even yet dream of, still unaware of the surveillance he was under. "They play folksongs," reported the FBI of one People's Songs event, "where the hoity-toity red intellectuals gather."

And a few weeks after George Sokolsky called out People's Songs in the summer of 1946, a group of film-industry figures were accused of having shadow Communist selves whispering in hidden red rooms, leading within a year to the Hollywood Ten hearings. In nearly every territory where the

Popular Front had advanced into culture, accusations now arose of subversive messaging.

George Sokolsky kept hammering at People's Songs. "It is important for Americans . . . to be vigilant when they see or hear a song issued by the People's Songs, Inc. or by the Almanac Singers, a related outfit," he wrote in a follow-up column. It was "propaganda designed to destroy the American form of government by every means usable including songs."

Republicans took the House and Senate in the midterm elections of 1946, gaining control of Congress for the first time in over a decade. Some began to openly equate the social legacy of Franklin Roosevelt's New Deal with an ongoing and insidious Communist corruption of government. The official-sounding Washington-based corporate lobbying group, the United States Chamber of Commerce, issued a twenty-two-page pamphlet in advance of the midterms, *Communist Infiltration in the United States: Its Nature and How to Combat It*, which spelled out many of the arguments that would grow familiar during the next two decades. Blaming the infiltration on "the broad-mindedness of the average liberal," it allowed that the New Deal was "humanitarian," but then the problem started.

Described in the language of infestation, "it was only natural that under these conditions, a considerable portion of Communists attained civil service status," the brochure read. "Some reached positions of authority. Once they had power, they behaved in a most illiberal manner. They were careful to appoint only like-minded individuals to offices under their control, and they schemed relentlessly to drive their opponents from government service."

In 1947, nearly as soon as the crop of representatives was sworn in, came the loyalty oaths, required for all federal employees by President Harry S. Truman. The attorney general prepared a list of "subversive organizations," including many from deep on the left. The Taft-Hartley Bill, meanwhile, made it possible for companies to sue unions for damages following strikes, effectively disempowering the American labor movement. The new policies and programs were not only a rebuke to Roosevelt's New Deal and the two decades the Republicans had been out of power, they were out-and-out revenge. Within the year, the House Un-American Activities Committee was en route to Hollywood.

One of the government's chief speechifiers was the unrepentantly anti-Semitic Mississippi congressperson John Rankin, the target of Lee Hays's "The Rankin Tree," who called the Communist menace in Hollywood "one of the most dangerous plots ever instigated for the overthrow of this government," emphasizing the eastern European given names of many of the accused, often Jewish. While there *had* been isolated cases of Russian espionage, none bore any connection to the American Communist Party, let alone the Popular Fronters now in the committee's crosshairs.

Just as the People's Songsters had their own dreams and hopes about the power of culture, so did the right-wing members of the House Un-American Activities Committee, who set out to investigate the influence of communism. Taking both at face value, the opposing sides shared a basic faith that culture *did* something, possessed of a transformative power over those who received it.

Possessing no legislative or judicial authority, except that which came in the procedural rules surrounding it, the House Un-American Activities Committee hearings were *investigative*, mere queries, really. Nobody was on trial. They just wanted to know the answer to a simple question: *Are you or have you ever been a member of the Communist Party?*

A person named Walter Steele called out People's Songs in a trial before the committee, naming the names of Pete, Lee, and many others. Steele's official title, as introduced by the HUAC's current chairman, was "chairman of the national security committee of the American Coalition of Patriotic, Civic, and Fraternal Societies." He was also the publisher of *National Republic*, "a magazine of fundamental Americanism."

"So important have the songs produced by People's Songs, Inc., become in Red ranks that the Communist school in Hollywood—People's Educational Center, the (Communist) California Labor School in San Francisco, the Jefferson School in New York, and the (Communist) Labor School in Oakland have inaugurated classes in the science of agitational song writing," Steele warned.

But if People's Songs wielded a fraction of the power that Steele ascribed, Seeger and the other founders would be happy musicians. As it was, American communism was in utter disarray. It was never anything like the organized pipeline conspiracy theorists like Steele described with such confidence.

The Iron Curtain was so tightly clamped that any official linkage was nil between the Communist Political Association and the Soviet Union. Alexander Bittelman, who shaped the CPA during the early Cold War years, received his "orders from abroad" by clipping articles from domestic and international newspapers that included reports on speeches by Russian party officials. Bittelman underlined the relevant passages.

I t was the most stressful tour Pete Seeger had been on yet. Some nights he didn't even get to perform. And in one hotel after another, he tried to focus. Everybody else went to the bar, but Pete went to his room. There, he juggled his banjo, a typewriter, and a collection of mimeograph stencils. His father had suggested that he write an instructional manual for the instrument. "The old books written in the nineteenth century, like Converse's and Briggs', really didn't show the folk styles," Pete would remember, adding another time, "they weren't very funny, didn't entice you to read further." Now, as the world started to push back at Pete Seeger, he found solace in the details.

He'd taken on some banjo students, and that had gone surprisingly well. In 1948, it was good for Pete Seeger to have something musical in which to have confidence. He'd toured and traveled plenty, on hitchhiking and train-hopping adventures alone and with Woody, or packed into a car with the Almanacs. In the spring, before this chaotic outing, he'd gone cross-country and back with his own PA and lighting system, selling a stash of People's Songs–related records and songbooks out of his car's trunk, trying to organize local branches. Pete was well accustomed to new situations, but being out on the presidential campaign trail was new for him.

Henry Wallace was their man, former vice president to FDR and now the newly formed Progressive Party's candidate against Republican Thomas Dewey and incumbent Democrat Harry Truman. People's Songs, and especially Pete, had joined the caravan, which is where Pete was in North Carolina when he and Wallace got pelted with eggs and tomatoes distributed by the Ku Klux Klan. It was rough out there.

That was also the night Pete saw Wallace crack, grabbing one of his harassers by the shoulder. "*Are you an American? Am I in America?*" the presidential candidate yelled.

"Get your filthy hands off me," the man replied to "Friendly Henry Wallace," as one of the People's Songs called him.

And it was hard to blame Wallace. Cast aside by FDR before the 1944 election in an effort to win the Southern vote, his third-party Communist-endorsed candidacy faced opposition on multiple fronts. Even President Truman referred to "Henry Wallace and his Communists," implying that the Soviet Union would be more receptive to his ideas. Perhaps he could go there "and help them against his own country."

But for People's Songs and the straggling remains of the Popular Front, there was virtually no other choice. Certainly Wallace was the only candidate willing to speak openly about the encroaching Cold War, calling it "an atmosphere of artificially created crisis." What's more, Wallace was a *singing* candidate, joining Pete both onstage and in private on the campaign plane.

Nearly every People's Songster recalls the early days of the campaign with a sense of blinding optimism. Via the ever-helpful Alan Lomax, People's Songs became the officially contracted musical coordinators, with a full-time desk at campaign headquarters in Manhattan. Rallies were soon peppered with *Songs for Wallace* pamphlets and enthusiastic song leaders.

Paul Robeson took to Wallace rallies singing "Battle Hymn of '48" (People's Song #223), which was "Battle Hymn of the Republic" altered for new duty. Filling churches and auditoriums with his rich voice, Robeson declared, "The People's march is on!"

Events began with a sing-along, often "The Same Old Merry-Go-Round" and "Everybody Wants Wallace," and the People's Songs office manufactured and distributed a pair of paper records, featuring "I've Got a Ballot" (People's Song #275) and Robeson's revised "Battle Hymn."

Ronnie Gilbert and friends hitchhiked to Philadelphia for the Progressive Party convention over the summer, camping out in a tent city in the parking lot near the Municipal Auditorium. Through the churn of People's Songs, the nineteen-year-old had begun to sing regularly with Pete, even recording a session. Onstage at the Progressive Party convention, Ronnie joined Pete, her girl-gang friends from the Priority Ramblers, and Paul Robeson himself, Ronnie's electric voice harmonizing with Robeson's world-creating bass-baritone.

"So much joy is not containable," she would later write. "I felt that it would burst through the walls and infect the country with hope and assurance. No one would be able to resist."

In New York, certainly, it seemed that way, with campaign money flowing into the People's Songs coffers, building toward a finale at Yankee Stadium. Fred Hellerman, still performing music for the dance troupe Folksay, and thinking about a career as an actor, recalled brigades of theater people volunteering at the overworked People's Songs office, and the subsequent attempt to employ them in song-laden skits. "It wasn't terribly organized, it wasn't terribly good, it was all sort of slip-shod," Fred said, "but in a way it was a very exciting time." It was an opportunity for many to get involved. Fred, too, found himself on a stage singing with Pete Seeger and with the former vice president of the United States.

The excitement was heightened, though certainly not in a way that Wallace or the Progressives wanted, when a dozen Communist leaders were indicted and arrested just days before the Progressive convention was set to begin in Philadelphia. They were charged under the Smith Act, which concerns "the overthrow and destruction of the government of the United States by force and violence." Besides the Klan, the Progressive Party's latest opponent seemed to be the Department of Justice.

These were drastic charges and many on the left were incredulous. Widely interpreted as a political move by the Truman administration against the nascent Wallace campaign, it changed the American political landscape in vast and unpredictable ways. The fallout would be felt for years. As a maneuver, it worked to destabilize what had already been a tenuous coalition. The CIO had been moving away from the left for a few years, and many of the remaining Progressive unions started jumping ship from the Wallace campaign almost immediately.

On cue, conservative columnists pointed out People's Songs and their connection to the well-disgraced Almanac Singers. One Songster who'd sensed trouble early was Lee Hays, but Hays always sensed trouble early. He'd moved back to New York late in the election season, and continued to churn out his regular column for the *People's Songs* bulletin. Always somewhat cynical, Hays's optimism seemed to swerve with his lifestyle, which favored long homebound nights, either hanging with friends like Woody and Cisco Houston, or hunkered behind his typewriter, and—in either case—filled with unceasing smoke and drink.

He'd ventured out to a few marches, and it hadn't suited him. He was *worried* by what he saw and heard, or more specifically *didn't* hear. Down Constitution Avenue in Washington, he remembered, "in the middle of a long line two girls and I walked singing, and half a dozen forlorn voices fore and aft tried to take up our melodies and sing with us." It didn't catch, and Hays blamed the lack of song training, the lack of material.

"[The] procession had about as much pep as a third rate funeral," Lee wrote, "and it was hot, and the marchers were harassed by the taunts of sidewalk Fascists, and gov't workers leaned out of windows to jeer and boo." He yearned to drown them out with music.

But Lee was right. The song power was failing, and not even Pete Seeger could save it. During the ill-fated Southern leg with the Wallace campaign, Seeger was confronted by an "absolutely livid white southerner [who] stood in front of me and said, 'Bet you can't sing Dixie!'" Seeger invited the man to sing along and added two extra verses he'd picked up during his song-hunting days in the army.

The mood on the campaign was grim and on-edge. At an integrated rally in North Carolina, instigators stabbed one Wallace supporter eight times in a melee. There was heckling, firecrackers set off indoors. "A number of people thought Wallace was going to be assassinated," Seeger remembered.

During the campaign, Wallace's favorite song wasn't a campaign song at all, but "Passing Through" (People's Song #249), written by a future English professor named Dick Blakeslee, which infused a sweet hymn-like melody with a rambler's grace, concluding, "we're all brothers and we're only passing through."

The song was part of another pitched battle People's Songs fought that summer, over the publication of the *People's Songbook*, banned in Quebec alongside Walt Whitman's *Leaves of Grass* and Leo Tolstoy's *War and Peace*, specifically for the inclusion of the "subversive" number "I Dreamed I Saw Joe Hill" (People's Song #179). When the *Songbook* finally made it across the border, a copy wound its way to a summer camp near Montreal, where a soon-fired Socialist camp director exposed it to a fifteen-year-old camper named Leonard Cohen, who—like Henry Wallace—fell in love with "Passing Through."

"I started learning the guitar, going through that songbook from beginning to end many, many times during that summer," Cohen would remember, recording "Passing Through" more than two decades later. "I was very touched by those lyrics . . . and that's when I started finding the music I loved."

It was perhaps with imagined readers like teenage Leonard Cohen in mind that Pete returned every night to the draft of his banjo instruction manual during those fraught and doomed days of the Henry Wallace campaign. Pete was ready to recruit for the peace army from miles or even years away. In time, his banjo instruction manual would have an even greater effect than the *People's Songbook*.

When Wallace's inevitable defeat came on November 2, 1948, receiving less than a million votes, it was resounding, finishing fourth behind racist South Carolina senator Strom Thurmond, running as a Dixiecrat. "DEWEY DEFEATS TRUMAN" read the *Chicago Daily Tribune*'s infamous miscalculated front cover. Henry Wallace's name appeared nowhere in the subheads.

Freddie Hellerman would remember it as a vast turning, "the end of the enthusiasm and the rah-rah of the Johnny-come-marching home period," he said. "All the hopes of the brave new postwar world came crashing down at the end of the Wallace campaign."

Over brunch in Sheepshead Bay a few days later, Ronnie Gilbert's girl gang bemoaned the results of the election.

"I thought we'd still get at least five or six million votes," one of them remarked.

Ronnie saw she'd been overly optimistic. "Wallace was supposed to *win*, wasn't he?" she asked, and realized he wasn't. It was a hard lesson, and a cold new world.

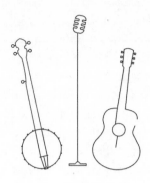

CHAPTER THREE

Warp and Woof

The new quartet came together along the banks of an ancient and secret waterway, an unstoppable source that wasn't a metaphor at all. A leg of Lee Hays's chair kept falling into it through the cracks between the floorboards when he leaned back during the group's long discussion sessions between songs. Flowing from an undammable spring twenty blocks to the north, Minetta Creek wound for nearly two miles beneath the rising Manhattan skyline, part of a network that fed into the Hudson River, a geology that caused some of the infamous zigs in the streets of Greenwich Village.

Once, the world around them had been different. Where they sat, Lee Hays envisioned, was "a winding course [where] lads and lasses used to stroll, perhaps to pause and sing courting songs. I don't know this for a fact, but the population has grown since then, so it's reasonable to assume that they did."

One of the creek's zags was through the basement at 129 MacDougal Street, where Pete and Toshi Seeger lived with Toshi's parents in a dilapidated three-story Revolutionary War–era house. "A low ceiling, dark shadows, stains of several memories," Woody Guthrie remembered the room as it stood a few years earlier, "filled with dim lights from two or three standing lamps, and hung full of Japanese prints, drapes, paintings, metal incense burners, ancient ash trays of bronze and copper, Japanese and Chinese paper lanterns. . . ."

Used for hoots for years, the basement was lately the rehearsal space for the new group Pete had started singing with during the last months of 1948.

Long thinking about people's choruses, the old Communist tradition that flourished in the 1920s, Pete had wanted to spawn one of his own. In the weeks after the 1948 election, he assembled just such a large group for the People's Songs Thanksgiving hoot.

In some ways, it was just another assemblage of the shifting pool of People's Songsters that had been turning over and over since the first Almanac House. "Pete wanted to put a chorus together," Ronnie Gilbert would remember decades later, "and so I was part of that chorus and Fred was part of that chorus."

Fred Hellerman would call the new configuration "almost a random, accidental thing," but it also might be seen as inevitable, the pool of musicians whose faith survived the electoral savaging. Pete was a relentless collaborator, working with nearly every size ensemble imaginable during the People's Songs years. Often, he returned to quartets and quintets, three or four men, one woman. He and Lee had recorded in a configuration like that with Hally Wood and former Priority Rambler Tom Glazer.

Three weeks after Henry Wallace's defeat, the night before Thanksgiving 1948, the People's Songsters huddled into Irving Plaza, the frequently hooted 1,000-capacity ballroom just east of Union Square. The chorus had already started to shrink, but it was starting to look recognizable. "You know, Pete Seeger has just returned. . . ." the People's Songs promotional postcard read, advertising the first hoot in nearly half a year, featuring "the new singing group of Lee Hays, Fred Hellerman, Jackie Gibson and Ronnie Gilbert," alongside the swelling chorus onstage and off.

They sang, Ronnie Gilbert would write, "as if the election results and the Cold War itself would melt in the happy flames stirred up by singers, songwriters, pickers, and, special for this night, dancers."

Pete and Lee, together again, were the senior hooters, the high voice and the high energy, the low voice and the gravitational center, neither their first nor last reunion. It wasn't just a chorus they were organizing. Both had yearned to assemble something like a less sloppy iteration of the Almanac Singers. Lee had even tried to recruit Oscar Brand into just such a cause. But in the end, the Weavers sprang from the full People's Songs tradition: script and gravitas by Lee, organization and enthusiasm by Pete, and electricity by all assembled.

When Ronnie, via Lee's script, offered thanks that "we can still be free to be here together and to sing and get acquainted," it was neither an idle nor un-fraught thanks. With the arrest of Communist Party leaders at the height of the 1948 presidential campaign, President Truman had escalated the Red Scare, and the ongoing Smith Act prosecutions now haunted the harmonies of the People's Songsters, demons hiding in the overtones. And so they hooted, at least after somebody plugged the People's Slide Projector back in, so they could run the lyric-aiding filmstrips.

It was there in the Thanksgiving singing that the Weavers became the Weavers, somehow focusing in on one another amid a larger group of singers. "I can recall hearing the sound of our voices, through all this other noise, just coming together like that," Ronnie said. Even if they didn't know it yet, the People's Songs Thanksgiving Hoot was the first performance by the Weavers, with some aspects that would stay in their repertoire for a decade and a half, some that would stay in their past, and all becoming woven into the emerging band's musical genetics.

Beyond reaffirming their belief in the progressive ideals of the Wallace campaign, the Thanksgiving hoot held its ground with union songs like the Almanacs' classics "Get Thee Behind Me Satan" (People's Song #151) and the old Wobbly tune from the *Little Red Songbook*, "The Commonwealth of Toil" (People's Song #262), which declared their "glowing dream of how fair the world will seem when each man can live his life secure and free."

And Pete led a sing-along on his translation of the unrepentantly Stalinist "Hey Zhankoye" (People's Song #173), originally in Yiddish, naïvely mythologizing the Jewish farming collective granted nationalized land by Joseph Stalin. In truth, the land was barren and the commune had collapsed. Pete's father, Charles, had left the party a decade earlier after reading transcripts of the Moscow purge trials. As with many of the brutal truths about Joseph Stalin's Soviet Union, it would take Pete and others at least another decade to recognize them.

In part, Pete's faith might be attributed to the other pieces of the emerging repertoire showcased at the Thanksgiving 1948 hoot, which included a growing body of reaffirming hymns. One was "Farther Along," a song Pete had repurposed on the spot earlier that fall in the face of two hundred jeering Dixiecrats: "farther along *they'll* understand why." Another, called "We Will Overcome" (People's Song #281), was once collected by Zilphia Horton at Highlander School in Tennessee and had its first New York performance at the Thanksgiving hootenanny.

At the Thanksgiving Irving hoot, there was also solidarity in the nonsense syllables of "Lolly Too-Dum," led by Freddie Hellerman, and the spooky resonance of Pete's clawhammer banjo on "Leatherwing Bat (The Bird Song)," found in the 1919 collection, *Songs from the Hills of Vermont*. To many, the unquestioned highlight of the Thanksgiving hootenanny was when a group danced to an arrangement that Pete and Freddie had worked up.

They were calling it "Around the World," and it linked global folk-dance standards in a way Walt Disney's composers would unconsciously imitate some twenty years later with an amusement park ride (see also: People's Song #24: "It's a Small World, After All"). When the proto-Weavers performed their globally unifying medley of dance tunes, it was a nearly radical sentiment.

On this night, they moved from the Arkansas square-dance number "Flop-Eared Mule" into a Polish folk dance ("I don't know the name of it but it goes like this," Pete announced) into the Hebrew circle dance "Artza Alinu" and straight into another irresistible nonsense chorus, the Bahamian "Hey Lilee Lilee Lo." The dancing was great, the audience *loved* the dancing, but it was the whole of the musical performance that did it: the sequence, the singing, the playing, the song choices. A powerful moment for all involved, it seemed a natural for the singing to continue until morale improved.

Down in Toshi's parents' basement, atop the burbling intrusiveness of Minetta Creek, they kept at it. Ronnie's girl-gang friends, Greta Brodie and Jackie Gibson, sang with them for another hoot or two, but soon dropped out. Left behind was a quartet: Pete Seeger, Lee Hays, Ronnie Gilbert, and Freddie Hellerman. Ronnie was working a series of jobs, from translating the tag lines of Mexican films into English for a local chain of movie theaters to the typing pool at CBS. Freddie was still a student, living at home. Going to the basement by Washington Square Park and singing was a pure joy. There were so many reasons to do it, and they all felt right.

For once, Lee Hays was right on time. A hypochondriac, Hays was less paranoid than he was fatalistic, his Southern dryness wrung into a wounded melodrama. He'd invested less of himself in the Wallace campaign than his People's Songs comrades had, which isn't to say that Lee Hays didn't believe in the cause. "We have had no greater cause in our lifetime," he'd written in his *People's Songs* column earlier in the spring. "Our jingles will help. But let us now write our fighting song!"

Lee's own answer was called "Wasn't That a Time" (People's Song #285), debuted by the American People's Chorus at Irving Plaza three days after the election—performed alongside international songs of struggle—and reprised at the Thanksgiving hoot. Written with Lee's sometimes dear friend Walter Lowenfels, it went quickly into service with the vocal quartet in the basement.

From the first six-word lyric—"Our fathers bled at Valley Forge . . ."—it linked the long left-wing struggle into the arc of American history.

The instructions for "Wasn't That a Time" gently suggested that potential singers shouldn't "let its apparent irregularities baffle you." The lyrics wound through other revolutionary struggles. Though Lee would rewrite the final verse for nearly every iteration, the earliest had the singers yelping *¡no pasarán!* in solidarity with the anti-Fascists of the Spanish Civil War. Written for a workers' chorus in an age when the workers' chorus was already on the verge of extinction, "Wasn't That a Time" was at once somber and triumphant.

"I had thought it was a patriotic song," Lee would remark later. "Even the worst of times can be considered a wonderful time because of the job that has to be done." The song sang like Emanuel Gottlieb Leutze's painting of George Washington crossing the Delaware.

In the weird invading gloom, Lee Hays found the oddest of times for a creative outburst, but perhaps it was what he'd been waiting for all along: a space dark and cavernous enough for his booming preacher's voice to fill with proclamations and proscriptions and other Socialist-tinged analysis wrapped in humor. Not long after he'd moved back to New York earlier that year, he'd kvetched to Seeger that he didn't like practicing, or even performing for that matter, but now he was doing both regularly. In addition, he began another endeavor so well suited to his temperament that it's a wonder Hays didn't try it decades previous: writing pulp fiction. Though he would never do it enough to make it his sole income, Lee's folk-dipped stories soon started to appear in *Ellery Queen's Mystery Magazine.*

Lee, who never again lived in the South after emigrating to Manhattan and co-founding the Almanac Singers in 1940, would always claim to be more a writer than a musician. And, as one future collaborator would note, Lee remained Southern all his life, his writing, singing, humor, and personality deeply rooted in his Arkansas past, constantly fighting to reclaim and redefine it and, by extension, himself. For a while, it seemed to be working.

It was a time to try the soul of man—as "Wasn't That a Time" put it, *a terrible time.* But down in Pete's basement, on the banks of Minetta Creek, that secret unstoppable stream below the pulsating city, was the faith-affirming answer that, somehow, Lee could feel coming when he'd written the song. "Isn't this a wonderful time?!" the song concluded on a triumphant harmony, placing itself and its singers on the crest of the glorious struggle.

The new group sang the songs of their friend Woody Guthrie, and they sang the songs of their friend Lead Belly, sixty-nine years old and falling into ill health. There was an early flash of success, with some seven hundred people turned away from the Christmas hootenanny at Irving Plaza.

Returning to the basement every Wednesday, it was Lee who now provided the push for them to keep going, to be a *band*. He got them booked on WNYC's *Folk Song Festival* radio show hosted by People's Songster Oscar Brand, where the four appeared as the No-Name Quartet, returning again a few weeks later. The *Daily Worker* was just referring to them as "People's Songs' new vocal quartet."

In what would become classic fashion for new bands, Brand put out the call over the airwaves for listeners to suggest a name.

"The audience was not completely complimentary," Brand would recall. Certainly none of the suggestions was quite right. The Undertakers? The Forlorn Four? The Off-Keys? At least two of the three suggestions Brand received would be taken up in future decades, but not by any of the former No-Name Quartet.

But between the time the postcard went out for February's Free and Equal Hoot and their next appearance on *Folk Song Festival* in late January 1949, they figured it out. "Out of somewhere, we don't know where, but out of somewhere, we did get a name," Lee informed Oscar Brand and their listeners. It was (collegiate studio drum roll): *The Weavers*.

"Did you have a special reason for choosing it?" Brand asked.

"You go buy soap, you go buy a dress, does 'dress' mean anything?" Lee shot back matter-of-factly. "It's just one of those ridiculous *brand names*."

"You must have had a reason?" Brand asked, exasperated. "You can't get away with that."

"The Weavers are *looming* over the horizon," Lee told Brand to a chorus of in-studio giggles as Lee threaded from the new symbolic language they'd claimed, "about to weave themselves into the *warp* and *woof* of American culture," Lee said, calling on industry terms. "I'm the woof . . ." More giggles.

It was Freddie who'd found the name through one of his English classes at Brooklyn College. It came from a play by German writer Gerhart Hauptmann.

"We wanted a name that didn't mean anything," Freddie would tell a reporter years later, concurring with Lee's description, in what would also become classic fashion for bands who didn't want to explain a choice they'd once made.

But the Weavers did mean something, and something specific. "There is a scene in which the weavers, out on strike, are marching from village to village singing protest songs," Fred would allow. They had their brand.

And if they remained coy about their new name's origins, it's perhaps because the Nobel Prize–winning playwright became associated with Nazis before his death in 1946. Of course, it wasn't why they became the Weavers. "It seemed to have a sound of rhythm," Fred said. Pre-industrial. A word from the time when Minetta Creek ran unfettered, free. "It rang a kind of bell."

Pete Seeger never liked working at an office anyway, and at this board meeting he was particularly distracted. People's Songs was broke. During the Wallace campaign, he'd lost himself in his banjo book. But there was no Wallace campaign to fund them in 1949.

The Worker Magazine published a bubbling story on People's Songs' upcoming third anniversary, and one can imagine Pete summoning up reserves of missionary optimism for the reporter. "This organization has become so much a part of American musical life that its absence would be unthinkable," they wrote.

The organization had kept trying new ideas. An excitable kid in the People's Songs office had organized a book- and record-buying club, but that had tanked. Lee was still very much on the filmstrip kick, and drew the new quartet into recording a soundtrack with Paul Robeson narrating Lee's script, dedicated to the Trenton Six, a civil-rights case unfolding in Jersey City. Now spread over two nights to solve the overflow problem, at least the hootennannies were proving popular. Even if everything else was falling apart.

But right now, Lee kept passing Pete notes during the meeting. They needed money and fast. Lee's notes weren't about that, though, but the newest manifestation of his latest creative outburst. Pete took a look and unconsciously added to it.

In the Adirondacks over the summer, the composer Marc Blitzstein played Lee his "Airborne Symphony," ending with its narrator's cry of "warning!" A Popular Front musician who'd written the controversial pro-union musical *The Cradle Will Rock*, Blitzstein likewise believed that singing was a form of battle.

"Since no song is entirely original, I borrowed his one word 'warning' and expanded on it," Lee recalled of the process that concluded during the long, boring People's Songs meeting. As the details of the organization's decline unfolded, Pete and Lee passed the paper back and forth, writing a line at a time, landing themselves in a more optimistic place.

The organization would fold soon thereafter, but—in time—it would prove to be the most productive board meeting either man attended. "The Hammer Song" made its debut at a June rally at the St. Nicholas Arena in New York and the *Worker* announced its performance with the same title that many would end up calling it anyway: "If I Had a Hammer."

It wasn't a Weavers gig, Lee and Pete appearing with other recovering People's Songsters. The organization had closed shop in the spring, much more suddenly than anyone wanted or intended. An overstuffed anniversary issue was scrapped when they couldn't pay the printer, and came out as a four-pager with only the gospel lament "This Old World" (People's Song #318), in an arrangement by Lee. "Let it out free," the note suggested.

The performance at the cavernous St. Nicholas Arena was for a typically dystopian good cause, the eleven Communists being charged at the so-called Foley Square trials. The case was central to the Weavers' world, and not merely in a legal way but an artistic one too. A professional informant with a growing celebrity named Louis F. Budenz testified that the Communists' texts were filled with what he called "Aesopian language." It said *one thing* but *meant another*.

It was a fantastic maneuver, to put it mildly, to suggest that when the progressive folk singers sang of "peace" they were actually calling for bloody revolution.

Anti-Communist arguments were increasingly sane, especially as trial transcripts and expatriates escaped the Iron Curtain. Yet, blind to numerous realities, Pete Seeger would keep insisting Stalin was merely "a hard driver" for many years. Even still, to insinuate that the advocacy of communism was an imminent threat to any American citizen was doubly insulting to people like Lee Hays, who'd spent their lives grappling with, and often rejecting, the ideas of the Communist Party. In the United States, violence and sabotage were far from the party platform. But those weren't the kind of nuanced arguments that Louis F. Budenz was making when he testified at Foley Square.

The decade after World War II was not a time for subtlety about communism. After the takedown of the Hollywood Ten, the movie industry had climbed on board too. A string of ludicrous features followed with informants as their heroes, like 1951's *I Was a Communist for the FBI*. Budenz was right, though, in the sense that a lot of Popular Front art brimmed with characters and plots that stood for broader ideas, designed to lead audiences to new in-tellectual spaces. But that's what art was for.

Poisonous circles closed around the Popular Front, the battle for pop music seemingly lost to moon/june rhymes, swelling orchestral productions, and a culture-wide anti-intellectualism casting a dull sheen on the American public's imagination. Overlapping in places with the freedom songs of the Underground Railroad, the Weavers' growing repertoire was filled with freedom songs of their own contemporary kind, not Aesopian at all, but there for anyone who wanted to consider the lyrics.

The Weavers had countless reasons to sing. What they needed were *places* to sing. Rolling their own hoots was one thing, but hopping on the subway circuit and making even half of a living wasn't quite as easy as it was in ye olde Almanac days of benefits and unions. Ronnie recalls tagging along with Pete to bookings when they could. But those were scarce too.

"Even people like Pete, who was then a star in his little orbit . . . was going out and getting maybe fifteen dollars for a booking," Fred would say. "And that was big time. So what kind of place could ever afford to pay the four of us?"

If there was a deference to Pete as the most accomplished musician in the lot, it wasn't because he demanded it explicitly. "He never acted or presumed to be our leader," Lee would say, "and we never rehearsed or performed with the concept of Pete as our leader," while acknowledging Pete's stature as their "sparkplug." The Weavers were at least nominally established as a democracy, and they were, the conversations and arguments built in to their rehearsal process.

Though Lee had started by zipping up new concerns into old hymns, he had turned into a substantially original songwriter on his own, even if he lacked the self-confidence to admit it at times. While he would swear for the rest of his life that he couldn't perform alone because he didn't play an instrument, he also wrote "Love Song Blues," performed at WNYC and elsewhere with Lee leading the song on piano.

"It was breathtaking how quickly songs came to us," Ronnie Gilbert would recall. Before a show, they'd meet up in the basement at Pete's place, at their personal wellspring atop Minetta Creek, and spend an hour or two running through material. If they didn't all personally save copies of the *People's Songs* bulletins in three-ring binders, all four were well versed in the canon that the senior two members, especially, had already helped shape. But they also had adventures learning new material. At one show, they performed a set of songs by Mao's Chinese Liberation Army. "The Weavers are frankly not 100 percent certain that they'll be singing these and other Chinese songs exactly as the victorious Liberation Armies and the toiling peasants are singing them," the *Daily Worker* noted. Lee was hardly confident in his ability to sing in other languages, with Ronnie often patiently coaching him through it.

Pete Seeger was six feet, four inches of high-strung passion, compared frequently over the years to his custom longneck banjo, and not inaccurately. Pete took on students, played private parties, and even occasional night club gigs. "I didn't know him in his everyday activities," Ronnie Gilbert would reflect later, remembering him as entirely and completely consumed with music. "I knew him only as a person who I sang with and did musical political activities with. And his moods swung very rapidly, very widely."

At one especially highfalutin birthday soiree with a good paycheck, Pete struggled to keep his mouth shut while one of the host's friends tore apart Henry Wallace and his campaign, until Pete was visibly shaking with rage, at which point a glass of Coca-Cola found itself splashed across a woman's dress.

Though it was nice to have his in-laws' as a home base, Pete now had two children to support, and his tolerance for the city was shrinking. By the late spring of 1949, as the Weavers were playing their first gigs, he and Toshi raised $1,750 to buy seventeen acres overlooking the Hudson River in Beacon, an hour's drive north of the city, and even quicker late at night after a gig in the Village. They spent the summer preparing the land for habitation.

One of the final issues of *People's Songs* had extolled the virtues of the Music Division of the New York Public Library, written in a can-do voice that is almost unmistakably Seeger's. And now Seeger returned to the Library, researching how to build a log cabin, which, quite earnestly, Pete Seeger began to do.

Pete Seeger *did* have a hammer. And an ax. And a pick. And friends. And most important, Toshi. If the Popular Front was closing, Seeger was staking his claim in the land itself. It was Americanism at its purest, both of the twentieth-century variety (as the old Communist slogan ran), but also the nineteenth or eighteenth, and back into pre-Revolutionary times. As the weather got cold, they borrowed a tent from their new neighbor, the painter Rockwell Kent.

The dark forces were out there nearby in the woods, Pete knew. Forces of another America that Pete hoped to transform with love and song. Pete could tell, heard whisperings around town, maybe just knew from all the haunted folk songs. It would take some good singing to shine the light just right, and even then he might see something he didn't want to.

It was a glorious green meadow under a cloudless blue sky that was, per-haps, to be the site of the biggest Weavers performance yet. Ronnie Gilbert and Freddie Hellerman got rides over from their summer jobs. For those born and raised in the boroughs, summer escapes were built into the rhythm of local life and were long built into the progressive world, becoming a reliable summer income source for those in the arts. Both of the former Camp Wo-Chi-Ca counselors now took work at Allaben, the Catskills resort operated by the *Morgen Freiheit*, the left-wing Yiddish daily newspaper associated with the party. Fred sent a third of his $15 weekly salary to Lee, back in Manhattan trying to follow up his mystery-story debut.

Ronnie's boyfriend Marty picked up Ronnie and some friends in his Dodge for a lift down to Peekskill, just a little to the south. Pete was performing that afternoon at a big concert, and invited them to join him, depending how the day unfolded. She was excited for the beautiful day ahead, a stellar bill featur-ing Paul Robeson, Pete, and more.

The Peekskill benefit for the Civil Rights Congress was the first major ven-ture by the reconstituted People's Artists, an outgrowth of the only part of People's Songs that had ever functioned successfully, its live events. A Paul Robeson concert in the idyllic countryside north of Manhattan was hardly a new proposition. As a left-wing hero, Robeson had performed there the pre-vious summers, drawing crowds from country houses and resorts whose cli-entele was rooted in various radical subgroups, like Camp Three Arrows (Socialist), Camp Unity (Communist), the Mohegan Colony (old-line anar-chist), Shrub Oak Park (labor Zionists and a broader coalition), and a full spectrum of left-wing subcultures. And in previous summers, such events had occurred without major hitches. But 1949 was different.

That spring, in Paris, addressing the Congress of the World Partisans of Peace, Robeson—taking the position of American workers—declared "We shall not make war on anyone. We shall not make war on the Soviet Union." Another quote, with blurrier origins but likely accurate, made an even bigger stir: "It is unthinkable that American Negroes would go to war on behalf of those who oppressed us for generations against a country [the USSR] which in one generation has raised our people to the full dignity of mankind."

Local newspapers boiled the quote even further. The report in the *Peekskill Evening Star* declared, "Robeson Says U.S. Negroes Won't Fight Russia." The long fallout from the New Deal continued, fears of socialism shooting out into local networks, out of electrical sockets and phone lines and into the local press, as news of Paul Robeson's impending concert arrived in Peekskill.

Working as a secretary at the *Morgen Freiheit*'s camp, Ronnie had perhaps glossed over the Yiddish headlines. Maybe copies of the *Worker* didn't make it there either. The unfolding events in Peekskill had been the subject of daily coverage. Somehow, in the late summer gloaming, Ronnie missed the details. When she refocused her memories with full knowledge of what had come before, she read the scene differently.

They were directed by local police to park over a mile from the concert site. Officers and state troopers stood by the side of the road, eating ice cream as they walked toward the entrance. An integrated crowd of Labor Day vacationers, locals, and those who'd made it out of the city filled in around her. Scattered locals occasionally jeered. Ronnie and her friends found themselves walking alongside a small marching band and a group of veterans in formation, protesting the concert that Ronnie and her friends were going to. Even if Ronnie didn't understand the full context, everything that followed did so with visible high-stakes drama, with all the symbolic forces taking actualized forms for a daylong encounter between the far sides of the American political spectrum.

"As we approached the main gate, our eyes met the most inspiring sight I have ever seen," Ronnie described to her mother in a letter a few weeks later. "Standing single file, elbow to elbow, in a snake line surrounding the entire hillside and lined up on both sides of the long road down inside the gate, were our boys, thousands of them, all of them with some identifying insignia— Local 65, UE, NMU, UOWPA, etc., etc., most of them with veteran insignias." There were some 2,500 of them, running anti-sniper patrols around the periphery of what was formerly the Hollybrook Country Club.

What Ronnie didn't know was that the concert had originally been scheduled for the weekend before. It was supposed to follow the day after People's Artists' inaugural Hootenanny Midsummer in the air-conditioned climes of the Astor Place Hotel, with Pete and Woody and Pete's Good Neighbor Chorus, a jazz combo, and more. But when Pete arrived with his mother for the initial concert in Peekskill, an evening affair, he was turned away at the gate of the picnic grounds, and told the show was canceled, which it was.

Those who'd arrived earlier, and were still inside, were well aware of the reason for the cancellation: an advancing angry mob, many drunk, throwing rocks, shrieking welcoming expressions like "Dirty commie!" or "Dirty kike!" or "We're going to finish what Hitler started!" and—looking for the absent Paul Robeson—"We'll lynch the nigger up."

A group in American Legion regalia physically attacked writer Howard Fast and his associates, who'd lined up in formation in front of the women and children. Fast and others retreated, locking arms and singing "We Shall Not Be Moved" as rioters tore apart the concert site, setting chairs and song sheets aflame in a bonfire. By the end of the night, there was a burning cross.

"I'll never forget the face of the man who struck me on the head, or the men who surrounded me, pushed me from one to another, grabbed me and hit me," said People's Songster Sylvia Kahn, who'd been one of the early arrivals. She'd been left crying against a car. "Why are you pulling an act?" a man in a Legionnaire's cap screamed at her. "Do they train you to put on acts?"

The initial anti-Robeson protest had been building steam during the previous week, participants taking offense in part because the concert was to be held across the street from a veterans' cemetery. "The time for tolerant silence that signifies approval is running out," the local newspaper editorialized. A parade coordinated by local veterans' organizations arrived at the entrance site in time to meet the concertgoers, and events had escalated from there.

The *Worker* covered their own angles to the story. "Paul Robeson should have the right to sing, speak or do anything he wants to," Jackie Robinson said from the dugout at Brooklyn's Ebbets Field. "If Mr. Robeson wants to believe in Communism, that's his right," Robinson said. "I prefer not to."

"Anything progressive is called Communism," the Dodgers infielder added.

At a rally in Harlem, Robeson announced, "I'm going back to Peekskill with my friends and they'll know where to find me."

With Robeson back on board, the rescheduled concert took on a new gravity, and progressives flowed in from around the East Coast. Shuttle buses ran from the local resorts. Lee and Woody got a ride up with a friend driving from Philadelphia. It was a short haul from Pete's new place in Beacon and he was, of course, scheduled to perform. The other Weavers would be happy to join.

Wanting them to witness it, Pete brought his whole family, including his two small children, against his father-in-law's wishes. After the media coverage the riot had received, Pete argued, nothing bad would happen. Still, the day before the rescheduled concert, at the site of his new homestead overlooking the Hudson, he'd received a note from the local Ku Klux Klan, thanking him and claiming they'd received 722 applications for membership in the past week.

The hills were alive with darkness. A banner appeared in town: "WAKE UP, AMERICA, PEEKSKILL DID" and the local newspaper urged further organization. Outside the concert site, a protestor distributed bumper stickers, BEHIND COMMUNISM STANDS—THE JEW! THEREFORE, FOR MY COUNTRY—AGAINST THE JEWS.

Just as Seeger had to clear the site of his future house, perhaps he needed to sing out across his new Hudson Valley home. A deindustrializing Republican stronghold, Peekskill was home to exactly the kind of people Seeger wanted to reach. So far it wasn't going terribly well. There were about 8,000 veterans marching outside, screaming threats like "You'll get in but you won't get out." The protesters even had their own song: "Roll out the Commies /We've got the Reds on the run." A police helicopter circled.

Ronnie remembered the concert as coming off flawlessly. In the throb of the afternoon, Pete didn't call up the rest of the Weavers, who only performed as part of the mass audience chorus that Pete led from the back of the flatbed truck during his short set. They were trying to wrap up the performance before nighttime fell. Pete did "The Hammer Song" and made way for Robeson.

Accompanied by a pianist, Robeson's set included "Go Down, Moses" and the mournful "Song of the Warsaw Ghetto," which Robeson had added to his set earlier that summer in Moscow upon hearing of the murder of Soviet-Jewish actor Solomon Mikhoels. Robeson sang "Ol' Man River," as well. Like Pete, he altered lyrics in his songs, changing the climactic chorus to "I must keep fightin' till I'm dyin'."

"The magnificent sound of Robeson's voice filled the hollow and swept the hillside," Ronnie wrote to her mother, the old-time fan for whom he was simply *Paul*. "Even the police helicopter overhead, which made as much noise as possible, could not drown out that voice." By four p.m., he was done.

Robeson was whisked off-site quickly, lying in the rear of a car with blanket-covered windows, a pair of trade-unionists lying on top of him, acting as bodyguards. But for the rest of the attendees, after the show was when the chaos began.

Ronnie couldn't find her boyfriend, or Fred, and after an hour of chaos, found herself on a packed bus hurriedly exiting the site. She could feel the vehicle slow to a halt "in a dark, leafy tunnel, under a canopy of overhanging trees," a moment of utter slow motion and late-summer silence, where "a young man in rolled-up shirtsleeves stood at the side of the road, a neat pile of rocks at his feet." The silence ended.

"Kikes!" Ronnie heard. "Jews!" The words were violent. "Go back to Russia, you dirty commies."

There was a pause, when Ronnie expected the nearby police officer to move in, to stop the man with the rocks. The officer stood there with his hands behind his back. He smiled. There was no help coming. The windows of the bus smashed inward, and the screaming started. Attackers threw milk onto the windshield, blocking the driver's view.

The assault was methodical, with the local police guiding it like an assembly line. The vehicles progressed down the exit road, were stopped by policemen, pelted with rocks, and continued on, before being stopped and pelted again.

In Pete Seeger's Jeep, the glass poured in like violent rapids over his children. Pete saw a police officer pull a driver from a vehicle outright and beat them with a nightstick. The banjo player screamed at the nearest trooper. "Aren't you going to do something? What are you *waiting* for?"

"Move on, move on," came the response.

Time magazine, too, reported police brutality: "One cop, reporting a brush with a Robesonite carload, announced proudly: 'We beat the hell out of them. I got two myself.'"

Lee and Woody experienced the attack from another bus, and Woody led the jammed-in passengers in "We Shall Not Be Moved," the Carter Family's "Worried Man Blues"—*"I'm worried now, but I won't be worried long"*—and Pete and Lee's new refrains of freedom, "The Hammer Song": *"I'll sing out danger, I'll sing out warning."*

Woody spat out jokes, too. "Anybody got a rock?" he called out. "There's a window back here that needs to be opened!" He yawped out the windows, taunting the rock throwers.

"I was literally scared shitless with Woody screaming at the Fascist pigs who had us surrounded," Lee remembered.

Lee's memory was of being trapped in a distant sylvan zone, the dark forces of the woods unseen on either side, "as if the air had changed, and there was no sun," Lee wrote. "Running through it was like being propelled through a long gray tunnel with no promised light of exit showing ahead."

As with the defeat of the Wallace campaign, there was a measure of comfort in gospel hymns and the power of folk music. Dozens ended up in hospitals, and coordinated stone throwing continued all the way south, into the Bronx.

Lee and others on the left claimed victory. "But we knew also that we would have to fight for it again as long as this state of war against culture and the people should continue," he wrote.

The *Worker* embroiled itself in the day-to-day news of the aftermath. Like Lee, the paper interpreted Peekskill as a triumphant moment, sneering at the local rock throwers as "imitation Storm Troopers," and rallying, always rallying.

But for musicians like Pete Seeger and others involved in the American progressive movement, there was nothing left for them in communism as it stood in any official capacity. It was in the summer of 1949, too, that Pete Seeger quietly ceased to attend party meetings. He would say later that it was because there was only one other Communist couple up in Beacon. But as the weather grew too cold to sleep even in the borrowed tent and the Seegers returned to the Village, Pete drifted away, his cheery intensity turned toward the same battles as before, following the same internal marching orders, now minus the procedural hassles.

The work was unlimited, as it always was, and if Wallace's defeat hadn't diminished his commitment, then Peekskill surely didn't either, as horrifying as it might have been. When clearing broken glass from his car the next day, Pete removed several rocks launched at him and his family, eventually building them into the wall next to the fireplace in his rising house on the Hudson, a reminder to never forget.

Ronnie Gilbert returned to Manhattan charged for battle, describing to her mother the "3,000,000 meetings and conferences and rehearsals I've had to attend since Peekskill." It was "one meeting after another[,] one duty after another—and so far as I'm concerned, there is no duty too much to ask of ourselves. Peekskill was a horrible experience—but I'm glad I was there. With my own eyes, I saw the cowardly, beastly face of fascism, the faces of fascists—screaming dirt and obscenity, hurling rocks with the viciousness they would use in hurling grenades, laughing at blood on the faces of women and children. . . ."

The Weavers' first proper assignment after Peekskill was organized on the fly by Mario Casetta, Pete's old army buddy, backseat passenger in Pete's Jeep during the attack, and proprietor of Charter Records. Wire recordings of Peekskill captured screams of "white niggers" and other taunts, and Mario was going to combine it with narration and music and make a record of it.

Constructed in the apartment of ambitious young engineer Tony Schwartz, "The Peekskill Story" cross-faded between the harrowing field recordings with matter-of-fact narration by Howard Fast, snippets of Robeson's performance, testimonials by Pete and Fred, and the Weavers singing the bold new song that Lee and Pete constructed, "Hold the Line."

Using a fighting chorus, Lee retraced the Battle of Peekskill around the ongoing movements of the peace army. On the material plane, they'd been pelted with rocks, their windows shattered, cars flipped. But there was a bigger fight, and they had stood their ground and *sung*. The two divergent Americas were once again visible in all their complexities. Peekskill created a historical turn that would grow sharper in a matter of weeks.

"A sort of political surrealism came dancing through the ruins of what had nearly been a beautifully moral and rational world," Arthur Miller commented about the unfolding events of 1949.

Woody, as charged up by the events as anyone, wrote almost two dozen new songs about the event, treating it as a major event in their collective timeline. On all planes of battle—local, global, symbolic, physical, personal, artistic, and political—Peekskill was a turning point.

Two days after the first Peekskill riot, in fact, a powerful new situation arrived, though news of it didn't reach American shores for a month: the Soviet Union's first successful test of nuclear weaponry. The Cold War gulf widened to vast new proportions before Boots Casetta could even get the two-side "Peekskill Story" into distribution.

In the safe harbor of Greenwich Village, the Weavers could feel choices coming on. They continued doing the work they'd been doing, the Almanac and People's Songs mission well intact when they signed up to sing for Vito Marcantonio, the only elected member of the American Labor Party in the House of Representatives, who'd quixotically decided to run for mayor of Manhattan.

Once the handpicked choice to replace New York's late beloved Fiorello La Guardia on New York's Upper East Side, the former Republican grew increasingly progressive through the years, forming the American Labor Party in 1936. Not expecting to win, he framed his opponents as "the big real estate interests, the bankers, and the Wall Street Gang."

Mario Casetta enlisted the Weavers and a brigade of People's Artists to the cause. Representing a deeply impoverished neighborhood, Marcantonio's platform countered police brutality against young blacks and Latinos, especially. Backing Laura Duncan, the singer who'd connected Billie Holiday with "Strange Fruit" a decade earlier, the Weavers performed on "Now, Right Now," a strident early civil-rights anthem. "*Why do the police treat my people so?"* Duncan sang. *"They beat us and they shoot us while justice passes us by,"* she continued, demanding freedom—with the allied Weavers harmonizing—*"now, right now."*

It was a battle they fought through the fall, and it had its triumphant moments. Instead of 15,000 people at Peekskill, the Weavers played to their biggest crowd yet during a late-October rally at Madison Square Garden, debuting a new version of Lead Belly's "New York City" with Lee's opening declaration ("New York City is a hell of a place/got every color of the human race"); a banjo/guitar duet, social commentary ("mighty fine place called Stuyvesant Town/but you can't live there if your skin is brown"); and an endorsement of the American Labor Party ("on November eighth, vote row 'C,' Marcantonio's the man for me . . .").

And if that weren't quixotic enough, Pete also signed up to sing for Benjamin Davis Jr., the black congressman from Harlem, the sole elected Communist in the House of Representatives, and certainly the only candidate running a reelection campaign while in jail. One of the eleven Communist leaders indicted on Smith Act charges, Davis was released less than a week before Election Day. A riot erupted at his comeback rally in Harlem.

Singing on the Marcantonio sound truck, the Weavers were pelted with vegetables. "Be glad they're not bricks," remarked Gordon Friesen, former Almanac House dweller, who'd organized the event. Then the campaign was over—one more old situation and a few more songs they'd never sing again.

L ee Hays had to be talked into the job. And, at the gates of very darkness, Pete Seeger plied him with assurances, the tall skinny Pete with the unbounded intensity convincing the deeply skeptical Lee of what could be done.

This particular gate was at the top of a narrow set of stairs on Seventh Avenue South that led down into the Village Vanguard, the nightclub where Agent Harwood E. Ryan had interviewed owner Max Gordon about Pete a few years earlier. Pete finally had his commercial group for Max.

You can go wait out the set breaks at the White Tower across the street, Pete told Lee, referring to the White Castle knockoff that (some think) was the inspiration for Edward Hopper's painting *Nighthawks* a few years earlier. *You can even go back to the basement at MacDougal Street, it's not far.*

It will be leaving our main job behind, Lee complained at the suggestion that they work in nightclubs. *It's a betrayal of the working class*, he moaned.

But it was Pete who made the key argument: the band would reach a new audience. If they did it right, perhaps, it would even be the exact opposite of a betrayal.

Pete Seeger wanted to make music that would be listened to by the humans who'd whipped rocks at them a few months earlier at Peekskill, the people who'd lobbed tomatoes at them on the sound truck, music that could carry all of their values and be unhampered by new situations to come.

What had provoked the conversation, though, was practicality. The Weavers had virtually no choice in the matter if they wanted to keep being the Weavers. While they continued to gather every Wednesday in Pete's basement, nearly everything they'd done in their year of singing together had been a dead end, and lately dead ends seemed to be coming quicker than ever.

They'd experimented with material and collaborators. The group integrated in the fall of '49 around the time of the election, too, with Hope Foye. Pete announced her addition to the lineup in the People's Artists newsletter. Sometimes called "the female Paul Robeson," Foye was a classically trained soprano who'd sung around the People's Artists scene, appearing on the bill at Peekskill, and with the Weavers on the Marcantonio sound truck.

Mysteriously, Lee didn't show up for those practices. "Always got sick or something other reason like having to stay home to work on a script," Freddie noted in a journal. They sang on WNYC and at the Marcantonio rally at the Garden. "I remember being told that I sounded like [when] on the Fourth of July, [the fireworks] go up and burst into beautiful colors," Foye told Ron Cohen. "They said I sounded like that in the background, because I would come out with one of my soprano tones."

In an attempt to keep the band together, Pete began to turn down other bookings unless he could bring the group with him. And even though he missed practices, Lee spat out a rambling fifteen-point Promotion and Publicity Plan over three extra-long pages. Point 12, in part reads: "Moses had Ten, and already I've got Twelve."

He proposed the Weavers go into "daily session": "daily meetings, assignments, reports each day on our assignments, also minutes and a record of our assignments." Of these "assignments," Lee suggested many, though they all seemed to go to other Weavers: Ronnie was managing them (she should get an extra 10 percent), Fred and Pete could write articles (Lee would be available for editing), they should all draft potential programs, and cease taking *all* outside work, following Pete. "The Weavers can't exist just as a group which meets once in a week and once in awhile gets a booking."

The new quintet recorded together for the campaign on "Skip to the Polls," Hope and Ronnie's voices sounding like two wavering currents of electricity not always aligned. Despite Pete's optimistic announcement, it didn't last. With her trained voice, Foye felt like she never fit in with the People's Songs world.

"After a few rehearsals and one or two appearances, Hope wisely decided to follow the road her operatic soprano took her instead of letting us try to mold it into Weavers shape," Ronnie would say. Hope Foye had her own career, and no interest in molding herself to Lee's pronouncements. Really, none of the Weavers had any interest in following Lee's fifteen points, with more coming at each further practice.

And as the fall wore on, the Weavers' colors dampened. Ronnie had been working as a CBS typist, trying in vain to "colonize" her coworkers into the union, now running on unemployment fumes. She and her boyfriend were thinking of moving to California and having kids. Freddie had finished college and, living at home with his parents, was still considering any and all options to avoid the family rags business, lately thinking about graduate work in literature at the University of Chicago.

This idea of Fred abandoning his Weaving for Chicago infuriated Lee, and perhaps stung even more (Fred thought) after some of Lee's other friends had moved away, including former Almanac Millard Lampell, who'd headed to Hollywood. "[We] used to be very close," Fred noted in his journal, "but now there was . . . friction."

As intimate and open and sweet and encouraging as Lee could be, he was also easily hurt. Especially when drinking, he could turn on people, lathering himself into an obstructionist attack mode. They were both sides of Lee that Pete knew all too well. Most of the time, these days, he could come to grips with it. "Pete always has to drive home or pick him up whenever we have to go anywhere," Fred noted.

But, like Ronnie, Fred liked singing with the Weavers too much to give it up. In the long days of '49, with the Almanac Singers gone and People's Songs shut down, the government attacking those around them, and the deeply shattering events of Peekskill barely in the rearview mirror, the value of having people to sing with was nothing to discount.

Lee, especially, was in a bad way. He'd missed Lead Belly's funeral, at which his three fellow Weavers sang. His only pair of decent pants were at the cleaner's, he said, and out of respect to the always-immaculate Huddie, Lee had to skip it. The Weavers played weekly semi-hoots on Sunday afternoons at the

Popular Front–spawned Photo League, a visual equivalent of People's Songs, also nearing its end. The basket money would usually go toward Lee's rent.

Ronnie sent queries to colleges and heard nothing back. Boots Casetta put out a single, Lee's blustering "Wasn't That a Time" backed with the Bahamian hymn "Dig My Grave." And while "Wasn't That a Time" was a smart and powerful cataloging of new situations since time immemorial, it was "Dig My Grave" that pointed toward the Weavers' future, simple and beautiful stacked harmonies. But the single went nowhere and Boots hitchhiked home to Los Angeles to start anew.

Finally Pete landed on what had seemed unthinkable to Lee: working in a nightclub. Hardly free of his own anxieties about the matter, Pete proposed to Village Vanguard owner Max Gordon that he book the Weavers, paying the same rate Pete received as a solo act. "I decided to stop congratulating myself on not going commercial," Pete would later say. With Lee finally assenting to descend into the Vanguard and sing People's Songs for the people of cozy Greenwich Village, the next step was to formally visit the 123-person-capacity club for a Monday audition night.

Fred and Ronnie, pop music fans both, shared none of Pete and Lee's commercial reservations, but Ronnie *was* terrified, and when she entered the club itself, she felt its long bohemian history, the "poets' ghosts [that] might be still creeping around inside the cracked walls of the shabby triangular room."

It wasn't what she thought a nightclub should look like. Lee, on the other hand, had no expectations in that regard whatsoever. "I don't know that I'd ever been in one," he would remember. Bars, yes. Hootenannies and rallies and marches and apartment hangouts, sure, but not this strange formalized place. Pete, the lightest drinker of the bunch, was the only one with any experience whatsoever playing nightclubs. A variety show's worth of hopeful comedians and other musicians circulated in the room while the white-haired Gordon sat at a center table, puffing on a cigar.

Ronnie felt a twinge of morbidity as Pete called for "Dig My Grave" as the opening song when they stepped onto the Vanguard's tiny corner stage. They followed it with an Israeli folk tune and a number of Christmas carols.

Lee's roommate had joined them to watch the audition and observed the competition. When they got home, he told Lee, "All those people [were] there breaking their backs, hoping Max Gordon would hire them, all of them wanting to get a job, and you're hoping he won't hire you."

But Max Gordon hired the Weavers at $200 a week to be split among them, plus cook-them-yourself hamburgers from the venue's backstage kitchen.

And so the Weavers opened at the Village Vanguard on Thursday, December 22, 1949, booked through the end of the year, and made their first trek from the kitchen, winding through the tables, past their smiling friends from the various hoots and Photo League Sundays, and to the Vanguard stage.

"Fred's look was unremarkably collegiate," Ronnie remembered. "Pete wore whatever he had on during the day (often jeans and a work shirt), and Lee had nothing presentable." She was somewhat aghast, but it was enough to get Lee down the Vanguard's stairs, let alone dress him up.

"Can you imagine singing 'Hold the Line' in tuxedos?" Pete remembered Lee once asking. At the very least, Lee made sure that their broke friends could either get on the guest list or have the drink minimum waived.

"We raced through our first 40-minute set in 15 minutes," Ronnie recalled. "When some singers are nervous, they go flat. When Pete Seeger is nervous, he goes fast." But they figured it out quickly.

Folk singers were hardly unknown in Greenwich Village clubs. After Red-baiting, only Café Society's Downtown location struggled on, that week featuring vocalist Sarah Vaughan, a jazz trio, and a comedian. But to see live music downtown remained a novelty in 1949, most of it living well above the Fourteenth Street latitude in midtown's neon-glow center around Times Square. "Let's go down to Greenwich and see the Village," one of the Weavers' early pieces of press joked, stressing the exoticism of the adventure.

There'd long been square-dancing at the Village Barn, but that was a tourist spot. Manhattan's music scene was far more oriented toward jazz and pop and dance bands. At Birdland, there was a two-hour show, running four times a night, featuring saxophone heroes Charlie Parker, Lester Young, and Stan Getz, as well as Harry Belafonte, a charismatic young actor and vocalist modeling himself on Josh White; he'd worked on the Wallace campaign and sung with the Weavers at one of the last People's Songs' hoots. But there was nothing that resembled the Weavers, with their folk songs and banjos and harmonies, all novelties that seemed to put them more in league with the satirists, telepathists, glee-club ensembles, cornball dancing at the Village Barn, and other miscellany scattered at dinner spots and hotel bars and other midtown nooks.

For their nightclub debut, they constructed a bridge to the audience from the People's canon of holiday songs like "We Wish You a Merry Christmas" (People's Song #206), "The Twelve Days of Christmas" (People's Song #208), and "Joy to the World" (People's Song #213), built into their repertoire from hoots past. On the first night at the Village Vanguard, they finished their final set with another old favorite, Lead Belly's "Goodnight Irene" (People's Song #178).

Huddie had succumbed to ALS a few weeks before the band opened at the Vanguard. The mournful waltz, in his repertoire for decades, had evolved in his performances out of a song he'd picked up from his uncles, becoming his signature. Perhaps ironically, its own roots would be traced to a nine-teenth-century Tin Pan Alley composition by Gussie Davis, or maybe even a half-related answer song, which made it even more authentic along the banks of Minetta Creek. With three of the four Weavers especially close to the late Huddie, "Goodnight Irene" became their closer nearly every night.

Pete acted as the group's first public voice, which had happened by default because of his professional stature. But, as Ronnie discovered, the job was suited to "anyone better than he, at times."

Lee came to the conclusion that Pete's "internal rhythm was twice as fast as that of most living human beings." He jumped into tunes before his band-mates were ready, and droned on in his introductions. Without protest from anyone, Lee swiftly took over. Where Pete tended toward the painfully ear-nest, Lee was quietly and thoroughly entertaining. The showman in the some-times shy Lee came to the fore at the Village Vanguard, "emulating [his] father" and cultivating his own kind of "ministerial presence."

For their perennial global medley, "Around the World," Pete gave the sing-song intro, "It's a collection of four dance tunes, all from different continents, and we won't even skip a beat, but we'll take a *real trip!*" (That's just great, Pete.) Other times, he'd be more overt: "In these days of a-bombs and hell-bombs, that kind of junk . . . we're going to show you that, no matter where you go, you find a lot of things in common with people."

Lee's take, with his soft and forceful preacher's intonation (as it evolved) ran: "It paints a picture of a *U*-nited Nations kind of world, a world in which people know how to get along together in perfect peace and friendship. Four different dance tunes, each one of 'em from a different country. We're gonna travel around without skippin' a beat and dance with the people and swap a few songs and court a few girls and vice versa. The first foreign country we're gonna visit tonight *is* the state of Arkansas . . ."

But it was the music that drove it home, the thrilling freshness of fluid next-beat segues between the Israeli circle dance and the polka and the Caribbean party jam. Most of all, the Weavers offered a blend of voices and intuitive harmonizing that at times might have seemed like a musical sleight-of-hand. They were four singers with only a banjo and guitar between them for instrumental support, but if any other quartet of musicians arrayed themselves in that configuration, there is little chance they'd come out sounding like the Weavers. Like a musical square dance, Ronnie and Pete might double up for a phrase or two, before switching partners with Fred, all thrillingly informal, Lee's ominous bass parts rumbling as if an underground freedom train had gotten loose in the subway system.

"There was no standard lead singer or backup," Ronnie would remember. "Someone might start with melody but then move to harmony, vocal lines crossing. Anyone could lead." The arrangement process, continued from the basement, was completely democratic, and filled with constant digressions and disagreements. Lee Hays was strong-willed and overflowing with opinions, but so was every other Weaver.

Quickly, the headquarters of Weavers activity shifted from the Minetta Creek–dampened basement on MacDougal to the kitchen at the Village Vanguard. "When we began working down at the Village Vanguard, all of a sudden we were called upon to perform many more songs than we had prepared," Fred recalled, and so the kitchen became a rehearsal room between Weavers sets as a trio led by pianist Clarence Williams played for the Vanguard crowd.

Drawing from their vast knowledge of the People's Songbook, and especially Pete's own wide reserves, they'd work up quick arrangements and take them to the stage. "And we'd improvise for the first night or two, and by the third night we'd have the parts down pretty well," Fred remembered. The quartet took on traditional songs, more Woody tunes, Spanish Civil War numbers, whatever they remembered on whichever particular night. Their old radical songbook stayed in play, too, including "The Hammer Song" and "Wasn't That a Time," though Lee continued to rewrite the last verse. The Weavers grew into a new shape to match their new home and ambitions.

"I remember being a little baffled by nightclub life," Lee remarked.

"I love your act," more than one Weaver was told. "*It's not an act!*" the Weaver would probably reply.

But it became that, too, and a matter of stagecraft. "We evolved a kind of choreography for four klutzes on the Vanguard's tiny stage," Ronnie recalled. "Pete displayed his virtuosity with the banjo, raising its long neck over my head to avoid hitting Fred in the eye as we exchanged positions at the single microphone." And there was Lee, the man *People's Songs* advertised as a "substantial singer," planted on the stage like a mostly immovable feature of the landscape.

Despite the chaos-wreaking doppelgängers emerging in the FBI's files, Pete Seeger was a smiling all-American boy on the Village Vanguard stage, a lean and tall New Englander only three years removed from his military service, in the fighting shape he would remain in for the rest of his long life. By the time of the thaw, he was chopping wood daily at his place in Beacon and commuting to the city. In the Vanguard kitchen, Pete Seeger helped himself to heaping piles of hamburger meat, broiling up half-pounders between sets, caught once by aghast club owner Max Gordon.

"Pete had, as always, a fantastic sweet tooth," Lee remembered, "and one of his main articles of diet was Coca-Cola which he used to drink at the club." At least until one day when a bandmate brought in a news clipping about a Japanese experiment where lab rats' teeth began to decay in response to the soft drink. The next day, Lee saw a deflated Pete change his regular drink order to distilled water.

"After a few weeks and [we] got the hang of it even at those low wages I started to enjoy it," Lee admitted. Perhaps too much. He never did wind up having to find a place to go between sets. When not actually working up material with his bandmates, "as it turned out later I wasted all that time drinking brandy and getting into trouble."

Generally speaking, though, the run was going well, and Max Gordon quickly extended the band's residency into 1950 and the new decade, upping their pay, but removing sandwich privileges. "I was always hungry in those days," Lee would recall, and he protested the new contractual term by acquiring a sack of burgers from the White Tower across the street and conspicuously consuming them at one of the venue's tables. He soon had his sandwich privileges restored.

Toshi Seeger, Pete's long-term level-headed ground control, volunteered to be the band's new manager. She and Ronnie declared that the boys needed to be outfitted for professional stagewear.

"It will lead to our being taken seriously as musicians and singers," Ronnie argued, "and not as a bunch of amusing characters who wandered in off the street."

Dragging the boys on perhaps the first coordinated clothes-buying expedition of their adult lives, they acquired almost-matching green corduroy jackets, finding one in Lee's size at an Army-Navy store. Fred described them as "bilious," still bristling years later at what he called "uniforms."

Positive press clippings accumulated. The *Herald Tribune* allowed that "they look as if they had just dropped in on the way home from the office." The *New Yorker* weighed in, too, noting their maroon ties and Lee's crumpled suit. "I leaned against the wall in the packed cellar and heard them do a blues song, a prison song, a militant Spanish piece, a sprightly number from Israel, a Zulu chant, and several other things that were entertaining and off the beaten track," the writer observed. "They are a refreshing group, the Weavers."

Material came together with a quick intimacy that was hard to square with where the songs would soon travel. The Zulu chant that the *New Yorker* writer heard was probably one of the songs that Pete Seeger discovered when he was home sick with a winter cold. Alan Lomax had brought him a stack of records from South Africa, and Pete finally had listening time.

One was Gallotone GB-829, where Solomon Linda and His Original Evening Birds performed their song "Mbube." Beginning with a long chant that Pete could almost but not quite make out, it sounded a little bit like the title on the record, but not really. What really grabbed Pete, though, was the high, wordless falsetto that floated on top and—most especially—where it landed, in a secondary melody, sad and sweet and a world unto itself.

He transcribed the parts as he heard them on scraps of paper and gathered the Weavers around a table at the Village Vanguard one night. Pete directed the session, almost incoherent with excitement, trying to describe the four vocal parts as he heard them. Maybe even that night he ran back over to MacDougal Street and brought back the record itself, but for Ronnie that didn't clarify anything either. "Where was the song?" she wondered at first.

But quickly they found it, the Weavers falling into the chant as best they could make it out: *wimoweh, a-wimoweh*, and on and on into what would prove to be cultural infinity. Onstage, with the Vanguard spotlight beaming down, it became a visual trademark, Pete standing behind them and away from the microphone and spotlight and letting loose with his most elongated falsetto, a swooping curling ghost of a transmission from someplace far away.

Ronnie wondered where it was from. "South Africa? Folksong heaven? Outer space?" she pondered. "Whatever it was, we were carried away together, sailing on waves of sound, measure after measure, the music meaning nothing and everything."

Max Gordon loved the band, and kept renewing their engagement even as weeknight attendance dwindled. At one performance, only one table was occupied, so the band headed out onto the venue floor, performing for the lucky customers. But empty houses were the least of what Max Gordon put up with from his beloved quartet.

The teetotaling Pete had taken the liberty of getting free Cokes at the bar, to keep that extra spark-plug glow. His less teetotaling bandmates likewise made use of their bar discount. Lee Hays discovered brandy with a vengeance.

By the early winter of 1950, it had caught up with him, and he began to call in sick from the Vanguard, claiming laryngitis. The sick days started to stretch out, eventually to weeks.

The other Weavers fumed, but they weren't stopping, continuing to add to their repertoire. Again, they called on Alan Lomax's recordings from the Bahamas in 1935 that yielded "Dig My Grave" and pulled out a song called "The Wreck of the John B." Collected by Carl Sandburg in 1927's *American Songbag*, the version sung by the Cleveland Simmons Group on Lomax's reel featured a layered harmony that Pete and the gang regularized against Pete's banjo approximation of a Bahamian rhythm. It was every bit as much of a transliteration as turning "Mbube" into "Wimoweh," and eventually would cause almost as much confusion when it migrated from the undefinable world of folk songs to the more legally bound institutions of pop music.

Ronnie, especially, was shocked that Max Gordon continued to book them, even as one-quarter of their ranks was absent. But Gordon had a genuine liking for the Weavers, paying Lee's weekly salary even in his absence. Not that the other Weavers were taking it lightly. "We may have to take the bull by the horn," Pete told Fred. "If we have to, we have to. I've done it twice before."

One potential replacement was Bill Dillard, a veteran bass singer and trumpet player who'd worked with Dizzy Gillespie and crossed paths with the Weavers at the Lead Belly tribute in January. "Not only was he a good singer," Pete pointed out, sketching an alternate-universe version of the Weavers, "but his trumpet playing would have worked in well. [Dillard] felt, however, that though he liked what we were doing, it would have represented too great a change from the popular song style which he had been working in for 20 years."

Word made it back to Lee that the band was seeking a new bass vocalist, at which point he got his act together and got himself back to the Vanguard. Claiming he'd learned his lesson, he would swear that "alcohol and music don't mix" but, while that was perhaps true in the moment, both would continue to play increasingly large roles in Lee's life in coming years.

Even when singing at the Village Vanguard, the band still hit the subway circuit for any number of good causes. They performed at PS 50 in Queens, at a benefit with Paul Robeson for a group suing the Peekskill police, and at the funeral for Bob Reed, the late *Daily Worker* music critic who'd given ample support to the Almanac Singers and People's Songs, a dear friend to Lee especially.

As spring wore on, the Vanguard crowds swelled. Alan Lomax brought the distinguished poet and song collector Carl Sandburg himself, and the band went home with a blurb that would serve them well for decades to come: "When I hear America singing, the Weavers are there," Sandburg said.

After that, the crowds grew even more. And, it was among these crowds that, one night, the band first heard the laughter.

CHAPTER FOUR

Irene, Goodnight

The high-pitched laughter came out of the darkness, over and over, night after night, "a great hooting sound," as it was once described: *hoo-hoo-hoo*. Lee's stage routines had tightened, and the hooting ricocheted around the Vanguard in perfect sympathy with the punch lines. The hooter saw the Weavers at the Village Vanguard for thirty-one nights in a row, by one accounting.

It took a few weeks for Lee's new fan to actually introduce himself. Pete remembered the "pleasantly drunk" man with the neat mustache and slicked-back hair. And it was up to Pete to explain to Lee who the nice man was. His name was Gordon Jenkins and he was one of the most famous musicians in the United States in 1950.

"I had never heard of Jenkins when we met him and knew nothing of his work," Lee admitted, "until [Pete] kindly explained to me what a big band was."

He continued, "This was coming towards the end of the time of the big bands which in my cultural experience had gone right over my head without my being aware of them at all."

And even Pete was only dimly aware of Jenkins's reputation. Devoted to the popular music of the 1920s and 1930s, Pete could still play much of the prewar hit parade, a music that informed his rhythmic sensibility at its deepest roots. Despite wanting the Weavers to perhaps make a dent in popular music, it was a world that was almost completely alien to the two senior Weavers. Ronnie and Fred knew better, though.

A bandleader, producer, arranger, and star performer in his own right, Gordon Jenkins's 1946 extravaganza *Manhattan Tower* was a tour-de-force multi-disc set celebrating midcentury Gotham at its most glittering, a concept album when 78s were still stored in actual bound albums. Wildly sentimental, dripping with strings and horns and choirs, it was nearly the polar opposite of the musical world that the Weavers inhabited, dismissed as middlebrow schmaltz by many a folkie. But Ronnie loved it as a pure pop pleasure, treating herself to a copy when she returned to Brooklyn after her stint in Washington with the Priority Ramblers. "That wasn't my New York by any stretch of the imagination," Fred would scoff.

But Jenkins's other recordings—with Peggy Lee, with Louis Armstrong, with Billie Holiday, with Ella Fitzgerald—were right up Fred's alley. "Being a big-band guy, I really just loved most of the work Gordon had done," he recalled. "Just knocked me out completely." He loved that Jenkins's arrangements seemed human, despite their scale, abounding with musical winks. One of Jenkins's trademarks was breaking down a full studio of musicians to a single one-handed piano part, which he played himself. In 1948, he'd been made a musical director at Decca, one of the country's five major labels.

"I just flipped over the Weavers," Jenkins told an interviewer. "I was hypnotized by the group."

Once he'd introduced himself, his love for the band grew even more boundless. Raised in small-town Missouri, Jenkins and Lee shared an easy country-boy rapport and became quick post-show drinking buddies. Often, while audiences filed in and out between performances, Jenkins would stay for the late set too. There was a night when he'd returned to California, but wanted to check in at the Vanguard, and called the venue's pay phone—in a boothless alcove in a hallway near the stage—and instructed club owner Max Gordon to leave it off the hook while the band performed. It wasn't long before Jenkins was promising the band a spot on Decca, and setting up an audition.

For Gordon Jenkins, it had nothing to do with politics. "I don't think he knew who the President was," Fred would say. Gordon Jenkins was an enormous Weavers fan and thought this combination of voices and songs needed to be heard.

The quartet tramped up to Decca's headquarters on West Fifty-Seventh Street to audition for the record company brass. Ronnie found the whole experience embarrassing, Gordon parading them in front of the executives. As soon as they'd walked into the office, a cheery bald man in a leather armchair leaned back, his mouth stretching into what Ronnie remembered as a "too-ready smile."

"Oh, yeah," he said, with a bright recognition, "I know you, Pete. Always liked you." This left Ronnie uneasy, especially when, looking at Pete, the smiler then referred to the Weavers as "your group." From that, Pete took it for granted that they knew about his background, and steeled himself for a lot more of the same. He'd reached this level of the game with the Almanac Singers. The smiler was Milt Gabler, a music-store owner and enthusiastic fan who'd jumped into production and eventually the executive end of Decca. A legendary record man in his own right who'd released Billie Holiday's searing "Strange Fruit," Gabler wasn't yet as convinced of the Weavers' salability as Gordon Jenkins was.

They ran through a half dozen songs as the executives sat around, "as if in someone's living room," as Ronnie recalled. Fred's memory amplified it to something like a Surrealist nightmare, a procession of company reps filing in and out of the room, all deeming the band unusable.

Eventually, the company president got up to leave, declaring the Weavers uncommercial, and one of the executives made a pronouncement that forced Lee to finally answer the familiar Question. "You're good," said one of them, "but you have to decide if you want to be good or commercial."

There is no dispute about Lee's answer: "We hoped we could be good *and* commercial."

The executive shook his head and lectured the band: How could they sing songs in Hebrew? What was all this "Tzena Tzena Tzena" nonsense? It would have to be in English, and it would have to be about a girl. . . . And eventually the man's voice just blurred for the Weavers and they showed themselves out. When they reconvened at the Vanguard later that night, a shaken Gordon Jenkins took Pete aside and promised he'd pull the band onto his next session, one way or another. But by then, the Weavers' world had lurched into motion.

Gordon Jenkins wasn't the only representative of the pop-music world lurking in the Village Vanguard's triangular cellar. "A lot of Broadway characters with fat cigars and big pinky rings began coming around asking who's managing us," Fred remembered. "As green as we were, we knew enough to stay away from *them*."

Pete proposed that, since they were going to be wading into the murky waters of professional music, it might behoove them to acquire a professional manager. Lee, for one, thought Toshi was doing a fine job. *Why do we need a manager? We already have a job. What's there to manage?*

Quite a lot, as the other Weavers knew, and—more important—far more that they didn't know. The band was pointed toward the next level, and Toshi already had her hands full with two kids, not to mention her cloud-dwelling banjo-playing husband.

The solution presented itself in the kitchen one night at the Vanguard when a thirty-year-old man named Harold Leventhal popped back to say hello. Pete only knew Leventhal casually. Before the war, Harold had been a genuine show-biz professional, hustling on Tin Pan Alley as a song plugger for Irving Berlin, pushing the songwriter's latest sheet music. He was well or-ganized and knew little about professional music management, but came with impeccable progressive credentials.

During the war, Leventhal had been stationed in India. Connecting to the local Communist Party, he received a letter of introduction from Jawaharlal Nehru, soon the country's first prime minister, to Mahatma Gandhi himself. When Leventhal arrived, the great activist was observing one of his weekly days of silence but wrote Leventhal a note suggesting he return.

When he did, Gandhi greeted him happily with a question for the New York Communist music scenester: *How is Paul Robeson?*

Whether Pete yet knew this particular anecdote, he instinctively invited Leventhal to manage the band. More so than Gordon Jenkins, Harold Leven-thal would play a pivotal role in the band's professional and personal lives, collectively and individually. One of his first acts was to partner with Pete Kameron, a childhood friend, to handle the band's day-to-day affairs. Harold had to tend to the family girdle business.

A complicated ally during a complicated era of a complicated quartet, Pete Kameron was a prewar show-biz hustler who'd worked all over, and had just returned from a high-stress road-managing gig in the still segregated South. The International Sweethearts of Rhythm were the first all-female jazz band in the country, and multicultural too. Living nearby, Kameron was using the Vanguard as his nightly hangout spot. In his version of Weavers history, he was responsible for bringing both Harold Leventhal and Gordon Jenkins into the Village Vanguard to see the Weavers.

A well-dressed smooth talker, he was "a breath of old show business," Ron-nie remembered, and seemed to match well with Leventhal's more obvious soft-spoken and mensch-like qualities. However he arrived, Kameron's hire paid off almost immediately, with a classic show-biz stratagem: He went to

Columbia Records and told them that Decca had been interested in signing the Weavers, and the band promptly received an offer.

"Don't do a thing!" Gordon Jenkins told them when they shared the news, just before they were to sign with producer Mitch Miller. "I'll call you back in half an hour." Jenkins played his cards hard, telling the heads of Decca that he would personally finance the Weavers' sessions, and would release them under his name, if it made them feel any better.

As they worked nightly at the Village Vanguard, the Weavers' professional life began to take undeniable shape and momentum. In a letter that spring, Pete described the band: "We got ourselves, after much searching, a good young manager, a Decca contract, and likelihood of steady work from now on, if we want it."

They had around fifty songs in their repertoire, Pete wrote. "Most of our arrangements are simple in the sense that they use traditional folk harmonies," he observed. "There is considerable subtlety even so."

Then Pete Seeger asked the Chicago-based vocalist Coyal McMahan if he'd like to join the Weavers. Describing themselves as "progressives" and friends of Paul Robeson and Josh White, they were looking for a second bass vocalist, though Pete didn't quite spell out why. Offering to pay McMahon's way to New York, Pete emphasized that it would be a democratic arrangement. "All of us take solos and leads on different songs, and we would want whoever joins us to take leads and us back <u>him</u> up on songs that he knows."

As the Weavers moved toward a professional career that would transport them far from the cozy confines of the Vanguard, Pete continued to seek a musical insurance policy on Lee Hays. Lee was a musical comrade, no doubt, but they'd made it this far, and if he were to disappear again, it would be a real setback. The addition of Coyal McMahan, whom Pete had connected with on the phone first, would likewise have integrated the Weavers, which they'd hoped to do the previous fall with the brief membership of Hope Foye.

From Chicago, McMahan politely declined. "You are a man after my own heart," he wrote Pete, recalling the time they had shared a stage during the Henry Wallace campaign two years earlier. Pete's letter had reached him in Chicago just as his own quartet was to make their debut after much rehearsal. Perhaps they'd cross paths sometime.

For the meanwhile, it was Lee Hays or bust. Mountains were hard to move. A week after receiving McMahan's delayed reply, Pete also received—on the occasion of his thirty-first birthday—a possibly drunken ramble from his old friend Lee. A roller coaster of emotion, the three-page letter veered from passive-aggressive to loving, from sweeping to self-pitying, unforgiving to tender. Some more of Lee's young friends were abandoning Lee to the depredations of the world outside, "living" (in Lee's judgment) "with no regard for the demands of life and history." The details of their betrayals were unspecified.

"Your life is an answer to all the corruption and tragedy of these lost ones," he told Pete dramatically. Sweet, unassailable Pete. They were due at Decca the next day for their first proper recording session, and perhaps the oncoming years were flashing before Lee's eyes, like premonitions of worlds to come, his Southern fire rumbling out over his typewriter.

"Have you ever looked at an old friend as through a mask," Lee wondered, "and seen a stranger, and heard from his lips the voice of the beast, the impostor, the demon come to devour the original spirit—

"?"

Lee's faith in the struggle would never waver, but the battle of life was another matter, and Lee's was perpetual. Where Lee oozed strange emotion, Pete collected his energies someplace inside, rarely articulating them directly. Certainly there is no record of Pete's response, but Lee knew him as well as anyone besides Toshi. United in the Weavers, their missions remained bound, assigned by fate to the same platoon.

It was during those months, too, that the Red Scare reawakened itself. The newest human face it occupied was Joseph McCarthy, stepping into the spotlight as the Weavers were gathering nightly around the microphone on the Vanguard stage. McCarthy ratcheted national Red-baiting to a dramatic new level, claiming he had *in his hands* a list of *Communists* in the *State Department*!

The fake list was real news, and with the Weavers preparing to enter into the surreal world of American pop, the tension crackled in the air as a mostly unseen force around them. Pete Kameron brought them to the William Morris Agency, and the first agent they encountered was the same rep who'd overseen the Almanac debacle of '42.

But navigating just-so, in the spring of 1950, the Weavers saw a clear sky into which they might hurl themselves on the rocketing colors of their entwined voices. In that moment, there was no one to stop them. Decca prepared a two-pronged launch: one single of the Weavers singing as their unadorned selves in their global-folk-songs guise, and one single of the Weavers paired with Gordon Jenkins.

So in the vast space of Decca's studio A, on the third floor of the Pythian Temple on Seventieth Street, vocalists assembled over here, strings over yonder, the Weavers gathered themselves around Gordon Jenkins's conducting stand. Staring them down from the far end of the room was a large caricature of a Native American woman, standing with her hands wide open. "Where's the melody?" a cartoon dialogue bubble asked.

"All my juvenile thrills at being part of a big important process with lots of competent people busy with their individual jobs in service of the broadcast came back in a wave," Ronnie recalled. Having a whole orchestra and coteries of backup singers was heaven itself.

When they were finally ready for the Weavers some two hours later, and Pete had risen from his nap on the studio floor, the band did something new: they compromised themselves. All they had to do was stand in Decca's Studio A and do what they did onstage at the Village Vanguard. Gordon had sculpted arrangements around them. What needed to change, as the too-ready smiler had called out during their audition, were the *lyrics*.

Sure, they could sing in Hebrew on their folk single, maybe the Andrews Sisters fans out there would buy that one, but on the main attraction—released under the banner of the Gordon Jenkins Orchestra—they would be featured guests, and Jenkins and Decca would have the final say. For "Tzena Tzena Tzena," Gordon prepared new English lyrics. Ronnie, for one, didn't mind and thought his take "capture[d] beautifully the feeling of the song and the internationalist impulse for us to be singing it." She almost liked the new lyrics better, considering the original Hebrew was the equivalent of an Israeli catcall. Making new lyrics for new situations was part of the folk process, as much Gordon Jenkins stepping into the Weavers' world as them stepping into his.

On the B-side, though, the new situation had the Weavers floating in on a bed of violins, as if on a movie sound stage, cooing vocalists and horns doubling the strings, the chorus swelling in, and then they were singing Lead Belly's "Goodnight Irene" (People's Song #178). The offending lyrics about suicide by morphine were part of Fred's verse, though Ronnie still got her beautifully haunted "Sometimes I get a great notion to jump in the river and drown." Lee sang the lines about rambling and gambling that Huddie had personally bequeathed to him at a jam session. Pete didn't get any verses to himself, but he didn't need them, his banjo cutting through the proceedings just as it did in chat-filled union halls, sing-alongs, or down the echoing avenue canyons during the Marcantonio campaign, a high lonesome signal in the noise.

Lee Hays stocked up on beans for the summer. They all did. "We were about to get a TV summer replacement show [sponsored by] Van Camp['s] Beans," Fred Hellerman remembered, "and we were all buddy-buddy with them and chummy-chummy and they were sending us all cases of their goddamn beans!" The global village was flickering on in America, families gathering by the tube glow, and it seemed to offer the most direct path to the widest audience, in Peekskill and everywhere.

In fact, the Weavers were right there at the start, making their television debut on the premiere of NBC's *Broadway Open House*, the very first late-night variety show on network television at the end of May 1950. But then, before their Decca single even hit stores, a prominent anti-Communist publication pegged the Weavers as Communists. *Red Channels*, a book published by a group of former FBI agents, provided a patriotically gossipy index of those who'd spent any time committed or even loosely connected to the vast network of causes surrounding the American Communist Party. Their regular supplementary newsletter, *Counterattack*, became the East Coast equivalent to the emerging Hollywood blacklist. The newsletter, treated like scripture by (among others) the virulently anti-Communist grocery mini-magnate Laurence Johnson, caused stores to pull advertising from any local or national television or radio network that worked with artists or actors stamped Red by *Counterattack*.

The band was "well known in Communist circles," the Red-baiting newsletter reported, which was accurate. But, the blurb continued, "the folk songs they sang for *Broadway Open House* are not the 'folk songs' they sing for the subversive groups they frequently entertain" like the "fighting songs of the Lincoln Brigade (which fought for Stalin in the Spanish Civil War) and other Communist song favorites." That was only partly accurate. They *also* sang "Venga Jaleo" and other Communist favorites at the Village Vanguard too.

Ronnie especially loved singing "Venga Jaleo," her bel canto voice soaring into the fighting anti-Fascist lyrics. "*Clap out the rhythm/Dream of a machine gun,*" the band's own translation ran when they collected it. But as with so-called Aesopian language, it would be a willful distortion to say Ronnie Gilbert was calling for any kind of physical violence; it was only a *dream* of a machine gun in the ongoing struggle for a more just world. Nonetheless, the bean deliveries ceased, the television offer was rescinded. They weren't very good beans anyway, Lee would note.

"It is our belief that folk songs will endure long beyond the malice of self-appointed traducers and inquisitors," Lee boomed into his typewriter, addressing those beansters who'd so recently wanted them so badly. "If a large company is not free to select the material it needs to sell its products to the American public, then we are indeed in a bad way."

Manager Pete Kameron hustled over to the *Counterattack* office and tried to broker peace. In Kameron's account, they asked for $5,000.

"I don't have $5,000," he recalled his response. "Why don't you lay off until me and the group can become capitalists?" Har-har.

Counterattack offered a follow-up on their meeting with the manager: "He had spoken to the 'boys' about the problem and felt that they were just gullible and well-meaning. He said that he would try to persuade them to cease their pro-Communist activity as individuals and, as their manager, would refuse engagements for any Communist front groups."

It was the first of many managerial moves Kameron would make without consulting the members of the band, actions they sometimes wouldn't discover for decades. Working earnestly on the Weavers' behalf, his decisions were often ones the musicians might not have come to themselves, but—for the moment—the Red-baiting ceased.

Communism remained on the American and world stage and was a touchy subject all around. Mao Zedong's People's Republic of China had entered into existence in the fall of 1949, just as the Weavers were preparing to turn pro. And on the Weavers' last night at the Village Vanguard, war broke out between North and South Korea. Vito Marcantonio, whom the Weavers had sung for the year before, was the only congressman to vote against the United States' entrance into the war. He was out in the next election.

Without air conditioning, the Vanguard closed down for the summer. After working nearly every night since Christmas, the sudden cancellation of their television slot left time for their first holiday, and the Weavers unwound. Decca was going forward with them as a band and had delivered their first $3,000 paychecks. For now, there was peace.

Ronnie and her boyfriend Marty Weg got married at city hall, threw a hoot of a reception at the closed Vanguard, and headed west in Marty's Dodge to see the glorious sights of America. Pete Seeger reverted to being Pete Seeger in the fullest way possible, in his spare time co-founding *Sing Out!*, a new folk magazine in the tradition of *People's Songs*, but mainly decamping to the homestead in Beacon with Toshi and the kids and a crew of volunteers that sometimes included Fred and/or Lee. The prospect of spending time out of the city during the summer was so cherished to Lee that the normally sedentary bass typist would even engage in manual labor.

While the Weavers enjoyed their summer vacations, their songs went to work. Pairing with a publisher named Howie Richmond, another ambitious Midtown song hustler, Pete Kameron began the process of retrofitting the Weavers' folk repertoire for the contemporary moneymaking pop world. Every Weavers song had come from a different faraway place, shaped by new situations en route, and now, via the Weavers' Decca recordings, the songs entered into the arcane and cutthroat world of American copyright.

Chaos immediately ensued. Pete Seeger had picked up "Tzena Tzena Tzena" (Sing Out! #8) from a People's Songster who'd learned it at summer camp, and so Howie Richmond treated it as a folk song, copyrighting it under a number of aliases, and hustled it hard. As was the norm at the turn of the 1950s, the *song* was the product, not the recording. That was familiar enough to the Weavers: a song was meant to be spread. By the time the Weavers' recording hit stores, nearly a half dozen others were already in production, by bandleaders including Mitch Miller, Ralph Flanagan, and crooner Vic Damone.

As the Weavers' version climbed into the top 30, the song's true authors emerged, a pair of Israeli songwriters, and they'd signed with a rival American publisher. "Rights Fight Turns 'Tzena' into a Dirge," *The Billboard* reported.

"I'd rather see the song wither and die than yield 5 cents' worth of interest to [rival publisher] Mills," Richmond said with a highly un-Weavers-like attitude. If the Weavers themselves were difficult and individual as people, their songs were the same and even more plentiful, each presenting its own idiosyncratic complications of authorship, some setting off chains of dispute that would last into the next century. Following a system devised by John Lomax, traditional songs were often given fictitious authors, pseudonyms for those who'd brought the song out of the public domain and into popular music, often splitting up the bounty among producers, folklorists, and musicians. It was an imperfect non-solution, jury-rigged for an existing system, but the Weavers didn't have much say at the moment.

Even if Mitch Miller and his gang made their own version of "Tzena," there was little else like the Weavers out there. Released into the world the same week were singles like Evelyn Knight and Dick Haymes's his/hers fantasia "Blind Date"; Lawrence Welk doing the "Dakota Polka" (no Israeli, Bahamian, or Arkansan melodies in earshot, though); ragtime showcases (Professor Turner's "The Entertainer's Rag"); jazz exotica (Stan Kenton's "Evening in Pakistan"); and a whole index of escapist big bands.

It was hard to tell what "Tzena" was. As much Gordon Jenkins's vision as the band's, it began with a fanfare, the Weavers singing at center stage. Immediately, they displayed what no other version could: their four voices and, audible at the edge of Jenkins's Orchestra, Pete's banjo. Jenkins's pocket symphony of plucked strings was like a drunken dream of clawhammer rolls, a vivid riot ending with the reentry of sober Pete Seeger, the other Weavers warping and woofing around him. Mitch Miller couldn't do that. By mid-July, the Weavers' "Tzena" was in the top 10. Less than a year after Peekskill, the Weavers' voices were coming out of radios and turntables across the country.

Ronnie and Marty first heard "Tzena" on the radio on their honeymoon, the DJ offering a botched Midwestern pronunciation: *Tuhzeena, Tuhzeena, Tuhzeena.* They heard it on jukeboxes, too, the Weavers' harmonies and Gordon's miniature movie remaking itself in unexpected places, more a celebration than an escape.

When the newlyweds stopped for a stay at the San Cristobal Valley Ranch outside of Taos, New Mexico, Ronnie's visit was treated as one of importance in the gossipy dispatch from the ranch's owner, a former People's Songster named Jenny Wells Vincent. (Right-wing New York gossip columnist Walter Winchell had noted Ronnie and Marty's nuptials, too.)

Another former People's Songster at San Cristobal that summer was the man sometimes known as Harvey Matt, arriving soon after Ronnie and her husband pressed westward. Though it wasn't widely known, Matt's record-buying club contributed significantly to the financial wreckage of People's Songs the previous spring. On the government payroll since just before leaving New York, Harvey Matusow installed himself at San Cristobal, providing license-plate numbers and thumbnail descriptions of the resort's guests at regular meetings with a local FBI agent.

Before he'd left New York, Matusow had told the bureau that they should keep an eye on the Weavers. But he wasn't telling the bureau anything new, just another checkmark in a file emerging and beginning to glow in the FBI's index of names.

As Matusow settled into San Cristobal for what turned out to be an extended stay, Ronnie and Marty arrived in Los Angeles to a telegram from Weavers' management asking them to return to New York posthaste. Pointing the Dodge back to New York, they heard the nation's DJs discover that they could flip over the "Tzena" 78 and play "Goodnight Irene." Ronnie returned to a different New York from the one she'd left.

At the Blue Angel, the high-class Midtown supper club where the Weavers opened after Labor Day, the headwaiter approached Weaver manager Harold Leventhal about the man outside. He wasn't presentable. With quilted walls and supper-club glitz (and matching miniature blue angels in the ash trays), it was part of a glittering New York to which none of the Weavers had ever belonged but were now employed to entertain with their new megahits.

Co-owned by the Village Vanguard's Max Gordon, the venue was a model of urbane sophistication and interracial audiences. With programming often guided by Gordon's partner Harold Jacoby, the Blue Angel was a direct connection from Gotham to the political cabaret culture of Europe. "There were nights at the Blue Angel when I never heard a word of English," Gordon would remember.

"Blue Angel regulars were a rarefied breed, very New York, mostly east siders," recalled Gordon's wife, Lorraine. "Smart, clever, well-dressed, and with a real knowledge of good entertainment. Plenty of gays, there were always lots of guys at the bar."

But sophisticated as they were, the Blue Angel didn't see fit to admit Woody Guthrie, so it was up to Harold Leventhal to get him in to see the Weavers. It was the kind of duty Leventhal was getting used to, Woody being his newest client. Granted, Woody wasn't looking or smelling great these days. Harold found a jacket for him, swiped a table napkin and tucked it under Woody's collar as a cravat, and smuggled the former Almanac Singer back into the venue through the kitchen.

Woody had come to see Pete at nightclubs before and it hadn't always gone well. A few years earlier, one such night had ended when Pete had performed Woody's "Union Maid" in his honor, and a young drunk man at the bar sang along with his own version of the chorus, replacing the phrase "I'm sticking to the union" with "I'm a capitalist" and Woody had threatened the guy with a beer bottle, telling him, "It's bastards like you who stayed home making millions while we was out fighting the fascists."

The Blue Angel was the type of place from which Woody typically made a point of stealing the silverware but, lately, even Woody had gone pro. "Long's I'm headin' this hit parade/My weavin's lots better th'n thievin'," he'd written in his new (and unperformed) "Weaver Theme Song," with verses for each Weaver. Besides a new manager in Harold Leventhal, for the first time, Woody had a publisher—Howie Richmond—who promptly purchased him a tape machine, paid him a weekly salary, and told him to record his songs. All of them. He'd signed Woody up even before "Tzena" and "Irene" had broken. There was a jackpot around here somewhere, and Woody was more than willing to go prospecting.

In the fall of 1950, the Weavers and "Goodnight Irene" were inescapable. "Irene" had followed "Tzena" up the charts and surpassed it. In its first three weeks on the market, the Weavers' single sold some 650,000 copies. The song was ubiquitous. "It is hardly possible that you have failed to hear a song called 'Goodnight, Irene' several times daily in the past four weeks," Washington, DC's *Evening Star* reported in August. They made the cover of *The Cash Box*, surely an irony not lost on a quartet whose members arrayed along the Socialist spectrum. When the Weavers played in Baltimore, the sound of people singing "Irene" in the streets floated up and into the open window of Lee Hays's hotel room.

"The folk song originally issued as the 'B' side of a Decca disk by the previously unknown Weavers group is looming as the biggest hit of the era," *The Billboard* declared. "Goodnight Irene" wasn't merely a hit, it was a milestone.

Like "Tzena," the alternate versions were expected and instantaneous, but the durable waltz flowered beyond all belief. Other chart contenders included a number-five version by anti-folkie Frank Sinatra (whose producers picked it for a comeback single), Jo Stafford (number nine), Ernest Tubb and Red Foley (number one on the country-and-western chart, number ten pop).

But by October, there were also recordings of "Goodnight Irene" by Eddie Grand, Gene Autry (two versions), Cliff Steward, Jack Shook and Dottie Dillard, the Harmony Bells Orchestra, Gunter Lee Carr, Lenny Dee, Ted Maksymowicz and His Polka Orchestra (translating it into Polish, "Żegnaj Irene"), Mad Man Maxwell, Moon Mullican (rewriting the verses), the Alexander Brothers, Dennis Day, and the Paul Gayten Orchestra, along with a straight knockoff of both sides credited to Ray Jenkins and Choristers (cheeky, cheeky). Thanks to the Weavers' apolitical savior at Decca with the hoo-hoo-hoot of a laugh, the People's Songs traveled farther than they ever had before, the Weavers proudly putting the *pop* in Popular Front.

"Goodnight Irene" had "already sold over 1,000,000 disks," *The Billboard* noted in its trend piece, meaning a combination of the Jenkins-helmed recording plus all the other releases. Even so, it might be possible to credit the whole million to the Weavers, too, their global folk vision spreading almost instantly into the pop marketplace. It was a kind of musical openness that—up to and including the Weavers' debut single—had been considered a novelty.

Mitch Miller, he of the hipster goatee who'd forced "Irene" on Sinatra, set himself on a global musical safari, including French tangos, country waltzes, half-Italian harpsichord-driven love tunes, and began to plumb the songbook of South African expatriates Marais & Miranda, who'd signed to Decca just before the Weavers broke big. American roots music edged decidedly into pop that year. Alongside "Irene," the year's other mega-smash was also in three-four time, Patti Page's "Tennessee Waltz." Jo Stafford, too, scored further pop hits with folk-ish material.

Decca would push the Weavers back into a studio soon enough, but their evenings were now filled with two nightly shows at the Blue Angel. And while the Blue Angel was a high-society gig, their afternoons were spent performing in another remnant of old New York show biz: four or five short sets at the Strand Theater on a rotating vaudeville bill.

There were dancers, and then a solo violin act, and then the Weavers, on a typical day opening with their old favorite "When the Saints Go Marching In" before a handful of Lead Belly–learned blues like "Rock Island Line," then closing with "Irene" (the audience bursting into applause after a few bars) and encoring with "Tzena" and "Around the World." And then on came the Three Stooges and the Harvest Moon Dancers. Weaver-mania was a strange phenomenon to behold. "The three boys and a girl singing team sold well, even to an apathetic house," noted *The Billboard*. The same could not be said of the Stooges. After all that came the featured movie.

Most of them enjoyed it. They'd received their first big paychecks over the summer, which was a shock to them all. Beans or no, the perpetually broke and Depression-weaned Lee Hays enjoyed his part of the Weavers' success to the maximum, loving dressing up, loving the new audiences, loving singing for a living. Fred moved out of his parents' place and into his own digs in the Village. Many nights, Ronnie and Marty dined at the Blue Angel, delighting in the Shrimp a la Jake.

There was the night when the Weavers were introduced to Blue Angel regular Tennessee Williams, his male partner, and their circle of friends. This time, it was the otherwise cultured Pete Seeger who was baffled. "Is it the custom here for young men to go out in couples?" he asked Ronnie. (Yes, Pete.)

Pete was born just after World War I, and Lee only months before its outbreak, the senior Weavers coming from worlds where homosexuality was shut so far into cultural closets that it wasn't even fathomable for the long-necked banjo player. For Pete, it was less a question of homophobia than awareness. He lived most of the time on Planet Pete, which didn't yet have any openly gay residents.

But the band's new status was getting a little boring to him already. "It's not so much fun now," *Time* quoted him as saying in September, reflecting on the Weavers' rise from hootenannies and the Vanguard. "Then we could improvise, sing what we felt like singing. Now we're so professional we have to rehearse, arrange, set keys and all that stuff."

The banjo player was now a commuter. Every night, he packed up his instrument and blazer after the last set at the Blue Angel and headed back north, up the Hudson River, to his homestead in Beacon. The house finally having become habitable over the summer, in part because professional income was no longer an issue, it was fifty miles from the Blue Angel to his driveway, which is where he was when he discovered Woody asleep in the back of his car, passed out sometime during the late set and still wearing the napkin cravat that Harold Leventhal had fashioned. Pete dealt with it in the morning.

Woody had always been fiercely independent and unpredictable, but lately it was uncomfortable. The most disciplined member of their scene by a long shot, Pete could easily grow tired of Woody's whims. What most took for drunkenness during the first days of booming folk were often, likely, symptoms of the Huntington's disease that slowly consumed Guthrie's body over the next decade and a half. His tics had been getting stranger than usual lately.

But he was still Woody, and it was one of his songs that Gordon Jenkins chose to follow "Irene": Woody's Dust Bowl classic, "So Long, It's Been Good to Know Yuh." The only problem, however, were the lyrics about the Dust Bowl. In addition to being dated, they were depressing, from a bygone age. They had to go, said Decca. And, sprawled on the floor of Gordon Jenkins's Midtown hotel suite, Woody was all too happy to scribble out some new verses to order on some paper bags for his most durable of favorites. What were some new lyrics between friends? He'd rewritten "So Long" for a tobacco sponsorship, and he'd rewritten "So Long" for Henry Wallace. Who was Gordon Jenkins, anyway, but another new situation?

Former Almanac Singer Sis Cunningham was incensed. "They changed and twisted one of our most loved songs of all time . . . just so some money-minded producer would accept it for recording purposes."

If the new lyrics weren't as good as the originals (and they most certainly aren't), they certainly paid better, with Woody taking home a $10,000 check, the most he'd ever made from any single musical endeavor. It covered the rent, bought the family a new car, cleared up some debts, and more. But Woody was not well.

"As he got sicker he acquired certain traits which can only be described as somewhat Messianic with phrases like 'my people' and 'oh, my people' and 'my Weavers,'" Lee recalled. *My Weavers*.

Changing Woody's lyrics hadn't been a matter of politics but commercialism. Lee, especially, had argued that—now that they'd *achieved* this *commercial* success—they might as well try their best to be *commercial*, and meet the demands presented by that particular challenge, no matter how uncomfortable it might be for individual Weavers. That's what being professional was.

Now came the choices. By Pete Kameron's decree, and to everybody's ready agreement except Pete Seeger's, it was time to sever themselves from left-wing causes or anything that might remotely be perceived as political. "You don't want to jeopardize the position you're in," he told Seeger.

And while there was rarely a *good* time to express sympathy for the Communist Party in the United States, 1950 was perhaps the worst. That September, as the Weavers' Popular Front harmonies echoed from the nation's jukeboxes, Congress passed the McCarran Act, also known as the Subversive Activities Control Act of 1950, giving the government the ability to create detention camps for groups they believed to be threats.

That fall, too, the Weavers' friend Josh White appeared before the House Un-American Activities Committee and renounced his past. He'd been fingered by *Counterattack*. "I Was a Sucker for the Communists" was the title of an essay he published in *Negro Digest*. He was blacklisted anyway. Pete shuddered at the whole situation.

After White's appearance, industry weekly *The Billboard* published an exposé on the Red-baiters, even taking a rare stand. "*The Billboard* does not believe that it is proper for a group of private citizens to control, or affect to a controlling degree, the lives and careers of show business people," they wrote, feeling "it is of considerable importance that everyone in show business know just what *Counterattack* is." It didn't do much good, as Pete Seeger knew better than anybody.

What Pete Seeger wanted was unwavering and the same as it had ever been: to get the music as far as possible. Everything was in the music. Whatever it was that he did or didn't believe about forms of government or utopia or how it might be achieved, that was in the music, too. He especially wanted to get the music onto television and into that mysterious ether on the other side of the screen. They'd made inroads, locally. Ronnie found television appearances tedious, a "repressive, alienating process."

It was something Pete Seeger wanted so badly that he was willing to forego singing at hootenannies or lending his name to fund-raisers for anything that might be construed as political. Sulking, Pete agreed. "I'll go along with it," he said, "but I will feel like a prisoner." And so Pete Seeger became trapped. Out went "The Hammer Song," although both "Wasn't That a Time" and "Venga Jaleo" remained in the band's sets on occasion.

By all accounts, it was a shift in dynamic, and Pete was never quite happy as a Weaver again. "Pete made us pay dearly for what pleasure there was to be had out of it," Ronnie would observe.

Lee, especially, enjoyed the pop aspects of the band's success, commenting that he never felt "more professional and more powerful" as when the band assembled at the center of a recording studio with an orchestra to support them. This sentiment must have been at its truest during the November session for "Lonesome Traveler," a signature Lee song at many a hoot, now given a choir-draped arrangement by his drinking buddy Gordon Jenkins.

For much of the year, when the Weavers weren't on the road (and even when they were), Decca pushed them in and out of studios with a series of producers and arrangers, looking for that elusive next "Irene." And if nothing was as *big* as "Irene," for the next two years, there were constantly Weavers recordings moving up and down various charts in *The Billboard* and *The Cash Box*.

If they couldn't sing for the causes that had set them into motion to begin with, they could at least carry themselves with the dignity they felt in their music. It had been a struggle to get them into the matching jackets at the Vanguard. But then Lee brought in a picture of Paul Robeson performing in a formal tux at one of his concerts, so it was agreed that the Weavers would get formal tuxes.

At the end of 1950, a year of maximum Weavering that had started broke and hungry at the Village Vanguard, they debuted their new stagewear at a Christmas performance at Town Hall, just off Times Square, their formal concert debut. After a year of slugging it out in the commercial trenches, they'd found a form that suited them: a night for them alone.

Beginning and closing with "We Wish You a Merry Christmas," the Weavers played their hits, their soon-to-be hits, and their favorites. Ronnie belted "Venga Jaleo" and the group stomped through "Wasn't That a Time," the hope ringing out on the final "isn't this a wonderful time?" And then there was the old hymn that Lee and Fred picked up "purely" (Lee announced) "for its anti-psychiatric intent," but it's easy to imagine it embodying the attitudes of a certain banjo-playing Weaver in late 1950: "I Don't Want to Get Adjusted."

Pete Seeger didn't smash banjos often but, when he did, he meant it. The problem was that no Weaver quite agreed on exactly what caused Pete to send his custom extra-long neck through a backstage table midway through the band's first extended tour in spring 1951. It had seemed like a moment of merriment until then too. Freezing the banjo in midair, then rewinding through the Weavers' tour, however, the accumulating strain was almost visible.

For Pete Seeger, just about to turn thirty-two, still looking for the best in everything—and filled with an equally intense world-saving fire—the Weavers' time on the road was a montage of projects that could only displace his wells of energy. From coast to coast, his activities were almost compulsively and surrealistically wholesome.

He transformed one hotel suite into a plaster blizzard, teaching himself to make casts of sculptures. He sketched pictures at the zoo. Elsewhere, he rolled out the family's holiday cards with a letterpress.

In Chicago, where the Weavers were staying at the upscale Palmer House while they were the featured act at the Empire Room supper club, Pete acquired a pawn-shop trumpet and a noise complaint from the neighbors. "He found laundries and boiler rooms and kitchens and the whole working apparatus of the hotel and not one single corner where he could blow his trumpet," Lee reported. Off he went to the lakefront, where (possibly, in Lee's recollection) he was stopped by the police.

Pete spent time devising schemes to transcribe a tape of African drumming. In Los Angeles, he found someone to teach him to hammer silver. In Texas, looking up old family friend John Lomax Jr., Pete and Toshi organized a field-recording expedition to a pair of local prison farms, bringing Fred along with them.

But besides occasional adventures like field recording in Texas, Pete was frozen musically inside the Weavers. His life became more an act of musical faith than ever, the opposite of the direct-action singing of the Almanac Singers and People's Songs. Now, everything *had* to be the music, and he could only hope that the music was fighting the battle as it should.

Sometimes that was hard too. At the glitzy Ciro's in Hollywood, the Weavers had gone into "Follow the Drinking Gourd," that authentic Minetta Creek freedom song, when one of the managers made his way to the stage. "People come to this place to forget their troubles," he told the band. "They don't want to hear those old slave songs."

"We were trying to sing songs to deepen people's consciousness of life," Pete would say with a sigh, still wounded a decade later. "This just ran counter to the purposes of his nightclub."

Toshi joined the band as their road manager, leaving the children, Danny and Mika, at home with Toshi's parents. But between the songs Pete couldn't sing and the people he couldn't sing them for, a banjo player could get mighty pent up.

The tension among the Weavers had emerged almost instantly, when the tour opened with two weeks at the Thunderbird Hotel in fabulous Las Vegas. Fred, Ronnie, and Ronnie's husband, Marty, had all dabbled in the dopamine thrills of gambling, much to the deep and judgmental contempt of their banjo-playing bandmate.

"When we attempted conversation, Pete's words would come clipped and icy through tight lips, a fine study in pure New England disdain," Ronnie would write.

On one of the nights at the Thunderbird, while the group was walking somewhere, Pete tossed a silver dollar into the hotel pool to show the waste-fulness of their ways. Ronnie's husband jumped into the pool and retrieved it.

The opposite of Pete, as always, Lee adjusted instantly to his new sur-roundings, discovering the wonders of room service and rented typewriters. Being forced into political inaction was no great strain for Lee. Like a gonzo folkie, he holed up as the Weavers moved from hotel to hotel, feeding off the television and radio news, firing off dispatches to friends and especially man-ager Harold Leventhal.

In another age, with a keyboard connected to the electronic networks, Lee surely would have been a voice on social media, dwelling in the seman-tic corners of unmeetable expectations. He consumed books rabidly, in-cluding trashy pulp paperbacks, earning eyebrow-raises from fellow Weavers. He compared it to "reading the kept press to know what the oppo-sition is doing."

"Lee would appear shortly before show time, bristling with the latest news," Ronnie remembered, "bloody battles over the 38th parallel in Korea; old Dr. W.E.B. DuBois [sic] dragged into court in manacles, charged with being a foreign agent." That spring, around the time his quips came to be occasionally reported in The Billboard, Lee even made contact with his siblings for the first time since his teens, flying to New Orleans for a visit during the Weavers' days off in Houston.

For Lee, the new lifestyle was a kind of fulfillment. Ever since the death of his father, the world had been one of continuous emotional and financial chaos. "When you're poor, in the first place, it's very hard sometimes to find clothing, it's very hard to keep clean, very hard to eat properly," he would say later. "That's why room service was so great."

Ronnie adjusted to the pop life in her own tentative way, making her bed every morning at the hotel until a chambermaid told her that she'd needed to unmake it each afternoon in order to put it to hotel specifications. Soon, she slipped into the habit of "recreational shopping," with every purchase thinking of her mother—the former International Ladies Garment Workers Union member—frowning a cartoon frown over her shoulder, but enjoying it anyway.

She studied the other show-biz troupes they crossed paths with out on the circuit moving from Las Vegas to Los Angeles to Reno to Omaha to Houston to Montreal to Chicago and beyond. She watched one woman from afar, a member of Chandra Kali and His Hindu Dancers, transfixed by her exotic power, until one night backstage she overheard the "Indian" dancer break character into a thick Brooklyn accent. Show business was an education.

Mid-tour, Ronnie sent a dispatch back to Harold Leventhal in New York using the nicknames she'd concocted for the Weavers. "All well here," she told the manager. "'The Messiah' is writing arrangements, 'The Drunkard' is only consuming 4 quarts of beer a night (who's counting?), 'Laughing Boy' bought a new shirt, and 'Camille' just spoke to her husband over the phone."

Lee's drinking had started to get frustrating to both of the junior Weavers especially. "Lee was again drunk for the second show," Fred noted in his journal one night in Texas. "As soon we walked on the stage and got the first whiff of him, Ronnie and I looked at each other and smiled—almost laughed through the first few songs. It was really impossible to stay near him. Pete, of course, noticed nothing." There were times when it was hard to be around him in public. Ronnie had tried to bring it up, but the conversation went nowhere.

"Lee has never admitted to us, even under questioning, that he has been drinking," Fred noted of the comedy that ensued one morning when the band encountered a British actor in the hotel lobby. "Lee was coughing and hacking away as is his usual custom after a hard night's drinking," Fred recorded.

"Been drinking too much brandy, eh, old boy?" the British actor asked.

"No," Lee said, always a bushel of health complaints. "It's my sinus trouble. This Houston weather, you know."

"Oh, come, come, old boy," the actor tutted. "I know brandy when I hear it!"

Fred, the "Laughing Boy," could be just as opinionated and moody as any Weaver, but at twenty-three years old with songs on the pop chart, he was also ready to meet the world. He found himself rubbing elbows with writer William Faulkner (at a party in Los Angeles) and country-singing pop mega-star Patti Page (at a hotel bar in Houston). A folk-singing ladies' man on the make, he looked for adventures, joining a speakeasy with fellow bachelor Harold Leventhal in Texas, and road-tripping on a stunning all-night desert drive with Ronnie and Marty from Los Angeles to Reno.

At the same party where he'd met Faulkner, Fred had befriended the host, actor Victor Killian. It was only a few days later that Fred was shocked to read of Killian's HUAC subpoena. "For the first time in his life [he has] a reasonable degree of financial security, only to have some viscious [sic] senatorial scum destroy his life's work with a few headlines," Fred wrote in his journal. He might have been writing about any of the Weavers, wondering when the committee might come for them, but Pete most of all.

That spring, with their songs on the charts, the other Weavers made it into the shadow world, too, their names appearing in the ever-swelling file dedicated to their Pete. The spook operators finally began to connect and cross-reference and re-stamp the documentation in such a way that connected the massively popular singing quartet to the overstuffed file on People's Songs.

"Confidential Informant T-18 stated that FRED HELLERMAN was a member of the Communist Party, in 1949." (Fred had maaaaybe fallen asleep at one of the meetings.)

"Confidential Informant T-9 advised that LEE HAYS was a member of the Communist Party [and] has written and published songs for the Communist Party." (Good luck getting through your agenda, Comrade.)

"During 1949, Confidential Informant T-6 advised that RONNIE GILBERT was connected with People's Songs, Incorporated, during the time that organization existed." The organization didn't really exist past the spring, and they'd missed Ronnie's previous three years of participation. Unrecorded, meanwhile, is how T-18, T-9, and T-6's harmonies were and whether they sang with a lightness in their hearts.

In many ways, the accuracy of the reports was of secondary importance. The Red Scare was ramping up to its fullest frenzy in 1951, exactly as the Weavers were at their miraculous peak. That summer, after the Weavers concluded their dreadful tour, Joseph McCarthy declared communism in the United States to be "a conspiracy on a scale so immense as to dwarf any previous such venture in the history of man."

Topping the bestseller lists were multiple books by pulp novelist Mickey Spillane, starring hard-boiled Commie-fighting private investigator Mike Hammer. In 1951's *One Lonely Night*, Hammer infiltrates the party and seduces the estranged millionaire's daughter he's been hired to find. She'd turned Red. After spending the night together, he concludes, "Maybe she'd go out and seek some different company for a change." She doesn't. And so, horrifically, Hammer strips her naked and physically abuses her. Spillane would write more than half of the decade's top ten bestselling novels. On the Academy Award nominee list for Best Documentary Feature that year was *I Was a Communist for the FBI*, a scripted docudrama starring real-life snitch Matt Cvetic.

And yet Weaver music continued to bop around the upper reaches of the charts, seemingly harmless in its harmony. "The Roving Kind," backed with "The Wreck of the John B," edged up to number eleven. Woody's self-doctored "So Long, It's Been Good to Know Yuh"—with Lee's "Lonesome Traveler" on the flip—made it even further, to number three, and earned its own cover versions by old-style bandleaders like Paul Weston, Ralph Marterie, and Les Baxter. Commercialism or no, even Lee was saddened when the band had to turn down a tour with Paul Robeson.

Ronnie made an informed report to Harold Leventhal from the front line at Weavers gigs. "'[On Top of Old] Smoky' must be doing good—even here in Omaha (ugh!) kids have been yelling it from the audience." Ronnie was right on the mark. "On Top of Old Smoky" would go on to be the Weavers' second biggest single, after "Irene." It was what *The Billboard* referred to as "a smash disking." Though it sort of had been already: like "Irene," a Weavers staple going back at least to the Vanguard, the group's version confirmed it as a folk standard.

Recorded during the band's Hollywood sojourn, Decca had paired them with a new signee they wanted to break, a fair-haired, fair-complexioned singer named Terry Gilkyson. It was not a natural collaboration. "They had already established themselves, and I was being promoted at their expense," Gilkyson would later say, fronting the band on the single's A-side, "Across the

Wide Missouri." During the recording of "Smoky," the 78's intended flipside, Gilkyson would remember Fred using his guitar to keep nudging the younger singer and his powerful baritone farther and farther from the microphone.

Leading the song with a technique he'd borrowed from Josh White, Pete sang the verses just ahead of the rest of the group, as if not only inducing his fellow Weavers to sing along but an entire invisible choir, breaking the fourth wall of the recording studio to pull listeners into participation. It was the most direct and radical way that Pete Seeger could express himself in the early days of 1951, in the hopes that there were other voices out there, echoing him. As with "Irene," DJs learned to flip the record over, and the B-side became the bigger hit.

If Pete was willing to put any faith in the metrics of capitalism, *The Billboard* noted that—while musicians had recorded "On Top of Old Smoky" before—the Weavers' version was the one driving the accompanying sales of sheet music. But the mainstream pop world felt like the only segment of the universe embracing the Weavers in early 1951.

At first, it was enthralling. "I remember once hearing my voice [on a jukebox], and all I could do was roll on the floor with my heels up in the air," Pete said, but by the spring of 1951, it had worn thin.

"I don't know about R., F., & L., but I'm getting awfully bored with singing the same songs over & over again for rich nightclub audiences," Seeger wrote to Pete Kameron. He signed the note as he often did, with an illustration of a banjo. This one had a prisoner's ball and chain attached to it.

Besides the finger-pointers at *Counterattack*, the Weavers now found themselves under fire from the newly established folk music magazine *Sing Out!* Despite the fact that the publication took its name from a line in Pete and Lee's "Hammer Song" (Sing Out! #1), and Pete had been a cofounder, his name had disappeared from the masthead around the time its new editor made his ascent. Irwin Silber had been a Brooklyn College classmate of Freddie's, where the future Weavers guitarist had performed in Folksay, the left-wing square-dancing group that Silber had organized. A hardline sectarian Communist, Silber's disciplined political aesthetic came up against the Weavers' pop status.

A Camp Wo-Chi-Ca alum and a fan of Pete's work outside the Weavers, the prole dancer came down hard on the band's cultural transgressions. He heard (not incorrectly) the "usual male supremacy of Tin Pin Alley" on one of the new "So Long" verses, though was apparently unaware Woody had rewritten it himself. Making himself the mouthpiece for one particular sect of folkies' response to Pete, Lee, Fred, and Ronnie's float in the hit parade, Silber's skepticism represented the most politicized end of the emerging folk spectrum, if only one viewpoint.

"Surely SING OUT readers need have no illusions that the 'success' of The Weavers signifies a new concern on the part of the entertainment industry monopolies with providing mass outlets for genuine expressions of People's Culture," Silber wrote. Through their ongoing conversation and the patient development of their material, they'd come to discover a new space in American music. But at present, they felt like that space's sole occupants, too polished for *Sing Out!* and too rough and intellectual for lifer pop musicians.

Grown in the hothouse of the New York political folk, on the road the Weavers now found themselves with sometimes unwanted chances to discover what the musical world at large thought of them. In Minneapolis, Fred had ended up drinking with one of the Andrews Sisters. Nearing the end of their own twenty-year career, they had been the first musicians to bring non-English songs to the American pop charts, People's Songs pioneers in their own way. Fred recalls the Andrews Sister in question being "a little bombed."

"The Weavers. Great group," she slurred at him. "Know why the Weavers are a great group? I'll tell you why. Imagine yourself at a diner someplace, bunch of truck drivers sitting at the counter, and a Weavers record comes onto the jukebox. One guy turns to another and says, shit, I could sing better 'n' that." Fred didn't entirely disagree.

Lee would likewise recall an encounter with a bandleader who told the Weavers' bass singer that he'd taken one look at the sheet music for "Irene" and tossed it in the trash, only to find it the most requested song of the year.

Even Gordon Jenkins would somewhat regret the success of "Irene" for the way it shook up the pop world. "[It] opened up a lot of doors I'd just as soon have kept closed," he said several decades later. "Everybody in the world started doing what they thought were folk songs, which developed into everybody on the street writing songs of their own, and it became just a flood of crummy songs and crummy groups."

Gordon Jenkins was correct in the sense that if three random men and a woman picked up a guitar and a banjo and started playing and singing, they would not sound like the Weavers. Pete Seeger was a virtuoso banjo player, and Fred had fastidious chops as well, his chord voicings moving in every direction but where a normal folk strummer might go, questioning their way toward elegance. While Ronnie's voice was an electric sound that transmuted the band's harmonies into something golden and shimmering, Lee's was a more unpredictable instrument. Like the soul outputting the words, Lee's phrasings and intonations were often different from performance to performance, a musical raised eyebrow here, a wink there.

Perhaps there were groups who could sing better, but there were virtually no groups that could sing *together* like that. For the tensions that emerged offstage, the Weavers would always continue to enjoy one another's musical company. But despite living in relatively close quarters in their hotels, there was less collaborative music making than when they'd been crammed into the Village Vanguard kitchen.

With manager Pete Kameron sometimes acting as taskmaster and fifth set of ears, they could muster collaborative energies, such as during sessions poolside at Houston's Shamrock Hotel. Seeger had remembered a lilting fragment of a melody that Lead Belly used to sing. Before he could recall the source, he'd written his own words for it, and pulled out a verse melody that Lee helped reshape. Their version was called "Kisses Sweeter Than Wine," and the Lead Belly song Pete remembered turned out to be "If It Wasn't for Dicky," which Huddie rested on a signature twelve-string guitar groove.

But Huddie, for his part, had learned the song at a Greenwich Village house party, where he'd heard an Irish musician named Sam Kennedy perform it, and subsequently pulled Kennedy into the relative quiet of the apartment's bathroom until Kennedy could show him the song "Drimmen Dow," about a recalcitrant cow, whose spirit now traveled from Ireland to poolside at the Shamrock Hotel by way of a New York bathroom and subsequently down the hit parade.

To Fred, however, the process had started to grow labored. "We didn't work together at first," he would observe a few decades later, "we just sang." Success had changed that. "When we began to work on an arrangement in the kind of self-conscious way that was unkown [sic] in our earliest days was when there occurred a significant loss. I still feel an embarrassing unease when I think of us sitting around the pool at the Shamrock in Houston nit-picking, 'working,' phrase-by-phrasing to death a sweet little song called 'Round the Bay of Mexico.'"

The band stayed in high demand, which only ratcheted up the tension even further. At a band meeting in mid-March, Pete Kameron announced he'd extended the band's tour until June. Though the banjoist had agreed to it in principle months earlier, with several more months of real touring under their belt, Pete and Toshi were deeply upset. They missed the kids. If the Weavers kept touring like this, Pete would have to quit the band.

The bad vibrations could be felt from afar. Barely a month into the tour, while the Weavers were out west, back at the progressive Union Square Music Shop in New York, the author of the Weavers' latest hit, Woody Guthrie, encountered a floating piece of gossip "that the Weavers have busted up—argument about what kind & types of bookings to take and to turn down," though he noted that it "may be just hearsay." The rumor wasn't true, but the Weavers were unquestionably fraying.

Lee placed some of the blame on Pete, and Pete blamed it on too much time without a real break. His resentments about the current new situation were getting very old and were pushing ever-closer to the surface. This life was not for him. Though it wasn't his preference to repeat the experience, he would almost surely rank being egged by Southern Dixiecrats on the Wallace campaign as preferable to being stuck in a sequence of hotels while his band-mates boozed and partied it up.

Adjacent to Planet Pete, however, the situation felt quite different. Ronnie and Freddie, especially, had often felt awkward about their interactions with the popular-music world around them, feeling self-conscious about their highfalutin political folk roots in relation to the working lives of the actual touring musicians they encountered. These were fellow workers and, lacking in some of the traditionally accepted skill sets of their new profession, the junior Weavers had yearned for acceptance from them.

In Omaha, they appeared for several days with old-time big bandleader Tiny Hill, a veteran of the circuit they now shared with a new class of fellow travelers. Backstage, Fred met Duke Ellington, who'd just finished his own stay and had come back to grab a few items. Like Gordon Jenkins before him, Tiny Hill fell instantly head over heels for the Weavers. A large man, larger than Lee, Hill was about to embark on a string of one-nighters—249 in 270 days that year.

The Weavers and Hill's ensemble hit it off, and by a few days into the run were invited to a post-show birthday soiree for one of Hill's touring party. It was a great hang. "The party was on a real friendly, personal, intimate level," Fred noted. Ronnie encouraged the boys to get their instruments, which Pete didn't seem too terribly happy about, but there was a jam under way. Ronnie wanted Pete to join in the fun with these lovely new friends. Out came the brass and some woodwinds. Even Lee Hays, so shy in his musical abilities, sat down at the piano and hammered along. Pete sat across the room, joining in halfheartedly.

Fred took a verse, directing it at the Weavers' undisputed musical leader: "*I'd sing high and I'd sing low, if I could hear that old banjo*," Fred sang.

"Whereupon Pete rose, [and] grabbed his banjo back by the neck," Fred recorded in his journal. "He swung at the table, and the banjo broke at the neck. So did the drum. Pete strode out of the room. There was a hushed silence."

Lee, with his back to the incident, picked up the piano rhythm again, but the jam puttered out. As Toshi started to follow Pete, Ronnie confronted her, and soon both women were in tears. "You shouldn't have forced him to sing," Toshi said.

Pete's memory of the incident would prove to be only partially compatible with Fred's journal entry and the subsequent resignation letter that Ronnie drafted in her hotel room. To Pete, many years later, the trigger was their insistence that he join them in drinking. As he recounted to biographer David King Dunaway, "I don't like to be forced to drink," he told his bandmates. "If I don't want to drink, I don't want to drink!" Then: smash.

The party broke up. Tiny Hill, a sensitive and open man, truly understood, or tried to, assuring them of his unbroken love. The three other Weavers adjourned for a late-night coffee. "Lee's utterly defeated, although he's standing up very well," Fred noted. "He certainly amazes me, the way he can become quite sane and natural in time of serious crisis."

"As effects go, this one went," Lee observed of Pete's gesture.

In her resignation letter, Ronnie addressed Pete directly: "For in the eyes of all present (save possibly a Weaver or two) there was no apparent reason for such action—the party being the celebration of the birthday of a member of the cast, it being gay if noisy, and the above-mentioned coworkers doing everything possible to make The Weavers feel a part of the whole (a slightly reversed situation than the usual)."

She was mortified beyond words, running out of them after five full pages, front and back, on hotel stationery, before finally breaking off mid-sentence. It was never sent, tucked instead into her luggage, if not out of her mind.

Fred was equally incensed and, on paper, perhaps even more dramatic. "He's a _dangerous_ man," he wrote in a long entry of his own. "This man is capable of anything—renegade, maniac, fascist, genius—terrifying."

Pete offered his profuse apologies the next day, to both his bandmates and the woman whose birthday it was. Cooler heads prevailed, and the Weavers' uneasy truce continued.

Lee was delegated to get the banjo repaired. He agreed on the condition that Pete explain to him what happened. In Lee's memory, Pete told him, "Sometimes I feel like I've got to kill someone or smash a banjo down through a table." So often opposites, one deeply embedded tendency in both Pete Seeger and Lee Hays was to turn a memory into a parable.

Tiny Hill continued to pour out his heart for the Weavers. Before the final show of the week-long residency, he gave them an impassioned speech (in Lee's summary) about "how much we meant to him, how much he loved us, how he had never spoken to any other act as he was speaking to us, how God had put us on the earth for a purpose, each of us, and how wonderfully the Weavers were fullfillinf [sic] God's purpose on earth—which is apparently to entertain and amuse the people, not to mention making money while doing so. We should accept God's dictate and learn to say 'to hell with the rest of it': and especially we should learn to work with Tiny on one-night stands, where the money is. He cried. Ronnie and I were moist-eyed over his deep feeling, too." Tiny extended an open invitation to join his troupe.

Pete Seeger kept himself contained, continuing to channel his frustrations toward the pop-minded Pete Kameron. "This is a discussion of what is bull-shit and what is not," he wrote in one letter, in a sharply un-Seeger like voice.

"We need time, time, time to rehearse and rehearse (not just an hour or two here and there, but solid weeks of concentrated work)," he wrote. "And it needs singing for different audiences besides these upperclass nightclubs and besides the workingclass theatres where our repertoire is limited in another way." He continued to press for the Weavers to be free to play for whatever causes they thought worthwhile.

Ronnie knew the problems went deeper, working her thoughts out in another unsent letter on hotel stationery about "why we four people have not been able to overcome our problems well enough to function constructively." The deepest issue, she thought, was *fear*. "I believe sincerely that as a group we have been afraid for the last 2 ½ years to see realistically the new world we had entered . . . above all, been afraid to face honestly that we had become a part of it." Her ideas were progressive.

They needed to learn more about publishing, about how folk music is treated, she surmised. Would Pete *please* stop walking through the nice hotel lobbies in filthy jeans and raggedy sweaters, causing scenes? Some of it would perhaps be discussed, much of it wouldn't.

By the end of the tour, *Counterattack* had gone back to work, reminding readers that the Weavers properly belonged on the index of unreformed Reds, this time even reprinting some of the lyrics of "Banks of Marble" (Sing Out! #3). Another minor panic bubbled up and a call-in campaign ensued, this time resulting in the Weavers' dis-invitation from their scheduled appearances on Dave Garroway's popular and respected Sunday-afternoon radio show, with a follow-up on his NBC television show later in the month. NBC issued a press release bogusly attributing it to "conflicting schedules."

More so than their yanked-away bean sponsorship the previous summer, the Garroway cancellation stung both Lee and Pete. Part of the experimental Chicago school of television, Garroway's program was a refined part of the emerging popular culture to which Lee especially was excited to contribute. "Damn it, the Weavers belong on it," the preacher's son from Arkansas rumbled. Television was a place of cowboys and Indians, serious white men in suits, cigarette ads, children's programs, and a vast array of local variety. It was where the system perpetuated itself, anyone could see.

Suddenly, now, bright-eyed Pete Seeger could feel the forces at work, almost see them amassing their invisible blockade, sending out their agents.

It wasn't just Pete Kameron restricting them from doing benefits, though that was part of it. There was something more ominous emerging, pulling at the Weavers, trying to find its way inside.

When Pete and Toshi finally returned from the road, their kids didn't recognize them at first. Toshi resigned as road manager immediately, but nobody quit the band. There was more work ahead, a job at New York's Café Society, maybe a few well-paying summer fair gigs.

Lee was typically fatalistic in one of his last dispatches from the road that spring. "There is a certain feeling of living under the axe and not knowing when it will fall," he wrote. The shows weren't great, everyone in the band was irritable, and the guys' new trousers didn't fit.

"Oh, well," Lee concluded, "history will soon come to our relief in these small matters."

The press met them at the airport in Akron, and it was too much for Lee Hays. The Almanac Singers' old Red-baiter, Frederick Woltman, had launched a round against the Weavers in the *New York World-Telegram* and his syndicated column. In part, it reported that—*scandalously*—Lee had spoken at the funeral of *alleged Communist Bob Reed.*

Was it true? they asked Lee.

No, Lee replied in his slow, low voice, his Southern blood on the boil, "Bob Reed was a *known* Communist. He was known and loved by more non-Communists than any Communist I've ever known. He was my neighbor and my lifelong friend. If any more of my friends die, I don't care whether they're Republicans or Communists, I'll be at their funeral to speak if asked."

It was a moment that Fred Hellerman would remember and value, Lee maintaining poise and humor as reporters pounded them with questions about their past affiliations. "I think if I know anything in my life about dignity, it's from that moment," Fred would say.

It was a tough and peculiar time for all of them, unwilling to disavow their pasts, but equally unwilling to admit their affiliations. Pete claimed he'd never been sponsored by People's Songs, "a [Communist Party] outfit which entertains at party conventions," according to Woltman. It was *technically* true. Pete had put more of his own money into the organization than any sponsorship they ever provided him.

Fred did his best to dodge as well. "We don't know who are in the audience, maybe some are Communists," he offered. Happy to play the innocent-woman card for once, Ronnie shrugged and was ignored while the press surrounded the guys.

The frothing scrum at the airport had generated itself after a building controversy. The Weavers had been booked for a week of shows at the Ohio State Fair, and for good reason. "On Top of Old Smoky" was still hovering as the number-nine jukebox record in the country, and both "Kisses Sweeter Than Wine" and "When the Saints Go Marching In" had just entered the top 30 in sales. While Decca's earnings had risen over the past half year, *The Billboard* reported the week before, they made sure to note that "the diskery hasn't been knocking down walls with its pop merchandise in recent months. Its hit lists boasted but one important disking of late, the Weavers' *On Top of Old Smoky*."

But then a citizen of Middletown, Ohio, named Roger E. Sherwood spotted an ad for the Weavers' upcoming appearance at the Ohio State Fair and, being a *Counterattack* subscriber, knew that this just couldn't be. He wrote to the governor, and the governor contacted J. Edgar Hoover. Who were these Weavers? Was it *safe* for them to play in Ohio? And, though it was strictly illegal for him to do so, J. Edgar Hoover sent off a bundle of clippings from the FBI's private files, sourced from the *Daily Worker* and such, with the promise that the governor keep mum about where he got them. When Woltman's article appeared, it built from much the same material.

The fair pulled the plug days before the band's departure, but the group decided to go anyway. They belonged to the American Federation of Musicians, and their agreement deserved protection like that of any other union member. When they arrived, the local press drew from Hoover's clippings, using their contents as ammo against the Weavers.

While they got paid, the trip was a paranoid nightmare. It was the most in-the-flesh confrontation and opposition any of the Weavers had encountered since Peekskill and the subsequent start of their pop career. With the Weavers staying in the *Counterattack* listings, the American Legion and other groups organized small attacks against them on as many cultural fronts as they could muster.

When the Catholic War Veterans of America protested a booking at the new club Iceland, the Weavers even lost a gig in the safe harbor of Mannahatta. "First instance of an act being cancelled out of a New York cafe because of an alleged leftist affiliation," *Variety* reported. The *New York Journal-American* was making a habit of forcing the issue, helping to get Lena Horne canceled from Ed Sullivan's show a few weeks earlier.

In Syracuse, members of the American Legion had been visiting local television and radio stations, jukebox distributors, and record stores, brandishing *Counterattack* and a copy of the "Banks of Marble"/"The Hammer Song" 78 that Boots Casetta had eked out. The A-side, with its lyrics about how "the vaults are stuffed with silver that the farmer sweated for," was bound to set anti-Commie radars bleeping.

The Weavers were "undesirable characters," concluded the chairman of Syracuse Post #41's Unamerican [*sic*] Activities Committee. Their music was inappropriate "to be broadcasting to the public in times like this with men laying down their lives in Korea," Vice Commander Dungey wrote to Decca musical director Gordon Jenkins, presenting the information about "Banks of Marble." "I would like you to investigate this at the earliest possible and let me know how you intend to cope with 'The Weavers,'" he signed off.

As it happened, the letter reached Decca's New York offices during one of Jenkins's Manhattan sojourns, which is likely how it ended up in Ronnie's possession. Whether Jenkins investigated anything is unlikely, save perhaps the charts for the Weavers session he was there to produce. Decca, and their musical director most especially, were sticking by the Weavers.

Gordon Jenkins loved the Weavers completely, and jumped vast conceptual chasms to make the band and their music work in the context of popular-music production. "We never met anyone else like Gordon when we started to become popular," Ronnie would observe. "He was a gentleman. He gave us the wrong impression of the kind of person we'd find in mainstream music. It wasn't him."

At one session, the band kept crashing takes when they followed Jenkins's conductor's baton, which fell intentionally a split-second ahead of the beat. Jenkins finally solved the problem by wheeling a chalkboard into the studio that blocked out his torso. Conducting the orchestra as usual, his visible feet tapped out the beat for the group to follow.

His latest arrangements were for the old cowboy tune "Old Paint," Lead Belly's "Midnight Special," and—at long last—"Wimoweh," featuring Pete's soaring falsetto over the band's mysterious one-word title chant.

For the South African song, Jenkins took perhaps the single most unusual piece of music in the Weavers' repertoire and arranged it into a form palatable to record-company executives, jukebox operators, and pop listeners. All of ninety wordless seconds in its original Weavers incarnation, Jenkins cushioned "Wimoweh" in a bed of dramatic, swinging brass that emphasized original lead vocalist Solomon Linda's last precious segment of melody, kicking up into a modulating swirl of trumpets that exploded toward the sunshine. Lee reported later that Jenkins told him that "on the sheet music, which he collected, a couple of the trumpet players had written on the scores things like, 'Holy shit, is he kidding?'"

Then the whole panoramic production broke down to one of Jenkins's signature one-finger piano melodies, rickety and human, and pivoted over to the Weavers, and the odd song Pete had transliterated. When Decca's promo men demoed it for jukebox operators they marked the beginning of the band's vocal with a piece of chalk, so they could jump from Jenkins's intro directly to the song's chorus.

It was an extraordinary cultural moment, all of Pete's Popular Front instincts channeled into a singular piece of art, with extraordinary side effects when it actually moved from Pete's purified existence into the harsher and more finite realm of song publisher Howie Richmond. Despite the fact that all pressings of Solomon Linda's original recording clearly read "African Music Research Copyright Control," the song wasn't copyrighted in the United States, and Richmond claimed "Wimoweh" as a folk song, crediting it to one of the copyright pseudonyms he'd established for the Weavers, Paul Campbell.

Another strange darkness loomed around the Weavers here, too, as the songs they'd collected became the fluid in a vast and largely unfair economic apparatus. Folk music could be complicated. They were tensions the Weavers would never fully resolve. As a matter of point, there was no songwriter listed on the Weavers' original 78 of "Wimoweh," only an arrangement credit for the nonexistent Campbell.

Though Pete would insist that money for "Wimoweh" be sent to Solomon Linda, his directive grew mistranslated in decades to come. The song itself would live many lives far away from the Weavers, but when "Wimoweh" came out of the Weavers' mouths, it was still just an unusual piece of music that Pete heard and loved, because he was on the hunt for songs to hear and love. Recorded with Gordon Jenkins in late October 1951, it was a last glorious peak of the era. The Weavers couldn't help but notice the facades crumbling around them. Even the temple of capitalism couldn't contain their contradictions.

After the song became a hit, they would learn more about its true origins. "Your record of it was quite popular down in Johannesburg," a South African woman would tell Pete. "But, you know, you should learn some of our older folk songs."

What the Weavers assumed was an ancient South African folk song about a sleeping lion was, in fact, a fairly recent pop sensation. What Pete wouldn't know for decades, though, was that the chiming melody at the end of the song—the one that Gordon Jenkins had highlighted up top, the melody that would eventually bear the lyric about the jungle, the mighty jungle—wasn't the "song" at all, but a fleeting improvisation by original singer Solomon Linda. All in all, just another authentic folk tune gathered along the banks of Minetta Creek.

A few days after the session, Gordon Jenkins joined them on piano for a rare live appearance at a society gathering, a Halloween Ball held in the Starlight Roof of Manhattan's posh Waldorf Astoria Hotel, a benefit for the Hospitalized Veterans Music Service. Along with the Lester Lanin Orchestra, the Weavers entertained a room full of New York elite, including William Randolph Hearst Jr., who'd succeeded his father as the head of the powerful Hearst publishing empire earlier that year.

It was a final splash of the Weavers in glitzy old New York. Two more Town Hall concerts closed out the year, where Pete continued to push the band into new directions. Besides being joined again by a jazz ensemble for a half-dozen songs, Pete and Fred introduced and sang along to the recordings they'd made at Texas prison farms earlier that year, and likewise led a miniature children's oriented set during the intermission.

Pete inserted his messaging as he could, introducing "Wimoweh" with a speech about the ills of South African apartheid. Interrupting Fred's intro to

"The Frozen Logger" one night at Town Hall, he added, "we'll sing about the teachers and their frozen wages," receiving a round of applause.

After that, it was back to the road, though not without dissent in the ranks. Pete Seeger was again ready to stop. He was outvoted, and the band pressed on into the darkness.

CHAPTER FIVE

Ballad for
Un-American Blues

The *Chicago Tribune* published Harvey Matusow's picture with the headline "Witness Tells of Sex Orgies by Red Recruiters." The twenty-five-year-old ex–People's Songster could've written that one himself. But the scale of Matusow's accusations was such that headline writers had a vast choice of angles with which to present his sociopathic information dump, fake news, and cagily worded half-truths.

By the end of his Washington performance in early February 1952, he'd been on the stand for the entirety of an afternoon session and into the next day, reeling off the names he brought with him not once, but twice, repeating them into the microphone in alphabetical order at the committee's request. Being a young Communist in the United States had once been a utopian act. But now, through a slip of language, it bordered on illegal. Being an *ex*-Communist, on the other hand, could be big business, which—to some ways of thinking—was perhaps even more utopian and surely more American.

Compared to the lurid sex-filled details Matusow offered about Communist-affiliated summer camps and Greenwich Village crash pads—not to mention a series of very serious accusations pertaining to New Mexico mining unions—his claim that the members of an extremely popular band were Communist Party members went comparably unnoticed in the wreckage.

"I think I remember Harvey," Ronnie Gilbert would recall many years later. "He was always walking up to people in a cafeteria and selling *Daily Workers*. We didn't take him seriously."

But in Akron, where the Weavers had returned for the first time since the cancelled Ohio State Fair gig, they had to take Harvey Matusow seriously, at least for a moment, when they came down from their hotel rooms to find their names in the paper again. "You could feel the violence in the air," Fred recalled of the vibe in Ohio.

After a year playing in fancy hotel ballrooms, the blacklist was starting to act as a fading agent, and they'd been demoted to a lesser circuit of supper clubs, despite their continuing success on the charts. When Matusow testified, the Weavers had recently concluded a week at Daffy's Stardust Room in Cleveland, where the American Legion had shown up, too. Owner Daffy Lightinan told them to get lost. "It's just music," he reportedly said. "Quit hassling me, or I'll get my boys on you."

It was during that week, too, on their way to the club, that Ronnie could feel someone following behind. She spun around and accosted the two men trailing her.

"Do you want your subpoena here or at the club while you're performing?" one sneered.

"*Here*," Ronnie said, and they presented her with a document informing her that she was due in Washington two weeks hence. A mysterious event in Weavers history until many years later, the band was unsure what to do with these documents that may or may not have been real subpoenas. They told manager Pete Kameron about it, and never heard anything again.

It was only in the next century that Kameron filled in the missing piece, explaining in a letter to Ronnie that he'd called HUAC chief counsel Frank Tavenner, laid on the charm, told the attorney that the Weavers' concert schedule was booked solid, and received a temporary reprieve. As unlikely as that seems, included with the letter were two telegrams from committee chairman John S. Wood pertaining to Ronnie and Pete: one referencing the January subpoena and rescheduling a hearing from February until March, the other informing Kameron that the March hearing was "postponed indefinitely." Why the hearing was postponed indefinitely and Kameron kept this from his clients for a half century remain unanswered questions.

As it happened, the day Ronnie was originally due in Washington was the same day Harvey Matusow testified. One wonders if Matusow would have made the same accusations with the Weavers in the room. Instead, cleared in secret by their manager, the Weavers found themselves canceled in Akron for the second time in a year. By the end of the day after Matusow's testimony, the Yankee Inn bought the band out of their contract for less than they'd been promised. On the last night, the club was packed.

The band hightailed it out of town, "feeling like we were an hour ahead of the posse," Fred remembered, though their other tour destinations didn't treat them much better. In Philadelphia, customers shouted them down at a hotel bar, their acoustic music and harmonies not quite enough to drown out the local trolls.

"Wimoweh" had hit the charts—number six with a bullet—before it, too, got shouted down. It was too unusual to be an instant standard, but too beguiling to be forgotten. Minetta Creek folk songs were meant to be rewritten, and the song formerly known as "Mbube" would continue to float through the American folk ether. Even as Harvey Matusow took to the stand later in February for a second set of flame-throwing accusations against the Weavers, bandleaders like Tommy Dorsey had picked it up.

A quick scan through the trade papers as the Weavers started to disappear in early 1952 revealed traces of them everywhere, most especially in the ways that "Irene" and the Weavers' eclecticism had helped crack open a door for previously marginalized music. A trend piece in *The Billboard* reported "Rustics Penetrate Major Night Clubs," and discussed the "rustic music field, which has firmly established itself via recordings during the past two boom years." Country music was just beginning its long ascent from regional dominance to national popularity, perhaps an even truer lineage of "people's music" than the folkies. And while that ascent had begun many years before the arrival of the Weavers—indeed, Woody himself had lifted plenty of melodies from the Carter Family—it accelerated in the post-"Irene" age.

In a lead editorial on the durability of pop ballads, *The Cash Box* lamented that "for a while it seemed that no song could be a hit unless it had a folk ballad and was done in a multi-voiced recording," but acknowledged that "all this has added a great deal of variety to our records and has produced a great number of smash hits." More and more, commercial song publishers were realizing both the vast scope of the material available to popular musicians, as well as the truly broad-minded tastes of record buyers.

A scan through the pages of *Sing Out!*, on the other hand, showed that—as they were fading from the music industry at large—the Weavers remained at the center of an explosive series of public conversations about contemporary music and the emerging folk-pop complex.

"Can An All-White Group Sing Songs From Negro Culture?" read a headline in January, reviewing a recent Decca collection of Weavers songs around the time the band was getting subpoenaed in Cleveland. "Because they are an all-white group, such a treatment [of "Easy Rider Blues"] seems to be an unintentional effect of cultural opportunism," claimed Lee's former Commonwealth College collaborator Waldemar Hille. Letter writers all but demanded that the Weavers integrate immediately, blithely unaware of the band's unfolding professional situation, the delicate dynamics that held them together in the first place, and the multiple attempts they'd already made to do so over the previous three years, most notably with Hope Foye.

In seeming response, Irwin Silber and People's Artists launched the People's Artists Quartet, a mixed-race singing group. "The idea was to keep it more political and less mainstream," said Ernie Lieberman, a former *People's Songs* editor and guitarist in the Quartet. "There was always a conflict on the left between making it commercially and staying true to your ideals. Part of Irwin's goal was to have a quartet like the Weavers, only they would be interracial." Lieberman remembers no particular ill will toward the hit-makers, only the notion of creating an alternative. Like a parallel-universe version of the Weavers, as if they'd never made it big and never stopped singing for the People, the new group found occasional gigs at places like the Freedom Festival, where they sang for the United Electrical, Radio & Machine Workers, expelled from the CIO along with other radical-leaning unions.

The more vicious *Sing Out!* attack began in March under the relatively innocuous title "Weavers Issue Folk-Song Folio," a review of the band's new songbook. Written by the hardline Irwin Silber, a disciplined party member who'd once presided over meetings of his square-dancing group with a gavel, the *Sing Out!* editor took offense to the songwriting credits attached to "Follow the Drinking Gourd" and "Midnight Special."

"The colossal presumptuousness of the editors of the collection in assigning authorship credit on these two folk songs to some writer from Tin Pan Alley is inexcusable," Silber raged. "When these two songs are products of the Negro people's struggle for full equality and freedom, we must characterize this statement for what it is—an arrogant piece of white chauvinism."

And Silber wasn't wrong entirely. But "Joel Newman," who received songwriting credits on "Midnight Special," "Kisses Sweeter Than Wine," and other Weavers recordings was, in fact, a publishing pseudonym for the late Huddie Ledbetter himself, invented to help direct funds to the late guitarist's family.

Folk music was complicated. As the process dictated, Lead Belly was only slightly more the original author of his songs than the Weavers were. Like Pete Seeger, Huddie was a song collector and performer who freely adapted material to his needs, which often included blurring their origins.

Earl Robinson, author of the Popular Front anthem "Ballad for Americans," then renting a spare room to Lee Hays, wrote in to correct some of Silber's finer points. "If the Weavers didn't copyright this material, twenty five other Tin Pan Alley publishers would," Robinson pointed out. "I personally would rather have the Weavers do it because I believe it will get better treatment artistically and from a content standpoint. . . .

"The whole practice of copyrighting folk material is, of course, idealistically bad and will sometime be changed," he admitted. "But that time is not now."

Silber wasn't buying it, going so far as to accuse "the Weavers themselves [of] doing a disservice to the struggle against the blacklist by conducting their professional lives in such a way as to alienate one of their most powerful allies in such a struggle—the Negro people."

It was as if Silber *did* have a hammer, and everything looked like a nail. Like his sometimes ally Pete Seeger, Silber was under extreme pressure in the early part of 1952. Both he and Betty Sanders, one of the People's Artists Quartet, had been subpoenaed themselves. And like the Weavers, they had their hearings canceled without explanation.

The shadow forms were reaching out from the other side, rising into the space between friends, making people wonder who actually was who, if they were the same people they'd always been. *Counterattack* and others had called out a legion of Weavers associates, and all handled it differently. Alan Lomax, for example, set sail for Europe in 1950 aboard the RMS *Mauretania* and simply didn't return to the United States for nearly a decade.

Oscar Brand, who'd hosted the WNYC show where the No-Name Quartet declared themselves the Weavers, gave a reproachful speech at Cooper Union in New York claiming that the Communists had a "pernicious influence upon the American folk-music field." They'd censored him, he said, when he'd wanted to sing the Confederate song "The Re-Constructed Rebel," questioning the "pro-slavery" perspective of the song.

Burl Ives, meanwhile, went a step further. In May 1952, the singer and actor became the first significant folkie to name names, names that (like nearly all names named) were almost surely known already in the secret files of J. Edgar Hoover's FBI. In this namer's case, it was fellow People's Songster Richard Dyer-Bennet and Ives's now ex-publicist Alan Meltzer.

"The future of Burl Ives should be interesting," Irwin Silber noted in *Sing Out!* "We've never seen anyone sing while crawling on his belly before." Though Ives would struggle for a few years, his name-naming was insurance that he might build a professional career as a genial and nonthreatening actor-singer. Even good-natured, find-the-best-in-everything Pete Seeger would call him a "stool pigeon" in print.

Harvey Matusow continued to pathologically spew names and numbers before various committees, as if experiencing an uncontrollable nausea having passed from the Red darkness into the national spotlight. There were 76 Communists working at *Time* magazine, he claimed. At the Sunday *New York Times* there were *126*! In actuality, the Sunday *Times* had fewer than 100 employees altogether.

Matusow babbled of hootenannies, spurted corn-fed square-dancing calls to one courtroom's amusement, and kept on disgorging about the Weavers. "They could integrate political songs into their program," Matusow said. "They could sing 'Old Smoky' and then could follow with a Spanish Communist song. They are good entertainers and the bobby-soxers would go for them."

"I sat in closed Communist meetings with three members of the Weavers," he declared, citing Pete, Fred, and Ronnie. It was a blind guess. Only Pete had ever been a real party member, and never anywhere near Matusow in any official capacity. Matusow levied a charge against Hope Foye, too, for good measure, citing her as an ex-member of the group and at least remembering what *Sing Out!* didn't. This time, even the *New York Times* picked up an item about Matusow's accusations. "Agent Calls Singers Reds," read the paper of record.

In New York, Pete Kameron convened a press conference, with Lee speaking as a representative of the band. "My reaction and that of my associates is that the charges are a lot of nonsense," Lee said. "We are singers and nothing else. Our job is singing folk songs."

It was maddening. All of it. The government. The lunatics like Harvey Matusow. The machinations and double-talk of the world they'd already felt so tentative about entering. The blowhards like Irwin Silber, who should know better.

Observing it from his always-dreamy vantage, Pete Seeger proposed to his bandmates a list of what he labeled "extraordinary possibilities." Maybe they could perform in Europe or Mexico or Canada? "Irene" had hit the top 10 in the United Kingdom, too, and a European audience certainly couldn't hurt. What about a residency at a progressive nightclub in New York? Or a more do-it-themselves concert tour? They could "build up contacts and independent outlets, so that if or when support from regular companies, agencies, is withdrawn, we are not stranded."

And there was another option, ignored for the time being, but the equivalent of smashing a perfectly good banjo: "Let us consider also: a fullpage ad in *Billboard* declaring the Weavers dissolution, and saying we will be back when the air is freer." The suggestion was rejected, and the never-ending tour continued as planned, though its itinerary was unquestionably limited.

This was Pete's worst nightmare. He wanted them to move forward, he wanted them to integrate, to do something. "What music we could could [*sic*] make!!" the banjo player concluded.

By this time, Pete Seeger was well and truly sick of it all. Agreements or no, that May, skinny Corporal Seeger slid back into his army uniform and marched with the May Day Parade down New York's Fifth Avenue. Protesters lined the blocks. DOWN WITH THE SCUMUNISTS, read one sign. But Pete and others celebrated their freedoms as Americans while violence broke out at parades in Tokyo and Berlin.

In a photograph that inevitably found its way into government files, Pete carries a large caricature of a microphone with a sign across the front of it, reading CENSORED. But on his face, he wears something not evident in the Weavers' recent publicity photos: a trace of a smile.

By June, manager Pete Kameron was bound for London, Paris, Stockholm, Milan, and Switzerland "to set a concert tour for the Weavers and dig up folk material," *The Billboard* reported. If he were acquiescing to Seeger's suggestion of cultivating a European audience, nothing would materialize from his efforts.

The Weavers were left to the dregs of the pop circuit: a Rotary International gala ("honoring and entertaining the ladies") in Pasadena, a private party for the president of a steel company in Indianapolis, a beer convention in Detroit. The bitter end could be seen manifesting itself in an ever-dwindling tour itinerary.

The year closed out, as it had the year before, with a pair of holiday concerts at Town Hall in New York, near the old People's Songs offices. There would be no jazz-pop ensemble to join them this time, but in the melee of 1952, the Weavers had also managed to completely turn over their repertoire for hometown fans. Of the thirty-four songs they played at their final concert in 1952 (thirty-five, if counting both opening and closing versions of "We Wish You a Merry Christmas"), twenty-four of them hadn't been played at their three Town Hall shows over the two previous years. They hit the hits, of course, but "Irene" was now buried mid-set.

Among the new additions to the set was "Die Gedanken Sind Frei" (Sing Out! #38), introduced by Lee as a new old song that had once been "used to bring Europe out [of] the Dark Ages," he said, "and then the song wasn't heard of for a long time." Adapted with new English words, Lee said, "like all good songs, this one has come back when it is most needed." Translated "Thoughts Are Free."

"*My thoughts give me power*," Ronnie sang, her voice soaring over the others, as always. "*No hunter can trap them.*"

As far as the Weavers knew, it was the last time they would sing together on a stage. Their dissolution was never announced. They just simply stopped playing.

Their names and songs continued to appear in trade papers. Decca insisted on one more studio session, anyway. "We took a sabbatical," Lee said in an oft-repeated quote, "which turned into a mondical and a tuesdical."

When Pete Seeger reported to work in Manhattan now, it was no longer to the well-appointed technician-run Decca studios but to a one-room record label on West Forty-Sixth Street. Moe Asch, the owner of Folkways Records, had a recording console built right into his desk. A trained electrical engineer, Asch did nearly everything at Folkways, from the recording to writing the liner notes, with the help of one assistant. "It's much easier for me to sit down at a typewriter and knock out the label copy than to tell someone what I want, right?" he once said.

Around the time the Weavers went on their hiatus and Pete became a Folkways recording artist, Asch's newest label was reaching full steam on the verge of transforming both the folk world and, eventually, popular music beyond it. Then in his mid-forties, Asch had been putting out folk recordings since before the Almanac Singers even existed, starting in 1939 with a 78 by the Bagelman Sisters, a pair of teenage girls singing updated versions of Yiddish folk songs. Discovering a market for Jewish music, Asch filled similar voids for Greek, Italian, Ukrainian, and—eventually—English-speaking listeners.

Miraculously surviving the war, *Time* reported, "Unlike most record companies, which have lavished their scarce shellac on surefire songs, Asch frequently stops making an album just when it is selling well, so he can put out something else—which may or may not sell. He has put out about 40 albums in the past three years, hopes to issue another 40 this year." Well heeled and schooled in Paris, Asch quietly and steadfastly carried the mission of the Popular Front into the '50s and well beyond.

In the postwar years, years of extreme cultural conservatism and mainstream blandness, his catalog spanned from Lead Belly to jazz saxophonist Coleman Hawkins, from calypso to Nat King Cole, from flamenco to Pete and his friends. His sessions with Woody between 1944 and 1949 would constitute the bulk of Guthrie's recorded work. The Folkways multitudes also contained Elizabethan ballads, John Cage, drum rudiments, and more.

And in 1952, as the last Weavers 78s were fighting their way up the charts, the market pushed Moe Asch in a new direction. Or, more specifically, his good friend Sam Goody pushed him in a new direction. Building from a used record store to a major operation that would soon go national, Goody was then slugging it out in the format wars. RCA was pushing their new 45 rpm 7-inch singles, and Columbia was championing their long-playing 33⅓ discs. Goody had thrown himself behind the 33⅓. But he needed more to sell, and was worried the format was going to go belly-up. He promised Asch that he would order 100 copies of whatever Folkways produced.

Goody was as good as his word and sold Asch's jazz compilations and spoken-word recordings, beginning with James Joyce reading his poetry. Issued that year, alongside *Drums of Haiti* and *Maori Songs of New Zealand* and others was a remarkable six-LP collection, spread over three double-LP sets and titled *Anthology of American Folk Music*.

Pete Seeger, the Weavers, and the Almanac Singers were nowhere to be found, nor were Woody Guthrie, Josh White, or Burl Ives. Instead, there were eighty-four songs collected between 1926 and 1934. A history of folk music generally ignored in the pages of *People's Songs* and *Sing Out!*, the songs political in their own complex ways. Assembled by a true eccentric named Harry Smith, the *Anthology* linked together blues singers and gospel ensembles and Cajun fiddlers and jug bands and banjo soloists and country harmonizers.

Where the Weavers had attempted global harmony through their post–Popular Front embrace of global culture, Smith's *Anthology* wove a winding thread through American regional music. Edited from Smith's collection of rare 78s, the *Anthology* amounted to a giant bootleg, though—given the loving assembly and Smith's copious notes—it could easily be argued that Smith's use of the material was entirely transformative. Another one of Smith's many interests was alchemy.

The *Anthology of American Folk Music* became a beacon, its news gradually spreading over the decade following its 1952 release. Veritably ignored by *Sing Out!* at first, the *Anthology* was a forking point, spawning a new generation of musicians whose interest swerved in different directions from progressive causes or even the smoothed-over urban folk the Weavers seemed to personify. Often raw and frequently surreal, the *Anthology* suggested worlds beyond the reach of politics and utopias and modernity. Its crackling real-life energy was a weirdness that rang like a rebellion against the conformist times, and even as a rebellion against the state of popular American folk music, a way of claiming personal autonomy. It began a new branch of the folk scene, those committed to tending to the music itself in its purest form, tracing Minetta Creek back to its sources in the Delta or mythical lands afar.

Yet right there alongside Harry Smith's *Anthology* in Asch's "encyclopedia" of a catalog was Pete Seeger, a regular in Asch's cramped studio office in the years after the blacklist dissolved the Weavers. Asch became a patron to Seeger, issuing over two dozen albums by Pete over the next years, including classical banjo arrangements, an instructional record, old mountain songs (including several collected on the *Anthology*), Jewish children's music, German folk, industrial ballads, skip-rope games, and Bantu choral numbers. Compared to the Weavers' records for Decca and Gordon Jenkins's sweeping cinematic arrangements, they were the model of nearly black-and-white austerity. It was a reclamation of a feeling that would allow Pete to cross over to the new audience of authenticity-craving folkies in a way the Weavers rarely would.

"I always believed in the 'one mike' theory," Asch would say. "I hate the stereo recordings, and mixing can never give you the accurate sense of the original sound. A hundred years from now it is as natural as the day I recorded it."

If this sentiment wasn't a direct rebuke to the past three years of Seeger's recording career, it was close. Though Pete would speak fondly of the band's work with Gordon Jenkins, he would regret many of the recordings the band made with other pop orchestrators. Pete felt right at home in Folkways' eclectic stable. Asch was a specialist in a very real way. The label's main source of income was from libraries, and Asch could regularly be found selling his 10-inches, LPs, 78s, and more at annual meetings of the American Anthropological Association and the American Library Association, in addition to marketing Folkways' products to art, science, and natural-science museums, even aquariums. Pete Seeger was again among the People. And the Fishes.

Living his life at the edge of the post-Communist countercultural network, Pete still hoped for and worked toward and woke up every day thinking about transforming the world through song. "Guerrilla cultural tactics" is how he would describe his musical strategy over the next few years.

With the Weavers scattered to the winds and the American public safe from their evil ways, Pete returned to the old utilitarian model of People's Songs. He and Toshi printed up promotional material and sent it out to a mailing list they'd accumulated of organizations that might be in need of a former Weaver to come sing children's songs or sea chanteys or union tunes or old hits or new topical songs or perhaps some combination thereof. Interested parties were encouraged to write or call.

During that first blacklisted summer, Harold Leventhal secured Lee Hays a job that Lee had been dead set against taking, working as a master of ceremonies at Schroon Lake, a left-wing folk resort in the Adirondacks. When the Weavers' obligations had finished, Lee had sworn he was done with the stage. "I detest [performing] so much that it is almost an obsession," he wrote to Leventhal.

"I think I have been through a nervous collapse," he said, "and only things like the tv set and my own work have kept me more or less in line." His first plan was to try writing for television, though he admittedly had never studied it as a craft, as such. He got some beer and planned to school himself. He didn't get very far.

Lee did better helping his friends Walter and Lillian Lowenfels clear land at their new cabin by the Jersey Shore, both keeping him outside and cutting down on his drinking. He'd even started putting ideas on paper again. "The good thing about my life now is that I managed to make such a large break with my recent past," he assessed.

Ronnie did the same and picked up on the California dream she'd deferred when the Weavers got serious. "Why not join the demographics?" she thought, ready to become the "typical, cozy American housewife [she] saw on TV." Her husband prepared to move his dentistry practice to Los Angeles, they packed the convertible they'd bought with one of Ronnie's first royalty checks during the Weavers' tumultuous 1951 tour, and took the long route west by way of Mexico.

Fred Hellerman wasn't quitting music. He *was* changing his name, though, at least for the purposes of continuing to make a living. Anything to escape the family rags business, still looming. Just because the Weavers were no longer pop professionals, that didn't mean he couldn't be, so—for now— "Fred Brooks" it was.

Wherever the former Weavers were, the blacklist loomed, either over them or their friends. It was a pervasive cultural condition, an affliction that came in the night. One could see it in the jobs lost, the names changed, and a general cultural flatness for which the decade would become caricatured. In the Weavers, Lee had felt it as a "blight of guilt and anxiety."

His emceeing went terribly. "I just made an ass of myself," he would sulk years later, still embarrassed. "[Harold] tried to make a standup comic out of me," Lee grumbled. "Even got me a professional material writer, a very well known one, who gave up on me because I had no use for his material." Oy.

The Weavers had seen the front lines of battle, but were now systemically exiled to the symbolic hinterlands. At times, the blight was hardly abstract at all, but brutal and cold and shocking. While Lee was stuck emceeing at Schroon Lake, the FBI raided the summer cabin of his old friend Walter Lowenfels at two o'clock in the morning, pulling the poet and activist from bed and arresting him on Smith Act charges. Depending on when one asked Lee, Walter was a collaborator on some of Lee's best-known songs, including "Wasn't That a Time." Other times, Lee might say, he'd only given Walter the credits to pay him back for years spent as a non-paying tenant. But Lowenfels's arrest sent the bass singer into a deep rage.

"I was flushed out of the mountains like a bull moose," Lee would say. It didn't take much to get him to leave the emcee job, and he immediately headed to Philadelphia to be with Walter's family.

A communal dweller since the Almanac days, give or take his room service–abetted sojourns on tour, Lee existed within and relied on the extended post-Communist counterculture. Since returning from the scarring first Weavers tour, he'd occupied half a floor in Brooklyn Heights, subletting from Popular Front composer Earl Robinson. A successful film composer until the blacklist came for him, too, he was helped immensely by Lee's $60 rent. The blacklist had reduced a vast movement into small communities.

True to his word, Lee Hays even started writing again. Some of it, given that he was blacklisted, he did under a pseudonym, sending pieces out under the name Christian Reinhardt, after a Southern relative who'd fought in the Revolutionary War. Another job he did under the moniker Mordecai Jones.

His Brooklyn neighbor was a pulp publisher specializing in nudie magazines, and paid Lee a healthy $35 a pop to write what Lee called "bawdy tales," adapting the *Satyricon* in a rural voice. It wasn't an entirely new genre to Lee, exactly. During the pre-Weavers days, he'd even tried writing a whole erotic novel. Toshi Seeger's father, Takashi Ohta, a deeply colorful character and friend of Lee's, had asked to read it, and the manuscript promptly disappeared into the vortex of the Ohta house above Minetta Creek.

But he did his most successful writing in the period as Lee Hays, returning to *Ellery Queen's Mystery Magazine* with "Banquet and a Half," a powerful and surreal tale based on the real incident of two young black boys accused of rape and executed during the time Lee was at Commonwealth College in Arkansas.

"A little gem, I thought!" Ronnie wrote to Lee from California. "I've loaned my copy to several friends."

Life was only sort of working out how Ronnie had envisioned. She and her husband Marty had welcomed their daughter Lisa into the world, and that was wonderful. But more than a year into her California adventure, Ronnie was having regrets.

Music still called. Pregnant and blacklisted in 1953, she'd been taken by Harry Belafonte's new hit "Matilda," an early sounding in the American calypso craze. Being a trained Weaver, she immediately made for UCLA's music library, enjoying what music they had from the West Indies. Belafonte's success signaled a new phase of the battle the Weavers had helped start, moving folk music into the public eye. Though often regarded as a fad of its own, the growing American fondness for calypso was nearly continuous with the early phase of the folk boom that the Weavers initiated. A veteran of the Wallace campaign and People's Songs hoots, Belafonte's first big gig had been at the Village Vanguard, about a year after the Weavers had left. Belafonte been named in *Counterattack*, too, but the American Legion never quite followed up, and his career trajectory soon carried him far past the Weavers.

Belafonte, of course, was black and had more sex appeal than Fred, Lee, and Pete combined, and calypso's rhythms were richer and more sensuous than anything the Weavers could muster, but the framing and production were often similar. Belafonte's productions weren't nearly as slick as the Weavers', but the idea was to adjust a regional sound into the bandwidth of mainstream acceptability. The American pop language continued to mutate, with the Weavers now encoded into it.

But even if they were encoded into it, the members were now forced outside it. Of the three non-Pete Weavers, Freddie had perhaps loved being a pop musician the most deeply. He was there for the cause, and a believer in everything he'd believed in as a People's Songster, but as a Weaver he'd discovered how to make a legitimate living at a craft that engaged him fully. Unlike Lee or Ronnie, Fred was an instrumentalist, services that could be useful elsewhere. Unlike Pete, he held no reservations about commercialism.

Befriending Robert De Cormier, a Juilliard-trained music teacher working at the Little Red Schoolhouse, Fred formed a new group, the Neighbors, which he conceived of as a "workshop for myself." If being blacklisted was like starting from scratch professionally, he'd still gotten more than his share of real-world experience. De Cormier expanded the guitarist's knowledge of voicing and harmony and arrangements. The Neighbors were a serious endeavor, but mostly played at home, working out complex vocal arrangements.

More important, it gave Fred a framework. "Come hell or high water before the Wednesday nights we'd get together, I always made sure I had a few new arrangements for things, or maybe even a new song," he would remember. For reasons that would later emerge, Fred would call it "the smartest thing I ever did in my life." If the Weavers couldn't get past the blacklist, the back end of the music business couldn't care less about Fred's connections. Fred Brooks set to work.

Not that Fred abandoned the folk scene either. Will Geer, the folk-singing actor who'd introduced Pete to Woody, moved back to New York after his own blacklisting and occasionally operated the Folksay Theater out of his apartment for fellow blacklisted actors and playwrights. Fred helped arrange music. Weavers manager Harold Leventhal worked the door. Sometimes, Woody Guthrie—his condition deteriorating—crashed in the basement, where he liked sleeping on the window ledge, waking up to the sound of people walking by.

Even if the Weavers themselves had given up on the idea of being Weavers, manager Harold Leventhal hadn't. Periodically, he wrote to each of them from his homey New York office, suggesting a reunion, a tour, or something else. Lee wanted no part of it. Ronnie didn't either.

But "housewifery," she confided to Lee, quickly "came to be somewhat less than totally satisfying." She'd gotten a sitter for a few hours every day and signed up for classes at a nearby college. In the morning, she sang with an a cappella choir. Twice a week, there was a basic musicianship course. And also a formal voice class, in part because it fit between the other two. She told Lee she'd entertain an offer if there were something specific and it involved a paycheck, but she had her hands plenty full.

"There are just too many other tangibles in my life to leave much room for daydreaming about nebulae," she told Lee. "It seems so ridiculous to ponder the problems of a job that doesn't exist and the why's and wherefore's [sic] of such hypothetical complications, when tomorrow's schedule includes 3 hours of classes, a load of dirty diapers to wash, marketing, house-cleaning, dinner-making, an hour of phoning for my club, and 2 hours of rehearsal at night for a far too ambitious job I took on (the vocal part in El Amor Brujo with the L.A. Community Symphony under Elmer Bernstein's direction!)." Maybe next year, Harold.

One afternoon, Federal Bureau of Investigation Special Agents Heinz Eisele and Trenwith Basford traveled to Dutchess Junction, New York, and followed a truck. Shortly after lunch, the truck stopped at the local elementary school and dropped off a child, after which the special agents approached the subject and identified themselves as representatives of the bureau.

A twelve-year veteran of the bureau already, during the war, Agent Basford had been deployed to track a troop of actual Nazis that had made landfall on Long Island's south shore via submarine. Now he was being sent to question this exceedingly polite thirty-three-year-old musician.

Pete Seeger greeted the men cheerfully. Barely two months since the Weavers' final recording session, spring had sprung on the Hudson. They were about a mile down the road from Seeger's home, and he immediately and cordially invited them over to talk. The agents declined and told the banjo player that they'd like to ask him about some of his past affiliations.

"When the purpose of the interview was stated his manner became reserved but he continued to be courteous," the agents' report read. "At no time during the interview did SEEGER lose his composure or appear to be uncertain or confused." But that didn't mean he wanted to talk to them.

"I think I had better just not say anything," Pete told them plainly.

"Shortly thereafter SEEGER again repeated that statement and indicated through his actions that he considered the interview to be terminated. He thereupon drove away in his truck."

"The interview was started at 12:40 P.M. and was terminated at 12:45 P.M." And that was mostly that. "No further action is contemplated by the NY Division."

Which is to say, the purpose of Special Agents Eisele and Basford's trip to visit Pete had little to do with gathering information from the banjo player. All they needed to do was pay him a visit, more or less just to let him know they were thinking of him.

For Pete, the blacklist was in especially full effect, with the bureau rolling out all kinds of bonus treatment for the former Almanac Singer and now Tuesdicaled Weaver. His sixty-six-year-old father, Charles, who'd renounced communism before Pete had officially joined the party, had his passport revoked in apparent retaliation for Pete's own alleged danger to the union's solidarity. A few years later, they would do the same to Pete's half sister Peggy. Since Communism was considered to be more or less an infectious disease in the 1950s, perceptions only grew even more distorted.

A year after the Weavers' dissolution, President Dwight Eisenhower spoke of the menace in his State of the Union address: "American freedom is threatened so long as the world Communist conspiracy exists in its present scope, power and hostility," he declared. "We should recognize by law a fact that is plain to all thoughtful citizens—that we are dealing here with actions akin to treason—that when a citizen knowingly participates in the Communist conspiracy he no longer holds allegiance to the United States." That is, lawfully convicted Communists should be convicted of treason and stripped of their citizenship.

A contemporary survey conducted at Harvard suggested that as much as 80 percent of the country agreed with the president. For that matter, 77 percent thought that Communists should be outright banned from the radio. It was just too risky. High school textbooks were about the same. "Unquestioning party members are everywhere," read one. "Everywhere they are willing to engage in spying, sabotage, and the promotion of unrest on orders from Moscow." It was a time of general oppression, and progressive ideas were often shunned and marginalized because of their association with Communist platforms.

Through these years, the HUAC parade continued, with a cavalcade of major and minor actors, writers, and musicians coming before the committee to reckon with themselves, with the government, and with the nuances of language and the law, where gestures and the slightest statements took on a horrible and magnificent weight.

There were "friendly" witnesses and "unfriendly" witnesses, depending on whether they did or didn't volunteer information or name names. Each tag carried a social branding of its own. To be "friendly," no matter the context or content of one's testimony, was to receive a stigma. That's exactly what had happened to the director Elia Kazan, then at the top of the entertainment world. A few years earlier, he'd picked up Best Director at both the Academy Awards and the Tonys, for *Gentlemen's Agreement* and *A Streetcar Named Desire*.

Unlike writers such as his friend and frequent collaborator Arthur Miller, Kazan rationalized, he needed a full support system to make films. That was his work, and there was no way to do it otherwise, and so he became "friendly," citing the names of eight actors he'd known during his Communist days, and ending his actual friendship with Arthur Miller, among others. Miller snarled that the "public exposure of a bunch of actors who had not been politically connected for years would never push one Red Chinaman out of the Forbidden City or a single Russian out of Warsaw or Budapest."

The "unfriendly" witnesses walked a narrower legal bridge, albeit with clear consciences. The Hollywood Ten had argued that their political beliefs and expressions were well covered by the First Amendment. But in a landmark case decided in 1951, while the Weavers were preparing for the final leg of their grueling six-month tour, the Supreme Court declared that they weren't. To advocate communism was to support the overthrow of the US government and was not covered under the freedom of expression.

Many subsequent witnesses stood behind the Fifth Amendment, the right to not self-incriminate. That offered little emotional consolation, forcing a public figure into a muted silence on a public stage, tacitly admitting the truth of the government's judgment that, yes, communism and Communists were dangerous. For progressive voices under attack, this was a great moral and logical and philosophical problem of the times.

It was a small window for expression, and the vast majority took the Fifth in situations when they were asked about their affiliations. One found an accidental third path during a Senate subcommittee hearing. "Are you or have you ever been a member of the Communist Party?" she was asked.

"No," she answered.

McCarthy ended the session immediately as assistant Roy Cohn beelined toward the subject's attorney. "What a clever trick!" he hissed. The woman had been summoned in a miscommunication, and wasn't a Communist. No others tried it.

Many did their best to get off parting shots before beginning to decline the inquisitors' questions. When HUAC passed through New York in the spring of 1953, they called the songwriter Jay Gorney, one of the composers of the Fred Hellerman favorite "Brother, Can You Spare a Dime?" Gorney wrote a new song for the occasion—"Bill of Rights"—but was interrupted when he tried to sing it.

If it hadn't been obvious for a long time, the trials were just for show. During HUAC's 1953 New York stand, fewer than half of the witnesses were what the committee deemed "cooperative." It was a time of narrow bandwidth, as the accused attempted to reconcile their public and private selves with their unknown doppelgängers waiting patiently in the strange rooms imagined by the FBI's secret files.

Even after the Weavers dissolved, Pete's file only continued to grow. Rebuilding his solo career anew in the nooks and crannies of the American left, it's quite possible that the bureau kept better records of his travels than he and Toshi did, and were perhaps his biggest followers in the most literal sense of the word. Even if Pete and Tiny Hill disagreed about drinking, there was one item that they might now come to see eye-to-eye on, should their long and winding paths ever cross again: the value of one-night stands. No longer confined to tedious hotel residencies, Pete was now in and out of towns in less than twenty-four hours.

Pete was surely happy in his new solo career not to discuss what was bullshit and what was not with former Weavers manager Pete Kameron, and he especially wasn't going to do it with Special Agents Eisele and Basford. He'd gotten back to work within weeks of the final Weavers session, as both the agents probably knew from having consulted their notes.

One of his first performances was the People's Artists All Fools Hootenanny at Manhattan's Webster Hall. "I haven't been as far as you might think," he told the crowd of 1,000-plus, who cheered him madly. If Pete had been remotely worried about the government's constant surveillance and persecution of suspected Communists, it was hardly reflected in his bookings, as he drove down from Beacon to Manhattan for a variety of causes.

The week before the agents' visit, at the same glitzy Manhattan Towers once idealized by Gordon Jenkins, Pete had appeared at a benefit dinner for Steve Nelson, a Croatian-born Spanish Civil War veteran convicted under the Smith Act that year. If the special agents thought they were going to intimidate Pete from future work, they were sorely mistaken. A few weeks after their visit, he was back in the city to play another benefit for another Smith Act defendant, former Communist Party cultural spokesperson V. J. Jerome, this time at the Hotel Capitol. Agents may have taken note of the event's name: "Culture Fights Back."

Other people could be blacklisted. Stopping Pete Seeger was impossible, short of physical detainment or worse. Pete and Toshi found a new circuit, filled with unlikely venues. Pete played People's hoots and lectured about ballads at the Jefferson School. He played for the American Labor Party in the Bronx and in solidarity with International Women's Day at the Yugoslav-American Cooperative Home in Hell's Kitchen, a regular venue for his solo performances during these years. He played house parties for the Labor Youth League (a recent derivation of the Young Communist League), numerous soirees for the American Labor Party; he turned up in Chicago to support trade and peace with China, and in St. Louis to entertain at the dance and social for the National Negro Labor Council. Over the summer, he ignored Tiny Hill's advice and returned to the Weavers' old ways of a residency, albeit this time at the Furrier Union–affiliated resort, the White Lake Lodge in the Catskills, for their summer music festival. In the darkness of the blacklist, Pete was able to find a full rainbow.

Pete Seeger was everywhere at once, it seemed, his shadow self reenacting his gestures in pantomime days later in the FBI's files, beamed to the ledger via informant or *Daily Worker* clipping. There were typos, and occasional inaccuracies as the shadow-Pete glitched out, trying to contort itself into something passable and sensical.

No matter how far they tailed him, Special Agents Eisele and Basford would never truly know Pete Seeger. Less cantankerous than the open-souled Lee Hays, Pete Seeger was also far more distant, filled with his own contradictions. "Only Pete knows Pete," Folkways owner Moe Asch once observed. "I don't think even Toshi knows Pete."

As conscientious a human as he tried to be, and as full-speed as he went, there were those who felt there wasn't much to Pete past his public persona and energy. Ronnie Gilbert always professed a hard time really *knowing* Pete. But even still, *that energy*, even if the person attached seemed to be aloof to the world he was trying to improve. As always, Toshi kept him grounded and organized, the mysterious bonding agent that allowed all his parts to be passable in the real world around them.

Possessed of a strangely blooming temper, Pete suggested to his biographer David King Dunaway, "Maybe I've got a little mental eraser that just blots things out." Perhaps he had no memory of why he'd once smashed a banjo in Omaha, Nebraska.

"We didn't see him lose his cool very often," one of his daughters would tell Elijah Wald many years later, "but when he did, he really did. He was totally unreasonable." Those were extraordinarily rare sightings.

Returning to the musical flexibility he had long yearned for, he now had achieved a certain kind of notoriety thanks to the blacklist. Almost certainly the smartest decision he made in this era from a business point of view—recognized as a guerrilla tactic circa 1953 but common sense soon thereafter—was to start performing at colleges and universities, hiring an agent just to book him into that circuit.

In a metric he would be fond of citing, in his first year post-Weavers, 1953, he played Oberlin College in northeastern Ohio, a left-wing bastion as far back as the Underground Railroad, and drew around 200 people. He would return the next year, tripling the crowd, and up to 1,000 the next.

They subpoenaed the wrong Lee Hays. Perhaps the Justice Department simply looked in the New York County phone book instead of the one for Kings County. Once the mistake had been made, agents were then compelled to assemble a file on Lee Hays, the actor, who was powerfully confused when he received a summons one Friday in July. Eventually, the document made it to the folk-singing Lee Hays on Cranberry Street in Brooklyn.

"Greeting," it welcomed him. "Pursuant to lawful authority, You Are Hereby Commanded to be and appear before the Committee on Un-American Activities of the House of Representatives of the United States."

Pete received one, too, a sleek black car pulling up to the still-in-progress homestead in Beacon. "Are you Pete Seeger?" the occupant inquired.

A hypochondriac in good standing, Lee had fretted about it for years. "I feel fairly sure that this is the year when we may be called by some group or another," he'd written to Howard Leventhal two years earlier. Since Lee was subletting a room from fellow blacklisted songwriter Earl Robinson, surveillance and harassment remained facts of life on Cranberry Street.

Pete stood for a long moment at the top of his driveway with the envelope in his hand as the car pulled away, the hammers hammering, their barn part raised. He too had expected this day to arrive, less paranoid than curious, though at least equally if not more offended than Lee. Finally he called out to his wife, "Hey Toshi, they finally got around to me."

The two ex-Weavers were to appear at Foley Square in New York, the site of the first big Smith Act trials, Lee at ten a.m. on August 16, and Pete two days later. HUAC was coming back to Manhattan.

The committee had never held any judicial power, but ensnared participants in the complex and formal drama of its hearings. Rather than simply accusing the witness of a crime with a set punishment, the toll was psychological and financial, a series of diminishing choices, public humiliation, and blacklisting via some unofficial channel like *Counterattack*. The discussion was not about the virtues or even the evils of any form of socialism, or even politics at all, but simply an abstract battle reenactment, the peace army going up against the dark forces of old.

On "Wasn't That a Time," Lee had described the battlefields of Valley Forge and Gettysburg. "The snow was red with blood," the Weavers had sung. Their fights had been at Peekskill, in Akron at the Yankee Inn, on union lines, not the drab interior of the courthouse at Foley Square. Now they all wore suits. Their signed inquisitor was Rep. Francis E. Walter.

Toshi Seeger found a progressive lawyer named Paul Ross to represent Pete and Lee. Had Weavers-mania not set in, Pete and Lee probably would have been representing Ross on sound trucks during his quixotic fall 1950 mayoral bid for the American Labor Party. As a lawyer, he'd helped integrate New York's Stuyvesant Town apartment complex, one of the causes when they'd sang for Vito Marcantonio. Mostly, he was there to keep Pete and Lee appraised of their extremely limited options.

It had now been nearly a decade since HUAC's Hollywood Ten show trials. It seemed violently absurd to Pete and nearly everyone he knew, of course. In the past six months or so, the public facade of the hearings began to crumble somewhat. By the end of 1954, Joseph McCarthy had been censured by his Senate colleagues for taking his persecution too far. They called it "contrary to Senatorial traditions."

McCarthy called it an "unprecedented mudslinging against the committee by extreme left-wing elements of the press and radio." None of it stopped the committee from truckin' onward into 1955, though.

Pete and Lee and more than two dozen others would go before a quartet of senators and their legal counsel over the course of five days, "but may require less time depending on how co-operative the witnesses are," the *Herald-Tribune* explained. The majority of those testifying were from the New York theater world. One was actor Tony Kraber, whom director Elia Kazan had fingered as a Communist. There was comedian Zero Mostel, on the bill for at least one hoot with Lee and Freddie. There was a concert pianist, a variety of stage managers, writers, playwrights, composers, a film importer, and a publicist.

"We'll find that a lot of people in the entertainment business, who have been Communists, have used large incomes they got from entertainment to further the Communist cause," the committee chairman told the press.

Lawyer Paul Ross outlined Pete and Lee's options. Most people these days took the Fifth Amendment, the right to not incriminate oneself. It had become a slur, "the Fifth Amendment Communists," a bullying shorthand. "Another Fifth Amendment Communist was finally dug out of the dark recesses and exposed to public view," the disgraced Senator McCarthy had once crowed. It's certainly not what Lee or Pete wanted to be. The other choice was to use the First Amendment.

As Pete would recall their lawyer's elegant explanation: "Using the Fifth Amendment is in effect saying, 'you have no right to ask *me* this question'; but using the First Amendment means in effect, 'you have no right to ask *any* American such questions.'"

Pete wanted to go further. "I want to get up there and attack these guys for what they are, the Worst of America, the witch hunters," Pete told the lawyer. Ross talked him down. At the very least, he needed to be courteous, or Ross wouldn't represent him. Every citation for contempt was the equivalent to a potential year in prison.

The First Amendment was a legally dangerous option, too, even if one remained polite about it. The Supreme Court had twice ruled that it wasn't a valid protection for Communists. The lawyer advised both Pete and Lee to take the Fifth. Harold Leventhal did the same. Pete Seeger made no promises.

For once in his life, Lee Hays was ready to take an easier path. Later, his quip-on-file about the whole period was, "If it wasn't for the honor, I'd just as soon not have been blacklisted."

For Lee, the humid summer day itself was a formality. His short journey from Cranberry Street over the Brooklyn Bridge to Foley Square was less like a march to a battlefield than a nervous trip before an impending medical procedure. There would be no statement by Lee Hays. The battle hadn't been lost by any means, but a second-rate HUAC hearing wasn't his platform, and a ballet of legal gambits wasn't where Lee Hays swung a hammer. He was a folk singer and a writer. The Weavers' career was over, what more did they want?

"I wanted to take the Fifth and be done with the whole thing," Lee would say. "I never did think much of the 'Hurrah!' side of the First Amendment." It was hardly a surrender, not like Burl Ives's name-naming, and that satisfied Lee's moral needs. To take the Fifth was to hold the line, like his and Pete's old song went. To take the First was to, in some sense, fire back. But even if Lee didn't want to tarry with the committee, he couldn't simply walk in, opt out, and go home.

The proceedings did not get off to a smashing start. Riding up to the seventeenth floor with his lawyer, "When I walked into the hearing room I passed two huge Irish federal marshals standing at the door," Lee would re-call. "As I passed, one of them said, 'I'd like to take them all out in the court-yard and shoot them.'" Lee waited his turn in the wood-paneled courtroom, the sound of scuffling feet on the marble lattice floor disappearing into the high ceiling.

Similar skirmishes and the quiet echoes of battle continued in other court-rooms, sometimes less ceremonial than Lee and Pete's turns. In Washington that day, a federal judge upheld the State Department's decision to revoke Paul Robeson's passport unless he signed a loyalty oath swearing that he wasn't a Communist. For a half decade, Robeson had been trying to return to Europe, where he continued to have a large audience. But he, too, had a line to hold. "Of course I won't sign," he said. "I consider it an invasion of every Constitu-tional liberty I have."

In New York, as Lee waited his turn, the morning's witnesses included the character actor Elliott Sullivan, making a reprise appearance in front of the committee. Two weeks earlier, he'd appeared in Washington in front of the committee's special subsection on Communist summer camps, and what ensued pertained both directly to the Weavers and how the committee per-ceived popular music—or at least for the purpose of public consumption.

Sullivan was an entertainment organizer at the left-wing New York resort Wingdale Lodge and—earlier that summer, over the Fourth of July weekend, only days after Lee had received his summons—put on an Independence Day revue. There'd been a mole in the house during the Saturday show and only weeks later Sullivan was in Washington, where the committee ran down the revue in detail, act by act, picking apart the performances.

It had begun with a chorus line of a half dozen girls (*hadn't it?*), followed by a satirical sketch about the Bill of Rights. The congressmen failed to find humor and grilled Sullivan. But then the committee turned their snouts to one of the musical acts on the bill.

A congressman from Virginia pushed the actor, "Do you recall that another skit followed in which an individual sang a song in which he referred to certain victories at different places, the victory at Valley Forge, for instance, with the verse concluding with 'Oh, what a time it was,' and then another verse regarding the victory at Gettysburg . . . and [the last verse] 'Our victory is endangered while free men are in jail. Oh, what a time this is.'

"You recall that; do you not?"

The mole's paraphrased version of "Wasn't That a Time" that Pete performed at Wingdale Lodge for Independence Day had struck a chord in the congressmen. They'd interpreted it correctly as a commentary on the Smith Act trials, though missed nearly everything else.

"Was that a means of getting over to the people in the audience, particularly the young people, the Communist Party view regarding leaders who were in jail as a result of Federal prosecution?"

Sullivan didn't know. *Who wrote it?* Sullivan didn't know. *Who sang it?* Sullivan didn't know.

And then it was back to Aesopian language, as they offered their official congressional interpretation of Lead Belly's "Midnight Special," which Pete had performed too. He'd introduced it that night as a freedom song often sung by prisoners.

"But in this instance," the congressman from Ohio insisted, "was it not used particularly in reference to the Communist leaders who are now in jail, and was it not intended to point out that each one of them in that audience was the light or the midnight special that was going to release those so-called freemen that were in jail?"

No, Sullivan told them, that was just, like, their opinion. When he returned to face the committee a few weeks later in New York, this time in the morning session before Lee himself took the stand, Sullivan unloaded on the committee.

"I believe that I am a [stauncher] defender of the Bill of Rights than you are in our relationship at this moment," he asserted.

The Ohio representative told him dryly, "We are trying to find out how far the Communist conspiracy has succeeded in its infiltration."

"All through the Berkshires," Sullivan replied, "and through the forests around Wingdale Lodge, and all over the place."

A quick flash in the Ohio representative's mind, perhaps, of a mycelium network propagating in the soil, an underground railroad eaten by some monstrous foreign force. On the stand for nearly two hours in New

York, Sullivan refused to invoke any amendment at all, an antiauthoritarian way of citing the First. He was cited for contempt, and would soon enter the tunnel of the legal system. The crowd cheered him as he left the stand.

Then it was Lee's turn. In the courtroom, Lee felt like a bumpkin. "I had a good lawyer, who wasn't allowed to speak," he would sigh. Ross could only sit at Lee's side and whisper advice and pertinent information into his ear. One of the first bits that he relayed was that their table was bugged, picking up any conversations they were having. "I don't think I have ever felt so damn alone as on that day," Lee would say.

They began with routine questions about his employment history, and Lee gladly told them about his time at the Cleveland Public Library. He left out the period he'd been employed at Commonwealth Labor College, and the committee's legal counsel called him out for it. "I have before me a photostatic copy of the *Daily Worker* . . ." the counsel began, flashing a piece of paper, and then the ordeal really started.

"You were not short in your memory about your employment," he grilled Lee. "You just were not going to tell the committee what your full employment had been; isn't that true?"

As they tried to pin him down on dates and places and jobs and sources of income, Lee's refusals to fit himself into other people's categories shined through, as the blurriness of his bohemian lifestyle made it into the public record, unable to account for the years he spent surviving on the goodness of his friends like the blacklisted Lowenfels and Robinson without bringing down any more shit fire on his or their heads.

"I believe in 1948 I was functioning as a folklorist," Lee told them. It was a truth of sorts. He told them he spent his time among libraries and conventions and record collections and, generally, people.

"Were you employed to do that type of research work at any particular place?" the counsel queried.

"I was self employed," he told them. Lee was living folklore, that year habituating among the Lowenfelses in Philadelphia and, as it happens, writing "Wasn't That a Time," before returning to New York to found the Weavers. "This is a lifelong profession, Mr. Tavenner," he told the counsel. "It is interspersed with many jobs, as they say."

To hold the line was also to tiptoe the line. "It was like having to walk a tight rope," Lee would say. They waved the clippings from the *Daily Worker* and *New Masses*, including an editorial in which Lee explicitly called for

Communist poetry to be of "a more rugged and revolutionary character" as part of a more complex treatment.

Asking Lee to cite some songs he was proud of ("Kisses Sweeter Than Wine," "So Long, It's Been Good to Know Yuh"), they turned to "Wasn't That a Time." By then, they'd figured out the title and author. Then they started in on the Wingdale Lodge program again. The place had formerly been known as Camp Unity, a Communist summer resort not far from Peekskill. After getting kicked out of the Almanac Singers, Lee had spent a summer there working as a night watchman. They hadn't figured that part out.

"It is the one that deals with Valley Forge, Gettysburg, and Bunker Hill," the Ohio congressman asked. "It sort of ridicules them, doesn't it?" he pressed, either willfully or actually misinterpreting "Wasn't That a Time," missing the shades of irony in Lee's lyrics, where the title and its variations veer between dejection and triumph.

"I was nervous and shaken," Lee said about that day, but the People's Songs theoretician surely stewed as this group of Washington nimrods ritualistically misunderstood one of his most wrought-over songs. Lee Hays had spent the better part of the previous two decades thinking about the roles of music, musicians, songs, lyrics, and the nuances of individual words, in helping to bring forth a better world.

"What I am trying to get at, Mr. Hays, is to learn to what extent the Communist Party has used you in its program to advance the cause of the Communist Party in this country."

Here, Lee Hays, the militant and careful writer, slipped into his actual self for his public inquisition. What did they mean by *used* exactly?

"You are asking questions which to me are highly argumentative and debatable," Lee told them, through the politely clenched teeth of an Arkansas minister's son, "and I don't propose to get into that debate and argument because it is an area that deals with associations and beliefs, and so I do decline to answer that under the reasons stated." Soon, but not soon enough, Lee was done.

The press and gallery couldn't help but note the lack of cooperation among the witnesses. *Do you think anybody will talk tomorrow?* the scrum shouted at the chairman. "We have hopes," the chairman replied dryly. Fond of the media attention, the chairman would later offer to dismiss playwright Arthur Miller for the small donation of being photographed with Miller's wife, Marilyn Monroe.

And so it was that Lee Hays became a Fifth Amendment Communist. The *New York Times* called him "a burly sandy-haired folksinger" and the other dailies speculated as to his weight. As procedures went, it was quite painful to Lee, even literally so. "When I got home my heart hurt and I place the beginnings of my heart trouble at that day," he told a niece decades later, not long before his death. The Robinsons were gone for the summer. There were letters, calls from friends.

If Lee had a doppelgänger in Hoover's files, it might find several shadow selves already occupying Lee's quarters when arriving to take his place. Even when the Robinsons returned, there was the long empty autumn, the cans of beer delivered from the corner store, and the television, which—his upstairs neighbor Doris Willens would write—Lee "watched until the channels signed off with their sermonettes and, to the music of 'The Star-Spangled Banner' or 'America the Beautiful,' their shots of warplanes, warships, exploding bombs, waving flags."

T wo days after Lee Hays, Pete Seeger took the stand, and it started much the same way: leading questions about his profession followed by a flashed photostat from the *Daily Worker*. Here, Pete Seeger's experience forked away from his bandmate's, and the banjo player faced the Un-Americans alone.

The first *Worker* clip had to do with one of Pete's appearances midway through the People's Songs era. If the committee planned to proceed by *Worker* clippings, it's quite possible that Pete possessed one of the longest rap sheets of the whole of the HUAC period.

"Sir, I refuse to answer that question, whether it was a quote from the *New York Times* or the *Vegetarian Journal*," he told them. Pete was ready to go. He sat calmly on the other side of the bugged wooden table in his checked shirt and corduroy jacket. If culture was a battle, Pete Seeger came ready to fight. Perhaps over-ready.

"I direct you to answer," the chairman told the banjo player.

"Sir, the whole line of questioning—"

"You have only been asked one question so far," the chairman pointed out.

Pete didn't pull punches and repeatedly stood his ground. Per the committee's formalities, they went around in linguistic circles, working out themes and variations and occasionally introducing new movements.

"There was a job that had to be done, I was there to do it," he assessed later, a little surprised that he pulled it off. "A soldier goes into training. You find yourself in battle and you know the role you're supposed to fulfill." If the real army had never put him into actual battle, the peace army certainly did.

One version of Pete's stance from mid-session: "I decline to discuss, under compulsion, where I have sung, and who has sung my songs, and who else has sung with me, and the people I have known. I love my country very dearly, and I greatly resent the implication that some of the places that I have sung and some of the people that I have known, and some of my opinions, whether they are religious or philosophical, or I might be a vegetarian, make me any less of an American."

With nearly each question, he and the committee would go back and forth in an attempt to clarify some point or another, but often found themselves trapped in backwaters that had nothing to do with Aesopian language and instead were spoken in the bizarre and forked tongue of midcentury legal-bureaucratic English.

They soon got around to the troublesome song, though the committee got the name wrong again, calling it "Now Is the Time."

A motif throughout his testimony, Pete volunteered to tell them about the song itself. He would sing it for them, if they wanted. Toshi had his banjo, though he didn't mention this. "I feel the songs are the clearest explanation of what I do believe in, as a musician, and as an American," he said.

Again and again, the congresspeople asked Pete about the circumstances of the song, of where it had been sung and when, never about the song's lyrics, about the blood spilled at Valley Forge and the freemen who'd gone to jail.

They flashed another round of photostats at Pete, documenting the Civil Rights Congress. In the middle was a notice about the Battle of Peekskill, as if it'd been just another function.

"I can only infer from your lack of interest in my songs that you are actually scared to know what these songs are like, because there is nothing wrong with my songs, sir," Pete told them. The congressperson from Ohio wanted to know which songs specifically he'd sung at Communist meetings.

Pete understood the absurdity of the affair too. "It seems to me that you heard my testimony, and that is a ridiculous question, because you know what my answer is," he said. Pete never broke into overt theatrics, but his calm was almost supernatural. There were no smashed banjos, actual or symbolic. On the stand at Foley Square, as when cornered by special agents a few years earlier, Pete was cool, his wits as close about him as his banjo usually was.

"I know many beautiful songs from your home county, Carbon, and Monroe," Pete told Tavenner, the congressperson from Virginia, speaking directly to the face of power. Ronnie had referred to Pete somewhat tongue-in-cheek on Weavers tour as "the Messiah." It was a benevolence that could border on passive-aggressive martyrdom, but also bravery, as on this battlefield, when Pete Seeger tried to bypass the cultural divide in front of him and perhaps find a human on the other side.

The Virginia congressperson introduced evidence into the testimony, a picture of Pete marching in his army uniform in the 1952 May Day Parade. "Will you examine it, please, and state whether or not that is a photograph of you?"

"It is like Jesus Christ when asked by Pontius Pilate, 'Are you the king of Jews?'" Pete replied, practically vibrating.

"Stop that," the congressperson said, as if swatting a fly in the battle they were fighting elsewhere.

"I'd always been amused by the 'Thou sayest' retort," Pete would explain to Alec Wilkinson decades later. "'Are you the king of the Jews?' 'So you sayest.'"

Pete Seeger was not a God-fearing man in the traditional sense. It wasn't until much later that he would admit he'd been raised as "a member of the Marxist church." Possessed of a deep and awe-filled sense of the universe, a love of nature would guide him out of the city and eventually up (and down) the river in a very literal way. And during the mid-1950s, exactly during the period he testified at Foley Square, he'd started to spend more and more time in houses of worship, in a sense forced there for refuge by the blacklist. With nightclubs and mainstream venues off the tour docket, Toshi and he found that churches were one of the places most receptive to his "guerrilla tactics," in part where he found a widespread children's audience.

It was here, too, that Pete gave the committee their biggest opening, and where they most completely failed to understand Pete's mission, not even understanding that their silencing mechanisms were incapable of stopping it anyway. As they tried to link him to a bigger conspiracy, Pete even baited them a little.

"I take it that you are not interested in all of the different places that I have sung," Pete told them. "Why don't you ask me about the churches and schools and other places?"

They didn't. "If you were acting for the Communist Party at these functions, we want to know," they demanded. Harvey Matusow had testified that indoctrination occurred at these radical summer camps, citing an alleged nursery rhyme thrust upon impressionable children: "Jack Sprat could eat no fat, his wife could eat no lean. Because the Congress done them in and picked their pockets clean."

But it was at these wholesome locations, for $20 a night, that Pete Seeger continued to perpetuate his most dangerous work, singing for the communist agenda with a lowercase *c* in front of impressionable young minds. He'd been doing it since the earliest days of People's Songs, and continued lately with his Folkways releases.

In the darkening, children's music had become a dependable outlet for other musicians who'd faced public scrutiny about their past ties, like Burl Ives and Tom Glazer. But, unlike Ives and Glazer, Seeger didn't curtail his activism. Though topical material made up less of his post-Weavers solo repertoire, his message only got bigger through the years. It wasn't, as Congress worried, his juxtaposition of "Wasn't That a Time" and "Midnight Special" that transmitted it, or even the lyrics of the songs, but the totality of it. Especially the singing along.

A few days before his committee appearance, he'd played a children's set at Camp Woodland, including "Die Gedanken Sind Frei" and "The Hammer Song." In an almost accidental but substantial way, Pete Seeger had moved from organizing unions to organizing a generation. At the summer camps and churches, it all rolled into a never-ending montage of ragged harmonies, the gospel song-leading techniques Seeger picked up from Josh White, and the repertoire he'd built in the decade and a half since the Almanac Singers. What he transmitted was as much structural as it was anything, training the young audience in the technology of shared voices and human-to-human social networks. Culture could be a battle, but it could also be a sing-along. There is power in a union, lowercase *u*.

They kept on listing organizations. Did he belong to People's Songs? People's Artists? Did he teach at the Jefferson School? What about the California Labor School? It was a map of real territory, American territory, without any substantial knowledge of the customs or their meaning, nearly as shallow as a bad ethnic stereotype.

Eventually, the chairman gave the word: "The witness is excused." A little bit after 12:30, he dismissed the room for lunch. Pete wasn't the first or last witness to be charged with contempt. Officially, a few days later, the charge would be with "depriv[ing the] committee of necessary and pertinent testimony." There would be more court proceedings to come.

After his testimony, Pete broke through the blacklist, however briefly. Outside the courtroom, in the hallway, Pete's banjo finally returned to his hands, he bid adieu to the committee, singing "Wasn't That a Time" for the cameras and the evening news.

CHAPTER SIX

This Land Is Your Land

None of the Weavers wanted to reunite, and so Harold Leventhal booked them a show anyway. It is a tale told along the muddy banks of Minetta Creek, and a happy and unconflicted one, for once. All four had turned down their manager's repeated entreaties. This time, he just went ahead and did it, telling each that the others had agreed. Such was the state of the Weavers' de-weaving that none was in close enough touch with the others to call Leventhal's bluff.

The story of the Weavers' resurrection has perhaps more tellings than Weavers. Town Hall *did* call Leventhal's bluff. He'd tried to get the cozy 1,500-seat theater first, where the Weavers had played their previous Christmas concerts, but it was either already booked or they refused the booking because of the blacklist. "Not us radicals!" remembered Pete. So Carnegie Hall it was, nearly twice the size.

Used almost exclusively for classical music, the venue's management was baffled by Leventhal's request, as Harold described it, thinking he meant that he wanted the small recital hall in the basement. They'd never heard of the Weavers, they said, or so Harold recounted. The Weavers had actually performed there before, as part of People's Songs' final hoot in 1949, with Pete and Lee appearing there at previous folk events. But that was a different world.

If Harold Leventhal had second thoughts about whether an audience remained for his act, he didn't show it when he ponied up money to rent the four-balconied venue on Christmas Eve 1955. Perhaps he just wanted out of the family girdle business. "It was all due to Harold," Fred would say. "It was one-hundred percent his doing."

The Weavers had their reasons for resistance, some more persuasive than others. "I was still mourning," Ronnie would say. She'd moved on. Like the others, she was hardly convinced that they had any audience left. She had a family now. Her daughter Lisa was almost two.

More than dampening their music, the blacklist had separated the Weavers as people, each with their own lives, at least three of the four on course for new places. Pete continued to ricochet around the country into new causes and networks and songs, in addition to having his own young family. Lee Hays sulked in Brooklyn, for reasons he would surely list, if you had a few hours. Fred Hellerman, meanwhile, was slugging it out as a musician in New York.

As Fred Brooks, he'd placed a trio of songs with Harry Belafonte, still trying to find a permanent audience himself after his early hit. (Ronnie couldn't fail to note that two were copyright-tweaked versions of songs she'd taught Fred out of the Priority Ramblers' repertoire.) "Folkish waltz-tempo ballad about a beauteous lass," *The Billboard* called "Pretty As a Rainbow." "Should get some spins." It was nearly pure schmaltz, but more successful—and a better sign of the times—was Fred's gentle arrangement of the more ancient-sounding "Delia." Gordon Jenkins and His Orchestra and Chorus recorded Fred's "I'm Just a Country Boy," surely both an honor and confidence boost. Folk-pop was far from dead, and Fred Hellerman knew from both.

He and Lee had even scored a session gig singing (uncredited) on "Goodnight Sweet Dreams," a suspiciously Weavers-esque waltz-time B-side by Jenkins and His Orchestra, during the summer leading up to Lee's blacklist testimony. Lately, though, Fred had been teaching guitar. More work was good work.

The Jenkins session had been nearly Lee's only paying job for 1955, Harold surely reminded him, as he motivated the bass singer into formally agreeing to the Carnegie Hall appearance. Lee was also Harold's client and Harold was his manager, though there was more to it than that. Harold oversaw Lee's expenses and income, even when it was obvious that Lee had only one of the two at the moment.

Moreover, as Harold perhaps knew more than anyone, the Weavers' needed resolution, both individually and collectively. He didn't want them to end by the choke of the blacklist any more than they did. What better time to fire back than immediately? Pete and Lee had been in the news, certainly. *It's a hell of a way to get a song on the air,* he'd ribbed them. Harold Leventhal was an altruistic human being and a mensch, but he also *was* a manager.

Pete had needed no ribbing to fire back. Less than two weeks after the committee had picked apart his July Fourth performance of "Wasn't That a Time" at the Wingdale Lodge, Pete returned there for a Labor Day encore, as if to thumb his nose at his inquisitors. As he'd told the HUAC, "I have sung in hobo jungles, and I have sung for the Rockefellers, and I am proud that I have never refused to sing for anybody." It was now time for him to return to sing for and with the Weavers and their audience.

Tickets for the Carnegie Hall performance on Christmas Eve 1955 sold out almost instantly. There'd been some posters and small business card–size ads utilizing the band's old advertising tags: "America's most popular Folk Singers" and, more important, "Together Again!" That's all it took. *The Billboard* noted the sell-out with mild surprise a week before the event, reporting that another two hundred temporary seats were added behind the band on the stage itself. If a return to the trade papers hinted at the Weavers' pop past, the musicians themselves were committed to the new era, especially Pete. He'd been blacklisted already, hauled before Congress. He wasn't returning to the straight and narrow of a full-time pop career. No one was going to keep him from performing when and where he wanted.

Over the course of the autumn, he played—as he told Congress—for anybody who would have him. In Philadelphia, he performed for the last remnants of the Progressive Party, about to call it quits. Even Henry Wallace had abandoned them three years earlier. In Chicago, he sang for the Midwest Committee for the Protection of the Foreign Born. The same week the Weavers were due to return to the stage, he was in Philadelphia, singing at a Christmas/Hanukkah party for the Friends and Family of the Smith Act Defendants. All were duly noted in Pete's files, thanks to the vigorous reportage of informants T-36, T-24, T-28, and others. Great job everybody!

In Louisiana, in one musical endeavor not noted in his files, Pete wound up playing with someone who *wouldn't* have him. After a folk festival, he headed for a Cajun jam session at a nearby house, invited over to study some fiddle licks. When he arrived, the house turned out to belong to none other than Congressman Edwin Willis, a nearly silent inquisitor at Pete's HUAC hearing. Singing commenced. That was one occasion when even Pete Seeger consumed alcohol. After a while, the congressman cornered the banjo player in the kitchen, and—at the congressman's insistence—Pete split town before playing the gig he'd set up at a local school.

The audience at Carnegie Hall had no such reservations about welcoming the banjo player, though, or any of the Weavers. Ronnie had arrived in New York a few weeks early with her daughter, Lisa, with pleasant but low expectations. The band got their set ready, joined by bassist Percy Heath of the Modern Jazz Quartet. And then Christmas Eve came.

"I will never forget what it felt like, out in the wings waiting to walk onstage," Ronnie recalled, still in awe years later. "The SOUND of the audience—after all, I'd heard many many audiences, you know, over the years that we'd been working, but the excitement, the electricity, just reached out onto the stage and around the baffle walls and through the door and into the wings; it was amazing."

She remembered the "breathless feeling, coming onto the stage and feeling what was going on with the audience before they even started applauding. The minute we got out there, there was a split second where you felt the 'Ahh!' and then the applause."

Just like old times, they opened with "We Wish You a Merry Christmas." When they finished, the applause kept rolling and rolling, as much as a full LP's side by one account. Everything about the night glowed. Lee charmed unfailingly, as he always did when put on a stage. "Yes, you've got to look on the bright side," he told the crowd. "I always do. I've been bowled out and balled up. Held down and held up. Bulldogged, blackjacked, walked on and walked over. Cussed and discussed, lied to and lied about. Boycotted, blacklisted, talked to and talked about."

Lee Hays was a breathing reminder that the Weavers were part of some kind of continued resistance, or at least solidarity, "traveling in the footsteps of those who came before," as they reminded listeners when they followed their holiday caroling with "When the Saints Go Marching In." "The audience, on intimate terms with everything taking place, was almost as much a part of the show as were the actual performers," the *Herald Tribune* observed.

Beginning with Carnegie Hall, Weavers concerts became a rallying point as the 1950s trudged onward in oppressive black and white, the overtones of their harmonies seeming to find a new and more vivid spectrum while Ronnie's voice beamed outward from the center. They sang in Hebrew and in Spanish. They sang black gospel songs and white gospel songs and songs of indeterminate origin, all with the battery of Pete Seeger's banjo, as always a perfect meeting of musician and instrument, impossible to say if the propulsion was coming from the banjo or the player. And, despite their formal appearance, back in their old proper eveningwear, there was a scent of danger, of an America not fully revealed, of truths unspoken.

The Carnegie Hall reunion would be noted as a turning point in folk magazines and fashion outlets like *Mademoiselle*. Folk clubs were springing up in colleges, and the vacation-time concert was a destination for the new strummers, the reunion buzz firing back into the campus network. As television drew families into living rooms, participatory folk singing was not only an alternative activity but an open window to the worlds of the songs: the worlds of the people who wrote and sang them, and the worlds of the other people singing along.

In the audience at Carnegie Hall was a new generation who hadn't seen the Weavers the first time around, too young to be aware of them or even get into the nightclubs they performed at. A not insubstantial subsegment were teenagers who'd discovered the band's music through Pete himself on his endless circuit through summer camps and other kid-friendly venues. One was Mary Travers, a nineteen-year-old member of the Song Swappers, a teen folk group that had recorded with Pete for Folkways. Travers was part of a generation of musicians that Pete seemed to be influencing personally. But she'd never witnessed the power of a fully operational Ronnie Gilbert, hearing her clearly as "the voice of a strong woman, someone able to stand on her own two feet and face adversity." The future member of Peter, Paul & Mary would even meet one of her future bandmates that night.

Irwin Silber, the sometimes-aggressive editor of *Sing Out!* who'd harshly criticized the band at the height of their success, wrote of "the contemporary inquisition" and interpreted their return with typical grandeur. "If proof were ever needed that peace is the indispensable ally, the Weavers' concert is a small but important documentation," he concluded. The Weavers were back and they were going to save the world. Again.

For Harold Leventhal, the Weavers' return was slightly more prosaic, but only slightly. "Frankly I had expected each of us to come out with more money," he admitted to his clients, but there were more expenses than he'd anticipated. The extra chairs onstage. The rental of the spotlights and sound system and marquee. The reels of recording tape they'd sprung for. But they'd done OK. By the first week of 1956, before Harold had even finished his accounting from Carnegie Hall, more calls were coming in and further shows were booked in the Midwest for later in the spring.

Four months after Pete Seeger and Lee Hays had been compelled to appear before the House Un-American Activities Committee, the singing peace army was even bigger than before. To some, they were American heroes.

Lee was forty-one, Pete was thirty-six, though each now qualified as elders in their own ways; though "Lee was always an old man," Fred would note, "and I mean o-o-o-ld." Both had long drawn a circle of younger musicians around them, including Fred himself at one point, but now the difference was nearly generational. As Pete mentored musicians in innumerable ways, from technical banjo skills to pro road tips, Lee's passing-on of wisdom could take unusual forms, as much talk as music, sometimes as simple as hanging out with Lee, watching television.

"Young musicians who'd attended the Christmas concert came to see Lee as they would a guru," wrote his upstairs neighbor, Doris Willens, who was also drawn into Lee's world and would eventually become his biographer. He was certainly filled with stories, many of them even true. A decade and a half, a World War, and a massive cultural ravaging now separated the present from the Almanac Singers and the heart of the Popular Front. The kids constantly wanted to hear Woody Guthrie stories.

Woody was still around, though, and the most recent stories weren't pleasant. When Fred was working at Will Geer's rogue Folksay Theater during the Weavers' Tuesdical, he recalled, Woody "was tottering and it was just drunk Woody again," and there would be awkward silence. But it wasn't that. Suffering from Huntington's, the same mysterious and awful disease that had slowly destroyed his mother, Woody Guthrie would become a tragically literal shell of his former self, trapped inside a deteriorating body.

Not long after the Weavers' reunion at Carnegie Hall, a meeting was convened at Earl Robinson's apartment, downstairs from Lee, with Woody's ex-wife and eternal guardian Marjorie, Harold Leventhal, Lee, Pete, and others, where they discussed what to do about Woody, then in residence at the Brooklyn State Hospital, and how to support him and his family. Feeling inspired by the Weavers' success over the holidays and the newly visible crowd of old lefties and budding folkies, they began with a benefit concert at the Pythian in New York.

Lee served as narrator, his stentorian voice rolling out through the nearly sold-out venue, an audience made up of the same new generation of folkies that had taken the Weavers as their heroes. The long script, written in part by former Almanac Singer Millard Lampell, linked together the threads of Woody's music and life, his poetry and his prose, from the songs he'd learned

An early incarnation of the Almanac Singers, 1941, the radical music collective at the top of the Weavers family tree. Butch Hawes, Millard Lampell, Lee Hays (playing autoharp), and Pete Seeger.

Working to create a "singing labor movement" in the postwar years with the People's Songs organization, Pete Seeger and Lee Hays rehearse for a pair of hootenannies at New York's Town Hall, May 1946.

Photos: © and more bears

Above: At left, former Almanac Singer Woody Guthrie performing with a young Fred Hellerman, circa 1947. Guthrie would be an erratic mentor at best, but Fred would absorb dos and don'ts at the feet of Guthrie, Seeger, Lead Belly, and many others. Hellerman Family Collection

Below: Pete Seeger and Fred Hellerman sing with Henry Wallace during the former vice president's disastrous 1948 presidential run on behalf of the Progressive Party. Photo by George Silk, Getty Images

in his Oklahoma youth like "Goin' Down the Road Feeling Bad" to Dust Bowl classics like "So Long, It's Been Good to Know Yuh," plus union songs, topical numbers, political parodies, morale boosters, and excerpts from his WPA-sponsored cycle about the wonders of the Columbia Dam.

At the end of the night, Pete led the crowd in a song that had begun its life in 1940 as another one of Woody's parodies, skewering what he believed to be the empty patriotism of Irving Berlin's "God Bless America" to the tune of an old Carter Family song. But just as Woody tossed off endless first drafts, he also kept reworking ideas, eventually transforming this particular one into "This Land Is Your Land." It'd passed into the common repertoire, and Pete had the audience singing along.

As the song wound to a close, organizer Earl Robinson whispered into Pete's ear to lead the crowd through one more chorus. While Pete did so, a spotlight illuminated a balcony box near the stage, where Woody himself struggled to his feet. He'd come into the theater just as the show started, and watched quietly. Speaking was hard, and singing was impossible. With the crowd now singing his song—their song—for him, Woody (at least in some accounts) raised a single clenched fist in solidarity.

The whole spot-lit moment "almost proved too melodramatic," even Pete admitted. "It couldn't have been planned." But it had happened. It was the first attempt at framing the mercurial Guthrie's lifetime of impulsive, inspired work as a single canon. In direct proportion, the event transformed Woody from a disappeared songwriter into an outright countercultural hero, and—in the present moment of 1956—caused its own amount of irreparable damage.

Feeling energized by the event, Woody checked himself in and out of the Brooklyn State Hospital with increasing frequency and was soon wandering around town, a-rambling once more. It was a bad scene. He nearly burned down Harold Leventhal's office with a lit cigarette. Another time he staggered to Lee's place, confusing a young group of Woody fans, who made him dinner before Woody stumbled off into the Brooklyn night. Picked up soon thereafter in New Jersey, Woody was placed in a new hospital, one where he couldn't wander out for the night, or even the afternoon. Woody Guthrie was grounded. It would take some time for Harold Leventhal to locate him, the hospital staff hardly believing Guthrie's stories about being a famous folk singer.

But Woody Guthrie's songs were very much not grounded. As always, Pete sang them nearly everywhere, now to increasingly bigger crowds. "This Land Is Your Land" was prominently showcased in the Weavers' repertoire when they tentatively returned to the road in the spring of 1956 following their

Christmas reunion. After a return visit to Carnegie Hall in May, they were off to Chicago, where they opened and closed with Woody's anthem, all of their socialist hopes coded there in Woody's panorama.

At Orchestra Hall, a stink bomb delayed the show's start. They demonstrated Pete's latest obsession, steel drums, and introduced songs with pedigree and humor. But, Lee announced with a solemn wink near the show's end, "We're gonna sing a song now that I got absolutely nothing to say about," before the congressionally investigated "Wasn't That a Time." "It's just a song for singin', not for talking about." After the Spanish Loyalist song "Venga Jaleo," they concluded by defiantly, once again, insisting that "this land was made for you and me."

The protests and harassment of the group returned, as well, a reminder that the battle continued along the same planes, and it could remain genuinely unsettling. The night before the May show at Carnegie Hall, as the band arrived at the Leventhals' apartment for a celebratory dinner, Ronnie returned a phone call to a "Mrs. Scatti," who'd called looking for her.

Thinking at first that it was somebody trying to get tickets to the sold-out show, she quickly found herself in an ominous and elliptical conversation. "My dear, even though you're married, we found you," the strange woman told Ronnie. "We can always find you." Ronnie was doubly puzzled, since she'd never made any secret of her marriage. Right-wing gossipmonger Walter Winchell had announced it in his nationally syndicated column. She and Marty were listed in the Los Angeles phone book.

The woman told Ronnie that "the Counselor" needed to meet with her. "Everything will be very private," the woman said. "We understand you are married now, and girls don't like to tell their husbands everything." Ronnie was thoroughly creeped. Harold helped her find a lawyer, and Ronnie called the woman back, telling her that she could be reached in Los Angeles. It was the last she heard of it, though she wondered about the incident for years.

Almost certainly, the woman was Dolores Scotti, a right-wing actress sometimes credited as the HUAC's "entertainment specialist." Turning up in other narratives, her methods sometimes read more like harassment than investigation, reportedly insisting that one actress speak directly with her, without the need of a lawyer. "Co-operate with us or we will tell your employers that you are a Communist," she told the woman, who testified the same day as Pete. "We've got plenty on you." In the case of Arthur Miller, she was deployed to leak news of an impending subpoena to the press.

More of the Weavers' harassment was at their performances. They hadn't seen the last of the American Legion, either, who continued to make cameos

Left: Ronnie Gilbert (center, with glasses) singing with Pete Seeger and former Priority Ramblers Greta Brodie (left) and Jackie Gibson (right) at a Henry Wallace rally, 1948.

Below: The People's Songs Thanksgiving Hootenanny at New York's Irving Plaza, 1948, weeks after Henry Wallace's crushing electoral defeat, the first time all four future Weavers sang together. Pete sings with Betty Sanders, joined by Lee, Ronnie, and Fred on the right.

Photos: © and more bears

The briefly expanded and integrated Weavers quintet with opera singer Hope Foye (her back to camera) at a rally for Vito Marcantonio, the only congressman from the American Labor Party, then on a quixotic Manhattan mayoral quest, 1949. Photo by George Silk, Getty Images

The Weavers record with their pop savior and biggest fan: bandleader, star, and Decca musical director Gordon Jenkins, who saw the band on thirty-one consecutive nights at the Village Vanguard. Despite Jenkins being one of the most famous musicians in the United States in 1950, Lee Hays had no idea who he was. © and more bears

The Weavers with manager Harold Leventhal at Ronnie's wedding party at the Village Vanguard, the night after closing their record-breaking six-month run, just as the "Tzena Tzena Tzena"/"Goodnight Irene" single hit stores. © and more bears

The height of Weavermania. Following back-to-back number-one hits, the Weavers play Broadway matinees (on a co-bill with the Three Stooges), followed by a dash to the ritzy Blue Angel nightclub for evening sets, fall 1950.

Photos: "PoPsie" Randolph, © estate of William "PoPsie" Randolph

Ronnie with pop-era Weavers co-manager Pete Kameron, backstage at New York's Strand Theater, fall 1950.
William "PoPsie" Randolph, © estate of William "PoPsie" Randolph

Harold Leventhal and Pete Kameron, co-managers through the Weavers' years as hit makers. They would lose their faith in Kameron and come to trust Leventhal completely.
Hellerman Family Collection

Lee with the Weavers' manager and all-time mensch Harold Leventhal, 1951, who would help the band—and especially Lee—through thick and thin.
Lee Hays Collection, courtesy of the Ralph Rinzler Folklife Archives and Collections, Center for Folklife and Cultural Heritage, Smithsonian Institution

Above: The Weavers with Toshi Seeger and country-pop bandleader Tiny Hill, backstage at Omaha's Orpheum Theater, April 1951.

Below: An after-hours jam with the Weavers (Lee on piano, Fred and Ronnie to his left) and Tiny Hill's Orchestra, moments before chaos erupts and Pete Seeger smashes a banjo through a table backstage at Omaha's Orpheum Theater, April 1951.

Photos: Ronnie Gilbert Collection, courtesy of Lisa Weg

Above: Front-page news: The American Legion glares at the Weavers from the front row of the Yankee Inn, Akron, Ohio, February 1952, just as the blacklist started to come down heavy on the band. Akron Beacon Journal

Left: Pete and Lee in the Hollywood Hills, circa 1957, following the band's miraculous restitution. Lee Hays Collection, courtesy of the Ralph Rinzler Folklife Archives and Collections, Center for Folklife and Cultural Heritage, Smithsonian Institution

The post-blacklist Weavers at Chicago's Old Town School of Folk Music, January 13, 1958, their last live performance before Pete Seeger left the group. Robert C. Malone, courtesy of the Ralph Rinzler Folklife Archives and Collections, Center for Folklife and Cultural Heritage, Smithsonian Institution

Pete Seeger, Old Town School of Folk Music, January 13, 1958, only days
before the band's calamitous rock 'n' roll session and weeks before their
infamous cigarette ad. Robert C. Malone, courtesy of the Ralph Rinzler Folklife
Archives and Collections, Center for Folklife and Cultural Heritage, Smithsonian Institution

Lee Hays, Old Town School of Folk Music, January 13, 1958. Lee would be the most wounded by Seeger's departure. Robert C. Malone, courtesy of the Ralph Rinzler Folklife Archives and Collections, Center for Folklife and Cultural Heritage, Smithsonian Institution

Ronnie Gilbert, Old Town School of Folk Music, January 13, 1958.
Learning to follow her muse, Ronnie asserted herself in the band's
dialogue in the post-blacklist years and would launch a solo career that
included jazz and blues LPs, acting, and becoming a licensed therapist.
Robert C. Malone, courtesy of the Ralph Rinzler Folklife Archives and Collections,
Center for Folklife and Cultural Heritage, Smithsonian Institution

Fred Hellerman, Old Town School of Folk Music, January 13, 1958.
Becoming an in-demand producer, accompanist, and songwriter, Fred
would absorb the finer points of the folk-pop business from mentor and
manager Harold Leventhal, eventually moving into music publishing.
Robert C. Malone, courtesy of the Ralph Rinzler Folklife Archives and Collections,
Center for Folklife and Cultural Heritage, Smithsonian Institution

The Weavers in their new lineup with banjo player Erik Darling, 1958. Replacing Pete Seeger earlier that year, Darling served in the band through 1962, creating perhaps the Weavers' tightest and hardest-swinging lineup, before short stints by Frank Hamilton and Bernie Krause. David Gahr, © Estate of David Gahr

Lee Hays, finally achieving peace, on his porch at home in Croton-on-Hudson, New York, 1980–1981, purchased with royalties after Peter, Paul & Mary turned "If I Had a Hammer" into an unexpected global standard. Lee Hays Collection, courtesy of the Ralph Rinzler Folklife Archives and Collections, Center for Folklife and Cultural Heritage, Smithsonian Institution

The Weavers gather at Lee's house in Croton-on-Hudson, 1981, a few months after achieving closure with a pair of concerts at Carnegie Hall, and half a year before Lee's passing. David Gahr, © Estate of David Gahr

throughout the remainder of the band's career, turning up in picket lines with the Veterans of Foreign Wars and other groups. While the Weavers' songs were perhaps very rarely heard on pop radio in 1956, they now played in larger venues than they had during their first go-round, including one with some 5,000 people in Chicago.

Even the mainstream press started to politely acknowledge them, like the massively conservative *Chicago Tribune*. "Everybody knows Pete Seeger," their classically inclined music editor reported from their sold-out show and professing his own ignorance of the other individual Weavers—but not failing to report the "sufficient loyalists" in the crowd.

"There apparently is a large revival of folk song interest at the moment," he observed. "Some earlier manifestations were accompanied not only by guitars, banjos, and the like, but grinding axes. This time it may be different." Maybe.

Members of the Weavers didn't often turn up at the Sunday jam sessions in Washington Square Park, but their presence was undeniable. For a few years when they lived nearby, Pete and Toshi had held the official permit themselves. The scene emerged almost imperceptibly a decade back with a core of People's Songsters who played every weekend in agreeable weather through the spring, summer, and fall, and crammed into friendly apartments when jamming outside wasn't tenable, maybe followed by dinner at Sam Wo's in Chinatown.

More than the various social connections, the Weavers shaped the music as it was played. "Folk music" before, after, and during the Weavers, was a catch-all term, catching anything that might be deemed "ethnic" music, from Southern fiddlers to Ukrainian harmonizers. *The Billboard*'s "Folk Tunes & Talent" column still mostly tracked country stars like George Jones. But as soon as the Weavers regularized the uneven harmonies and arrangements of the Bahamian songs "Dig My Grave" and "Wreck of the John B," they virtually invented a striking new way to occupy the concept.

This new unified idea of folk music was of the times, too, a mainstreaming process of the 1950s that contorted sounds and images and flavors into a melting pot, welcoming the old ideas to the atomic age. Politics removed, the Weavers created a rhythmic, harmonic, and musical standard for a new generation of musicians. Not that it all sounded like the Weavers.

The permit was good for Sunday afternoons, two to six p.m. From above, the scene that resulted might be observed as visualizations of literal circles of musicians scattered in the north part of the park around the fountain and

Stanford White's mock triumphal arch. Binding it together were the sing-alongs on staple numbers like "Blue-Tailed Fly" and "On Top of Old Smoky," but more nuanced groups reigned on the fringes. There was a squad from the Jewish summer camps. There were political pickers in the Almanac tradition. There were mournful balladeers. There was a group, as well, of extremely serious musicians devoted to traditional American bluegrass, played in arrangements as authentic as possible. There was crossover in the players and the musicians they listened to. And if the Weavers weren't responsible for many of them being there, Pete by himself surely was.

The pool of musicians that cut their teeth in Washington Square Park would cross into the Weavers' musical circles in coming years. It wasn't a singing labor movement at all. But it was singing. A lot of it. Rarely were the politics obvious. All that many shared, in fact, was the singing itself. The Weavers had hardly invented group singing, but it was one that they helped bring into the lexicon of secular American middle-class activity, from Pete's song-leading on the hit "On Top of Old Smoky" single to every concert they gave from their Carnegie Hall reunion onward. That unity, without a specific message attached, could be heard differently by all, though certainly the Weavers (and many others) coded their music as they saw fit and hoped for the best.

It was an increasingly foggy lineage. On a rare afternoon when Lee visited the park, he surveyed some of the assembled musicians, asking them "to tell [him] what they knew about Woody." Guthrie himself had been an occasional park visitor during his last stint in New York, showing up with an exploding beard and outward-curling hair, but he was already more a folk character than musician by even the late 1950s. "I remember getting ten or twelve different stories," Lee recalled. "Most of them legendary to my knowledge and mythical."

With the specter of Minetta Creek looming over and under nearly half of the square, it was a place for new myths to bloom as well. At its widest, in the early nineteenth century, the creek expanded where the square was now, its shoreline extending just to the edge of where the fountain's promenade stretched. Here, the folk worlds mingled, the spirits of Kentucky miners emerging from the warbling overtones of one group and meeting somewhere in the charged air with a folk song in Hebrew. It was neither a melting pot nor a patchwork, but a wide-eyed cacophony.

To other young New York musicians passing through the square, it was bogus. "It was essentially summer camp music," the ever-gruff Dave Van Ronk would assess, a Brooklyn-born teenage hipster en route to sessions with an emerging crew of jazz lovers. The sounds in the park, Van Ronk thought, were "songs these kids had learned at progressive camps that I came to think of generically as Camp Gulag on the Hudson," he told Elijah Wald. Van Ronk would rethink the park scene once he met some of its more studious players, but he also represented another corner of New York's many music worlds and cultural spaces.

If the Weavers' hopes were hard-coded into folk and folk-pop, whether the musicians wanted them there or not, many of the other emerging new countercultures actively sought different political configurations altogether, like the bebop-loving Beat writers, pledging allegiance to the spontaneous ecstasies of the universe. In time, the Beats and the folkies would meet up, but in the mid-1950s they quested in different parts of the same country and even the same neighborhoods, sharing the new interstate highway system while doing psychic battle with the American cultural morass from parallel existential planes.

But "if there was one thing that all the jazz musicians could agree on, it's that folk music was irredeemably square," Van Ronk would recall. Though even Van Ronk would be bowled over soon enough by Pete Seeger, give or take his ideas and his politics.

In a city of many thriving energies, other approaches to music pushed and pulled at the always-absorbent folkies, from the pop fantasies coming from the Brill Building on Times Square to the infinite vocal harmonies rising from street corners throughout the boroughs, community singing groups indistinguishable from music-centered gangs (and needing no encouragement from Pete Seeger whatsoever). It all started to increasingly come out in new combinations in the fingers and phrasings of the new generation of Minetta Creek ramblers.

One Washington Square regular from the early '50s had even started a convincing climb into the pop world. With past and future ties to the Weavers, Erik Darling was a onetime banjo student of Pete's, and had fallen in with the hardcore musicians at the park. Highly disciplined, Darling possessed a musical work ethic perhaps even more hard-edged than Pete's, with an equally musical curiosity that took him places the older banjo player would rarely venture. Darling saw Latin dance bands mambo into the wee hours at the Palladium, and absorbed the swing of guitarist Freddie Green and the big band of Count Basie over at Birdland. Erik Darling loved the music wholly, with room for neither politics nor any embarrassment about crafting the most likable songs possible.

A keen observer of the Weavers' popular success—largely with a blind eye to their politics and blacklisting—Darling was unabashed about his desires. "I needed a song that could capture the imagination of the entire country, as 'Goodnight, Irene' or 'On Top of Old Smoky' had done," he would later write. The song came first. Like any good Minetta Creek creation, it fused parts, two fragments fellow musician Bob Gibson had come back singing after a trip to the West Indies. Darling virtually formed a group to sing it, drawing from Washington Square pickers, including the young musician-actor Alan Arkin, also a new regular at the rolling salon at Lee's apartment in Brooklyn Heights.

Signing to a New York indie label, the Tarriers were first paired with singer Vince Martin and "Cindy, Oh Cindy," a rewritten version of "Pay Me My Money Down," a song from the Georgia Sea Island Singers, featured most recently at the Weavers' reunion concert. The song cracked the top 10, and the Tarriers found themselves Shanghaied into service as Martin's backing band for the duration of the single's success. Darling's discovery was shelved for the time being. By the time the Tarriers' "Banana Boat Song" hit the top 10 in late 1956, Harry Belafonte had stormed the charts with his own version, "Day-O," drawn from a slight variant, making a genuine pop sensation. Darling's instincts had been spot-on, and he knew it. He wouldn't stop trying.

Even non-commercial Pete could see the new audience for Weavers-like music. But radio wouldn't play the Weavers, and there was no way Decca or any other big label had any interest in them. Hero though he may have been to the burgeoning teenage folk set, Pete Seeger was something very close to a wanted man. Nearly a year after he'd testified, Pete was finally and formally cited for multiple counts of contempt of Congress, along with a batch of others who'd taken the First Amendment during the same period as him, including writer Arthur Miller. According to Pete, Toshi "felt quite complimented, in a way, to be in the same class with [Miller's wife] Marilyn Monroe."

The political air around Pete remained charged and ambiguous. He'd never denounced communism, nor admitted his former party membership. That year, news of Russian president Nikita Khrushchev's closed-door speech to the party leaked to Communists worldwide, admitting significant cruelties Joseph Stalin had undertaken in the name of politics. It would be some time before Pete himself would come to grips with the true scope of Stalin's atrocities, not to mention the increasingly obvious oppressions across Communist eastern Europe. Pete's past remained a source of perpetual anxiety, even night terrors.

But then, in the most natural way possible, a path opened for the Weavers, almost as if they'd prepared the ground themselves. Just as the blacklist had forced them from nightclubs into concert halls, where they discovered they could program an entire night of music, the blacklist also forced them from the pursuit of hit singles and into the burgeoning market for long-playing records.

The format hadn't yet taken off the way record retail magnate Sam Goody had hoped, and remained primarily a specialty. In the first part of the decade, the cast recording of *South Pacific* remained the bestselling LP for three years running. It wasn't even until the Weavers' first reunion year of 1956 that *The Billboard* even began compiling annual lists of bestselling LPs. Though the top sellers represented elements of the mainstream, the medium was a wide-landscape alternative to the narrow confines of the 78 or the 45, and the majority of the market was represented by experimenters like Moe Asch of Folkways, classical imprints, and entrepreneurs wondering what to do with all this new time. RCA had a new collection by a Memphis sensation named Elvis Presley, his wild trio now tamed into the more acceptable form of R&B called rock 'n' roll, surely nothing to worry about.

At the very top of the LP list was Fred's sometime employer, Harry Belafonte. His 1954 *Mark Twain* album, a sleeper hit, finally made it to the top 10 in early 1956, and Belafonte soon eclipsed himself with the smash *Calypso*, one of the era's most ubiquitous albums, at number one for more than half a year. It rocketed Belafonte to superstardom, and ushered in what is sometimes dismissed as the "calypso craze" but might be seen not-totally-simply as a continuation of the popularity of extra-American Weavers' hits like "Tzena Tzena Tzena" and "Wimoweh." The extremely progressive Belafonte managed to escape the blacklist himself and would become a mainstream ally to the Weavers and many others—and a sign that, perhaps, pop music and activism weren't incompatible after all. Fred didn't have any songs on *Calypso*, but his relationship with Belafonte would only tighten.

Even before Belafonte and the Tarriers' success, in addition to shelling out to rent Carnegie Hall when he'd bluffed the Weavers back into existence, Harold Leventhal had the foresight to spring for the extra cost of recording their comeback performance (a cost of $128.11, in his accounting to the band). It seemed like a completely natural idea for all of them to release a recording of the concert, an unavailable option during their first go-round due to technological restraints. Though editing and releasing the Carnegie concert had been part of the plan all along, when Decca released them from their contract, they'd prevented the band from re-recording any of their material for five years following the original session dates. But in 1957, the Weavers could now regain control of their songs, in some sense, presenting themselves as they really were, four voices and two instruments in a room *and* represent the newest pieces of their repertoire without the need to even think about entering a studio.

But this was just about all the Weavers agreed on, along with an utter distrust of any outside party to be able to edit the concert to fit properly onto an LP. Lee wanted to include song introductions by the four members (yes, good idea), and suggested that perhaps the second side could begin with a sequence of his own routines (shot down unanimously, causing no bitterness, no sirree). Maybe Fred should do it (everybody trusts Freddie), and Pete suggested an engineer but Fred declared him "a stiff." It was the Weavers' parliament in high session, Lee Hays fueling the questioning with his usual second-guessing curiosity (and also declaring that he planned to maybe release an album of *only* his monologues and songs, and reserved the right to keep his material separate from the proposed Weavers' live album until such time as he could properly investigate the potential profitability).

Lee grew floridly exasperated as usual. "I feel I have been dropping suggestions down a dark well," he wrote to Harold before signing off. "It's like I've been saying: nobody listens. Or maybe it's me."

The album was edited, carefully "cutting, blending and fading [the applause] so as to suggest the presence of the audience without overdoing it," as Lee recalled. "There is even one brief moment of silence which adds to the overall effect." The opening holiday carol was replaced with "Darling Corey," all four Weavers shouting "*WAKE UP, WAKE UP . . .*" in joyous unison while Pete frailed on his banjo, a call to arms.

Harold finally struck a deal with Vanguard Records, or more properly: the Vanguard Recording Society. Owned by the brothers Maynard and Seymour Solomon, Vanguard was a classical label that branded itself on its high-fidelity LPs. They knew little of folk music, but the Weavers *had* sold out Carnegie Hall twice thanks to Harold Leventhal's ingenuity, and they knew of Carnegie Hall.

Now, through the Weavers' association with Vanguard and regular performances at Carnegie Hall, folk became permanently associated with classical music, neither in the radical ear-liberating way Charles Seeger once had hoped, nor even the way in which Béla Bartók or other composers borrowed traditional motifs. In some ways, it was precisely what detractors of the

Popular Front dismissed as *middlebrow*, the art's juice sucked away in an un-satisfying compromise between a pure original and the perceived tastes of popular culture.

And yet there was Lee, deflating it from the Carnegie Hall stage and on LP. As he'd proposed, they introduced songs on the final record. It was a musical education that included Lead Belly, Woody Guthrie, the Fisk Jubilee Singers, "Venga Jaleo" (described on the jacket as "an imperishable Spanish folk song"), a coal-miner's lament, a modified Indonesian lullaby, the out-and-out romanticism of "Kisses Sweeter Than Wine," the exhilarating strangeness of "Wimoweh," and the promise that there was more to the picture than met the eye. The LP format was also perfectly fit for the "Around the World" medley, the piece of music that catalyzed the Weavers' debut performance in 1948. There was a sense that one could go to a Weavers show—or now listen to a Weavers album—and come away knowing more.

If the songs were toned down from their original incarnations, there was a seriousness of purpose and sense of decorum that unified the collection too. After weathering the pop whims of Decca's A&R Department and various arrangers, the Weavers were assuredly happy to represent themselves in mass-distributed recorded media. Besides minor squabbles that occurred when trying to bring the album into tangible existence, the Weavers maintained a mostly pleasant musical relationship, sharing a common vision of how they wanted their music to sound.

Nowhere on the LP did it mention anything about a reunion, let alone the blacklist. Sold-out crowds, yes. But the album was simply *The Weavers at Carnegie Hall*, finally set for release in the spring of 1957, almost a year and a half after it'd been recorded.

They came for Fred in early 1957, just after the New Year, when he was legally implored to appear in Manhattan on a chilly Thursday in early February. The official cause for inquisition were Communist activities at the Metropolitan School of Music, where Fred had taught briefly a year previous, near the end of the Weavers' hiatus.

His interrogators were two-thirds of a three-man subcommittee, a pair of congresspersons from California. One, Donald L. Jackson, had once declared that Russian composer Dmitri Shostakovich "has the same right to attend a cultural conference as a rattlesnake has to be at the altar of a church."

Also glaring back at Fred was Dolores Scotti, likely the woman who'd spoken so ominously to Ronnie on the phone a few months earlier, her role in the official transcript listed as "investigator" for committee counsel Richard Arens. Scotti was partially responsible for triggering a major lawsuit filed that year. Not long after Pete and Lee's hearings, she had tried to serve a subpoena on the radio personality John Henry Faulk, an old-time People's Songster. Scotti had arrived during breakfast, Faulk still in his pajamas, and attempted to push her way through the door. With the financial support of Edward R. Murrow of CBS News, Faulk would continue to push back against the unofficial blacklists created by *Counterattack* and *Red Channels*. But that was far from resolved.

It was Scotti's boss, Counselor Arens, also glaring at Fred, who'd been dressed down the summer before by Paul Robeson when he'd waved a *Daily Worker* clipping in front of the great singer. "You are the nonpatriots," Robeson had snapped back, "you are the un-Americans, and you ought to be ashamed of yourselves."

Not yet ashamed of themselves, the committee continued to investigate the deep-rooted Communist conspiracy, somehow never quite cracking it, though the hearings were starting to wind down. Their treatment of Fred was perfunctory, another left-wing musician run down the committee's assembly line. They asked about his employment and soon got to the portion of the program where they started waving photostats in front of him and Fred declined to answer, clearly stating his use of the Fifth Amendment.

Are you now, or have you ever been a member of the Communist Party? What about this Daily Worker *article? Are you connected to People's Songs?*

Fred downplayed the Weavers' return, as if describing the band from afar when he admitted that the band "reconstituted themselves for 1 concert in December 1955, I believe, and again for 2 concerts in 1956," and claiming that the Weavers were "not presently" in operation. Well, except for the currently planned "6 or 7 concerts for which the Weavers are reconstituting themselves." Fred himself was "engaged in a free-lance way presently."

Perhaps with Dolores Scotti whispering in his ear, the counselor had one final query for Fred before dismissing him: "Is Ronnie Gilbert with the Weavers?"

"As much as the Weavers work; yes." And Fred was done. He'd already been blacklisted and begun to climb his way back. But it was something he and a generation of left-wing citizens had to pass through, some making appearances in courtrooms, some merely wondering if they would. A cross between a sickness and time spent fighting in a war, the blacklist and invasive questions about one's past were an omnipresent fact of life in the 1950s for nearly all citizens to the left of the Democratic platform who wanted to work in any kind of public-facing occupation. Unlike nearly all of his peers, Fred was at least able to enter the courtroom with the feeling of recent Carnegie Hall ovations at his back.

Perfectly angry about the day-to-day situation of the blacklist, Fred came through the period mostly unscarred by the experience, give or take the Weavers' breakup, the subsequent economic damages, the psychic wounds endured via friends and bandmates, and the ongoing harassment. Possessed of his own deep and personal moodiness that shaped his daily life, relationships, and creative output in its own way, the blacklist was only a practical stumbling block for Fred. Achieving national success as a twenty-three-year-old with the Weavers, it took a determined work ethic to start again virtually from scratch. Much later, he would call it "the happiest time of my life."

While the Weavers had "reconstituted themselves," as Fred put it to the committee, they hadn't *really* come back. There would be increased work, but Fred's living increasingly came from elsewhere. In the late 1950s, Fred Hellerman remained on the cusp of folk-pop as it, in turn, remained on the cusp of the real world.

Throughout the Tuesdical, he'd played in the Neighbors with his friend Bob De Cormier, where Fred learned to read, write, and orchestrate music, and move himself to the next level as a musician. Eventually, the Neighbors even started playing out with some frequency, occasionally back at the ritzy Blue Angel.

It was at one of these Neighbors gigs that De Cormier caught Harry Belafonte's attention. The calypso folk star, progressive hero, and dashing young black sex symbol invited the composer on as full-time arranger and bandleader. The Neighbors lasted no further, but De Cormier's new job gave Fred an even stronger connection to Belafonte. Over the next year, Belafonte would record a half dozen "Fred Brooks" songs. With Harold and other Weavers associates as publishing-savvy guides, Fred's musical education jumped past the bounds of the fret board and sheaves of arranging paper.

One of Fred's other freelance endeavors was even stranger, an intersection with a new strain of folk-pop that threw him for a loop, an ungraspable portent of weirdness to come, like trying to grasp an object from a different dimension. Oddly, it was a union job.

As Fred testified, he was a member of the American Federation of Musicians Local 802. But this wasn't merely any union job. It was a union job that came from a peculiar international truce between the AFM and the United

Kingdom's Musicians' Union. For nearly two decades, the two organizations had fought their own kind of cold war, having nothing to do with communism so much as nationalism. British bands were refused visas to tour in the United States; American bands were refused permits to perform in the United Kingdom. The standoff was mostly concluded, except for a burp in the States, a side effect of the current boom for guitars unforeseen by Pete Seeger. There'd been nearly a half million sold in the States in 1955 alone.

With so many new guitarists out there, jobs for AFM musicians were drying up, and the union needed to protect the interests of their dues-paying members. While British musicians could tour the United States, guitarists weren't permitted. Not yet. Even for singers who played themselves, accompanists would have to be supplied by the AFM.

Lonnie Donegan was England's newest minted pop star riding the wings of an unstoppable single. And not just any single, but a single written by Lead Belly. Or, as was often the case, hammered into identifiable shape by Lead Belly. Like "Goodnight Irene," "Rock Island Line" had deep roots, originating in a song performed by a group of employees of the Rock Island train company in Arkansas, the Rock Island Colored Quartet, called "Buy Your Ticket over Rock Island Lines." The author was an engine wiper, Clarence Wilson.

The Weavers did their own version, learned from Huddie himself, in the set list during the Village Vanguard days and when they came back at Carnegie Hall. Over the years, Lead Belly had performed the song with a variety of spoken introductions that segued into the chorus. The Weavers had dropped that part, aiming themselves directly for the propulsive heart of the title hook.

Backed by a jazz revival combo, the Glasgow-born Donegan attempted Lead Belly's Texas accent, trying to make formal sense of what he thought he heard. It was a special kind of problematic. But when the music built, it reached a rockabilly-like intensity similar to what Elvis was channeling concurrently in Memphis, and the song took off—top 10 on both sides of the ocean in 1956. Capturing the British imagination, it set off an entire mainstream musical craze: skiffle.

So when Lonnie Donegan arrived in the United States for a string of television appearances, club shows, and tour dates in the summer of 1956, and the AFM prevented him from playing guitar, into the void stepped Fred Hellerman.

Like the jazz guitarists before him, Fred wasn't a good fit. Paired together for a residency at the Town and Country Club, a pure show-biz establishment out in deep Brooklyn, in Marine Park, on the water, Fred found that Donegan played the music his own way. "He had little sense of what these songs meant," the Weaver assessed coldly. "He was looking for a pop audience and doing it very badly." And, coming from a former member of the Weavers, that may have been an accurate perception. They didn't *sing along*, Fred remembered of the audience, at least not in Brooklyn.

But in the UK audiences did something even Pete Seeger would be happy with: they picked up guitars and started bands of their own, sloppy and wild and charged up by the song's locomotive rhythm. There'd been folk music in England for centuries, of course, but—despite the chart success of "Goodnight Irene"—no major contemporary revival of which to speak. Launched in 1954 after being inspired by *Sing Out!*, the British folk music magazine *Sing!* was struggling until the arrival of skiffle.

Sing Out! ran a "Don't Scoff at Skiffle" guest editorial by *Sing!*'s founder. "For years, people had been battling to get youngsters to sing, and not just listen and jive to the pops," John Hasted wrote. "And now, there are Skiffle groups starting everywhere." A brief but powerful explosion in British pop culture, skiffle was in its own way—without exaggeration—as significant as the discovery of atomic energy. Among the teen skifflers picking up guitars were future folk heroes like John Lennon, George Harrison, Paul McCartney, and Jimmy Page, who would take the electrified music down its own curious roads.

As a mode of folk-pop, skiffle took virtually no recognizable hold in the United States. Donegan eventually paired himself with a Memphis rhythm section and toured with Chuck Berry, but the deeper connections between folk and rock were yet to be welded. Out in the broad-stretching United States, there were those who listened to both, and would soon acquire their own guitars, but it would be a few years yet before they wove themselves into the story.

In New York, Lonnie Donegan was nobody's idea of folk-pop, the emerging industry (to which Fred now belonged) aiming for a more grown-up audience, with singers like Harry Belafonte considered to be the apex of the artistic world. It was music that aspired to sophistication while pulling from the mysterious waters of Minetta Creek and other sources, epitomized by Fred's jazzed-up version of "Fare Thee Well" recorded by Belafonte in 1958. Lee's old Question—of being good *and* being commercial—was still open, but not the final basis on which to judge Fred's new career.

Folk music, as framed by the Weavers, was a radically decentralized way of approaching song production. But even as the Weavers may have smoothed out the regional irregularities from the songs they performed, they emphasized their kaleidoscopic array of sources. Now, "folk music" was becoming a mode of songwriting and production itself, especially in New York, as the music industry and music industrialists gradually absorbed it into their own organism with musicians like Fred on call.

Though they were coming to define their own kind of folk-pop, the Weavers' recently achieved stature as LP artists on a classical music label put them on a new side of an audience divide. In the battle of the formats, the 45 had stuck as the platform of choice for pop singles, earning itself a young market. Many older fans (and those of any age that didn't want to spend the money to upgrade to a new turntable) simply continued to buy 78s, which remained the dominant platform for R&B and country; not coincidentally, two genres that *The Billboard* and other talliers would systemically undervalue for the next half century.

And yet pop is what the Weavers aspired to when they assembled, hoping to bring their music as far as possible. But by 1957, the Weavers were in no commercial position to go reaching for the ears behind the stone throwers at Peekskill in the same way they once had. They were reaching a new class of popular music listener, part of a national tier of performing acts in the midst of discovering something beyond the singles market. There was a growing audience on college campuses, as well as the swelling professional world. Mostly, though, the LP market was a new and unsettled place, more suited for the blacklisted likes of the Weavers, anyway.

The Weavers at Carnegie Hall was a nearly instant smash. "A must for any folk record collection," *The Billboard* said. By the end of March, the same week that Pete pled not guilty to ten charges of contempt of Congress—each potentially carrying a sentence of one year in prison—the band's new album hit the number-three slot on *Variety*'s LP list. It didn't quite do the same for *The Billboard*, but by early summer the Solomon brothers were declaring it Vanguard's biggest ever seller.

Pete's not-guilty plea, meanwhile, triggered another new situation. They could cover the $1,000 bail (Fred wrote the bond), but Pete was legally forbidden from leaving the Southern District of New York without explicit permission from the court. His lawyer quickly worked out a new but still invasive arrangement, whereby Pete would only have to telegram his intended whereabouts and methods of transportation to the district attorney. Still, it was a helpful settlement because the Weavers were scheduled to imminently open their first real tour in a half decade on the other side of an international border, at Toronto's Massey Hall, discovering at the last moment that they were due there even sooner than they thought: the day after Pete's arraignment.

Shadow Pete and his vaporous friends kept up with all kinds of new activities in the FBI's files, continuously nurtured by a dark and trembling ecosystem of informants. T-13 produced a copy of *Sing Out!* (splendid job, T-13), allowing them to determine that Pete, indeed, served as a vice president. T-12 reported back that Pete had performed at a hootenanny. They missed the fact that the Weavers were playing ten shows in two weeks, all one-nighters, as Tiny Hill would've wanted. The spooks could've just checked *The Cash Box*.

M any years later, Lee Hays would tell manager Harold Leventhal about his frequent awful dreams about being onstage again. Funny, Harold responded, "My recurring nightmare is that I'm back on the road with the Weavers."

Harold had joined them for the string of dates mostly concentrated on the West Coast, through folk-friendly cities like San Francisco and Los Angeles, but also smaller markets, like Ogden, Utah, and Fresno, California. Working with a new Michigan-based promoter named Paul Endicott, the Weavers began to blaze a folk circuit of theaters and colleges flush with entertainment budgets. As a template for a new mode of the Weavers' ongoing financial sustainability, it worked fantastically well, yielding excellent ticket sales and glowing reviews. Endicott would book the Weavers, Pete's solo ventures, and many other acts over the next decade. On their first real tour of one-nighters, the Weavers moved quickly enough that not even Pete could get bored.

But the right speed for Pete was several speeds too fast for Lee, and perhaps everything was going too well, anyway. Taking care of Lee and his many ever-questioning demons, Harold quickly started feeling more like a personal assistant and less like a manager. Lee drove him crazy with increasingly specific demands, from checking the cabin air pressure on planes to procuring wheelchairs to make airport travel faster.

Ronnie recalled Lee's road behavior, and perhaps put it mildly: "As a fellow worker, brilliant, funny, and colorful Lee Hays made excessive demands on everyone's comradeship and compassion." But despite his constant kvetching, the Weavers' latest comeback had clearly energized him. The Weavers' newest success had taken *everyone* by surprise, not the least of whom were the Solomon brothers.

While the tour came to a conclusion and the live album kept selling, it was determined that 1957 would be the year of the Weavers, at least for the time being. As the late spring flowed on in New York, a half dozen plans were hatched for the band's future.

Most easily accomplished was another live album. They'd received a $1,200 advance for one in the spring—about $10,000 in current terms—and taped a night in Salt Lake City for that purpose. The recording didn't meet their standards, but recording future shows wasn't a problem. The ambition scaled from there.

Maynard Solomon suggested a "prestige" studio LP, but also what he called "personality albums"—solo projects for each Weaver. Lee, especially, took this seriously, and began poring over his repertoire with the band, in addition to the talking routines nixed from the live album and how to turn that into something usable. Somebody else had suggested a Weavers children's album, which was a natural enough concept too. And someone, somewhere in the vicinity of the Hellerman/Leventhal/Seeger axis, and more likely the guitarist and manager, had decided that now was the time for the band to reclaim its status as hit makers, keeping the *pop* in the Popular Front.

Certainly, this wasn't the Vanguard Recording Society's idea of a next step. They'd barely ever put out any folk albums before the Weavers, and never any singles. But Vanguard had established a reputation for high-quality LPs, and the Weavers had only boosted their reputation. What better way to get into the market than with those experienced hit makers, the Weavers? They announced it in *The Billboard*, a series of non-album Weavers singles, with the first to hit stores in the fall of 1957.

While it was a time of cultural monochromatism, the upper reaches of the pop charts were beginning to open up somewhat that year, with new kinds of voices coming out of radios many miles from where they originated. It wasn't the people's music as People's Songs envisioned it, nor was it pop music as New York music industrialists hoped to organize it, but some hybrid.

Whereas 1956 was mostly dominated by the likes of Pat Boone and Elvis, then en route to his ballad period, there'd also been hits by Little Richard and Fats Domino. But by the end of 1957, the charts had made room for fiery rock 'n' roll guitarist Chuck Berry from St. Louis; for mannered songwriter Buddy Holly from Lubbock; for the richly harmonizing Everly Brothers from Kentucky; for lots more Elvis; and for the soulful singing of Sam Cooke, not to mention the Tarriers, Erik Darling's group of Weavers-loving folkies from the scene around Washington Square.

Beneath the staid technocratic surface of the period, new tools came and evaporated, simultaneously a broad consumerist rainbow and an ongoing experiment in platform making. Just below one of *The Billboard*'s postings about the forthcoming Weavers singles, Vox announced the arrival of a new vinyl format, the XL disc, playing at 16 ⅔ rotations per minute, allowing for hour-long sides, such as for symphonies or lectures. Had Pete Seeger not been so preoccupied with court dates and Weavers tours and saving the world and raising a family, he might have come up with a few good uses. Neither XL discs nor the proposed Weavers singles turned out exactly as planned.

As had happened more than fifteen years earlier with the Almanac Singers, Lee came back from the cross-country tour fired up with ideas, typing out open-ended manifestos in the form of letters to the other Weavers, sometimes all carbon copied along with Harold, sometimes in sub-threads. Lee's creative ideas almost always were framed in a state of perpetual wound, as his own perceived shortcomings erupted into logistical nightmares as only he could envision. He'd been working on songs, recording small demos, fragments mostly, sometimes accompanied by young friend Alan Arkin. Playing them for others, including Pete and Harold, he received what he perceived to be a lukewarm response at best, and—in turn—transformed this into even more personal hurt.

The idea emerged for a Weavers summit at Pete's place in Beacon, where all four could dive into a new batch of songs and prepare for the proposed singles and more. But even organizing this summit proved difficult. A pre-organization meeting in Beacon with the three local Weavers, Harold, and Toshi, minus the California-grounded Ronnie, had not gone well at all. Lee felt railroaded into the concept of recording singles, wanting to focus on what he had not unrightfully felt was a breakthrough in the LP format.

Even off the road, much of Harold's job consisted of calming Lee down, reminding him "the Weavers are not re-constituting themselves for full-time work." In another letter, after Lee had bitched him out for even reuniting the band, the mensch-like manager patiently cataloged the reasons why. Harold loved the Weavers, as a musical group, as clients, as individuals, and his patience for Lee, especially, could seem like a feat of nearly holy grace, as if his wartime encounter with Gandhi had left him with a certain glow capable of handling the lonesome Arkansas traveler.

"Words, words, words," Lee scribbled on that envelope.

Though he'd reestablished contact with his family since the Weavers' success, Lee's day-to-day life was mostly an extended network of friends.

Anchored by Harold Leventhal, who oversaw Lee's not inconsiderable expenses, the Weaver continued to live the bohemian lifestyle of a semi-functioning alcoholic folk singer and writer. Without a permanent partner, besides Harold, Lee could lash out at the slightest feelings of betrayal. Far away from his bandmates, all busy with their own lives, Lee found it hard to muster up excitement from them about his "personality" album, which he envisioned as a group endeavor. Never short on ideas for the Weavers or just about anybody else, Lee seemed to possess almost no imagination about himself as a featured performer of any kind.

Ronnie, ever-encouraging, pointed out that this should be a *Lee* album, and that there *must* be a way to showcase him without taxing the Weavers' strained time, a conversation that grew to illuminate the bandmates' relationships as they found their way through the acrid fog of the blacklist. "I think I can understand and sympathize with what I think is a need on Lee's part to surround himself with The Weavers," Ronnie observed in one of the group letters, "perhaps even slightly more than can others, since in some respects it's not too far removed from my own feelings of insecurity as a performer."

Maintaining a constant affection for her bandmates, though sometimes preferring it at a distance, Ronnie Gilbert was perhaps the most affable Weaver with whom to work, without the saintly aloofness of Pete, the wired and confident energy of Fred, and the prickles of Lee Hays, the Arkansas cactus. Though that hardly meant she was accommodating for its own sake. Especially after the Weavers re-formation, Ronnie took a more assertive role in her participation. Even so, it was tough going. Looking back, Ronnie would assess that it was less about chauvinism than an ongoing form of "male competition" among her coworkers.

"If I demanded an equal place, if I demanded my way, I got it," she would say, with many years of hindsight. "But I don't like to do that, you know? It was who I was and I didn't really want to be that." Dissecting the Weavers' dynamics, she saw the existing "very fierce competition" between Pete and Lee, and "Freddie the younger guy trying to make his way with those two powerhouses."

More enthusiastic about some of her bandmates' suggestions than others, there was one song that grabbed Ronnie and for which she became an immediate and unwavering advocate: "This Land Is Your Land."

"If at all possible, I think we should record and release this as soon as possible, even if we have to go into a studio on the day I arrive to do this and a song to back it that wouldn't suffer by a Weavers-only-plus-bass instrumentation!" It was so obvious.

"This is a Weavers type song," she declared, "we get our characteristic big sound on it, and as the weeks go by, I realize what an opportune time this is for such a song to be released commercially, a feeling I've never had before." The Tarriers, the pop-makers from Washington Square Park, had picked up on the song too. They'd picked up on a lot of the Weavers' makings lately, including attaching themselves to former Weavers' manager Pete Kameron. But Ronnie was determined. The more the merrier, especially if Vanguard could release their version concurrent with the Tarriers' single.

Even with Ronnie's positivity, Harold's patient coaxing, and Pete's ever-fired enthusiasm, it was still hard to break Lee out of his sulks. After not hearing back from one missive to Pete, Lee had fired off a supremely passive-aggressive letter to Toshi. But who knows where Pete was when the letter arrived. He was like a planet orbiting the sun at a higher speed than his fellow Weavers. Since the band had passed through Southern California during their April tour, Pete had already returned to the area two more times by the time collective letter writing commenced in early summer.

And, oh, the letters flew. The logistics closed their time together to a week, which incensed Lee even more. "Let the other three work up the songs and tell me what to sing," he moaned to Harold, "I'll be glad to oblige."

But all Weavers would descend on Beacon anyway, and the week would come and go quickly, harmoniously, and productively. They didn't record "This Land Is Your Land" the day Ronnie arrived, as she'd proposed, but "the rural, laid-back atmosphere served to reconnect us," she would recall. "Lee was at his best in sylvan surroundings and especially with children." With Ronnie's daughter, Lisa, hanging out and playing with the Seegers' kids in the summery hillside overlooking the Hudson River, the scene was about as idyllic as anything the Weavers ever collectively achieved.

The Weavers' repertoire took on a mass of new songs, some familiar to them all, some newly repurposed. Many, they didn't all agree upon. Oftentimes, it wasn't that the band's choices were a compromise to the world of popular music, but to one another. Ronnie could put a good spin on it when she wanted to. "As you all know, I've never shared the fondness you guys apparently have for this," she noted in one of the preliminary letters about one such choice. "But I've had my mind changed before by you remarkable guys, and time having mellowed my likes and dislikes somewhat, I'd go along for the kicks."

In terms of recorded and released output, the summer of 1957 would prove to be perhaps the single most productive season in the band's history, yielding material that would find itself spread across three LPs and several singles over the next few years.

The simplest task at hand was an appearance at the lefty-friendly Music Barn in Lenox, Massachusetts, down the road from Tanglewood, the renowned outdoor classical music venue. Offering a jazz and folk alternative, a New England country inn had converted its back porch into a stage, the adjacent lawn fitting a not-insubstantial 750 folding chairs, soon covered in a tent. Part of an event season that included Ella Fitzgerald, the Weavers drew the hugest crowd, and found themselves invited back over Labor Day to help close out the year.

And in between the two dates at the Music Barn, they tracked some twenty-four songs over a three-day session at Brooklyn's Masonic Temple in Fort Greene, a short ride from Lee's apartment. With a reputation for high-quality classical recordings, Vanguard Records had contracted legendary producer John Hammond after reading an article he'd penned lamenting the quality of current jazz. Finding the Masonic Temple, Hammond hung a single microphone from the ceiling, as album sides had been cut decades before. Though it would be Vanguard co-owner Seymour Solomon that engineered the Weavers' sessions there, and in stereo, the Masonic Temple was a natural solution for recording music.

The first day was devoted to the proposed singles, and—to accompany them and convey the Weavers' idea of pop music in 1957—they brought in a group of hardcore jazz survivors, led by trumpet player Ruby Braff, then occupying the Weavers' old residence at the Village Vanguard. *Downbeat* even reported the details of the four-song session. With fanfares and snare rolls, the band tried "Tina," a Spanish-flavored global-party-type song, perhaps in the spirit of "Tzena," and an extended version of "Hey Lilee Lilee Lo," the Bahamian tune usually featured as the concluding section of the "Around the World" medley, with room for a trumpet solo from Braff. They did some gospel and a Weaverfied version of a ballad collected by a British folklorist.

The other two days were for the less adjusted Weavers lineup, with the occasional presence of a harmonica player and bassist Justin Arndt. Though they'd made demos in their early days, been shepherded through recording studios by a parade of producers at Decca, and all spent time in studios over the years as individuals, recording was never the band's home. Grown from the People's Song hootenannies, with ample space given for Lee's rambles and

Pete's crowd-leading, the Weavers' concerts *were* the Weavers. It was all of it, the dynamics of the band, the focus of performance, the participation, and the context of simply being there, band and audience alike, at that time and place in American history.

Whatever it was that animated the Weavers' music to its fullest capacity, though, it only came in small flashes during their first set of formal studio sessions in five years. While they put a remarkable amount of music on tape in August 1957, their attempt at a pop session was deemed unusable for the debut of Vanguard's singles line, but almost everything else would find some released home.

Most immediately, the live recordings from the Music Barn were shaped into *The Weavers on Tour*, added to some Carnegie Hall leftovers, plus a handful of studio recordings from the Brooklyn sessions with dubbed-in applause. The album captured another slice of the band's enormous repertoire, getting down songs they'd known for years, including more of their Decca-era sides stripped of their Decca-era arrangements. Where Pete had led songs on records before, and the *Carnegie Hall* live album had demonstrated the powerful echoing boom of a crowd singing together, *On Tour* got right into Pete's song-leading, breaking down "Michael, Row the Boat Ashore" into its component harmonies and goading the audience into joining.

The album highlighted, as well, what Pete Seeger had learned in his time apart from the Weavers. He led the songs with a new confidence, his voice no longer quavering in the young, overexcited way that often characterized his early style. Lee would sometimes call Pete "the most commercial singer I've ever met in my life," not implicating Pete's motivation but his sheer devotion to crowd work. "Oh, he knows all the tricks," Lee would explain. "Staging, timing, programming, dynamics. All these things he would vigorously deny."

On Tour was a glimpse of a thirty-eight-year-old Pete Seeger reaching artistic maturity, after seventeen years on the road, with Woody, the Almanacs, People's Songs, Henry Wallace, the Weavers, and mostly by himself. It was a skill set he hadn't fully understood when he'd started to assemble it, the combination of social-justice organizer and singer, and he'd only *really* achieved success as the latter, but it was a job description that he'd dreamt up as a product of the Popular Front. In the same way, it now brought the Weavers to their own fullest expression, with all of their hopes and dreams still occupying their active repertoire. While lacking the Manhattan electricity of their *Carnegie Hall* album, the Music Barn tracks on *The Weavers on Tour* were—at the time—the most natural and casual documentation of the Weavers as popular entertainers.

As with *Carnegie Hall*, the resultant LP was divided into four earnest categories, like "Songs That Never Fade" ("On Top of Old Smoky") and "Tall Tales" ("The Frozen Logger") (People's Song #264) on the A-side, "History and Geography" and "Of Peace and Good Will" on the flip.

Filed under "History and Geography"—perhaps with a knowing wink— was "Wasn't That a Time." Less than two years since the HUAC grilled Pete and Lee about the song's alleged contents, they kept on singing it. The song was now written (and sung) into American history on the wings of its own chutzpah and Congress's own misunderstandings. Providing the information that Lee and Pete wouldn't provide to Congress, the jacket slyly noted, "A patriotic song composed by Lee Hays celebrating the great crises of American history."

The year had been at least a partial vindication for the former Communists and fellow travelers of the American left, winning a series of Supreme Court fights that began to slowly legally justify Pete Seeger's belief that he was only practicing his right to free speech. In June, as the band was bickering via the United States Postal Service, came what the McCarthyites and other House Un-Americans called "Red Monday," with the Court handing down four separate decisions that reversed more than a dozen convictions, including contempt-of-Congress citations for refusing to answer the committee's questions. In the fall, the Court overturned the Smith Act once and for all by a 5–2 majority, ruling that the advocacy of communism was, in fact, *not* the equivalent of advocating for the violent overthrow of the government. It was the difference between "instruction" and "concrete action," a legal acknowledgment of (and victory for) the nuances of language.

The real battle, though, was always changing, and Pete had come to accept that. His great hope had always been to help the country unionize. An outgrowth of what historian Michael Denning calls "the Age of the C.I.O.," the union battle had grotesquely transformed into the Cold War in large part when unions began to expel Communists, ending that epoch and making Pete's dream untenable.

At the beginning of the Weavers' year, Pete had gone from his arraignment directly onto the Weavers' tour. And following the band's last date of the year—their return to the Music Barn—Pete departed immediately for Tennessee, where the Highlander Folk School was celebrating its twenty-fifth anniversary. Like Commonwealth, where Lee had taught, the school had been a breeding ground for progressive thinking and action. Unlike Commonwealth,

Highlander had managed to persevere, and was now at the center of the growing civil rights movement.

Pete had first visited with Woody in the summer of 1940 during their cross-country hitchhiking trip. It began a lasting association with the institution, with Pete even ducking up for a weekend on leave from army training, around the time he was first being investigated for possible subversive activities. The school's co-founder, Myles Horton, had invited Pete to perform at the school's twenty-fifth anniversary.

That weekend, Seeger met two of the movement's leading lights: Rosa Parks, a Highlander graduate who'd initiated the successful yearlong Alabama bus boycott in 1955, and Dr. Martin Luther King. King had organized the Southern Christian Leadership Conference that year, a group that would shape the next decade of the civil rights movement and help forge connections between the folk underground and the ongoing protests.

But the civil rights movement didn't need folk musicians to know how to use music. The "freedom songs," as they called them, were Baptist and Methodist hymns, repurposed for new duty, exactly in the same manner that had inspired Lee Hays. It was Highlander's Zilphia Horton who'd helped introduce songs like "We Shall Not Be Moved" into the freedom-song repertoire. Dying in an accident in 1956, she wouldn't live to see "We Shall Overcome" transform into the anthem it became.

An "extraordinary young man," Pete thought of Dr. King, who was about a decade younger than the banjo player. The reverend watched Pete perform in the book-lined library, and someone snapped a picture during the performance. Eventually the photo would be circulated around the South, plastered on roadside billboards and the front pages of newspapers, with the traditional and unimaginative Red-baiting headline, "Martin Luther King at Communist Training School," with circles and arrows pointing out King and the various alleged Communist agitators surrounding him. For Pete, it was a moment where music and the battles of the world—the real battles of the real world—began to once again come together.

Back in New York, the Weavers' world pressed onward. There were schedules to make and shows to organize and albums to produce and singles to delegate. When they'd started, it had been a whirlwind, and Pete committed to riding it out. In resurrecting the group, Pete now found himself only a part-time Weaver. It wasn't the worst new situation he'd ever faced. Even Pete could recognize the band's pop ambitions as a grand project, an ongoing experiment in contributing to the vast and undying Popular Front.

Carnegie Hall was still selling briskly, anyway, up to 20,000 copies through the fall—an astounding number for an LP of a live folk concert. Moe Asch's old friend Sam Goody had reported it as the number-three top seller in his shops, the metric for its ranking on the national *Variety* chart. And when *On Tour* followed in November 1957, it quickly sold 15,000 copies of its own before the end of the year. The singles would wait until early '58, Vanguard announced, now part of a slate that included former Count Basie vocalist Jimmy Rushing, and young rock 'n' roll singer Candy Reed. With a royalty statement, Harold assured the Weavers the first release would be out in the second or third week of January. The Weavers prepared to return to the world of pop music.

CHAPTER SEVEN

Twelve Gates to the City

The Weavers' new single did not come out the second week in January. Instead it became part of a sequence of events leading to the day that Lee would never forget and of which Pete would never again speak. But when 1958 started, the quartet seemed right on schedule, once again using their voices to blow down barriers set in their way. By the end of the year, the pop music world had been transfigured permanently under their influence, but not quite in the way anybody could foresee.

They began their working year in Chicago with their first television appearance since the blacklist, appearing with Mahalia Jackson and Richard Dyer-Bennett and Josh White on Chicago's local WGN, part of a series of televised concerts. Jackson joined the Weavers for "When the Saints Go Marching In." The *Chicago Sun-Times* called it "worthy of replay on a network." There was a jam session, too, at the Old Town School of Folk Music, a new local institution opened only a month before by a pair of local folkies, including self-described Pete Seeger acolyte Frank Hamilton. It was a blissful excursion to the Midwest, and a peace before the trauma. But in Chicago, in that moment, the four Weavers had gone before the cameras and sang one more time through the airwaves, one small veil removed, at least for a moment.

Two days later, the Weavers reassembled back at Vanguard's Masonic Temple studio in Brooklyn to once again try to stake their claim in pop music. Though the band had initiated the project of making singles, Vanguard hadn't liked what they'd come up with at the August 1957 sessions. It didn't match the commercial vision of the brothers Solomon, who now took matters into their own hands.

With Vanguard contracting an outside arranger along with jazz saxophonist Budd Johnson and His Orchestra, the Weavers reported for work in the Fort Greene studio much as they had done in the Decca years, except now they were handed arrangements of songs they'd never performed before, nor even rehearsed. Bandleader Budd Johnson had played with the Weavers once before, at the first Town Hall concert in 1950, but they hadn't rehearsed for that either. For this session, he returned to drums, his first instrument, bringing a pair of bassists and a trio of electric guitarists, including Joe Puma.

It was to be the Weavers' attempt at something like a rock 'n' roll record. In fact, it was the heart of rock's first golden age, with Jerry Lee Lewis and Buddy Holly and others all dashing in and out of the charts, not to mention declarative novelties like Danny and the Juniors' "Rock and Roll Is Here to Stay." The Weavers were going electric. Sort of.

Fred, who'd been writing proper arrangements for a year or so, was disappointed that he hadn't been considered for the task. If one of the Solomon brothers had picked up the current issue of *The Billboard* the week the Weavers went into the Masonic Temple, he'd see it reported that Fred had been named musical director of the fledging folk label Elektra Records. Lee had hoped Earl Robinson might take a crack. Fred met with the guy who'd done it, though nothing resulted. Pete was too busy, Ronnie was on the opposite coast, and Lee was conveniently ill.

Both songs that wound up on the single were somebody else's idea of how the Weavers might translate to the newest version of popular music. The A-side was a rewritten tune from Lead Belly's repertoire, which was hardly the worst idea, but the old chain-gang song "Take This Hammer" now became the saltier and decidedly less edgy "Take This Letter."

"Hearing the arrangements at the session . . . was a shocking experience," Lee wrote to Harold. "Only the work that Fred and Pete did in reducing and changing and re-routing the arrangements into something more nearly like our style saved what we finally did get."

Lee had followed the single into the mixing phase, too, offering his input, which—according to him—the engineers accepted. Still, "Manny [Solomon] called in some engineers to listen and their approach to the sound of the tapes was only how it would sound on the juke boxes," Lee said, scandalized. The whole of it had been a discomfiting experience, to say the least. When his test pressing arrived, Lee thought maybe he'd received a defective copy, but they all sounded the same.

What's worse is what happened when Lee played the single for his friends. "The Weavers don't sound like the Weavers," reported one.

"Leave that kind of stuff to the Crickets," said another. Lee refused to even play it for housemate Earl Robinson. It wasn't, he assessed, "the heroic effort our friends seem to expect of us to break in with new standards, new ideas, new ways of reaching the pop market." He braced for "a certain period of embarrassment which I fully expect will follow the release of this record."

While "This Land Is Your Land" would eventually come out as a Weavers single, it would still be another two years. Perhaps they should have listened to Ronnie. Or even Lee. When "Take This Letter" was finally released in March 1958, it completely tanked. It barely even registered in *The Billboard*, falling into the category of singles reviewed by the magazine's staff and "rated 70 or less." There were too many other early rock mutations that week alone to give fuller consideration to the Weavers' first stab at electrified folk-rock, like Dwight Pullen's rockabilly "Sunglasses After Dark," and rock's own version of the folk process, answer songs. There were two of them out that week, too, responding to the Silhouettes' "Get a Job"—the Heartbeats' "I Found a Job" and the Tempos' "I Got a Job."

The Cash Box liked it, relatively speaking, rating the two sides B+ and C+ respectively. "A rockin' item with a pleasant folk flavoring," they said of "Take This Letter." "A powerful contender for hitdom." But they were in the decided minority. More than a half century later, their review and subsequent "Best Bet" designation remain the only historical traces of any positive memories of the Weavers' attempted return to pop music. The single vanished virtually without a trace, its release date incorrect in record guides, too forgotten to even be collectible. Eight or so months later, Vanguard's conception of what constituted commercial folk music might be substantially different. In the moment, the whole process had been deeply demoralizing. The Weavers had gone electric and almost nobody noticed.

Within months, Maynard Solomon would apologize to the band about the whole affair. Still, Lee would note, "every last one of us went along, nodding agreement at every turn—including Pete, by God—and it was only after the stinking thing came out that we turned on them and blasted the record as if we had been raped. I frankly did not know it was so bad until I heard it; but I did not give it any thought." The single would be virtually never spoken of again by the Weavers, perhaps in large part because of what almost immediately followed its recording.

By the time "Take This Letter" came out, the Weavers had a much, much bigger problem on their hands. Though their albums continued to sell, Harold hadn't been able to secure a spring tour for them, but he *had* found some other work, and what's more it would be yet another assault on the blacklist. Through the well-heeled Madison Avenue firm of Dancer Fitzgerald Sample, they were contracted to record a singing commercial.

More than the local appearance on WGN, this was considered a return from the blacklist, paradoxically in the form of mainstream capitalism's nurturing patronage, welcoming them back from the cold. In the value system of late-1950s America, the Weavers had reached a cul-de-sac in their sometimes lonesome travels as Popular Front balladeers, carrying their melodies and ideas through thick and thicker to bring folk music into ears across the country through any means necessary, now reaching the question of literal commercialism. Coming only days after the "Take This Letter" session, this was a new challenge.

The product, and the sticking point, was L&M Cigarettes. All the Weavers but Pete were smokers, and band practices were a constant haze, a constant irritant to the banjo player. Even during the Almanac days, he would bolt from the room if it got too smoky. On top of that, Toshi's mother had recently been diagnosed with lung cancer, the connection between nicotine and the illness only recently established. Pete had nothing against the premise of a commercial, only the product.

A band meeting was convened after the offer came in, with Pete the sole Weaver dissenting. "Why couldn't it be for yogurt?" he asked.

"Lee argued that we owed it to fellow blacklisted performers to take advantage of the possible thaw," Ronnie recalled.

"You have a solo career," Fred pled with the banjo player. "We need this." So they voted, three to one, and soon thereafter recorded the cigarette commercial. Pete joined them, and they sang the assigned jingle, backed by a big band. Pete had sung many hundreds of different songs over the years, from many hundreds of origins. As he'd told the HUAC, he'd "never refused to sing for anybody." But that didn't mean he wouldn't think very hard about whether or not he'd do it again. He fretted over the commercial.

That night, immediately following the session, Pete called a band meeting at Harold Leventhal's apartment. That was it, Pete told the Weavers when they assembled, he was out. He "would have nothing more to say about the matter, ever."

"Won't you discuss it even?" Lee asked him, pained. Pete only sat there cold-faced. "And that hurt me as much as anything else, that he wouldn't discuss it," Lee said. "I figured if he had grievances or some ways he wanted us to change, to adapt to his views or his way of life that in a group I felt he should say so."

But that was that. In the end, Pete Seeger only refused to sing for the Weavers. He was breaking up with Lee Hays again, just as he had when he asked Lee to move out of Almanac House, just as he had when he'd asked Lee to resign from the People's Songs board, and it added another layer to Lee's collection of open emotional wounds, one of the deepest and most perpetual hurts that he carried. Pete's decision wasn't *only* about the commercial, of course, just as it wasn't only about no longer being able to work with Lee Hays and his endless accusatory and passive-aggressive decision-making. And it wasn't only about recording somebody else's idea of the Weavers doing a rock 'n' roll song. But those were all parts of it.

"Fred and I were shocked at Pete's departure," Ronnie recalled. "Lee was devastated and bitter."

Always dramatic, Lee would forever refer to the evening Pete announced his resignation as "that dreadful night." The bass singer returned to Cranberry Street in tears, certain that it meant the end of the Weavers.

"It came out in the guise of going ahead to do something pure and noble," Lee said, "which had the effect of making the rest of us feel guilty as hell for going on, as if we were doing something wrong, as if he was telling us we were doing something wrong."

Ronnie, too, wondered what was to happen. "Loss of income aside, I was deeply angry at the probability of our demise," she would say. "To give up now that we had popular approval to be onstage seemed to me like a slap to the public's face." Like both of her bandmates, Ronnie would hold a great sadness about Pete's departure for many years to come. She'd come to admit that maybe "Pete was never really happy as a Weaver."

With his own side work starting to take off, Fred understood perhaps more than the others. "If you get your way 25% of the time you're getting your fair share," he recalled of the quartet dynamic. "That's not enough for any artist! And I'm sure that that had to tell, after a while." Fred wasn't unfamiliar with the feeling. By now, Pete was already headlining Carnegie Hall without the Weavers anyway, headlining a show with Sonny Terry just before New Year's, which, by April, was in *Variety*'s top 15 LP chart (via a Folkways recording) along with the Weavers' original *Carnegie Hall* LP, plus another collection of Pete's ballads.

Though all remained on speaking terms, and even friends and occasional collaborators, a dark cloud hung between Pete and his former bandmates for years to come, even as all understood the reasons for his departure. As Lee was fond of pointing out, now that Pete had found a huge audience to join his sing-alongs, he no longer needed a quartet to harmonize.

But as Pete made clear, the last thing he wanted to do was silence the Weavers. Still, his weird formality about the whole affair underscored how institutional the Weavers had become, or maybe always had been, as if Pete were only resigning from some People's Songs singing subcommittee—which perhaps he was. They easily possessed what Fred called "the Weavers sound," an approach and sense of musical decorum that all four understood, despite infringements like "Take This Letter."

Pete assigned half (but only half) of his monies from the cigarette commercial to *Sing Out!*, the perpetually struggling folk magazine. To the people he'd known for decades, he sent a handwritten letter via Harold.

"It would be a real understatement to say I feel real regrets about not singing again as one of the Weavers," he wrote in what was essentially a break-up note. "I hope we are all going to see each other again, anyway, even though at this time our professional paths are no longer going in exactly the same direction." It was both straightforward and completely sidestepping any of the real emotion that his decision had upturned in any of his bandmates. He had made his decision, and would live by it. The cigarette ad never got picked up anyway. But the cigarette ad had never really been the issue.

Equally earnestly and sincerely, Pete offered to help the Weavers find a replacement. As often, Pete's suggestion was an effective solution. But perhaps most unusually, it was even practical.

The Weavers' new banjo player didn't immediately know he'd been drafted into the quartet. He'd received a card from Lee when he was in Paris, wrapping up an engagement with his trio, but Lee hadn't mentioned it directly. Like the Weavers, the Tarriers were at a turning point. They'd had a good run in the City of Lights, but they were at the end of a path. Over the past few years, they'd had a few hits, including their version of the "Banana Boat Song," appeared on *The Ed Sullivan Show*, and had done the mainstream circuit. They were all in their early twenties, too young to be anywhere near the blacklist. But now one of their number, Alan Arkin—one of Lee's young friends—had decided to return to acting.

Back in New York, the band's leader, Erik Darling, rode the subway in a haze, basking in Manhattan's cultural melt, his band taking up a residency with a new bassist and reconfiguring themselves. Also managed by Harold Leventhal, Darling had perhaps unconsciously been waiting for what Leventhal was about to propose. A musician with a deep sense of precision and a massive amount of pop ambition, he'd seen the Weavers' first holiday concert, at Town Hall in 1950, when he was seventeen, and was struck with nearly blinding inspiration when they performed "Wimoweh."

The "performance shifted my sense of self," Darling would say many years later. "From that moment on I knew that I understood something about the value and ecstasy of this kind of art," he put it. "It had something to do with the essence of life."

After that, "I wanted to be in a group like that," Darling would recall. "That was my impassioned teenage dream." The Weavers, and especially Pete, had been heroes. He'd even gone backstage once to get his banjo signed. He played a custom model with an extra-long neck, just like Pete's, a modification not yet commercially available. To Darling, the alteration made the instrument look "heroic." For a musician who confessed little awareness of politics in his youth, Darling certainly picked up the outer cadences of Pete's Popular Frontism.

A onetime student of Pete's, Darling had honed a tight, virtuosic banjo style around the Washington Square Park fountain in the early 1950s. For Darling, as a young musician, the Weavers were the absolute pinnacle of folk music. There was absolutely no contradiction in the Question, as phrased by Lee Hays, about the tension between being good and being commercial. Holding musical craft and accessibility as equally high virtues, Erik Darling saw only Answers. The problem was finding the *right* songs.

Six years younger than Fred, Darling had grown acquainted with the Weavers' guitarist while rising through the folk-pop ranks. Darling played banjo with a level of obsession beyond what Pete had achieved, in many ways closer to the fast-picking style and musical devotion of Kentucky bluegrass. His mind centered on the music, all else pushed to the edges. As a musical presence, the twenty-four-year-old Darling possessed an ebullient energy of his own, a bouncing, giggling giddiness that curved into the outer edge of his voice.

"I can't remember us considering anybody else," Fred recalled. There was barely an audition. They didn't offer him the full-time job right away, though, framing it first as a way to finish the so-called prestige LP for Vanguard they'd started recording with Pete. That had worked out just fine, recording five songs in a two-day session in late April. Less than a month later, the album was in stores.

Released with the appropriately timid title *At Home*, around the time Pete Seeger departed for the first vacation of his adult life—a cross-country sight-seeing trip with his family—the Weavers' founding banjo player still featured in the group photo on the album's cover. Darling was listed in slightly smaller print on the LP's back as a guest artist, with the notes referring to Pete's status in the band in the present tense. Describing the band's arranging process, the sleeve records that "Weavers' rehearsals consist of ten percent singing and ninety percent discussion (sometimes heated)."

Opening with "This Land Is Your Land," two years after featuring it at their earliest reunion performances, the album did carry the Weavers forward in the Popular Front tradition, calling the song out for its "patriotic vision" on the jacket notes.

"Another wonderful album from the marvelous folk singers," *The Billboard* crowed, singling out the album in an extended review with no reference to the band's bombed single of less than three months earlier. "Excellent cover photo of the group should help spark sales." And sales were brisk, almost 8,500 copies in less than the first two months, though it was the first *Carnegie Hall* LP that continued to be their biggest hit.

It wasn't until the end of the year, when Vanguard formally extended the band's contract, that the group officially informed their label that Erik Darling had replaced Pete. But his assimilation into the band was virtually instant, receiving the same relative percentage as Pete did on the album for his work on one-third of the songs. "No one was boss," Erik observed.

Besides being a complex and thought-filled human, Erik Darling wasn't much like the other three Weavers, but he got along with all three instantly, and in three very different ways, each fully indicative of both Erik and his new bandmates. "I was treated with the utmost respect, as an equal participant, not as the new kid on the block or someone who had to earn tenure," Darling would write. "Everything else was a head-trip of my own."

He and Ronnie got along easily but, genuinely outgoing Ronnie got along with nearly everyone. "Ronnie was eager for life as a whole, no matter what it contained," Erik would say. "Ronnie was the center of gravity that allowed the rest of us to spin out of orbit at times."

Though more present than she'd been in the band's earlier iteration, especially after she divorced and moved back to New York the following year, Ronnie had continued to opt out of the "male competition" that tended to infect the dynamic of the remaining members of the quartet.

"I loved singing with Erik," Ronnie would say, "blending my alto with his high, thin tenor, and listening to him play." Like Fred, she loved how Erik's "musicianship was buoyant and contemporary, stylistically in tune with the rising generation of good players and youthful audiences trained, ironically, by Pete to look beyond him for inspiration and education." His musical ideas were both fresh and completely in line with how the band understood their own music.

Fred Hellerman, for one, absolutely adored playing music with Erik Darling. He brought "qualities that were just super," Fred said, "Just super. And with all the virtues that Pete has, the group never *swung* with Pete the way it did with Erik."

For his part, though, Erik never felt fully comfortable around Fred, though they got along perfectly well. Some of it wasn't personal, he knew. He observed that Fred was impatient with *everyone*. Erik "couldn't help but look up to the man," even while he "never knew what to make of him or how [he] fit in."

"The meaning of the word 'hyper' could have been coined around Freddy [*sic*]," Darling's then wife Joan would recall. She would remember her own relationship with Fred fondly, though "his whole energy ran so fast, I don't think he took the time to absorb the information he got."

Perhaps most crucially for the ongoing situation, though, Erik got along with Lee Hays, nearly nineteen years his senior. "We had both grown up in the country, and that gave us a kinship, I think," Darling would recall, raised in rural upstate New York, far from the battles that had forged the Manhattan folk scene. Neither a compulsive self-educated reader like Lee, nor raised in the Communist milieu of New York in the '40s, he knew nothing of the Popular Front, and it's possible he'd never even heard the phrase before joining the Weavers.

"I must say Erik was a very good audience," Lee said about their rehearsals, where he was working up a new batch of stage routines. "He was easy to crack up." In the same way that Erik had picked up on Pete's self-worn heroism, even minus the politics, he'd instantly absorbed Lee's humor and cadences, minus the other parts. To Erik, Lee was just Lee, his years of experience only manifesting in the strange Arkansas man who was now his conversation-monopolizing bass-singing coworker, often with reference points that didn't naturally resonate with Darling. The humor came through loud and clear, though.

"In my father's house, there was seldom a newspaper, to say nothing of political discussions," Erik would recollect. "He'd always say, 'Somebody got married, somebody died, there's a war going on and I don't need a newspaper to tell me that stuff.'" But the Weavers had created Darling's "very essence," and this was the opportunity of a lifetime. If he hesitated, it was only slight. "I came to the conclusion that if somebody wanted to brand me a Red, so be it," he decided.

By 1958, though, it was fair to say that the Weavers were terribly sick of politics, at least as they pertained to their professional career and music. Their fight was implicit, built into what they sang. The politics weren't done with them, however. There were still cancellations and signs of the Un-American fog-outs.

The Weavers' politics were internal, anyway, most often just centered on appeasing and containing Lee Hays. As Harold began to put together their first real outings with their new banjo player, new strategies were required. For convoluted reasons of his own, Lee insisted that the band perform only on weekends. Fred chalked it up to "Lee's nature, inclination, hypochondria—well he's too tired, whatever."

Fred hated the abbreviated touring regimen, frequently complaining that all their income was going to the airlines. All the same, he was busy with his own life. "I was working my ass off during the week," he would remember. "Then on the weekends I'd have to go out with the Weavers." Most of Fred's income came from his jobs at Elektra and writing for Harry Belafonte. "Yet emotionally," he emphasized, "the Weavers had first call on my time." But even that wasn't always true. While Fred would easily block time for Weavers tours and rehearsals, oftentimes, his identity grew more entwined with his studio work, his creative energies focused on scores and arrangements and song choices for other artists, and less for the artistic battlefield of Weaver work.

Practicing was a roller coaster. Lee might show up. He might call in sick via Harold. He might cancel and show up regardless. Other times, he'd arrive early. "Very patiently, he'd stack up the medicines he was taking at the time," Harold remembered. "Slow. A lot of side talk." Lee could preserve a grudge as well as Alan Lomax could collect a folk song.

Onstage, though, it was a powerful and transformative experience for Erik Darling. "I could feel each of them extending their power, timing, and eagerness to me, helping me live in that moment," he would say. "It was as though they had been given a gift of some sort, and I was given the privilege of visiting there, in the temple they sang from."

That glow of four voices continued to create an energy field of its own. The proverbial jury was still out on whether the Weavers and their fabulous machines killed fascists. Pete's trial hadn't yet started. More interesting to the Weavers in later 1958 was whether that special Weavers glow could be used to sell commercial products.

With Pete gone, Lee fully embraced what he had declared to be the Weavers "brand" back in 1949. Along with Erik, who had become a quick friend, and other collaborators, Lee masterminded a number of jingles on spec, submitting through the same producer who had organized the failed cigarette ad. Lee and his patient friends powered through draft after draft that summer and fall, the world of advertising tags integrated into the structures of folk songs. He and Erik tried to interest Gold Medal Flour in buying a talking blues, one of Woody's most durable templates: "If you want better biscuits, let me tell you what to do. . . ." Like the Weavers cigarette jingle, none of Lee's ads made it into national distribution.

Harold was working on fall dates, but it was a rough time with the Weavers, despite the musical revitalization Erik brought. Vanguard owner Maynard Solomon had hoped their recent efforts would sell more. Lee admitted, "It is obvious that we have not come up with any 'big' numbers, comparable to Wimoweh, Venga, etc., but instead have come up with a spate of folksong pastiches which lighten our repertory instead of strengthening it." As when it had come time to release the single, Lee again forgot about their anthemic "This Land Is Your Land," as much the Weavers' song as anyone besides Woody. A further Vanguard LP combined new tracks with Erik with the last of the Pete era.

They continued to fit fragments together, looking for the elusive transformative pieces that would turn a small bit of discovered melody into something magical and whole, the way a song from Minetta Creek ought to sound.

For all the precision that Lee demanded in language, sometimes, and for all the global love the Weavers expressed, there could also be a carelessness about their assemblages. Though Lee had called himself a "folklorist" to the HUAC, all four Weavers also carried a confidence and assumed privilege that *they* could alter the songs however they saw fit.

That had always been how they all understood folk music, that it was source material to be altered or preserved as needed or desired. One of the last pieces Fred and Pete had worked on together before Pete's departure was a chantey called "Greenland Whale Fisheries," fusing a scrap of Bahamian melody with a New England ballad. Lover of good stories as he was, though, Lee could often present his song lineages as their own kind of performance, in print or onstage, enacting his senses of humor and copyright-controlled blurriness by setting them into the historic record in the form of LP jacket notes. But that was an age that was soon coming to an end.

The liner notes to *Traveling On* described the process in highfalutin but not inaccurate terms: "The unseen portion of work is editing, rewriting, polishing, re-emphasizing phrases, clarifying motives—all of the painstaking, thoughtful work of rebuilding songs that has gone into the product we call Weavers' songs." If it was overly earnest and covered their tracks, it was the 1950s, and to frame themselves as an idiosyncratic Fordist assembly line was highly modern and not fully wrong, only that they needed some mechanisms greased up. They were beginning to fall into the rhythms of the new popular music landscape. Harold got spring tour dates arranged, including the Carnegie Hall debut of the Erik Darling lineup of the band.

At the Weavers' now-branded home, Erik—as harsh a self-critic as one might find—grasped his way through what he would recall as a "mostly unpleasant" and panic-stricken performance. In the audience that night was Pete himself, now a full year removed from walking out, watching from a balcony box at stage left.

Erik's wife, Joan, and others eyed Pete occasionally to see how he reacted to the show's various moments. "When you first sang, he sort of led the applause," she told Erik. "Then, at the end, when you sang 'Wimoweh,' he led the standing ovation for you."

For Darling, though, it was a strange experience through and through, replacing his teenage hero onstage at Carnegie Hall. "It was not the magic and total cure-all for your life that you thought it would be," Joan would recall of Erik's feelings.

But the implications of that didn't fully register just yet. *The Billboard* raved over the show, calling out Darling's "spectacular yodeling and banjo-picking." For their first Carnegie Hall show in two years, the room was once again packed, "with so many stage seats there was hardly room for [the band]."

The *Billboard* critic also observed a new phenomenon at Weavers shows: a "predominantly teen-aged audience." Both the Weavers and Erik Darling had been wise to persevere. The seismic harmony had come.

A pair of ghosts crept onto the radio and out into millions of households in 1958. They'd both been killed nearly a hundred years earlier in North Carolina. He'd murdered her, and had been hanged for it. Their memories became a song, then many songs, sung in the mountains, collected by visiting folklorists, printed in books, and soon enough heard around the Washington Square Park fountain. The Kingston Trio claimed they first became aware of "Tom Dooley" (People's Song #225) on audition night at San Francisco's Purple Onion, and attached their own words from a printed collection. Others suggested they'd picked it up from a Stinson recording made by Erik Darling and friends.

But it was the Kingston Trio, based in Palo Alto, and their recording of "Tom Dooley" that detonated the great American folk boom when the song became a massive hit in late 1958. An LP track first, the song blew up big after a Salt Lake City radio station put it into high rotation. The expression "folk revival" had circulated for at least a decade, but no one had conceived it on this scale, maybe not even Pete Seeger. Just as with "Goodnight Irene," in popular American folk music, there was before "Tom Dooley" and after "Tom Dooley."

Of course, the Kingston Trio's hit hardly arrived in a vacuum, but traveled in the footsteps of those who came before, even if the new stars weren't always sure what that meant. Dave Guard, the trio's banjo player, was inspired to pick up the instrument after catching the Weavers in San Francisco on their reunion tour in 1957.

"It was the *big* experience of our lives," his bandmate Nick Reynolds would say. "We were all in tears from the first note they sang to the last," Reynolds would say.

After struggling their way around the San Francisco peninsula in a series of acts, they re-assembled as the Kingston Trio. "We were sort of trying to sound like the Weavers," Guard said, "It was really Weavers energy."

They did everything they could to channel it. The band planned to perform songs from the Spanish Civil War, too, because they were "very ballsy-sounding," but their manager nixed the idea. "Politically we didn't know what was going on," Guard would admit. Profiles of the band emphasized their utter domesticity and general vanilla qualities.

It wasn't *only* the Weavers energy. Their name referenced the still-sizzling calypso craze, and there was more than a hint of island rhythm incorporated naturally into both Guard's banjo playing and their arrangements. Where their debut album drew heavily from the Weavers' songbook, including "Bay of Mexico" and "Wreck of the John B," the calypso phrasings carried the songs into a new era. Likewise, the Hawaiian upbringing and subsequent California migration of two-thirds of the band instilled their playing with a laid-back air the Weavers could never achieve, either as people or musicians. In some ways, the Kingston Trio provided a linkage between folk music and the equally au courant fad for exotica.

But the Weavers' influence was unmistakable on the Kingstons and many of the other folk acts breaking through to the mainstream. Another group of Bay Area folk-pop contenders, the Gateway Singers, pre-dated the Kingston Trio and were left-wing through and through. Led by comic Lou Gottlieb, the integrated quartet had glimpsed the folk-pop future only a blink before the Kingstons arrived, pulling liberally from the Weavers' repertoire and empha-sizing a sophisticated swing, even adding a jazz combo for their debut LP (on Decca, no less). At first, Gottlieb had simply called them the Re-Weavers.

The damage the Weavers had sustained from the mainstream culture was not soon forgotten, either. When Gottlieb reached the end of his tether, he was replaced by former People's Songster Ernie Lieberman, a folk singer back into the Henry Wallace days. "When I joined the Gateway Singers, they were concerned about getting on television," he said. "They had a very difficult time because they were interracial, and the Southern market would cut away when an interracial group played on a network show. They were concerned about my left-wing credentials, that there would be further blacklisting, so they asked if I would mind changing my name." He became Ernie Sheldon. Even as the blacklist era began to wind down, it still hovered in folk music like a barely repressed memory.

Lou Gottlieb, meanwhile, went on to form the Limeliters, following the Kingston Trio into pop ubiquity, and making their own version of "Hey Lilee Lilee" a centerpiece of their live shows. Once the concluding segment of the Weavers' "Around the World" suite, the Limeliters created an audience partic-ipation extravaganza featuring improvised stanzas. "Here's another of the original verses . . ." Gottlieb would announce when they performed the song, before launching into a couplet that most certainly didn't source from Alan Lomax's 1935 recording, lifted straight from the Weavers' globalist songbook: "Sing this song in every land/dance together hand in hand. . . ." In some small way, the energy of People's Songs remained luminescent as the dark, strange decade of the 1950s began to run down.

The Kingston Trio and "Tom Dooley" uncorked a passageway to a far-off world of spirits. By the next summer, Columbia Pictures had pushed out *The Legend of Tom Dooley* starring Michael Landon, the Kingston Trio's album lingered on the pop chart for 114 weeks, and folk music entered popular culture. Like so many other crazes, it became a catch-all for adjacent cultural ideas. The specters swirled, as the Kingstons, the Weavers, Pete, and associates became entry points that might lead listeners to Woody Guthrie, the weird historical rifts of Harry Smith's *Anthology of Folk Music*, or any number of other mysterious discs on Moe Asch's Folkways label.

The debate raged in the pages of *Sing Out!* In one editorialist's estimation, the Kingston Trio brought "good folk music to the level of the worst Tin Pan Alley music, and is even worse because it is advertising itself as folk music." The clean-cut trio oftentimes seemed totally separate from the impulse that had driven the Almanac Singers and People's Songs and their descendants. But the Kingston Trio might be credited for landing a durable bridge back to the mainstream. Much as Alan Lomax had self-consciously championed the accessible blues and folk of Josh White and Burl Ives in the early 1940s in an effort to broaden public ears enough for the more unfiltered version he favored, the Kingston Trio was a new way to make folk palatable.

What the Kingston Trio and others carried from the Weavers wasn't politics except in that most very basic energy. There was power in a union and there was power in group singing, using collective action to reaffirm individual identity. While the Limeliters' goofy sing-alongs may not have resembled protest music, it was a derivation of the very goal with which Pete and Lee had begun, to use singing as an organizing tool. The collective action had become the singing itself. While the music's shared cultural space perhaps grew from the coalition-building strategies of the Popular Front-era Communist Party, it was now a virtual and still-evolving coalition-building handbook available to all.

The Kingston Trio became an inflection point when the history of folk music turned practically non-linear, existing everywhere, a singularity with a dozen or more quickly changing zones of influential musical activity existing in parallel for the next seven or eight or ten or twenty years.

In New York, an entrepreneur named Izzy Young, possessed with Pete-like levels of energy—and chutzpah to spare—opened the Folklore Center, a block from Washington Square Park, near the corner of Minetta Lane. It became a center of activity for all kinds of folk, but especially those who venerated the old-time recordings. One of the hottest young pickers among these was a Seeger too: Pete's younger half brother Mike, who'd formed the New Lost City Ramblers with a pair of hardcore Washington Square folkies. There was a Folksingers Guild and new rooms booking a variety of folk flavors, including the Village Gate. Scenes bubbled in Cambridge, Massachusetts, and Berkeley, California, and Denver, Colorado, and people's songs—no matter what form they took—suddenly seemed to share space in a transformed marketplace.

Another metric was the frequency with which Weavers publisher Howie Richmond now sought to protect Weavers-related copyrights. It had begun just before the Kingston Trio, when a young pop crooner had a hit with "Kisses Sweeter Than Wine," his label trying to pass it off as a piece in the public domain. Richmond was on it. By the end of the year, he was addressing the annual BMI dinner. "I'd especially like to thank the boys at Roulette Records who worked on the tune just as hard as they might if it had been their own," he quipped, accepting an award.

The Weavers had entered into the serious world of copyright in the Decca era, though were seemingly erased almost as quickly. Now, with the ascent of the Kingston Trio, the Weavers began to regularly accumulate outside royalties. Just like the Weavers, many of the new acts continued the practice of tweaking melodies slightly to achieve their own copyrights, but on some songs, "authorship" was indisputable. Lee received attribution for "Lonesome Traveler" and Paul Campbell got a nod for "Wimoweh" on the Kingston Trio's popular . . . *from the 'Hungry i'* live LP, another mode they owed to the Weavers. As a brand, the Weavers' arrangements now began to appreciate in value.

Fred Hellerman absorbed it all. Like Lee and Pete, Fred had developed his own specific and now virtually complete skill set as a folk musician. Lee specialized in song collecting, editing, theorizing, storytelling, bass singing, and general bullshitting. Pete was Pete, with his memory and pro chops and song-leading and charisma and energy and organizing and secret superhero weapon Toshi. Now Fred was fully Fred, with his guitar playing and singing and songwriting and sense of taste and arranging skills and lifetime badges of honor from both the Weavers and the House Un-American Activities Committee (though, in Fred's case, technically a subcommittee, but who was counting?).

With a devoted manager and close friend Harold Leventhal, Fred learned the inside-out of the folk-music business in real time. As the industry boomed in the wake of the Kingston Trio, Harold Leventhal—with his flawless politics and altruistic love for his musicians and his jolly mutton-chop sideburns— became a new kind of music industrialist. Fred was right there ready to boom with it, both a respected ten-year industry veteran with the Weavers, but only thirty-one and excited to make himself a career as a folk-music professional.

During the Kingston year o' '58, Fred placed a half dozen songs on various Harry Belafonte–related releases, such as the Belafonte Singers, the backing group franchised into a performing band of its own, led by Fred's Neighbors collaborator Robert De Cormier. In his guise as musical director at Elektra, Fred produced two albums for globetrotting folkie Theodore Bikel, who would credit their success to Fred's arrangements. "He knew much more about recordings than I," Bikel observed. "He was also able to get a lot of music out of relatively few instruments." In addition to touring and recording as a Weaver, Fred charted arrangements and performed on the LP debut of Ronnie Gilbert, fully titled *In Hi-Fi . . . The Legend of Bessie Smith*. The first of the proposed Weavers' so-called "personality" albums, it was a fine concept at what proved to be an odd time.

The band was filled with bona-fide jazz all-stars, including longtime Duke Ellington trumpet player Cootie Williams, and several Benny Goodman collaborators. Conceived and released just before the Kingston Trio broke big, the tribute to the blues singer was less in line with the folk revival than the LP market's demands for new varieties of novelty and sophistication. It also came at a moment of new interest in Smith's music, one of several full-length tributes released that season, including discs by Dinah Washington, LaVern Baker, and Juanita Hall.

Reviews were downright cruel, bordering on sexist. "She sounds more like a social worker than a blues singer," sneered *HiFi and Music Review*. The jazz stalwarts at *Downbeat* were even worse. "I suppose the best thing to say about [it] is that they sent a girl in to do a woman's work." RCA released her from her contract for the follow-up, which would arrive instead on Vanguard.

It had been a singularly shitty time for the usually indomitable Ronnie, with or without cranky reviews. She and Marty were divorcing, and the custody battle over their daughter heated up around the time both *The Legend of Bessie Smith* came out and Erik Darling began to integrate into the Weavers as a full-time member. And, reviews or no, it hardly stopped her. There would be plenty more singing for Ronnie in the coming years, but first she had to move herself and her daughter, Lisa, back to New York City.

It was during this auspicious folkie dawning, too, at the Robinsons' brownstone in Brooklyn Heights, that Lee Hays created his most major work outside the Weavers. It was at once the most unusual, surprising, and successful recording to come out of a Weaver during their non-Weaving time, Pete excluded. Lee had started with the idea of making a "personality" LP of his own, but wound up with something else, a project uncommonly suited for capturing Lee Hays, the Brooklyn folklorist, in his natural habitat.

Lee had befriended the couple upstairs and, always at his absolute best with kids, became part of their young baby Jeffie's upbringing. Doris Willens and her husband had been making up playful songs for and with their infant, and Lee joined in, instinctually spewing out little bits of folk nonsense as Jeffie learned to climb the stairs. Soon, Jeffie was joining Lee, adding nonsense to Lee's couplets.

One of Lee's younger folkie friends was Alan Arkin, Erik Darling's ex-bandmate in the Tarriers, who'd moved to the neighborhood with his family to focus on an acting career. The son of a pair of veteran People's Songsters, Los Angeles division, and the nephew of Earl Robinson's wife, Helen, Arkin found himself in the living room with the big sliding doors amid the rolling left-wing folk salon on Cranberry Street largely due to Lee. "I don't think Earl would have ever said hello to me if he wasn't married to my aunt," Arkin observed. But Lee would, always ready to make a new friend. Thanks in part to Arkin's handiness with a tape recorder, the two struck up a partnership.

"I was very into technology and especially technology in order to be creative on one's own, without outside help," Arkin remembered. He had a tape recorder and a microphone and they went from there.

Using the songs Doris Willens had been making up with baby Jeffie, a new group began to assemble around the accumulating body of children's music. Almost exactly twenty years Arkin's senior, Lee became a mentor to the ex-Tarrier. "He was endlessly patient and he was endlessly kind," Arkin recalled.

Lee excelled, jumping in with his full skills as an editor, a recognizer of structure and melody and historical pedigree, all those years of half-loafing folklorism paying off now, working in an environment where he could simply lead in a minimal, noninvasive way. It was perfect. The songs emerged from the child-rearing atmosphere around him, and all he had to do was gently encourage and take note. It was perhaps the best platform Lee Hays would ever find outside the Weavers—and it became a band of its own, featuring the journalist and young mother soon known as "Sister Doris."

"Without ever feeling hysterical, or without ever feeling pressured or pushed, there was a wonderful ease about the creative work we did together, and watching him work," Arkin remembered. Arkin marveled at the slowness that could be frustrating to the Weavers. "He would just take his time. Everything was slow and orderly and not pressured. I learned a lot from many aspects of being with him and that was certainly one of them." Arkin and his wife also picked up cooking tips, watching Lee work in the Robinsons' kitchen.

Recording at the Robinsons, the group made what Doris Willens called "possibly the only children's albums ever recorded in a beer-filled bed-sitting room." Perhaps inspired by Lee's friend Tony Schwartz, the legendary New York aural ethnographer, the Babysitters were a locally sourced production through and through.

Arkin edited the album himself. "You just had the tape recorder and a roll of editing tape, a little bar where you put the tape, and a razorblade," Arkin remembered. "You made your cuts and splices and, if you didn't like it, you made sure you hung on to the little tiny pieces and could tape them back together." As Arkin recalls, when they turned it in, he'd only thought of it as a collection of demos, "and they decided to publish it just exactly the way we recorded it."

Released by Vanguard under the name the Babysitters, the formal title was *Folk Songs for Babies, Small Children, Parents and Baby Sitters*. "Songs for imagining and pretending," read one description point on the Babysitters' debut. Then working as a columnist for the Hearst-owned *New York Journal-American*, on the album Doris Willens used her married name, Kaplan, to sidestep her notoriously conservative employers.

"Breathes there not a Spock-marked parent who has ever run out of inventions to keep the kids occupied?" Lee asked in his liner notes for the album. Dr. Benjamin Spock, too, was a Popular Fronter. Drawing from his regular column on child care for New York's progressive daily newspaper *PM*—defunct by 1948—Spock's *Baby and Child Care* was a global change in parenting, recognizing the need for open play and flexibility.

Here, Lee and Pete and their other folk-singing brethren fit right in, finding an even more secret new market for their music. Pete had been recording children's music and performing at summer camps for years, and the postwar baby boom kept on booming into the early 1960s. While much was made of the new market for teenagers, children's music grew into its own dependable market force, too, with the Weavers as true pioneers, individually and together, their popular folk never being too far removed from children's songs to start.

Reviews of *Folk Songs for Babies, Small Children, Parents and Baby Sitters* were generally glowing, with praise oozing from the *New Yorker*, the *New York Times*, *Time*, *Catholic Messenger*, and *HiFi and Music Review*. The *Catholic Messenger* raved, "This is easily the most popular record, so far as this reviewer's children are concerned, that has come into the house."

With all of this, the Weavers had now generated what might be described as a truly all-ages fan base: the kids who loved Pete and Lee's children's recordings, the teens and collegiate audience who perhaps discovered them through the Kingston Trio, the grown-ups who appreciated the tasteful arrangements and high-fidelity recordings, and the even older lefties who still remembered the Almanac Singers. Pete Seeger could be in so many places at once that he also remained an invisible but tangible presence at Weavers shows, like the ever-restless song-spirit of Woody Guthrie, a folk ghost of his own. Though Pete had left the band in early 1958, it wouldn't be until 1960 that the Weavers would release an LP that didn't feature him, and (to Lee's displeasure) Pete continued to loom large over Weavers performances.

Pete Seeger had become the living avatar of folk music. Long bordering on caricature, especially now that he'd reached an international folk celebrity, he likewise achieved parody. The New York singer and guitarist Dave Van Ronk, a playful and far-left anarchist who'd initially dismissed the Washington Square Park scene as music for summer campers, co-authored *The Bosses' Songbook: Songs to Stifle the Flames of Discontent*, featuring titles that might ring bells with ex-Almanacs, including "Which Side Are We On?," "This Land Is Their Land," and one that took direct aim at Pete, "Ballad of a Party Folk Singer." To the tune of "The Wreck of the Ol' '97":

> *Well, they gave him his orders*
> *Up at Party headquarters*
> *Saying, "Pete you're way behind times*
> *This is not '38; this is 1947*
> *And there's been a change in that old party line."*

But even as the folk scene seemed to fold into the vanilla pop-music world, Pete often served as a transcendental figure. Peter Stampfel, a helium-voiced young folkie from Wisconsin, dismissed the Weavers as harmless and fell in with a cooler crowd that existed at the periphery of the local folk music and the Beat scene. But going to see Seeger perform was a revelation for Stampfel, as the cooler-than-thou bohemians made an exception for the ex-Weaver.

"He was just *gooder* than anybody else we'd ever seen," said Stampfel, who would soon move to New York and co-found the Holy Modal Rounders. "He seemed to radiate goodness that was intense and powerful, and everybody in the audience seemed to be good by reflection," he told Elijah Wald.

Constituting a natural resource, Pete was a hard presence to replace in the Weavers. And while Lee, especially, might have felt resentful about Pete's departure, the banjo player's missionary musical work more than helped sustain the new world that the Weavers inhabited, even if (as Lee put it) the band now had to "work ten times as hard to accomplish the same goals."

Opportunities awaited the group known as "America's Most Popular Folk Singers," but it was here, too, that the Weavers began to get stuck in time. The band was a slow-functioning democracy under the best of circumstances, with Lee Hays working on a geological scale compared to his younger bandmates. At some point during this period, they would change their tag from "Most Popular" to "Most Loved." And now the folk-singing universe accelerated to Pete-speed around them. As the band concluded their spring 1959 tour with Erik Darling, a draining-enough experience by itself, the nonlinear all-around-them events continued to transpire.

That summer saw the first installment of the Newport Folk Festival, featuring Pete (of course), the Kingston Trio, bluegrass heroes like the Stanley Brothers, banjo pioneer Earl Scruggs, old-timey newcomers the New Lost City Ramblers, gospel-blues songwriter Rev. Gary Davis, and—the unquestioned breakout star of the weekend, Joan Baez. Like the Kingston Trio, the eighteen-year-old singer and guitarist from Cambridge was deeply inspired by the Weavers' 1957 appearance in San Francisco. Inspiring a minor record label frenzy, Baez soon signed to Vanguard, primarily because it was the home of the Weavers.

Even separated from the Weavers, Pete, too, continued to think about folk's possibilities. But Pete's musical sensibilities seemed firmly and increasingly grounded in an earlier era. He closed out the first night at the first Newport with "Careless Love," the timeless folk song that had effortlessly become a pop standard without the help of Pete or Alan Lomax or any other folklorist.

"Let's sing that chorus once again for every patriot and revolutionary the world ever knew," he told the crowd at Newport, "who perhaps loved humanity not wisely but too well—and their hearts are often broken." In the first flowering of the here-for-real folk revival, Pete Seeger was still a wanted man, court decisions suspended over every chord.

Only weeks after the Newport Folk Festival, police raided the Highlander Folk School, the social activism center in Tennessee where Pete had met and performed for Martin Luther King Jr. the summer before. At Pete's recommendation, the young songwriter Guy Carawan had revived the music program there. Working with the NAACP, Carawan had sung at events around the South. He discovered that some People's Songs standards like "Passing Through" and "This Land Is Your Land" didn't often work in the new civil rights era. (In coming decades, Native Americans would pose the question of exactly whose land Woody was laying claim to, anyway.)

What resonated—and what the students sang the night of Highlander's police raid—was another People's Songs standard, "We Shall Overcome" (People's Song #281), the old hymn collected by Zilphia Horton, edited and slightly rewritten by Pete and others, and sung back by Guy Carawan. The new edit propagated throughout the South, and would eventually be placed controversially under copyright by Weavers' song publisher Howie Richmond. Though royalties were directed toward civil rights groups, many would see it as the height of arrogance: putting a legitimate song of the people under any kind of control. The song moved faster than ever around the South, where the civil rights movement grew by leaps and bounds.

But as folk music exploded into new importance and prominence in both the commercial marketplace and the currency of social action, the Weavers were seemingly silent.

When they received news of the impending tour at a band meeting, Erik Darling could see the color nearly drain from Lee's face. "Had he drank [*sic*] less beer, been from somewhere else, and weighed less, he might have been delighted," Darling would assess many years later. The new banjo player had done time in Europe with the Tarriers, fulfilled his sense of adventure, and didn't feel the need to go back, but neither did he feel the need to rock the boat. "Lee's silence and passive-aggressive behavior had me believing he'd get the job done," Darling recalled. It didn't.

It was due to the slow recession of the blacklist that Lee Hays soon found himself across the ocean, hunting down strange typewriters. Lee's friend

Rockwell Kent was to blame, in some regard. The government had denied the blacklisted painter the right to travel internationally, and he'd sued for his passport. Fighting the case all the way to the Supreme Court, they finally ruled in Kent's favor in 1958, declaring that the secretary of state could not lawfully deny someone a passport over their political views.

The implications of *Kent v. Dulles* rippled out. Paul Robeson, who'd been in court about his passport the same week that Pete and Lee testified—and in limbo ever since—could finally travel again and resume a performing life that had always been more lucrative abroad, before he'd been grounded by the State Department. Less than a month later, Robeson departed for Europe, not returning to the United States for a half decade.

Without Lee and Fred's HUAC appearances hanging over their travel, the friendly skies beckoned, and a promoter appeared with an offer for a five-week tour of Israel, of all places, with more than forty shows. They would pass through England on the way there and back, keeping them abroad for the entire summer of 1959.

The Weavers descended on London in late May, a few weeks after Erik's Carnegie Hall debut, and they were suddenly someplace new. Fred's time in the Coast Guard had brought him to many exotic locales, but this was different. To Ronnie, the sites of "London [were] names out of books," and she was ready to enjoy it the best she could, still feeling the emotional weight of her divorce and custody battle. Ronnie's daughter and mother would join her for parts of the adventure, sometimes staying with friends, sometimes traveling with the band.

Lee was already in full form, beginning a series of nearly daily dispatches to Harold Leventhal back in New York, part professional check-in, part diary, part score-settling, and largely just a sounding board for complaints of all genres. "We have been here a day and a half and already half the group detests the other half, so everything is normal," Lee began his first missive.

Typed out onto Air Letter sheets, folded and sent back over the ocean, the letters quickly proved Lee's literary mettle as a world-champion kvetcher. "London is drab, noisy, the hotel rooms are grubby and the beds smell of stale semen, bathtubs are long and narrow; food is greasy and poorly prepared, though service is pleasant," Lee detailed for his manager. "I ordered a glass of milk which must have come from a desiccated old heifer who had long since forgotten the taste of green grass, and tepid as swamp water." It went on from there.

The separation among the Weavers was vast. When they'd checked in, Ronnie had wanted to go for a walk to nearby Piccadilly Circus. Worried about being a single woman alone in a strange city, she steeled herself and went to the lobby, and then: "whom should I meet downstairs but Fred, restless like me and ready for a long walk." It hadn't occurred to her to check with her fellow Weavers. The two jet-lagged Camp Wo-Chi-Ca alums wandered through Piccadilly Circus across the Thames to the Royal Albert Hall.

Lee, meanwhile, made his own Piccadilly stroll by himself, just after dawn. "There was not a soul to be seen," he told Harold. "No coffee shops." Back in his room, he ate breakfast alone. "It isn't like room service at all," he wondered. "It is a custom, and the hotel people are sort of hurt if you don't order." There would be many new customs for Lee Hays over the next few months, not all of them as pleasant.

He'd befriended Erik and Joan Darling, though Lee was sometimes bemused by the younger Weaver's somewhat kitschy taste in pop culture. For their parts, the Darlings had a genuine affection for the large Southern bass singer, smiling involuntarily when in his presence. The young banjo player was learning about the complexities of humans in all their weird glory, Lee Hays becoming a mostly benign teaching specimen. "There was a hauntedness to him," Darling would say, "a sadness over something we never learned much about."

It was a feeling that Babysitter Alan Arkin shared. "There was a sense of isolation and sadness," Arkin described. "His past was something you didn't talk about."

No one wanted to coordinate with Lee about sightseeing or strategy for their scheduled TV appearance and Radio Luxembourg sessions. Later, he found out that other members of the Weavers had been out carousing in the clubs, jamming and performing with local skiffle acts, though Lee's letters home don't detail which ones. Nobody had invited him.

The skiffle scene had mushroomed quickly after Lonnie Donegan's initial hit with "Rock Island Line," a genuine national craze that mutated in numerous ways around the United Kingdom. Not long before the Weavers arrived, the London skiffle scene had even gained a political consciousness. There'd been an escalating series of racially motivated hate crimes on the city's West Indian community, often perpetrated by Teddy Boys, rockabilly-loving street gangs sometimes connected to the burgeoning Fascist movement. Donegan and others were quick to condemn the violence, speaking out for racial equality. Short-lived but influential was the Harmony Club, London's first interracial folk club, aimed at local teens. It barely lasted into the spring, and was closed by the time the Weavers arrived.

Over their first week in London, it became clear that the band's travel plans weren't as well laid as they may've hoped when boarding their transatlantic flights. This pass through London was to serve mostly as a promotional effort, laying the ground for a fuller tour after the main purpose of the trip: a month-long tour of Israel.

One of the movers behind the Weavers' international effort was Pete Kameron, the band's wily manager during the Decca epoch. He'd been too show-biz for Pete Seeger before, organizing the band around his own private strategies, and the post-blacklist Weavers would discover that he hadn't changed much. Without prompting, Erik and Joan Darling formed the same opinion. But, even as they'd blazed a new alternative trail in the States, Kameron continued to manage the Weavers from the crossroads of Lee's Question and its Answer: whether or not the Weavers could be a genuine mainstream pop act.

Kameron went to work setting up a tour with Lonnie Donegan in the fall. In addition to the skiffle scene, there was likewise an equally self-serious folk scene, anchored in part by Pete's half sister Peggy and her husband Ewan MacColl, as well as the *Sing Out!*-inspired *Sing!* that much more closely resembled the People's Songs world from whence the Weavers sprang. There was a folk audience there, they could sense, but they hadn't found it.

But it was a productive time in London just the same, with the band trucking into Radio Luxembourg's London studio, tracking sixty-three songs in a marathon two-day session. It was, Lee noted to Harold, every single song in their repertoire, and Lee felt rushed, but when didn't he? For less than a full year with Erik in the band, it was an impressive number. It included plenty of staples that they'd once done with Pete, with Erik bringing new life to his mentor's old parts. Erik especially loved singing "Wimoweh," and it remained his anchor on nights when he struggled through the set. On songs like "Rock Island Line," especially, it was easy to hear the difference between Pete's enthusiastic banjo playing and the hard percussive drive of Erik's phrasing. "Venga Jaleo" was in, but "Wasn't That a Time" was out. For the moment "This Land Is Your Land" was missing, but "Take This Hammer" was there, and so were some twenty other songs new to the repertoire since Pete's departure.

One number that Darling had taken over from Pete was another that had floated into their repertoire from the Bahamas, "Run, Come, See Jerusalem!" With Erik singing and the other three giving him the supercharged Weaver energy, it came out with pure gospel power, but as Pete noted when the song was reprinted in *Sing Out!*, it was a topical song about a shipwreck, maybe even a parody, not a hymn. Sung on Radio Luxembourg, this was perhaps prophetic.

"When we stepped off the plane at the Tel Aviv airport, it was like stepping into a total inferno," Erik Darling would recall. "The heat came from in front, from behind, from below, from both sides." He was an unhappy camper from the start.

But the Weavers were received as heroes. "Nobody gave a damn about America's blacklist outside the United States," Ronnie quickly realized. Nearly everywhere they went, their concerts were mob scenes, overflowing with fans. There were near riots and gate crashes and screaming pop fans everywhere, especially kids. Girls insisted on carrying their instruments.

"As everywhere, children hung around outside the hall, and climbed walls to hang on window ledges outside our dressing rooms," Lee wrote in his new bulletin, *A Newsletter from LEE HAYS*, distributed via Harold's office. "It is quite an experience to go to the toilet and sit there quietly beneath a window grill, then become conscious of being stared at from behind, and then to turn and see four pairs of bright eyes inspecting every move."

The kids trailed the large Arkansan around, surely a strange sight in the Old World. At first, Lee made the best of the situation, diving into sightseeing with the band, sometimes even pairing off with Ronnie's mother, Sarah. The scholarly Lee was up to his ears in ironic juxtapositions and historical wonders. The folklorist began absorbing local slang, jokes, and other color. Learning some of the ranks of the Israeli Army, Lee adjusted his stage introductions. He was the *Rav-Aluf*, the major general. Fred was the *Aluf*. Ronnie was the *Aluf-Mishne*, and Erik was *Turai*, a private.

From somewhere, the promoters had manifested old New York City taxis, DeSotos with jump seats and a distinct lack of air conditioning, repainted a sandblasted tan, which became the heart of the Weavers' desert convoy. They toured the *kibbutzim* circuit in four cars with local roadies and their own sound system. Though they tried to work their way through the situation with folkie harmony, the band's Israel tour grew harder by the day. On their "Around the World" medley, they'd offered stop-offs in the Bahamas and Germany and Israel, each lasting barely a chorus or two. Extended to a whole trip was a vast strain.

The closest the Weavers got to a reprieve while in Israel were rapturous receptions from the crowds. "The heat never ceased, even at night," Erik would remember. "Under the stage lights, it was next to unbearable." Lee wrote to Harold about one night when Ronnie steadied herself on Lee's back for the last part of a performance.

"It seems America is 183 years old today," Lee noted on the Fourth of July. "I feel older."

Fred had a better time, absorbing the majesty of the holy land, seeing the *kibbutzim* and the wonders of a new country, floating in the Dead Sea, and connecting with relatives, including one who'd helped bring electricity to the Sinai Peninsula.

The band would come away with a few shared road stories, like the night that their local hosts overheard Lee pining for American food and somehow acquired some highly un-kosher bacon on the black market. But they had no idea how to prepare it, serving it nearly raw, with Ronnie eventually quietly taking the host aside and teaching her how to fry it in a skillet. The other shared memory was slightly more harrowing, their convoy taking a shortcut through a disputed zone, and having to pull over to change a flat tire, one of their drivers pulling a pistol from the glove box in case something should go awry.

Erik Darling, especially, observed Lee's deterioration. Lee had complained about his health since the Almanac days, and the other Weavers had long since tuned it out. But one day in Israel, under the strictest of confidence, making them promise not to tell the rest of the band, Lee had shown Erik and his wife the "red welts . . . the size of silver dollars, all over his body." Darling and his wife tried not to freak, and kept to their word. In his countless pages of moaning to Harold Leventhal, it remained a secret as well, give or take vague notes about his "physical distress."

The heat made everything more surreal. "I thought I was going to get away from lefties here, but they come up in the same numbers as in the [States]," Lee confided to Harold. One told him that the Weavers didn't have as much "courage" as when they sang at hootenannies.

"In Jerusalem, of all places, I was challenged with: What happened to PS?" He didn't clarify if the inquisitor meant Pete Seeger or People's Songs, but they'd always been the same anyway.

And then even Ronnie's mother—a lifelong Socialist—made a similar remark about the band's music: "Of course you are reaching a broader audience, but with what?"

Fred was there on his own song-collecting mission in the folk-pop importation business, looking for the type of song that perhaps the Weavers could perform or, even better, Harold Leventhal and Howie Richmond and Fred could work with. But he was coming up empty there, too. "It's a little difficult since most of them are [already] published," he admitted to Harold, though he might bring back "a few loose ones." Fred was more than ready to return to the music business of New York.

Lee's narrations home remained colorful. "Beautiful fields of grapes, bananas, oranges," he observed on one drive. "Fresh turned soil as black as Mississippi gumbo where once there was only sand, and a stones [sic] throw from the sea."

There was a night, too, when their hosts treated them to a roadside picnic, illuminated by headlights, blasting Harry Belafonte and Ricky Nelson music. Lee did not take to the falafel, but enjoyed the cognac and the warmth of the fire. Their driver "pulled out his pistol and began firing at the constellation of Orion" before a swerving hour-and-a-half drive back to Tel Aviv, an equally drunk Fred Hellerman clutching for safety in the repurposed cab, and Lee Hays, collector of bemusements, bemused.

Erik and Joan dreamt a vision of the erudite storytelling Lee seaside on the Riviera drinking a Campari on ice, wishing they could give him some relief. The senior Weaver was in a very bad place. It manifested onstage and off. The Darlings found their own place of serenity in the mornings by the pool in the courtyard at the Tel Aviv motel near the Yarkon River, where the breakfasts were "the best part of the entire trip."

Joan Darling had recently come across a book by the esoteric Russian thinker P. D. Ouspensky, a disciple of the equally esoteric human-potential pioneer George Gurdjieff. Not usually much of a reader, Erik made his way through the collection, *The Psychology of Man's Possible Evolution*, expounding what he called the School of the Fourth Way. By the pool, before the day's temperature rise was tangible, Darling tried meditation, his eyes closed except to watch for the lizards, letting the world and the Weavers and all the harmonies blend into the flow of the universe, where all might be as one.

CHAPTER EIGHT

Hammer Songs

It was happening again. All signs pointed clear, the Weavers were finally going to bypass the blacklist and make it onto national television on NBC, just a few days after the New Year 1962. The world was on the mend, somewhat. But then the black fog came curling up from the trapdoors and through the station switchboard. One night, it'd been announced they were going to be guests the next day, and the next day that was no longer true.

The network presented the band with loyalty oaths, right there, with those same tiresome questions: *Are you now or have you ever been, etc., etc.*

Now Fred was the spokesperson. "We resent the indignity that such a request implies," he told the Associated Press. "Moreover, we feel very strongly that no private business establishment such as NBC has the power or the right to require proof of any citizen's patriotism."

Harold Leventhal filed a notice with the FCC, which admitted that it was the first time they'd ever received such a complaint, saying that any such loyalty oaths were decided upon strictly by the network. The year before, the band had appeared on local television in New York, on a show hosted by the successful folk-pop singer Theo Bikel. At first, the station balked, but Bikel's sponsor—the kosher soap company I. Rokeach & Sons—stood by him. The Weavers appeared for Bikel's Passover festival, playing the folk songs of Israel.

But NBC was a different story. "It seemed so ridiculous," Lee pointed out. "If we were truly subversive we'd have signed anything."

Whether intentionally or not, that spring, Vanguard's newest Weavers 45 was almost comically on the nose: the hundred-year old "Rally Around the Flag," a Civil War union cry, was on the A-side, and "Fight On," a freedom song collected at the Virginia State Penitentiary in 1936, was on the flip. "*We're almost down to the shore*," the Weavers sang on the chorus and, in 1962, they needed to believe that they almost were.

Having survived the shipwreck of Israel, more lately it seemed as if they'd been trapped. Vanguard continued to put out singles, but they were just drawn from the band's LP releases now. Maybe one would take off, but—after the Kingston Trio, especially—Vanguard could let the market come knocking if they had a hit on their hands. After Israel and a not particularly fertile return pass through England, they'd given Erik his undivided Weavers debut via another *Carnegie Hall* live album.

But creatively, they seemed stalled out as the folk world sped up around them. Far in the distance, they could see battle fronts they no longer occupied. Ronnie, full of creative energy after moving back to the East Coast, could feel it acutely. She reconnected with Ann Shepherd, a member of the progressive Group Theatre who'd lost her soap-opera acting career around the same time as the Weavers got fogged off the networks. Taking a group vacation with their kids, the two compared professional notes, "weeping, guffawing, and commiserating, forging the kind of woman-bonding I'd known before the Weavers—and very much missed." Ronnie began to think of acting again.

When Lisa went to spend part of the summer with her father, Ronnie rejoined the Weavers to prepare for their appearance at the second Newport Folk Festival. They were trying out shape-note hymns. In storytelling mode, Lee recounted to the band how shape-note singing in Southern churches was often staged with the singers facing one another—which sounded like a great idea to Ronnie.

No one responded well. "It's very uncomfortable," Lee told her.

"It feels so unnatural," Fred offered.

Fred had sensed the stall-out occurring too. *The Weavers can only do what they've been doing*, he told Ronnie around this time. It felt to Ronnie like the "worst kind of fatalism," but Fred was feeling the band's energy slowing, even suggesting to Lee that they think about breaking up. He, too, could see and hear the folk world changing at a pace they weren't matching.

At Maynard Solomon's request, Fred had accompanied Joan Baez on her self-titled debut album for Vanguard, whose spare arrangements and somber mood further rearranged the world of folk music, supplanting the collegiate good nature of the Kingston Trio with a solemn channeling of spirits. Along with its follow-up, it hit the charts in late 1961, remaining there for much of the next two years. What's more, Baez had been politicized while attending high school in Palo Alto—coincidentally, the same town in which the Kingstons had solidified—though Baez had made her way to Ira Sandperl's Peace Center, a local folkie activist hangout and crash pad for wayward bohemians.

Though Fred was fully taken with Baez's music, he wasn't as enamored with the new wave of musicians who'd started to turn up around Greenwich Village. With more than a decade of experience under his belt, Fred was now a folk veteran and possessed his equally fair share of opinions, held firmly. When Robert Shelton raved in the *New York Times* about a new singer appearing at Gerde's Folk City, Fred cornered him on the street. "How on earth can you say that he is such a great this-and-that?" he grilled the newspaper's folk champion about his review of twenty-year-old Bob Dylan. "He can't sing, and he can barely play, and he doesn't know much about music at all. I think you've gone off the deep end!"

To Dylan, observing the scene while camped out in the Village's cafés, Fred was one of the "heavy people going by." But even after the Minnesota songwriter started writing original material, transforming old folk songs in new ways, it was an opinion Fred continued to possess; in the People's Songs days, he'd thought Woody was pretty sloppy as a performer too. In what was emerging as a generational divide, Dylan's rhythmic energy came, in part, from someone who'd spent his early teenage years immersed in rock 'n' roll and R&B. Fred's notions of musical propriety landed him in a different place, maybe best exemplified by his elegant adaptation of the Carter Family's "I Never Will Marry," recorded during early studio sessions with Erik in 1958. Fred retained the basic country-folk shape of the song, but added his own verses, extrapolating the changes into richer harmonies that landed at the familiar chorus, framing it with a new sophistication. It became part of an expanded Hellerman catalog, the type of holding now possessed like a long-term investment. Ronnie, on the other hand, loved Bob Dylan, ever eager about the new music that might come.

Lee, too, grumped about the new wave of topical songwriters. After some deeply hard years, emotionally and financially, Pete and Lee's old Almanac

Singer compatriots Sis Cunningham and Gordon Friesen reemerged, launching a small do-it-themselves magazine called *Broadside* to create an active exchange of topical songs to supplement *Sing Out!* As always, Pete was gung-ho. Lee found a point to bemoan, arguing (as Friesen remembered) "that no good songs would be written because it was impossible for anyone to write a worthwhile song about something outside his or her personal experience."

It was a ridiculous point, and Lee probably knew it, having written many such songs himself. But Lee Hays made ridiculous points. With financial support from Pete Seeger, Sis and Gordon edited *Broadside* anyway, publishing it from their small apartment and providing a platform for a new generation of songwriters, including Bob Dylan, Phil Ochs, and many others. Not that Pete loved all of it either. He took particular offense at the spate of novelty variations on "John Henry," a favorite song that he held up as a symbol of American folk music. But this new generation of Almanac-like creators were like an infinite folk-song generator, spitting out new tunes while digging up and re-animating old ones, using a vast spectrum of approaches and configurations and levels of skill, creativity, and luck.

Perhaps most able to comprehend it was Pete Seeger himself, who'd long ago been to the top of that mountain and insisted the land beyond existed. He stayed as busy as possible, expecting jail time soon. He signed to Columbia Records, his first major-label record deal since Decca had dropped the Weavers, preparing simultaneously to record his Columbia debut and head back to court yet again.

Jail was a very real threat. He'd been convicted by a jury on ten counts of perjury the year before. Before his sentencing, he was allowed to address the court. The case was a sensation, the gallery overflowing with supporters. The judge had once seen the Weavers, back at the Blue Angel.

"Some of my ancestors were religious dissenters who came to America over 300 years ago," Pete said. "Others were abolitionists in New England in the 1840s and '50s. I believe that in choosing my present course, I do no dishonor to them, or to those who come after me." He didn't mention it, but there was also his uncle Alan, most famous for announcing "I have a rendezvous with death," shortly before dying in the Battle of the Somme.

Holding his banjo, Pete asked the court once again if he might sing "Wasn't That a Time," at the center of the committee's questioning. He was denied.

"Do I have a right to sing these songs?" Pete asked. "Do I have a right to sing them anywhere?"

In a dramatic scene, the judge sentenced Pete to ten concurrent sentences for his ten counts of contempt of Congress: 366 days, no bail, beginning immediately. With his banjo still on, Pete was handcuffed, Ronnie's sardonic image of him as a Messiah coming true, as Toshi stepped forward to take his instrument from him.

Pete's lawyer, Paul Ross, got him released several hours later on appeal, and the court case proceeded from there. The banjo player remained unflappable, at peace with the fact that he might be headed to jail. During the contempt trial, the *Daily News* reported, "the menace Seeger sat through the proceedings slouched and far away over distant hills."

In May of 1962, as the Weavers were straining, Pete's case went to the Court of Appeals. Paul Ross prepared a sixty-eight-page Defendant-Appellant's Brief in which he laid out the ways the US government had blacklisted Pete Seeger, drawing out the way the publishers of *Red Channels* and *Counterattack* seemed to have access to unpublished government documents, plus a host of other arguments about the illegitimacy of the committee's purview as a legal body. "Lacking a legislative purpose, the inquiry violated appellant's First Amendment rights," Ross argued. Pete wanted to bend the case back on the Un-Americans as hard as he could.

The ruling came down: The indictment was faulty and, just like that, Pete was free for good. Ecstatic to be liberated from endless court proceedings, he was also upset that the ruling had ignored the First Amendment argument Paul Ross laid out. Nonetheless, it was hard to argue with freedom.

In other courtrooms, however, the battles resolved more conclusively. A month after Pete had his sentence overturned, John Henry Faulk, the radio entertainer and former People's Songs associate, won his lawsuit against the blacklisting grocery store magnate Laurence Johnson and former *Red Channels* editor Vincent Harnett, whom Ross had called to testify in Pete's trial. Having been harassed by the same group as the Weavers, including Ronnie's investigator Dolores Scotti, Faulk won a $3.5 million settlement that provided some of the vindication that Pete Seeger's trial lacked. After appeals and fees, Faulk only received a tiny fraction, but the blacklist's fog grew less persistent.

The years combined. To Erik Darling, the space between the band's trip to Europe and his resignation from the quartet seemed like a matter of months. In his memory, he quit the Weavers almost immediately after they'd returned home. On more recognizable calendars, it took him nearly another two and a half years. To Ronnie Gilbert, too, the period flashed by when she put the years of her life together later, given barely a sentence or two of thought.

The junior Weaver banjo player had revelations in Europe. Not in Jerusalem, though perhaps the heat and the meditation and the stress contributed, but starting in Italy. They'd stopped briefly there, with the promise of never-materialized Weavers shows on the French and/or Italian sides of the Riviera. Erik and his wife found themselves in Florence, visiting Michelangelo's sculpture *David*. Darling's father was an artist with a profoundly singular worldview, leaving a deep impression on the way the younger Darling absorbed the world, including a genuine and emotional openness to art. The musician experienced a sense of deep ecstasy upon hearing the Weavers' "Wimoweh" in concert in 1950, and now—in the presence of Michelangelo's great work—had another transformative experience.

"I had to affirm who I was," Darling summarized, "apart from all other things and events." It was a genuine artistic revelation as much as anything else. "I had to find what it was about me that I wanted to express about being a person, an artist, a person who sings about matters of life." He needed to break apart from his onetime heroes and truly define himself in all ways. But that wasn't the only revelation, nor was it the only reason he would come to leave the Weavers.

He had never had much political consciousness, another remnant of his proto-bohemian father. "I don't recall ever having a political conversation with him," his former bandmate and close friend Alan Arkin said, remembering their shared distaste for organizational logic. "If I'd questioned him, I think we would have been exactly aligned."

But Darling's thinking slowly began to change, though in his typically methodical and freethinking way, Erik Darling was unsure how at first. He'd never been much of a reader, but near the end of the Israel trip, he'd moved from P. D. Ouspensky to another book recommended by his wife: *Atlas Shrugged* by Ayn Rand. He struggled his way through it. His takeaway in part was "to think about the idea of actual freedom, and motives of human behavior, the matrix of political thinking."

Erik Darling had known all along that, like his musical direction, his politics didn't fully align with that of the Weavers. "I still didn't have a lot of certainty about where I should stand," he admitted, "just that I wanted to stand." As he did, he came out further to the right than even he might've expected. He resigned from the Weavers in the early part of 1962, not long after the hullabaloo over the loyalty oath on NBC.

"Another career shot out from under me," Lee groused when Erik announced his departure at Harold Leventhal's office. The line was part of Lee's own growing treasury of bitterness. The Eleventh Commandment is "never give up a grudge," he once told Pete.

It was a rough blow for the group, having rebuilt themselves so improbably with Erik. But for once Lee seemed to work to not hold a grudge. The newest ex-Weaver underscored his human-to-human connection with Lee. "When I talked to you about people or performing or what ever, I always got what I think of as a strait answere [sic] from somewhere in the realm of reality," Darling wrote, "without colorations or 'hip talk' or guessing games."

But just as Pete Seeger had built himself an audience who could fill-in the Weavers' harmonies wherever he went, he'd also trained a generation of banjo players in something like his musical image. In the late '50s, Vega had begun to manufacture its own Pete Seeger model banjo with an extended neck and sold several hundred by the turn of the decade to a new crop of musicians playing in ways that banjo players couldn't before the arrival of Pete Seeger. One was twenty-eight-year-old Frank Hamilton, the son of a Socialist college professor who'd found his doorway into culture through the Popular Front. A self-described Seeger acolyte, he would say, "I want to believe Pete's view that the world can change because of a song."

Deeply embedded in the national folk scene, most lately he'd been on the founding faculty of Chicago's new Old Town School of Folk Music, where he'd played with the Weavers just before Pete's departure. As a teen picker, he'd hung out at the musical Topanga Canyon commune run by blacklisted actor and Almanac pal Will Geer, and traveled into the South in the summer of 1953 with Guy Carawan and Ramblin' Jack Elliott. Stopping at both Pete and Lee's for advice, the trio hit the road, meeting A. P. Carter in Virginia, stopping at the Highlander Folk School in Tennessee (where Carawan would return to teach), the experimental Black Mountain School in North Carolina, and the Asheville Folk Festival in North Carolina, overseen by Bascom Lamar Lunsford.

There, they climbed the hill to Lunsford's tent to meet the man who'd inspired Pete Seeger to pick up a banjo. Carawan announced them politely from outside. Then, as Hamilton would remember, "This booming voice roared at us in the night from inside the darkened tent, 'YOU BOYS COMMUNISTS?'"

Lunsford, then seventy-one, collected the year before on Harry Smith's *Anthology of American Folk Music*, hadn't appreciated the nuances of the progressive folk music. By the time Hamilton replaced Erik Darling in the

Weavers in the summer of 1962, the South was beginning to come north, at least from a musical perspective, to the Newport Folk Festival and residencies at Greenwich Village folk clubs. While Lunsford never made the Newport trek, others with a whole spectrum of backgrounds and beliefs were an increasing presence on the diversifying folk scene.

The Weavers' authenticity was of its own kind, a professional operation with a manager and agents and publishers. A formal press release announced Frank Hamilton's new position, with a luncheon at Al and Dick's Steakhouse on Manhattan's West Side. Industry events were regular parts of the Weavers' schedule. But a Weavers luncheon still wasn't quite like any other.

Pete came down from Beacon for the symbolic exchange of banjos. But the party had an even more special guest: Woody Guthrie. Almost completely hospitalized and barely capable of speech, he'd been on a few outings lately with his ex-wife Marjorie, visiting his son Arlo at school in Stockbridge, Massachusetts. His mind perfectly alert, but his body almost fully uncooperative, communication was sometimes limited to blinking, and Marjorie would soon devise a system of cue cards.

Hamilton had previously played with Woody at Will Geer's place in Topanga Canyon, and—recognizing him again in New York—Woody could only greet him with a one-word, "California!"

It wasn't the usual first day on the job for a banjo player. And if the Weavers weren't quite pop musicians, they weren't quite folk musicians either, but a new form in between. Increasingly, they were recognized for the pioneers they were. Fred remained an on-call arranger and musician for A-list folk records, playing guitar on the 1961 debut of young singer Judy Collins, and appearing on the Chad Mitchell Trio's *Live at the Bitter End*. Tony Bennett recorded Fred's blues-pop "The Way That I Feel."

The Weavers were starting to earn mainstream recognition as pioneers. A *Billboard* cover story called out the trend of live albums, a concept radical outside the jazz world at the time of *The Weavers at Carnegie Hall* only four years earlier. Now, *The Billboard* pointed out, there were four different Carnegie Hall albums on the chart that particular week in late 1961: *Judy* [Garland] *at Carnegie*, *Belafonte at Carnegie*, the not-actually-recorded-at-Carnegie *Jimmy Reed at Carnegie Hall*, and the new Erik Darling edition of *The Weavers at Carnegie Hall* (with a few punched-in studio tracks of its own). Salty Jewish comedienne Belle Barth had a Carnegie Hall recording scheduled soon too. Live albums were catching on. There were nine on the charts, and thirteen more on upcoming release schedules. Jazz artists had utilized the form, but—as with some of their songs—it took the Weavers to bring it to the pop market.

DJs and other music industrialists tried to analyze the reason for the spike in popularity. "Deejay thinking is that the spontaneous nature of 'live performance' albums—with their applause and audience asides—sparks a livelier pace for a wax show," the article observed.

Or as Lee Hays might've told them: live music is people's music, capturing the sound of the human voice and instrumentalists unvarnished in front of an audience, not trapped like a ghost in an air-locked studio. As the '60s dawned, Lee and the Weavers were finally starting to get some real songwriting recognition too—and, more important, some money.

Both *The Billboard* and *The Cash Box* reported—likely from the same Howie Richmond–sourced press release—that Lee had songwriting credits on new albums from the Kingston Trio and Harry Belafonte, and Jimmie Rodgers had just had a hit with "Wreck of the John B." Lee would eventually note to Harold that he was perhaps the only Weaver that *didn't* have a hand in rearranging "John B" into its current state of bobbing harmonies and forward motion, but it was nice to have the checks.

After the Kingston Trio had done "Wimoweh," the song transmogrified again. A New York quartet called the Tokens turned the title chant into something like doo-wop, but their record company decided that Pete Seeger's ineffable and wordless arrangement could never sell. They contracted a lyricist, and—focusing on the tiny bit of melody that Solomon Linda had improvised in the studio—rearranged the song with a new lyric, based on the vague understanding of the song's title, and it became "The Lion Sleeps Tonight."

As a process, it was no more inauthentic than when Gordon Jenkins tried to capture "Tzena Tzena Tzena" in English, or how Pete and Lee and everybody turned Lead Belly's song about a cow into "Kisses Sweeter Than Wine." The Tokens' version went to number one and became a global phenomenon beyond anything the Weavers had ever known. In one version of the story, Beach Boys founder Brian Wilson was struck by the power of the song perhaps nearly as much as Erik Darling had been, having to pull off the road. Like others before, the Tokens' label initially tried to pass it off as an original but Howie Richmond got on it, earning the credit "based on a song by Paul Campbell" and many new royalties.

Though Pete insisted he signed his share over to Solomon Linda from the start, he was no less aloof about the actual mechanisms of royalties than when Ronnie had called him out a decade earlier. It would be many years before the

proper funds made their way to the family of "Wimoweh" songwriter Solomon Linda in South Africa, a mess still being sorted into the next century.

By 1962, it was a dozen years since their Decca debut, and the Weavers
machine powered a certain corner of folk music. Not everybody was buying
it. The hardcore young folkies who ran the *Little Sandy Review*, from the same
Minnesota cadre that produced Bob Dylan, sneered that the Weavers and
their second *Carnegie Hall* album were nothing but "folkum."

"They are able to play both sides off against each other and come out with
lots of money and much folk critical acclaim as well," they barbed. "They have
that sanctimonious, heavy-handed religiosity toward folk music and themselves: they wear peace songs on their sleeves and expect to be applauded
wildly for mere mention of World Peace or any such subject."

Perhaps so, but it was during the next year that Lee Hays became one of the
most-heard songwriters in the world, even if the song had been written over
a decade earlier, and had been considered too controversial for the Weavers to
sing. It was during the summer of 1962 when a new trio of Weavers fans
called Peter, Paul & Mary released their debut LP, and the album zip-zoomed
to the top of the chart, with a top-10 single to follow: "If I Had a Hammer."

It was a literal People's Song, its lyrics worked out on a piece of paper
during an executive meeting in 1949, part of a collaboration so intimate that
Pete and Lee could write a song without even speaking. After a discarded,
barely heard Weavers version, Pete had recorded it during his endless Folkways sessions at the height of the blacklist, putting it on an album cheekily
titled *Love Songs for Friends and Foes*. Now a young trio was taking it to the
toppermost, and soon so was a pop-rock singer named Trini Lopez.

It should have been the Weavers' time. They were part of a cause, too, back
in the public eye in early 1963, when the loyalty-oath question thrust them
into the national news yet again. A new ABC show called *Hootenanny* required that musicians pledge allegiance. They wouldn't have Pete, who'd been
responsible for introducing their show's title into the American lexicon. He
didn't meet commercial standards, the network claimed, which perhaps stung
even more.

But now there was a whole anti-*Hootenanny* movement, becoming grist
for the folk-pop mill, artists refusing to play the show. Joan Baez and Bob
Dylan and other emerging artists signed petitions against the networks'
passive-aggressive blacklisting. The Weavers, too, signed on in solidarity.
They even had a college show in New Rochelle canceled over the protest. By

that point, though, that was perhaps the easiest decision the group had made in years, to *not* perform somewhere.

There was a magical night during those years that Ronnie and Fred spent wandering the West Village, not far from the Vanguard, staying out in the giggling streets into the early-morning hours. The two old Camp Wo-Chi-Ca friends were experiencing a period of extreme turmoil in their shared professional lives, but the night had nothing directly to do with their duties as Weavers, nor even as musicians. But it wasn't unrelated.

Ronnie had been the instigator in some regard, and in that way, it was intimately connected to the Weavers' gradual unwinding, but mostly just life in general. The band had picked up touring with Frank Hamilton, with their usual engagements scheduled at the Music Barn and such, but she felt it all at a dead end. Not just the Weavers, but the world. It came falling over her like a shroud during the summer, convulsive tears, and a sequence of days where the normally effervescent Ronnie Gilbert just couldn't face the world. Nor could she bear the thought of now-traditional Freudian psychotherapy. "I don't want to get adjusted," so went the hymn that Lee Hays picked out for its "anti-psychiatric intent."

But an acquaintance recommended an experimental psychiatrist on the Upper East Side working with a new kind of therapy using LSD-25, the psychedelic compound discovered by chemist Albert Hofmann in Switzerland two decades earlier and used by doctors in a range of experimental treatments over the course of the '40s and '50s. Almost exactly concurrent to Ronnie's introduction to LSD, the substance was starting to leak onto college campuses and into various artistic and musical undergrounds, but remained legal and in the purview of psychiatrists like Dr. James Watt.

Ronnie couldn't help but observe what she recalled as "a serious record player" when visiting his office, and it was through this turntable that Ronnie stepped into the psychedelic world, listening as the music turned into "long satin ribbons, pale lavender and yellow swirling skirts, and festoons of bright brass buttons on vivid red jackets."

She opened her eyes to ask what the music was. *Sibelius*, she was told.

"Duck!" she cried out to her therapist. "Here it comes again!" The tears of laughter sent her into a delirious spiral of free association and visual language that led her into the serious questions of therapy. There were long discussions, journal entries, and letters to Watt—often written through multiple drafts—as

Ronnie worked through the worlds and sometimes grotesque scenes she encountered.

When her nine-year-old daughter asked what she was doing with this new doctor, Ronnie told Lisa, "He teaches me to remember how to have fun." Her daughter observed that her mother no longer got mad at minor household transgressions. From both their perspectives, life in general and their relationship got measurably better.

One evening, Ronnie was at home, not on the night of an LSD session, and all she wanted to do was *dance*. "I danced, really danced—like I've danced in my head for years," she told her doctor. "Like I just couldn't tire myself out. I only got happier, happier, happiest! Lisa didn't find it strange at all for some reason."

Ronnie and the doctor went for walks, the singer gasping at the wondrous fixed and impermanent architectures of Manhattan. Other times, he had trusted friends hang out during their sessions. And so it wasn't long afterward that Ronnie sat with Fred Hellerman as he tried LSD for the first time, listening to records and talking through the vivid worlds. She watched Fred struggle at first and thought of her latest session, the day before, which itself had been a difficult trip, fighting with words and where her mind took her. Sometimes the sessions or their comedowns would be paired with Indian classical music, a combination of sitars and psychedelics that pre-dated the Beatles by a few years.

Like Ronnie, Fred had a bundle of deep-seated issues. They were complicated, as they were for any human, related to family and life and deeper meanings and such. Fred's mind was capable of going to some dark places, which Ronnie might have known.

After the session, Ronnie and Fred headed toward the Village, where Fred lived, ending up by the Hudson River. "It was very calm and beautiful," Fred recorded. "Occasional flashes of orange heat lightning from New Jersey. Although I was getting more and more turned off, there would be surges of getting turned on again. For example, while sitting there and watching the water, I began to see thousands and thousands of white rabbits jumping around on the water."

He was glad that Ronnie was there, he noted, "largely because she was able to understand what I was experiencing and seemed to have her own 'being at one with it.'" When Fred decided that he wanted some food with a lot of *really interesting things* in it, the ever-game Ronnie was up for shish kebab with peppers and rice, and soon the two Weavers found themselves giggling and eating with their hands.

Subsequently, Fred would spend several years taking LSD with James Watt. As with Ronnie, nowhere in the voluminous sheath of session reports—including both their notes on their evening together—does the subject of the Weavers ever come up in more than a passing way. Whatever weighed on the group wasn't an issue about which either had any conflict. There was plenty else going on in their interiors.

After a year and change in Dr. Watt's psychedelic therapy program, Fred reported a substantial improvement in his general well-being. "The other night I walked into the Village Gate for Leon Bibb's opening," he noted in one document. "Saw [former Neighbors collaborator] Bob De Cormier, whom I hadn't really seen for quite some time. His comment to Harold: 'Gee! Freddie looks great! I've never seen him so relaxed.' This was said in the first minute after I walked in."

For both Ronnie and Fred, LSD was a revelatory and changing experience, steeling their cores for the years to come, putting Ronnie especially in touch with an ability to shift her life and creative paths with an elegant and enthusiastic fluidity. "I think I preferred you the other way," Lee would tell Ronnie sharply.

Neither would jump the barricades and join the rising psychedelic culture, and Fred especially likely looked down on it, but both Weavers were in their mid-thirties, and both had some of their most rewarding work ahead of them.

It happened like a movie there at Club 47 in Harvard Square. Bernie Krause was onstage in the middle of a set of Weavers parodies—"puerile," as he later described them. Perhaps it was "If I Had a Hammer (I'd Bash Your Fuckin' Head In)" he was playing when the twenty-three-year-old musician looked into the audience and saw Lee Hays sit down in the front row. Krause recognized him immediately.

The songs were topical in the sense that the Weavers were in town and Bernie was bored. Krause wasn't interested in seeing "America's Best-Loved Folk Singers," even if the local edition of *Broadside* did pronounce them their favorite group. He'd grown up on Pete Seeger's music, starting at summer camp in the People's Songs days, and seen the Weavers enough, starting with their 1955 comeback show at Carnegie Hall. But Bernie Krause was no Pete Seeger acolyte. By the time he got to college in the late '50s, "the buzz going around the folklore society was that things like the Weavers weren't terribly current," he remembered.

An eclectic listener and thinker, Krause had arrived in Boston as a post-grad to study communications systems at MIT, with jobs on the side working at WBZ radio and in the office of folk promoter Manny Greenhill. He loved folk music, but he loved jazz and blues and R&B and much else. When he'd briefly landed a music programming job at NBC Radio in New York, he'd lost it for playing too many black artists like Ray Charles and Nat King Cole. Other than his job with Greenhill, he wasn't really part of the Boston folk scene, though, mostly hanging in the jazz clubs.

Nor, for that matter, were topical songs his bag. The decision to play Weavers songs was only barely premeditated. "My parodies were mostly pretty stupid, it didn't even feel right to me," he remembered years later. "I was too lazy to even really think about. They were not really well-considered and not terribly funny, just gross. It caught Lee's attention only because it was so out of the ballpark." He hadn't announced it in advance, he'd just done it. And yet there was the baby-faced Bernie Krause and there was Lee Hays, Weavers eminence, who'd come across the Charles River to check out what was going on at Club 47, a rare post-show excursion for the bass singer.

"You're a wise guy," Lee told Bernie when he came offstage. He told him Frank Hamilton was preparing to leave the group. It'd only been a matter of months, but it wasn't a good fit. Relocating from Chicago with his family, Hamilton was going through a bad time outside the band, having a hard time adjusting to New York. "I left, basically because my personal life was in turmoil at that time," he would say, "and I wanted to go back to California where I thought my kids could have a decent lifestyle."

It is possible, too, that Lee Hays made his way to Club 47 to check out the night's main act, Keith and Rooney, featuring prodigy banjo player Bill Keith, who would soon make a contribution to bluegrass banjo playing forever known as "Keith style." Perhaps Hays missed Keith, and arrived during the open-mic part of the evening. However he got there, Lee invited Bernie to submit a demo tape for the soon open position. They struck up an affectionate correspondence, Bernie joining Lee's circle of younger friends. By early 1963, Bernie had made a demo tape in a local studio, paid for by Lee, and was in the running to be in the Weavers. He auditioned for Lee and Fred and Harold, meeting Ronnie later. There were other people scheduled, he remembers, perhaps Eric Weissberg, but they didn't cross paths. "It baffles me even today, I got the job," he said more than a half century later.

"That was a time when Lee was so grumpy and so disagreeable that we were willing to go with anything or anybody if it made him happy," Fred would admit in hindsight.

By early spring 1963, Bernie was headed to New York for his new job in what was now called "the Pete Seeger chair." Harold Leventhal had booked the band a two-night fifteenth-anniversary extravaganza at Carnegie Hall for early May, and it would include *all* of the Weavers banjo players. Bernie's addition wasn't announced yet, but word circulated in the folk press. "Pete Seeger and Erik Darling will appear with them," *Broadside* of Boston reported, around the time Bernie Krause landed at his new digs in Brooklyn, "plus a surprise." That was an understatement.

"I was paid 150 bucks a week living in New York, which is not terrific," Bernie said. "And so I couldn't really even afford an apartment at that time. So it was suggested to me by Harold that I should go and live with Lee Hays for a while."

For a moment, it was nice. After hearing him sing on a demo, Ronnie went over to meet Bernie. "[Lee] fussed like an old lady over his protegé [*sic*]," she noted with some affection in a journal. "It's love!" Bernie, too, thankfully, "turned out to be as likable as his voice."

But if it was an arrangement that Bernie didn't quite understand at first, he quickly grasped it. "Things got weird immediately with Lee and Harold," Bernie said. "I had no idea what I was getting myself into when I joined the Weavers. One of the reasons that I was asked to join is because I could probably handle the music, but I was hired because I was [to be] a caretaker for Lee Hays. It turned out that way. It was not my choice. That's what Harold had in mind and that's what Freddie had in mind."

Lee had moved out of the apartment on Cranberry Street a few years back, settling in a new place nearby, down the block from Alan Arkin. For an unattached Brooklyn bohemian with an occasional houseguest, the small apartment was the perfect arrangement. For forty-nine-year-old Lee Hays and now twenty-four-year-old Bernie Krause, the humor of the odd-couple situation drained almost immediately to borderline terror, with the new banjo player stashed in a tiny bedroom of the three-room 800-square-foot folknik bachelor pad.

"He was smoking all the time and drinking and being drunk," Bernie remembered of his new roommate. "Whenever I wanted to entertain my dates, he'd come stomping into the room unannounced, or without knocking or anything like that." The singer would hover awkwardly. "I had no privacy and couldn't concentrate," Bernie said. "I couldn't prepare for the performance scheduled for May. So I told Harold I had to get the fuck out of there."

Harold Leventhal was only somewhat sympathetic to the new Weaver's plight, but was able to send Bernie up to Beacon to stay with the Seegers for two weeks of Weaver training and nearly literal woodshedding, living in the barn. "[Pete] would get me up early in the morning to chop wood," Bernie recalled. "We talked about certain kinds of performance techniques on banjo and 12-string guitar that were unique to him." They talked political topics, too, and while they perhaps agreed on the broader issues, Bernie didn't exactly see eye-to-eye with Pete on the day-to-day strategies of the civil rights movement or folk-song-publishing rights.

"I was pretty much left to my own devices," Bernie said. "Pete had his own things that he was doing and he was very busy, and Toshi had hers, and left me pretty much in the barn alone to read and just stare at the Hudson River."

Soon, it was time for Bernie to head back to the terrifying situation in Brooklyn, though Pete did send him home with a custom long-neck Pete Seeger–model banjo, perfect for playing Weavers arrangements. And then it was back to Lee's place and the beginning of the group's rehearsals for the two nights at Carnegie Hall.

As expected, not everything ran smoothly. Pete brought his usual flaring energy and a batch of new songs. The group rejected his suggestion of a few by Bob Dylan. They didn't have enough of a group-singing element. They were too abstract. Pete tried to defend the abstraction to Lee, but gave up.

Other times, though, it all wove together as naturally as ever. Like "Tzena Tzena Tzena," Pete picked up "Guantanamera" on the summer-camp circuit, and it had an equally complicated songwriting lineage, causing the Weavers' publishers no small amount of trouble when it became a hit for the Sandpipers that year. It was one of those rare latter-day moments where the Weavers didn't have enough time to think about it and fell to what Fred called the "old way" of working: "Pete says, 'Hey! Here's a new song I learned,' begins playing 'Guantanamera' and we all fall in line."

Erik Darling was traveling a hard road in his quest for personal expression. Like Ronnie and Fred, he'd been gripped with deeper emotional questions. He would spend years grappling with deep depression, and his own experience with LSD that was nearly the polar opposite of theirs. But after splitting with the Weavers to work solo, he *did* find the number-one song knew he had in him. On "Walk Right In," Darling's one-off Rooftop Singers trio channeled the joyous jug-band craze, tightening the anarchic party music into a crisp arrangement for two twelve-string guitars and three voices. It scaled the chart and hit number one in early 1963.

Where Pete had offered Lead Belly songs and wood-chopping skills as his advice for a new Weaver, Erik offered his own suggestion to Bernie: *Atlas Shrugged*, by Ayn Rand.

"When I first met Erik, during rehearsals for Carnegie Hall, that was the one thing that he wanted me to read," Krause said. "He was greatly influenced by that horse shit. I said to Erik, 'this is *such a bad writer*.'"

"And he said, 'I don't know much about literature, since this is the only book I've read, but it's changed my life.'"

"I said 'okay.'"

With Pete on board, the tickets for the two shows sold incredibly well, a jolt of energy. They were all fresh from the *Hootenanny* non-spectacle, heroes to new generations of high school and college students. The shows included the first Weavers' performances of "The Hammer Song" since perhaps even before the Village Vanguard, and now known by its Peter, Paul & and Mary–era name, "If I Had a Hammer" and featuring (over Lee's objection) a new intersex chorus.

Erik and Frank, friends since long before their Weavers days, duetted on "San Francisco Bay Blues," their guitars playing "horn parts, like in a Dixieland band, not too tightly arranged," Darling remembered, and the song unfolded into a stumbling but inventive human free-flight. When the inevitable live album was made, Darling had to be talked into using the more imperfect but ecstatic version, a mind wound so tight that "part of me thought I was selling out artistic values under group pressure by even wondering if they were right."

After the shows, they were back to just Weavers again. Just over a month after the Weavers' two nights, Pete sold out Carnegie Hall as a solo performer, recording a new live album that included a pair of Dylan tunes, and set off for a year traveling the world, part concert tour, part family vacation. Frank Hamilton finished out another month of shows with the band before passing the banjo chair along to Bernie Krause once and for all.

For Bernie Krause, the nightmare continued. He eventually moved into his own apartment nearby Lee's, and continued to attempt a collaborative relationship, working on some proposals for commercials and some vague song ideas of Lee's. The awkwardness and Lee's weirdness continued unabated. Fred and Ronnie were too busy with their own lives to show much energy. Their joint LSD session was only a few days after Carnegie Hall.

"I think that what Lee was expressing was a profound inability to express himself sexually," Bernie observed. "And I think he was probably gay, and that was fine with me, I didn't care. But he was certainly not attracted to women. And so he surrounded himself with all these young people: Millard Lampell and Alan Arkin and me and others who passed through his life."

The group performed a small number of summer engagements, but it was simply getting harder and harder for them to operate, mainly because of Lee. It wasn't Bernie's fault that he'd entered into such a clearly twisted dynamic. But—as a rhythmic battery and novice banjo player—he could hardly provide the energy that Pete or Erik did. Musically, he had a hard time gelling with the rest of the band, who—he realized very quickly—were ready to be done with the Weavers, more interested in their own projects or their LSD therapy. Fred never took him seriously, Bernie could tell, nor made time for him as a musician, telling him to refer to the LPs for any questions about arrangements. Ronnie was unfailingly supportive, but that only went so far.

Bernie would go on to be a successful electronic musician and pioneer of soundscape recording, but his time with the Weavers was almost entirely fraught.

"Lee was hanging around drinking and calling Harold and complaining that we weren't doing concerts," Bernie recounted, "and then when we were doing concerts, he was complaining that it was too much work and that there was no time for rehearsal. And when we had rehearsals, he wouldn't show up." Occasionally, he would send dramatic telegrams announcing he had quit the band, and Harold would talk him down. Though the band conferred every night before they went on, writing out a new set list, the four Weavers never practiced together again after the initial prep for Carnegie Hall.

That summer was the Civil Rights March on Washington, where Peter, Paul & Mary sang "If I Had a Hammer" to an estimated quarter-million people gathered down the Mall. It never even entered onto the Weavers' radar that they might attend, individually or collectively. The battle raged, the country convulsing into transformation.

Sometime in the fall, the quartet played at a Connecticut college, taking a limo out from the city. As they entered the campus, they passed by clusters of protesters picketing their appearance. They'd been doing this for a long time now, even the former junior Weavers, Fred and Ronnie. They were very tired. Seeing the protesters and the dark fog that possessed them likely made them even more tired. A rock or two landed on the car's hood. Bernie felt pangs of fear, and looked to Lee. "All we have to do is outlive them," the elder Weaver told him soothingly.

By the fall of 1963, Harold Leventhal's office circulated a press release announcing that the band was dissolving due to Lee Hays's impending retirement, which was certainly news to Lee. He raged at Harold, spinning into deeper bitterness, trying to clench onto a last bit of the Weavers. He proposed weekly rehearsal sessions followed by a "final Final FINAL F*A*R*E*W*E*L*L CCOONNCCEERRTT!" at Carnegie Hall. "But later."

No one was biting. The Weavers were simply untenable. Nobody was happy. He performed the dates, but wouldn't speak to Harold for months.

It is also possible that around this time that Harold Leventhal performed calculations pertaining to the incoming royalties for Lee's songwriting now that "If I Had a Hammer" was a global standard and realized that Lee Hays was sitting on a retirement fund that might ease him from the pain of having to Answer the Question night after night and never hearing either the same way twice. With some irony, it was the very song written in support of Communist leaders that, run through the music industry, created enough lasting value to turn into food and beer and shelter for the rest of his days.

N ot that Pete Seeger *watched* a lot of television, but Pete Seeger was fairly obsessed with the glowing boxes that had spread into American homes, predominantly in full color by the mid-'60s. His first mission remained getting folk music, the real seed of every idea he held, into the homes of the United States.

"I'm doing my damnedest to get on network TV," he wrote in a *Sing Out!* column. "There are 200 million American people out there, all sizes, shapes, and colors. It would be a crime not to try to reach them."

He worked desperately to do so, writing rejected project proposals. He pioneered *Rainbow Quest*, a UHF-bound show that ran from 1965 to 1966 with an extraordinary array of guests from across the folk world, including Elizabeth Cotten, Mississippi John Hurt, Johnny Cash, Roscoe Holcomb, and many more—visual field recordings from the global village. But at the time, almost nobody saw it, buried as it was at the far end of an obscure dial in a limited number of cities.

In the summer of 1967, a pair of singing comedians called the Smothers Brothers—representing one show-biz extension of the Kingston Trio—invited Pete onto their primetime ABC show. He could sing "Wimoweh" as well as his new hit, "Waist Deep in the Big Muddy." Set in Korea, the song was impossible not to be heard as allegory for the raging Vietnam War. It was really going to happen. Pete Seeger was on network television in the United States, *in prime time*. The blacklist was over.

But nothing was ever that easy. He'd performed both songs, only to see "Big Muddy" sliced out of the program before it aired. It was happening again: more censorship, more fogs, more creeping creeps. Yes, he was singing against the Vietnam War—"*the big fool says to press on*"—but it wasn't just the Vietnam War, or the big fool, but all the fools, all the creeps, all the wars, all the obstacles humans put in the way of other humans. They let him back on not long thereafter. The mission was always the same.

This big fool hadn't started it, but one of them had. And there were others out there to stop yet.

CHAPTER NINE

This Too Shall Pass

Nine months after the expanded Weavers exited the Carnegie Hall and world stages, around the time Lee Hays's proposed FINAL F*A*R*E*W*E*L*L might've taken place, the Beatles entered. It was Carnegie Hall's first rock show, and the audience participation was a very different sort than Pete Seeger ever envisioned. A year later, in 1965, the Liverpudlian heirs to skiffle pioneer Lonnie Donegan played Shea Stadium, Bob Dylan plugged in an electric guitar at the Newport Folk Festival, Pete Seeger probably didn't threaten anybody with an ax, and the Weavers seemed to disappear from the folk dialogue. Absorbing the surrealistic machinations of Dylan and the raucous drive of rock, folk's new audience now seemed to prefer sounds with a roughness around the edges.

And yet, hoisting itself up the charts in 1966 was a new version of the "Wreck of the John B," a few chords and the title changed, recorded by the Beach Boys. The California band may have even tried a primitive version of it before they'd even landed on the idea of writing songs about surfing.

"I was interested in knowing more about folk music after discovering the Kingston Trio, and I found this album *Live at Carnegie Hall*," said Al Jardine, the Beach Boys' folkiest member. Like the Kingston Trio, where Jardine initially heard "Sloop John B," Jardine was "excited and absolutely dumbstruck by the quality of the recording and the quality of the songs." But what really shocked Jardine were the harmonies.

In the United States, great swaths of the musicians on the emerging California rock scene had gotten their starts via coffeehouses, music stores, songbooks, weekly hoots, and other standards of the folk world. The Weavers could be discerned audibly in many acts. For Paul Kantner of Jefferson Airplane, the Weavers turned him onto "the idea of people singing together and getting other people to sing along with them and to join them in their ideas and their joy of life," as he told writer Mike Greenhaus. It wasn't a singing *union*, but it was a new form of generational solidarity.

"Most importantly," Kantner noted another time, the Weavers taught him the value of "having an extremely powerful female singer."

And in Palo Alto in the early '60s, a pair of teenagers found a doorway into American music through the Weavers. Part of a suburban folk scene that included living-room hootenannies but also access to Kepler's Bookstore and the Peace Center, teenagers Jerry Garcia and Robert Hunter and their friends quickly sized up the locally rooted Kingston Trio as phonies, recognizing the blacklisted Weavers as authentic class- and history-conscious members of an emerging American counterculture, as real as the Beat writers they were starting to absorb.

The earliest recording of the future Grateful Dead songwriters captures the pair at the birthday party of Garcia's girlfriend, Brigid Meier. "The Weavers are back in town," someone jokes. The pair does a range of songs originally associated with Pete and Lee and company, including Lee's arrangement of "Follow the Drinking Gourd" and Hunter doing his best Pete bellow on "Oh Mary Don't You Weep."

"The Weavers songs weren't performances, that was really important," says Brigid Meier, "they were sing-alongs, so they helped coalesce this community. You didn't just sit there passively. That's a huge demarcation, when you're a participant." Robert Hunter was known to lead crowds in wonderful versions of "Wimoweh."

Also on the birthday tape is Garcia's version of "Wasn't That a Time," Lee's long-abandoned ¡no pasarán! verse resurrected from a songbook or other source. In the next half decade, the self-taught and open-eared Garcia would accelerate through the New Lost City Ramblers, Harry Smith's *Anthology*, Bill Monroe, Bill Keith, and hundreds of other sources and thousands of hours of practice. Plugging (back) in with the group that became the Grateful Dead, Garcia would both help define his own form of countercultural politics and, with Robert Hunter, contribute new modes to the American folk tradition.

But for many of the new musicians, the Weavers' politics were nearly invisible, despite the politics they would soon develop themselves, or in some cases were a cautionary tale. "There's just some point where you cannot confuse your musical image with your politics," said Al Jardine, who would become an environmental activist. "We learned that, probably, as a result of what happened to them."

Even for David Crosby, son of a preeminent blacklisted cinematographer, it was the Weavers' voices that drew him when his mother brought home a stack of 10-inch LPs during the band's first wave of success. "They were a really good harmony group!" says Crosby, who contributed to the three-part vocal weave of the Byrds with fellow Weavers-lover Roger McGuinn, who'd worked in the New York folk scene under his given name, Jim McGuinn. Though Crosby, especially, would connect music and activism, it was through a different kind of progressive politics. The future Crosby, Stills & Nash singer would maintain Pete was "wrong about Communism."

His Byrds bandmate Roger McGuinn had been a student of Frank Hamilton at Chicago's Old Town School of Folk Music, was a regular at the Weavers' performances at Orchestra Hall, and grew up playing a Vega long-neck Seeger-style banjo. When Pete came to teach a class, McGuinn watched in astonishment as Pete used a fellow student's inexpensive run-of-the-mill banjo. "He made it sound so incredible," McGuinn said in awe more than a half century later. "It was my first introduction [to the idea] that it's not the instrument, it's the instrumentalist."

Following their first number one with Bob Dylan's "Mr. Tambourine Man" in 1965, the band brought Pete back to the top of charts at the end of that year, recording his "Turn! Turn! Turn!," its lyrics adapted from phrases in the Book of Ecclesiastes. When it hit big, Crosby says, they got a letter from Pete, thanking them. "He said that he wasn't real popular around [Beacon] because he'd been a Commie," Crosby recalled. Just as the Byrds' new hit ascended the charts, local conservatives were protesting an appearance at a school near his New York home. But, Crosby reported, "now that 'Turn! Turn! Turn!' had come out, they were coming up to him and saying, 'Oh! Pete! You're wonderful! Lyrics from the Bible, pretty neat!'"

It didn't require a subcommittee to draw connections between the Weavers and the first crops of major '60s rock stars. If the quartet's particular styles of group singing and song arranging were no longer the dominant modes, the conversations around the Almanac Singers and People's Songs continued unabated into folk and rock magazines of increasingly larger circulations and with socially conscious musicians of all genres. Half-forgotten pioneers, the Weavers and their friends had been among the first to tap into this particular energy source: the power of music to unite, organize, and transform.

Skiffle could still be heard deep in the Beatles' Mersey beat and, even if Fred accepted neither Bob Dylan nor the barbaric Rolling Stones, he could still come to deeply appreciate John Lennon and Paul McCartney's songwriting, not to mention the finer pleasures of getting stoned and listening to *Sgt. Pepper's Lonely Hearts Club Band*.

That same Summer of Love, Fred found himself working with a Guthrie again, producing twenty-year-old Arlo's *Alice's Restaurant,* an eighteen-minute "anti-stupidity" story-song in the finest Guthrie tradition. Decaying with almost infinite slowness in a hospital, Woody himself passed away a month after his son's debut was released, just as the song's jingling chorus was entering the counterculture lexicon.

The proceeds from the collaboration allowed Fred to buy a house and build a recording studio of his own. He'd married Susan Lardner, *New Yorker* "Talk of the Town" writer, from a family that was literary and blacklisted in equally serious measure. They migrated out to Weston, Connecticut, near Harold Leventhal's place, and soon started a family. Though he would stay musically active, Fred also took a desk at Harold's office, joining the Weavers' manager in the financial and mechanical gear work of the folk-song universe. By the end of the '60s, he and Harold were running a group of publishing companies together, Fred following in his father's entrepreneurial footsteps. Their office in the Fisk Building became a magnet for folkies and comedians.

When Arlo starred in a feature adaptation of *Alice's Restaurant* in 1968, he drafted Lee Hays into service as the actor he always was, playing an itinerant preacher. It was a rare emergence for the ex-Weaver. The years since the band's dissolution had been especially hard on Lee, perhaps even harder than he anticipated. It was a time of stalled-out projects. In the early '60s, he'd taped endless interviews with his and Woody's old pal Cisco Houston, and over the next decade tried and repeatedly failed to shape them into something usable.

Recording a final Babysitters album around the same time in a studio at New York's Chelsea Hotel—with Willens, Leventhal, and Arkin kids on board—they did not cross paths with Leonard Cohen or any other of the other new folk cognoscenti. Alan Arkin soon moved on to a wildly successful acting career, first as a part of Second City in Chicago and later in Hollywood, bringing Lee along to hang out during his first major role in *The Russians Are Coming, The Russians Are Coming*. Besides that, Lee made starts and stops at songwriting and demo-making, occasionally discussing potential collaborations with correspondents, such as middlebrow pop-poet Rod McKuen.

He worked, too, on what he called (in typical Lee fashion) his "posthumous memoirs," sometimes typing, sometimes rambling into a tape recorder, sometimes trailing off to drunkenness. Always a drinker, his alcoholism manifested itself more visibly to his friends when there were no more Weavers or blacklists to occupy Lee's time. In 1968, he joined Pete and others onstage at the Newport Folk Festival for a tribute to Woody, but that was the last time he would perform in public for many years. He ceased publishing his newsletter.

By then, though, Lee Hays had finally found his place. Along the river in Croton-on-Hudson, twenty-five miles south of Pete and Toshi Seeger, Lee Hays literally retired to a street called Memory Lane, steps away from People's Song–era roommate Harold Bernz. A town so steeped in progressive culture that one of its landmarks was Red Hill, once home to Communist journalist John Reed, Croton was the green and leafy sanctuary that Lee craved when escaping the confines of the city. For the first time in his life, Lee owned a home of his own, purchased with his earnings from "If I Had a Hammer" and other windfalls, and orchestrated entirely by the saintly Harold Leventhal, arranging a $2,500 guarantee per year from BMI—a partial retirement fund for his years in service of popular music, gathering songs, and generally being Lee.

Moving to Croton, his retirement was total, and if it wasn't fulfilling in the traditional creative ways that late life might be, he would find a new mode of being, transforming easily into the old man he'd been waiting to be all along. A perfectly sedate and heavily Jewish village along the Hudson with curly headed kids on bikes and a picture-book Main Street, the progressive Croton was home to a thriving teen musical culture.

"I remember him showing up with a folding chair," said Jim Brown, then a seventeen-year-old musician playing in a jug band at the local park a few blocks from Lee's new digs. The Weaver introduced himself, and invited the gang over to hang out. Lee's place became, once again, a center for a new crop of friends far younger than him. "He had good stories," said Brown, who helped Lee tend to his new garden, and would hang out and watch television and drink beer with Lee after. "And when his friends showed up, *they* had great stories. I learned a lot."

Lee found a kind of peace in his small bungalow with a garden in Croton, mentoring a generation of neighborhood youth. A settlement on his own terms, it was a reckoning, too, making peace with old friends turned enemies. Or not, as with "Wasn't That a Time" coauthor Walter Lowenfels, whom Lee often insisted had little to do with the song's writing, despite the recollections of Pete and others. But, now, living not far from Peekskill, he came to accept that he and others misjudged those who'd attacked them, calling them "Fascists." They weren't quite that. They were just scared Americans.

A fatalistic hypochondriac to the bone as he approached the age of sixty, Lee preferred a quieter path. "Life is fairly simple," he wrote to Harold. "I go to bed when tired, arise when rested, eat when hungry, drink when dry, and if a tree don't fall on me, I'll live till I die."

Pete, still flying at the pace of a manically frailed banjo, would occasionally dispense with letters, gently encouraging his former songwriting partner to return to some sort of minimal action in the peace army, suggesting lines of songs he might use as starting material.

He tried to be optimistic and helpful, ever Pete. Though Lee was once again civil with the banjo player, he'd certainly never forget the three different careers Pete had "shot out from under him," in the Almanac Singers, at People's Songs, and in the Weavers.

"I think what is needed is a Croton Folk song club of some sort for you to keep singing with friends," Pete suggested another time. "Take care of your health, this is just your Thursdical."

Ronnie rolled her eyes when an LP showed up in her house with a dedication. *To Ronnie Gilbert: a woman who knew how to sing and what to sing about.* By the early '70s, Ronnie was done with new music. She thought most people got the Weavers all wrong anyway. She wrote to Lee after hearing a documentary about them on a public radio station in Berkeley, where she'd moved, bristling at the characterization in which "you and Pete were the Yin and Yang, Fred was the Pencil, and I was the Voice."

"Shall I consider that a cut above The Femme, The Chick and the Thrush?" she added parenthetically. "It feels much the same."

The Weavers had been a collective endeavor, each with their own roles that were rarely easily characterized. Pete and Lee had been the senior voices and forces, certainly, with worlds of experience to offer, but they were hardly the only Weavers involved in creative decision-making. "Did you know that Fred wrote our arrangements?" Ronnie asked Lee. "How come no one told me. . . ."

She'd kept recording and performing for a few years after the band's dissolution, the only original Weaver besides Pete to pursue a performing career, forming both a friendship and working bond with guitarist Sam Brown. Released at the height of the folk boom, 1964's *Alone with Ronnie Gilbert* continued her assured jazz-folk fusion and Weavers-weaned sense of good taste, singing new material by Phil Ochs and Bob Dylan, a pre-Byrds version of "Turn! Turn! Turn!," and a trio of songs by F. Hellerman. She'd kept up with the scene, picking up on the excellence of Simon and Garfunkel's "Sounds of Silence" before producer Tom Wilson added overdubs and turned it into a hit. Ronnie performed out in New York for a while, but her heart was less and less in it. The theater called, and her career there blossomed.

But by 1970, she was done with that, too, for the moment, her energies shifting again. She relocated to the Bay Area, though it did nothing to stem the fogging depression. Becoming involved in Arthur Janov's experimental primal-scream therapy, Ronnie Gilbert's force-of-nature voice now found a way to access a space even more hardwired than music.

"Music interested me, so I sang," she would say, "Theater interested me, so I acted; therapy interested me, so I practiced therapy. Doing these things woke up stuff in my imagination, and when I pushed it a little they became vocations."

Soon enough, she departed the primal-therapy movement, earning her master's in clinical psychology and moving into her own practice as a therapist, fitting right into the Northern California landscape of progressive, open-minded practitioners with her experience with socialism, LSD, group singing, group screaming, and other radical ideas. By the time her daughter brought home Holly Near's *A Live Album*, with its dedication to Ronnie, the former Weaver was preparing for a new adventure, and music played no direct part in it. At age forty-nine, Ronnie was getting ready to relocate to deep British Columbia, build a new practice, and—in the tradition of Pete and Toshi Seeger—a new home.

But then here was this record, which—to her surprise—Ronnie quite enjoyed. Holly Near was no folk singer, at least in the sense that her music wasn't about strummed guitars, but it grew from a space that lay between social awareness, deep personal empowerment, and singer-songwriter expression. Based out of Ukiah, California, north of the Bay Area, she and Ronnie soon met up. Near apologized for thinking Ronnie was dead, a sign of how completely the '60s had erased the Weavers from popular culture.

Beginning as an antiwar songwriter, Near was a leader of a burgeoning women's music movement. A new age of independence dawned over the '70s, musical scenes and countercultures seizing the mechanisms of production, and Near and her friends—almost all women—did just that, establishing

Redwood Music and a network of festivals and venues. En route to her years in the non-figurative wilderness, Ronnie was astounded and deeply moved by both the breadth and depth of the music and dance she witnessed.

Pete Seeger had been right about the power of song as an organizing tool, and the model multiplied, a basic toolset of the media landscape. Music and art weaponized in countless new ways. Counterculturalists like Detroit's Trans-Love Commune (with its flagship band, MC5) and New York's Yippies repurposed the concept of People's Music, reborn as a modern folk culture in the global village.

Concerns and conversations once arcane in *People's Songs* bulletins were now commonplace, music was used for nearly every social (and commercial) purpose imaginable, from the overtly political and symbolic Jamaican reggae that arrived on American shores in the early '70s to the on-the-beat journalism of hip-hop. There were commune-dwelling punks of every Socialist/Anarchist stripe and avant-garde protest conceptualists, radio pirates and hyperlocal music movements, protesters who jettisoned songs entirely and protested with pure sound. Sometimes their stories could be packed and polished into neat shapes that Pete Seeger could recite like a parable.

Pete himself could often be seen a-sail on the Hudson River aboard the sloop *Clearwater*, bearded as of his fortieth birthday and looking more and more the part of veteran Messiah. A re-creation of an eighteenth-century Dutch river-craft, the *Clearwater* was built to raise funds and consciousness to help clean up the Hudson. When first launched, the floating environmentalist project sailed the Northeast, Pete and company performing in harbors and acting as the boat's crew. More manageable efforts prevailed, notably the annual Clearwater Festival, established in permanent form by 1978.

Moving comfortably back into the folk underground, Pete recorded his last album for a major label in 1979, the end of his service on that particular battlefront. Produced by Fred Hellerman at Fred's home studio in Connecticut, *Circles and Seasons* was neither folk nor quite pop, mixing Pete's sensibilities with Fred's most tasteful arrangements, a glockenspiel here or an electric bass there. Fred sang with Pete, too, on many tracks. One other production trick the album contained was the presence of Ronnie Gilbert, harmonizing with two of her three former Weaver partners on the album-closing "Allelulia/ Joy Upon This Earth."

She wrote to Lee about it. "It was wonderful to sing with [Pete] and Fred" at an Abraham Lincoln Brigade luncheon in New York. "But F. Hellerman in a studio as a record producer [during the session for Pete's album] frying with tension, I can do without."

There'd been talk of Ronnie coming to New York to perform at another one of Pete's regular events, the Thanksgiving concert at Carnegie Hall, a continuation of the People's Songs holiday hoots and the Weavers' own Christmas concerts. Up in Croton, Lee Hays was roused. If he didn't exactly come charging down Red Hill like a bull moose, the Weaving signal was too much to ignore. But despite Lee's commitment to what he called his "dignified silence," life was even more complicated than usual. His Thursdical was coming to an unusual end.

"I'm Lee Hays, more or less," he'd taken to introducing himself. It had started with his small toe, amputated in 1972, and then his left leg in 1975, finally his right in 1978. An advanced hypochondriac with chronically bad health habits, Lee's late-stage diabetes was diagnosed just after he turned sixty, a hard-lived folk life catching up to him. His young extended family continued to tend his garden, and now helped him adjust to a new phase of existence, installing wheelchair ramps throughout the house.

But life in the bungalow on Memory Lane grew wilted and smaller. The substantial bass singer shrunk in physical stature and ambition and became even more depressed, "suicidal almost," in the words of his friend Jim Brown. He continued smoking, drinking, and plying himself with sweets.

Singing with the Weavers again required patience and negotiation, as Lee Hays often did. First he wanted to beam into Carnegie Hall via video. Jim Brown, his young friend, had become a television producer. Easily enough it turned into a proposal for a documentary, *The Weavers: A Living Room Reunion*, with the idea of bringing the quartet together at Lee's place to discuss their career, sing a few songs, and get it onto public television.

The first step, though, was for the rest of the Weavers to get on board. "Harold has heard the proposal and likes it and you will undoubtedly see it soon (when Harold tells each of the 4 that the other 3 have agreed)," Lee wrote to Pete. Lee was to write a script to build the film around. They scheduled a day in Croton for May 1980, and—just as during their formation in 1948—Lee pulled himself out of his torpor. He quit smoking, did vocal exercises, even push-ups. Lee's low vibrating spirit began to hum back to audible levels.

The Weavers' letter-writing network activated itself and, before a note was sung, the Weavers had re-formed, picking up directly with all the comradeship and fraught dialogue they'd long ago put aside. With group letters distributed via the Leventhal office, where Fred continued to work as a song publisher, the new round of Weavers conversation included both the mechanics of their upcoming reunion, but—with Lee's health so precarious, with so many years gone by—also reflections, reckonings, and wounds accidentally reopened.

Fred compared the band to a "good marriage," adding "I consider that the Weavers did have a good marriage for a long time." It was, Fred wrote, "a sharing, an intimacy, a reservoir of common viewpoints, attitudes, secrets, private jokes that allow for a great deal of unspoken-ness. . . . It's getting up from the table at a dinner party and announcing that it's time to go <u>knowing</u> that my wife feels the same."

But not all Weavers remembered their musical youth in quite the same way. "I hate to say it, Fred," Ronnie bristled, "but your description of how you leave a dinner party reminds me of nothing so much as how pissed and pained I used to feel at your unilateral decisions and pronouncements. They in fact rarely represented my opinions, wishes or needs . . . although you used to seem to think they should." And so the Weavers restrung.

Tensions aside, the quartet remained generally supportive of one another, especially Lee. Though inspired, Lee needed extra-special attention. "I sure as hell ain't going to make it through this one without a lot of extra energy from you, mainly," he wrote to Pete. "I hope you have got it to spare." As usual, Pete did.

Much of the time, it brought out the best in them and the plan escalated to a backyard picnic for their family and friends, scheduled for a May day in 1980. Flipping through scrapbooks and running down songs around Lee's living-room table, the inside jokes emerged quickly, marriage or no. When they tried out "Irene," Pete imitated Gordon Jenkins's violin arrangement and everybody broke into laughter. They soon found themselves in the soft-reflected green of an adjoining backyard on Memory Lane belonging to former People's Songster Harold Bernz. Sitting around a table, they cleared their throats and began "When the Saints Go Marching In."

"We are traveling in the footsteps of those who came before," they announced again, and by now the trail extended in both directions, links in a chain, back to Woody and Lead Belly and Aunt Molly and Joe Hill, and off into visible and unseen futures, through musicians they admired and musicians of which they were unaware. Even within the space of a generally liberal epoch that had bloomed in the '60s, cycles of counterculture and politics had risen and fallen like miniature civilizations with their own social orders and musical expressions, but all still fought common enemies of stupidity and racism and oppression and all the dark, looming forms behind the veil.

Like the songs, the enemies remained the same, almost literally. As the Weavers assembled for their picnic in Croton, former California governor Ronald Reagan was pulling ahead in the Republican presidential primaries, sweeping through the South with the same anti-Communist fervor he'd displayed as a Hollywood FBI informer in the 1940s. His ascent marked a new phase in the Cold War that had begun concurrently with the Weavers' formation.

Now, in the Bernzes' backyard, they sang for the same reasons they always sang, regardless of what compelled them to assemble, the forces and spirits in their voices undiminished. It was a beautiful day for all. There was a world to change, as usual, and they'd long since settled on their methods, their joined voices harmonizing, the overtones rising into the sky like loose vibrating particles of change, and out into the universe at large.

Pete was overjoyed. Lee could do it, he knew, and made sure Lee knew it too. What had happened in the Bernzes' backyard wasn't merely a picnic but a rehearsal. Lee would perform at Carnegie Hall, he was sure, as part of the Thanksgiving show, if only for a few songs. Lee resisted and continued to work on his script for Jim's film, but finally he gave in, accepting that the Weavers would gather officially again onstage. The letter writing accelerated. Lee wondered if "The Hammer Song" still worked at all, and ordered an Esperanto dictionary to see if he might be able to rewrite some lines.

"I vocalize every day and I sound about as mellow as an old rooster," Lee noted to Pete. As always, he was unsatisfied with the ending to "Wasn't That a Time" and wrote more new verses. They all had their own hopes for the projects, most of them tied gently to a sense of closure. Ronnie brought up Erik Darling, but he was far away, in his own new life. She hoped that the film could let her absolve the guilt "over the error of my ways for pushing us into tuxes and gowns—not because our previous garb was more working class, as Pete used to argue, but because dressing like showbiz acceptees was silly and conformist and pleased nothing but my Greedy-'50s little heart!"

By the time tickets went on sale, one Carnegie Hall show had turned into two and it was now billed as the Weavers. They had a week and a half of rehearsals scheduled for the fall at Lee's house to adjust what loose threads they could. It didn't quite work out smoothly.

Neither of Pete and Lee's new efforts took. One they rehearsed endlessly, not getting it. "We simply couldn't get the song to catch fire," Ronnie remembered. "But we needed material that would relieve the nostalgia and show that we still had a lively interest in the world."

She pulled out a tape of Holly Near's most recent album, *Imagine My Surprise!*, in which the Weavers-inspired songwriter had tackled a wide range of contemporary issues with an eclectic and modern variety of approaches. Ronnie cued up the last two songs, the haunting "Hay Una Mujer Desparecida" and "Something About the Women," to a fully impassive reaction from her bandmates. It crushed her. Lee kvetched about learning the Spanish. The song had too many chords, Fred fretted. Pete didn't think it was for them.

The next day, both Pete and Fred arrived at rehearsal with arrangements. They'd come around to the haunting "Hay Una Mujer" (as it became known on the Weavers' recording), a memorial for disappeared Chilean women. No one besides Ronnie was quite satisfied with "Something About the Women," with Fred stonewalling Ronnie when she prodded him to open up, but they performed it anyway. A new Hellerman composition, too, written on the set lists as "Fred's Lullaby," was a recent song about his young son Caleb: "Tomorrow Lies in the Cradle." By one estimate, they had nearly two hours of material ready to go for the two shows.

And if Lee's new songs weren't going to make it to the stage, his new song introductions certainly would. At the center of the movie-in-progress, the Weavers' reunion shows in 1980 were very much about the earthly and earthy presence of Lee Hays. He prepared new stage patter. "It has often been said," pause, "by me," he would announce: "The future ain't what it used to be: and what's more it never was."

When they day arrived, the logistics went off as planned, getting Lee to the city, where he hadn't been since having his toe amputated eight years earlier. "His mind was terrific and his sense of humor was terrific," Jim Brown said, "but we were all afraid he was going to have a heart attack and die. His doctors were there and encouraged him to do [the show]."

The film crew interviewed folk luminaries in the audience, including Mary Travers and Arlo Guthrie. The tapes rolled; on the second night, the cameras filmed; the Weavers sang.

A few weeks before the shows, Ronald Reagan had run away with the American presidential election, defeating Jimmy Carter and confirming the newest situation. Lee tried out variants in his drafts for the stage banter: "Democracy gives us a choice of which machine to vote with," ran one dark turn. "Or choose which brand of razor blades," ineffable pause, "you'd rather cut your throat with."

He went with one that ran toward the more cosmic: "This too shall pass," he said of the oncoming Reagan years. "I've had kidney stones and I should know."

Lee Hays remained a Weaver until the end. They would play one more time. Pete wanted them to sing at the fourth version of his Clearwater Festival, just down the road from Lee's, at Croton Point Park. And, as soon as they agreed to do that, the agonized decision making began anew, hilariously on cycle. It is what made them alive.

Since they had no time to meet up beforehand, they would bill the show as a public rehearsal, sitting around with a songbook in the afternoon and hoping people would sing along, much as they had at the Photo League, before they'd broken big at the Village Vanguard. Then there was the heated discussion about whether they'd allow the show to be taped for broadcast. Oy.

"I might have a few words to say, if I can figure out which local institutions to insult," Lee promised the *New York Times*. Holly Near joined them onstage and Lee and his friends sang out freedom one last time on the banks of the Hudson. Lee was gone two months later.

The singing didn't stop, which is what Lee would have wanted, not that it seemed to do much good in the early 1980s—but why would that ever stop Pete Seeger? It continued to foster and nurture communities. And the Hudson River got appreciably cleaner thanks to his efforts. When Jim Brown's documentary was released in 1981, now titled *Wasn't That a Time*, it became a staple of PBS affiliates across the country, a solid fund-raiser during pledge drives in the age of video stores. When it screened, it beamed the Weavers, their singing, their songs, Lee's stories, and beautiful folk music into homes across the country, just as Pete and Lee always wanted.

But that was hardly the end for the Weavers. Relocating to an apartment near Manhattan's Tompkins Square Park, Ronnie had begun touring and recording with Holly Near. She slid happily into the womyn's folk revival, all-female crews connecting a circuit of festivals, clubs, theaters, publications, labels, and listeners. The two joined Pete and Arlo Guthrie on tour in 1984, billed as HARP, an acronym for their first names. They did Weavers standards like "Wimoweh" and "Oh Mary Don't You Weep" and expanded their repertoires further, something like an updated version of the group, releasing a live album the following year. It was during this tour, too, that Ronnie fell in love with a woman nearly twenty years her junior, moving with joy and surprising ease into another new life.

There were more semi-Weavers performances too. In 1988, Doris Willens—Lee's onetime neighbor and collaborator in the Babysitters—completed her biography of him, *Lonesome Traveler*, and Pete, Ronnie, and Fred returned to the Village Vanguard to celebrate its publication. Even without Lee, though, there could still be well-considered friction about the band's repertoire. This time it was Ronnie, sitting out "Wasn't That a Time" itself. There was no discussion, though, other than the simple drama of removing herself when Pete struck it up.

The hyper-male lyrics didn't sit well with her. "It starts out, 'Our fathers bled at Valley Forge,'" she later pointed out, "so that was what we had at the time . . . [we] had clichés about humanity . . . which always were masculine. Whenever it was that kind of statement, it was masculine, and all of the songs were like that."

But that only began a new conversation between Ronnie and Pete, with Pete proposing a rewrite of the verses in a letter to Ronnie.

"I love that you're taking on the problem of this song which has been so central in our lives, certainly yours," she wrote him. She had some verses of her own, and proposed one.

> *"Our fathers bled," we always say*
> *And never give a thought*
> *To all the women raped and slain*
> *In wars their fathers fought*

The weaving continued into the twenty-first century, finally winding down for real more than a half century after it started. Pete had handed his Carnegie Hall concerts over to Arlo Guthrie not long after the Weavers' 1980 reunion, though he returned frequently.

In 2003, the younger Guthrie staged a tribute to eighty-four-year-old folk management Buddha Harold Leventhal. The Weavers would be there, joined for the first time since 1963 by Erik Darling, with Pete's former student Eric Weissberg taking up the bass parts. The Weavers played last, and the all-star show ran overtime. The band bombed from a musical perspective, at least in Darling's estimation.

In the next year, they would get one more try, playing in Toronto, of all places, for the opening of a new documentary about their former manager, directed by Jim Brown. This time, they did it right. Pete's voice had long since shattered beyond repair, still good for song-leading, but far past the ability to hit the high notes in "Wimoweh" or elsewhere. Erik stepped in, singing for his life, reaching a whole tone above his highest note at the end of the song for an extra harmonic explosion.

"It was like reaching for hope, or survival, or destiny," he would write. Pete noticed, as he always did. "These people cared about life in a way that was truly electric, but without electric guitars," Erik observed. It was the closure he needed. They all kept singing, Pete and Fred together on occasion until 2010, even. Fred, too, stayed in the gear work, continuing to commute to the office, performing on occasion, and working happily on an album of beloved vaudeville songs, entirely sung, arranged, and performed by him, with intricate and playful electronic arrangements, eventually released as *Caught in the Act*.

Pete Seeger, meanwhile, got shot out into the main arena of culture again when Bruce Springsteen recorded an album of wildly reconceived songs associated with Pete, entitled *We Shall Overcome: The Seeger Sessions*, pulling a Grammy, and another new audience for Pete. "Bruce blew my cover," Pete remarked.

But the horizon and the visionary cities kept rising and falling on the hills, each a different shape with a different set of architects and a different set of goals. There was often music. Pete Seeger wasn't far behind. When Barack Obama was inaugurated in 2009, there was Pete right next to Springsteen in front of the Lincoln Memorial, raspily leading the crowd in "We Shall Overcome," just as he had led crowds of protesters during the second Gulf War a half decade earlier, and the first Gulf War a decade before that. And when the Occupy movement claimed territory on Wall Street and elsewhere in 2011, manifesting temporary autonomous zones to protest the whole entire system, Pete was right there marching and singing with them, the People's Microphone echoing and amplifying his ninety-two-year-old voice.

The chaos wrought by Pete's aloofness continued to surface in the twenty-first century, too. The "Wimoweh" argument had burped along for years, and emerged again into the open when South African author Rian Malan wrote a long article in *Rolling Stone* in 2000 on the injustices of the song known to much of the world as "The Lion Sleeps Tonight." Pete's transliteration had most recently been heard in Disney's mega-musical *The Lion King*. He continued to struggle with the consequences of what he'd ignored in the early 1950s, until Ronnie had to virtually ask him to unsubscribe her from further letters on the matter.

Ronnie's politics had grown blunter and, in a way, moved even further to the left as she'd grown older. As the new century dawned, she'd joined the Women in Black, a radical street theater troupe, and found herself yet again experiencing a look-see from the FBI. It was all too familiar.

If the Weavers themselves perhaps fell into the far mists of pop music and social-justice histories, the songs they chose to sing certainly didn't. But it was never about the Weavers. It was about the singing along, the harmony and the connection. It was the space between the threads; the singing, not the song or the singers. It wasn't about the Weavers, but the weaving.

Erik would pass in 2008, Pete in 2014, Ronnie in 2015, and Fred in 2016, the links becoming part of the chain. And in the second decade of the twenty-first century, music and activism seemed more tied together than ever, a self-reinforcing chain under constant Question-and-Answering, just as Lee would've wanted. One decision Pete might have supported came in 2018, when "We Shall Overcome" returned to the public domain. Publishing had reached a (somewhat) more civilized age, with songs being less exploitable than they once were, and Alan Lomax's paternalistic copyright practices gradually disappeared.

For the Weavers, the Questioning would remain built into their existences —thoroughly modern humans who happened to be born in the first part of the twentieth century. Into the '90s and Pete's seventies, he and Ronnie continued to exchange occasional verses for "Wasn't That a Time." FBI file-keeping on Pete had stopped long ago, not that it would have ever stopped him from exchanging new verses for the congressionally investigated song on open postcards.

They are perfectly normal sentiments now, formerly considered on the far-out fringe. Still, some of his new lyrics about bloody wars and the planet's end might have raised the brows of any curious eyes scanning the cards between Beacon and Berkeley. But they *had* to save the planet. Now was the time, the Subject knew, dashing off one more tightly written postcard to the Weaver he'd known for fifty years, sharing one more hopelessly hopeful dream in song. It was definitely worth further investigation.

ACKNOWLEDGMENTS

First and foremost, enormous loving thanks to my mother, Jill Stamberg Jarnow, for soundtracking my childhood with Pete Seeger and the Weavers, a perfect first musical doorway, and for bringing me to an early theatrical screening of Jim Brown's *Wasn't That a Time*.

Bottomless thanks to my sweetheart Caitlin for semi-willing cohabitation in book jail.

To all other family members: Al Jarnow and Lizzie Crowley, Peter Stamberg and Paul Aferiat, Allen Farbman, plus all assorted Potters and Dembiecs.

And especially to my late grandmother Lois, who faced down blacklisting supermarketer Laurence Johnson in the 1940s, and—in her nineties—made sure I knew about his defeat at the hands of John Henry Faulk; and who still swooned over Paul Robeson.

Praise be to my editor, Ben Schafer, and my agent, Paul Bresnick, for believing in the power of a good sing-along. Many thanks, as well, to Justin Lovell and Lissa Warren at Da Capo, and big acknowledgments to production editor Michael Clark, copyeditor Rachelle Mandik, indexer Kate Bowman, cover designer Kerry Rubenstein, interior designer Cynthia Young, and anyone else who contributed to making this book into an object.

Proper respect to those who've written about the Weavers before me (see Sources), but extra-special thanks to the generous Ron Cohen, who—in addition to his scholarship—pointed me in many new directions, opened many new paths, and patiently addressed queries and helped with the manuscript. Likewise to Dave Samuelson, who helped clarify many finer points of Weavers, folk, and pop-culture history, in addition to checking over my work.

Much gratitude to Lisa Weg and Caleb Hellerman for their help, hospitality, and willingness to delve into their respective family histories and boxes of papers, and to graciously try to answer perhaps unanswerable questions about their parents' work.

Love to Barry and Judy Ollman for a hair-raising tour of the magical mystery paper trails. Thank you to Brian Miksis and Dennis McNally for providing the Garcia connection.

Big ups to every institution that aided in research, as well as to their respective librarians and archivists and benevolent keepers: Cecilia Peterson at the Ralph Rinzler Folklife Archives and Collections at the Smithsonian, David McMullin at the Performing Arts branch of the New York Public Library (and all those who maintain the digital microfilm scanners), Aaron Smothers at the Southern Folklife Center at UNC.

For proper introductions, technical assistance, and more: Robbie Lieberman, Spud, Scott Bernstein, Amir Bar-Lev.

For incredible aid in tracking down usable images from many decades ago: Richard Weize, Mychael Gerstenberger, Michael Randolph, Bobby Ward, Kim Barth.

Secret Buddhas of the underground, forging connections and opening doors: Steve Silberman, Mitch Blank.

For travel cheer: Tyler Wilcox, Zac Cohen, Joe Beef, Ned W. Lagin.

Colleagues/comrades/editors: Mark Richardson, Jeremy Larson, and RJ Bentler; David Lemieux and Ivette Ramos; Caryn Ganz, Dave Mandl, Judy Berman, Dominic Umile, Patrick Doyle, Mike Greenhaus, Pete Shapiro, every present/past comrade DJ at WFMU (especially those who filled in for me while I was on Weaving duty: Sasha Jones, David Suisman, Mary Wing, Amanda Nazario, Joe Duffy), Sean Howe, Corry Arnold.

All united abetters, pals, and adventure providers: the Sloppy Heads fam, Bill and Gabby, Ariella and James; Georgia, Ira, Joe Puleo, Kurt Wagner and Lambchop; Lisa Jane Persky and Andy Zax, John Colpitts, Joel Berk, Jack Chester, Matt Van Brink, Mark Suppes, Frode Stromstad, Andy Battaglia, Tyler Roy-Hart, Rick Harris.

And finally to the Weavers, who knew how to sing and how to get others to, as well: Ronnie Gilbert, Lee Hays, Fred Hellerman, and Pete Seeger; Erik Darling, Frank Hamilton, and Bernie Krause. And, of course, Harold Leventhal.

SOURCES

For a pop band with a string of enormous singles, a run-in with the government, and a later reemergence, the Weavers often seem to exist only on the periphery of other cultural narratives about the Red Scare, folk music, and even Pete Seeger himself. So ubiquitous throughout the 1950s and into the early 1960s (and at affordable prices in used LP bins ever since), they sang in another century, in another time.

It was an honor to be able to directly interview several Weavers associates, including Ernie Lieberman of People's Songs (and later the Gateway Singers), Alan Arkin of the Babysitters (and a few other credits), 1963 Weavers banjo player Bernie Krause (who would help revolutionize both pop music and field recording), and documentarian Jim Brown (whose *Wasn't That a Time* documentary cemented my young Weavers fandom). It was likewise a thrill to speak with several musical descendants of the Weavers, including David Crosby, Roger McGuinn, and Al Jardine. Bottomless thanks to Brigid Meier for speaking about the connection between the Weavers and the Grateful Dead, as well as for preserving the recording of Jerry Garcia singing "Wasn't That a Time."

Special thanks go to Ron Cohen and Dave Samuelson, for personal guidance and research resources, but especially their archival work on the *Goodnight Irene* and *Songs for Political Action* box sets, as well as Ron's indispensable books *Rainbow Quest*, *The Pete Seeger Reader* (with James Capaldi), *Deadly Farce* (with Robert Lichtman), and *Folk City* (with Stephen Petrus). Likewise, enormous debts are owed to Doris Willens and David Dunaway, biographers of Lee Hays and Pete Seeger, respectively. In addition to their wonderful music, both Ronnie Gilbert and Erik Darling left behind soulful, colorful memoirs that capture lives fully lived. Elijah Wald's books made me rethink the relationship between folk and pop music in the 1950s, especially.

Large parts of this book are also built around paper trails, and enormous thanks to the rangers and custodians of those source documents. The Lee Hays Papers at the Smithsonian's Ralph Rinzler Collection are almost entirely digitized, and the Smithsonian staff was able to provide amazing long-distance support. Similar miracles were provided by the Southern Folklife Collection at the Louis Round Wilson Special Collections Library, University of North Carolina. As always, the New York Public Library and the Performing Arts Division provided access to a wealth of material on microfilm (as well as now mostly working and entirely amazing microfilm scanners). Long live these institutions and their keepers.

Other paper trails had more private guardians, and special thanks to Caleb Hellerman and Susan Lardner, Lisa Weg, and Barry and Judy Ollman for access to an incredible array of virtually unseen documents, as well as the human context that reanimates traces of songs sung.

And, of course, this book travels in the footsteps of those who've gone before and, hopefully, those who will come after. While copyright laws exist to protect from piracy and exploitation, fair use remains a shared legal bedrock of writing, folk music, and virtually all forms of public creativity. Friendly correspondents welcome.

Bibliography

Aldin, Mary Katherine. *Wasn't That a Time* (liner notes). New York: Vanguard Records, 1993.

Bragg, Billy. *Roots, Radicals and Rockers: How Skiffle Changed the World*. London: Faber & Faber, 2017.

Broven, John. *Record Makers and Breakers: Voices of the Independent Rock 'n' Roll Pioneers*. Urbana: University of Illinois Press, 2009.

Cantwell, Robert. *When We Were Good: The Folk Revival*. Cambridge, MA: Harvard University Press, 1996.

Cohen, Ronald D. *Rainbow Quest: The Folk Music Revival & American Society*. Amherst: University of Massachusetts Press, 2002.

Cohen, Ronald D., and James Capaldi, eds. *The Pete Seeger Reader*. Oxford: Oxford University Press, 2014.

Cohen, Ronald D., and Dave Samuelson. *Songs for Political Action, Folk Music, Topical Songs and the American Left, 1926–1953* (liner notes). Holste, DE: Bear Family Records, 1996.

Cunningham, Agnes "Sis," and Gordon Friesen. *Red Bust and Broadsides: A Joint Autobiography*. Amherst: University of Massachusetts Press, 1999.

Darling, Erik. *"I'd Give My Life": From Washington Square to Carnegie Hall, A Journey by Folk Music*. Palo Alto: Science and Behavior Books, 2008.

Denisoff, R. Serge. *Great Day Coming: Folk Music and the American Left*. Urbana: University of Illinois Press, 1971.

Denning, Michael. *The Cultural Front: The Laboring of American Culture in the Twentieth Century*. London: Verso, 1997.

Dunaway, David King. *How Can I Keep from Singing? The Ballad of Pete Seeger*, updated. New York: Villard, 2008.

———. *A Pete Seeger Discography: Seventy Years of Recordings*. Lanham: The Scarecrow Press, 2011.

Fletcher, Tony. *All Hopped Up and Ready to Go: Music from the Streets of New York, 1927–77*. New York: W. W. Norton, 2009.

Gilbert, Ronnie. *Ronnie Gilbert: A Radical Life in Song*. Oakland: University of California Press, 2015.

Halberstam, David. *The Fifties*. New York: Fawcett, 1993.

Jenkins, Bruce. *Goodbye: In Search of Gordon Jenkins*. Berkeley: Frog, Ltd., 2005.

Klein, Joe. *Woody Guthrie: A Life*. New York: Delta, 1980.

Koppelman, Robert S., ed. *"Sing Out, Warning! Sing Out, Love!": The Writings of Lee Hays*. Amherst: University of Massachusetts Press, 2003.

Lichtman, Robert M., and Ronald D. Cohen. *Deadly Farce: Harvey Matusow and the Informer System in the McCarthy Era*. Urbana: University of Chicago Press, 2004.

Lieberman, Robbie. *"My Song Is My Weapon": People's Songs, American Communism, and the Politics of Culture, 1930–1950*. Urbana: University of Illinois Press, 1989.

Matusow, Harvey. *False Witness*. New York: Cameron & Kahn, 1955.

Navasky, Victor S. *Naming Names*. New York: Viking Press, 1980.

Noebel, David A. *Rhythm, Riots and Revolution*. Tulsa: Christian Crusade Publications, 1966.

Petrus, Stephen, and Ronald D. Cohen. *Folk City: New York and the American Folk Music Revival*. Oxford: Oxford University Press, 2015.

Sakolsky, Ron, and Fred Wei-han Ho, eds. *Sounding Off!: Music as Subversion/Resistance/Revolution*. Brooklyn: Autonomedia, 1995.

Samuelson, Dave. *The Weavers, 1949–1953* (*Goodnight Irene* liner notes). Holste, DE: Bear Family Records, 2000.

Seeger, Pete. *The Incompleat Folksinger*. New York: Fireside, 1972.

Turner, Fred. *The Democratic Surround: Multimedia & America Liberalism from World War II to the Psychedelic Sixties*. Chicago: University of Chicago Press, 2013.

United States Congress House Committee on Un-American Activities. *Investigation of Communist Activities, New York Area: Hearings Before the Committee on Un-American Activities, House of Representatives, Eighty-Fourth Congress, First Session, August 15 and 16, 1955, Vol. 6.* London: Forgotten Books, 2015.

Van Ronk, Dave, and Elijah Wald. *The Mayor of MacDougal Street.* Boston: Da Capo Press, 2005.

Wald, Elijah. *Dylan Goes Electric! Newport, Seeger, Dylan, and the Night That Split the Sixties.* New York: Dey Street, 2015.

——. *How the Beatles Destroyed Rock 'n' Roll: An Alternative History of American Popular Music.* Oxford: Oxford University Press, 2009.

——. *Josh White: Society Blues.* Amherst: University of Massachusetts Press, 2000.

Weissman, Dick. *Which Side Are You On? An Inside History of the Folk Music Revival in America.* New York: Continuum, 2005.

Whitfield, Stephen J. *The Culture of the Cold War.* Baltimore: Johns Hopkins University Press, 1991.

Wilkinson, Alec. *The Protest Singer: An Intimate Portrait of Pete Seeger.* New York: Alfred A. Knopf, 2009.

Willens, Doris. *Lonesome Traveler: The Life of Lee Hays.* New York: W. W. Norton & Company, 1988.

NOTES

Ronnie Gilbert Collection, courtesy of Lisa Weg (LW)

Fred Hellerman Collection, courtesy Hellerman Family (FH)

Lee Hays Collection, Ralph Rinzler Folklife Archives and Collections, Smithsonian Center for Folklife and Cultural Heritage (RR)

Courtesy of Barry and Judy Ollman Collection (BJO)

If information within a short range of text is drawn from a single page range within a source, that source is cited only once.

Prologue: The Loathsome Traveler

1 **front-page news:** Milt Freudenheim, "Sing Under Surveillance: Show Goes on Despite Disfavor of Legion," *Akron Beacon Journal*, February 5, 1952, 1.

2 **gorgeous summer day:** Lee Hays, "Simon McKeever at Peekskill," *The Sunday Worker*, September 13, 1949.

2 **instant American standard:** Elijah Wald, *How the Beatles Destroyed Rock 'n' Roll: An Alternative History of American Popular Music* (Oxford: Oxford University Press, 2009), 158.

2 **"The quartet comes through":** "The Billboard Picks," *The Billboard*, January 12, 1952, 44.

3 **recent holiday shows:** December 21 and 22, 1951, Town Hall, New York, NY (recordings), FH.

3 **"When people have asked":** Freudenheim, 2.

4 **same week in Washington:** Robert M. Lichtman and Ronald D. Cohen, *Deadly Farce: Harvey Matusow and the Informer System in the McCarthy Era* (Urbana: University of Illinois Press, 2004), 51.

4 **"There was Pete Seeger":** *Communist Activities Among Youth Groups (Based on the Testimony of Harvey Matusow): Hearings Before the Committee on Un-American Activities, February 6 and 7, 1952* (Washington, DC: United States Government Printing Office 1952), 3297.

5 **"They played to":** "Akron Stay Cut Short by Weavers," *Akron Beacon Journal*, February 7, 1952, 1.

5   **the band had been served:** Ronnie Gilbert correspondence with Pete Kameron, LW.

5   **a paper trail connecting:** David King Dunaway, *How Can I Keep from Singing? The Ballad of Pete Seeger*, updated edition (New York: Villard, 2008), 95.

Chapter One: The New Situations

7   **Agent Harwood E. Ryan:** "FBI File on Pete Seeger," 2016, https://archive.org /details/PeteSeeger, Section 1, 73.

7   **lingering questions:** David King Dunaway, *How Can I Keep from Singing? The Ballad of Pete Seeger*, updated edition (New York: Villard, 2008), 120.

7   **invented a pretext:** "FBI File on Pete Seeger," Section 1, 61.

8   **Agent Laubscher:** Ibid., 52.

8   **nicknamed the young musician:** Dunaway, xxii.

8   **"Badly pimpled face":** "FBI File on Pete Seeger," Section 1, 112.

8   **his superiors received notice:** Ibid., 137.

8   **throughout the South:** Stephen J. Whitfield, *The Culture of the Cold War* (Baltimore: The Johns Hopkins University Press, 1991), 21.

9   **"not an overthrower":** "FBI File on Pete Seeger," Section 1, 73.

9   **his own interview:** Ibid., 129.

9   **Hanging on the wall:** Ibid., 73.

9   **Seeger's former landlord:** Ibid., 77.

10   **impresario Max Gordon:** Ibid., 76.

10   **Café Society:** Elijah Wald, *Josh White: Society Blues* (Amherst: University of Massachusetts Press, 2000), 102.

10   **Village Vanguard:** Ibid., 91.

10   **"Woody is just Woody":** Joe Klein, *Woody Guthrie: A Life* (New York: Delta, 1980), 160.

10   **Back at the base:** "FBI File on Pete Seeger," Section 1, 84.

11   **Hoover still wasn't happy:** Dunaway, 118.

11   **knock on the door:** Doris Willens, *Lonesome Traveler: The Life of Lee Hays* (New York: W. W. Norton & Company, 1988), 66.

11   **stayed at Harvard:** Alec Wilkinson, *The Protest Singer: An Intimate Portrait of Pete Seeger* (New York: Alfred A. Knopf, 2009), 51.

11   **intervening years:** Ibid., 55.

11   **Hays could engage:** Willens, 66.

11   **former protégé:** Ibid., 53.

12   **"early religious brainwashing":** "Lee on Woody Guthrie, 1975," RR, Box 5, Folder 49.

12   **mother's mental health:** Willens, 14.

12   **"if I didn't get a ride":** "Lee Hays Interview by Jim Capaldi, 10/27/79," RR, Box 5, Folder 48.

12   **"The system faced":** Ibid.

12   **"Every book":** Ibid.

12   **"Somewhere along in there":** "From 'The Post-humous Memoirs,'" in Robert S. Koppelman, ed., *"Sing Out, Warning! Sing Out, Love!": The Writings of Lee Hays* Robert S. Koppelman, ed. (Amherst: University of Massachusetts Press, 2003), 57.

12   **Christmas 1938:** Willens, 54.

13   **Emma Dusenbury:** Ibid.

13   **Bascom Lamar Lunsford:** Dunaway, 49.

13   **drown out Salvation Army:** Klein, 83.

13   **Sarah Ogan Gunning:** Ronald D. Cohen and Dave Samuelson, *Songs for Political Action, Folk Music, Topical Songs and the American Left, 1926–1953* (liner notes) (Holste, DE: Bear Family Records, 1996), 56.

14   **Seeger was crashing:** Klein, 190.

14   **"I could change":** "Lee Hays with Don McLean (transcript)," RR, Box 5, Folder 48.

14   **Seeger hadn't cut it:** Dunaway, 82.

14   **Doc Rockwell:** "Lee Hays Interview by Jim Capaldi, 10/27/79," RR, Box 5, Folder 48.

14   **first booking:** Willens, 66.

14   **big stage debut:** Robert Koppelman, "Lee Hays, American Culture, and the American Left," in Koppelman, 23.

14   **Ballad of October 16th:** Klein, 191.

15   **Pete's mentor:** Dunaway, 70.

15   **Woody had blown into town:** Klein, 190.

15   **best sports section:** "Lee Hays Interview by Jim Capaldi, 10/27/79," RR, Box 5, Folder 48.

15   **early rent parties:** Klein, 196.

15   **Popular Front:** Michael Denning, *The Cultural Front: The Laboring of American Culture in the Twentieth Century* (London: Verso, 1997), 4.

16   **boarding school:** Dunaway, 32.

16   **had a subscription:** Ibid., 45.

16   **composer Charles Seeger:** Denning, 66.

16   **"Communism is Twentieth-Century Americanism":** Ibid., 129.

16   **Young Communist League:** Dunaway, 54.

16   **Popular Front was officially abandoned:** Denning, 12.

16   **like Woody Guthrie:** Klein, 134.

17   **"We are in the peace army":** George Lewis, "America Is in Their Songs," *Daily Worker*, March 24, 1941, 7.

17   **"Like roving reporters":** "Folk Singers in Original Revue Tonight," *Daily Worker*, May 15, 1941, 7.

17   **Lee's constant analysis:** Klein, 199.

17   **"I can't remember that anybody":** "Lee Hays Interview by Jim Capaldi, 10/27/79," RR, Box 5, Folder 48.

17   **Mike Gold:** Ibid.

17   **Music Room:** Ronald D. Cohen, *Rainbow Quest: The Folk Music Revival & American Society.* Amherst: University of Massachusetts Press, 2002, 29.

17   **Within a few weeks:** Ibid., 30.

18   **Madison Square Garden:** Dunaway, 83.

18   **"Talking Union":** Klein, 192.

18   **One Sunday:** Dunaway, 90.

18   **made it to the White House:** Klein, 198.

18   **"On Account of That New Situation":** Dunaway, 293.

19   **small third-floor bedroom:** Agnes "Sis" Cunningham and Gordon Friesen, *Red Bust and Broadsides: A Joint Autobiography* (Amherst: University of Massachusetts Press, 1999), 209.

19   **"He would get up":** Dunaway, 89.

19   **portable turntable:** Ibid., 102.

19   **bulletin board:** Cunningham and Friesen, 211.

19   **Lee Hays is the cook:** Klein, 199.

19   **"nice young man":** Cohen, 34.

20   **Woody beat Lee:** Willens, 71.

20   **Officially becoming a member of the Communist Party:** Robert Cantwell, *When We Were Good: The Folk Revival* (Cambridge, MA: Harvard University Press, 1996), 126.

20   **"pretty seditious stuff":** Lawrence Emery, "Union Idea, Fine Music in 'Almanac' Records," *Daily Worker*, August 6, 1941, 7.

20   **"strictly subversive":** Carl Jochim Freiderich, "The Poison in Our System," *The Atlantic Monthly*, June 1941, 661.

20   **San Francisco's Longshoremen's Hall:** Dunaway, 95. Twenty-five years later, Longshoremen's Hall would host the LSD-laced Trips Festival, a culminating Acid Test by Ken Kesey and the Merry Pranksters, organized in part by future Whole Earth founder Stewart Brand and the San Francisco Tape Music Center's Ramon Sender, featuring the Grateful Dead, among other bands.

20   **between gigs:** Ibid., 100.

20   **the wee hours:** Cunningham and Friesen, 216.

20   **Panning down to the basement:** Ibid., 211.

21   **One basement frequenter:** "Lee Hays Interview by Jim Capaldi, 10/27/79," RR, Box 5, Folder 48.

21   **asked to resign:** Victor S. Navasky, *Naming Names* (New York: Viking Press, 1980), 48.

21   **She would share:** Klein, 214.

21   **Hays also made friends:** Willens, 100.

21   **"the creative power":** Ibid., 74.

21   **"I had no doctor":** "Lee Hays Interview by Jim Capaldi, 10/27/79," RR, Box 5, Folder 48.

21   **It was up to Seeger:** Dunaway, 93.

21   **Woody happily reconfigured:** Klein, 225.

22   **theatrical Almanac Players:** Ralph Warner, "'Sign of the Times': Spirited Labor Revue," *Daily Worker*, May 17, 1941, 7.

22   **A former organizer:** Cunningham and Friesen, 339.

22   **Alan Lomax's suggestion:** "The Almanac Singers [Pete Seeger] to Son House," in Ronald Cohen and James Capaldi, eds., *The Pete Seeger Reader* (Oxford: Oxford University Press, 2014), 72.

22   **Pete had run into:** Klein, 238.

22   **"Oklahoma-style":** Cunningham and Friesen, 217.

22   **"a smattering of Junior League":** Elijah Wald, *Josh White: Society Blues* (Amherst: University of Massachusetts Press, 2000), 76.

23   **led off *This Is War*:** Cunningham and Friesen, 212.

23   **Navy Department:** Cantwell, 129.

23   **billed as *comedy*:** "Comedy in Spotlight," *Mason City Globe-Gazette*, March 27, 1942, 2.

23   **William Morris:** Dunaway, 111.

23   **joined the Local 802:** Ibid., 113.

23   **"Singers on New Morale Show":** "Singers on New Morale Show Also Warbled for Communists," *New York World-Telegram*, February 17, 1942, 3.

23   **Palmer Raids:** Clancy Sigal, "John Ashcroft's Palmer Raids," *New York Times*, March 13, 2002.

24   **"Bring on the girls!":** Cunningham and Friesen, 220.

24   **THIS MACHINE:** Klein, 243.

24   **he typed away:** Cunningham and Friesen, 221.

24   **Sailing away:** Dunaway, 124.

Chapter Two: People's Songs

27   **In her new bedroom:** Ronnie Gilbert, *Ronnie Gilbert: A Radical Life in Song* (Oakland: University of California Press, 2015), 42.

27   **mother was sick:** Ibid., 39.

27   **doing that all her life:** Kate Weigand, "Voices of Feminism Oral History Project: Ronnie Gilbert," Sophia Smith Collection, Smith College, 2004, https://www.smith.edu/libraries/libs/ssc/vof/transcripts/Gilbert.pdf, 3.

28   **rang a bell with her mother:** Robbie Lieberman, *"My Song Is My Weapon": People's Songs, American Communism, and the Politics of Culture, 1930–1950* (Urbana: University of Illinois Press, 1989), 21.

28   **Sarah had dragged Ronnie:** Gilbert, 4.

28   **"when this man":** Weigand, 4.

28   **"I'd never heard":** Weigand, 4.

29   **"The artist must take sides":** "The Artist Must Take Sides," in Philip S. Foner, ed., *Paul Robeson Speaks: Writing, Speeches, Interviews, 1918–1974* (New York: Citadel Press, 1978), 119.

29   **"politics, power, and songs":** Gilbert, 5.

29   **playing field drum:** Ibid., 24.

29   **taking the elevated train:** Ronnie Gilbert, undated draft, ca. 1997, LW.

29   **"When I was about 10":** Lieberman, 48.

29   **"there's not another camp":** Gilbert, 26.

29   **"an integral part":** Lieberman, 61.

29   **"dangerous ideas":** "Introduction," June Levine and Gene Gordon, *Tales of Wo-Chi-Ca: Blacks, Whites and Reds at Camp* (San Rafael: Avon Springs Press, 2002), vii.

30   **she became Ronnie:** Gilbert, 28.

30   **"very organic part":** Lieberman, 21.

30   **Her supervisor:** Gilbert, 44.

30   **"only stereotypical female thing":** Weigand, 7.

30   **"Jackie and friends":** Ibid., 6.

30   **"singing started early":** Gilbert, 45.

31   **Ronnie didn't readjust easily:** Ibid., 48.

31   **"You couldn't really call it":** "Fred Hellerman, Part 1 Final," interview with Weston Forum, 2016, https://www.youtube.com/watch?v=1I__la7_8Ow (accessed May 16, 2018).

31   **radio operator:** "Fred Hellerman: In His Own Words," The Weston Forum, September 10, 2016, https://archive.thewestonforum.com/68715/fred -hellerman-in-his-own-words/.

31   **the Hellermans' corner:** Lieberman, 21.

31   **Young Communist League:** Ibid., 62.

31   **"When I was 12 or 13":** Hellerman, "In His Own Words."

31   **Ray had heard about:** Fred Hellerman, "Daylight to go . . ." term paper, Brooklyn College, late 1940s, BJO.

32   **"chronic truant":** Bruce Jenkins. *Goodbye: In Search of Gordon Jenkins* (Berkeley: Frog, Ltd., 2005), 227.

32   **dramatics counselor:** Gilbert, 48.

32   **"I'd go to a movie":** Weigand, 4.

32   **postwar Manhattan:** Tony Fletcher, *All Hopped Up and Ready to Go: Music from the Streets of New York, 1927-77* (New York: W. W. Norton, 2009).

33   **"If you're interested":** Jenkins, 227.

33   **American Folksay:** Hellerman, "Daylight to go . . ."

33   **by both the left and right:** Besides Folksay, see: Robyn Pennacchia, "America's Wholesome Dancing Tradition Is a Tool of White Supremacy," *Quartz*,

December 12, 2017, https://qz.com/1153516/americas-wholesome-square -dancing-tradition-is-a-tool-of-white-supremacy/.

33   **"They weren't rollicking affairs":** Agnes "Sis" Cunningham and Gordon Friesen, *Red Bust and Broadsides: A Joint Autobiography* (Amherst: University of Massachusetts Press, 1999), 48.

33   **"A lot of kids":** Hellerman, "In His Own Words."

33   **After singing:** Hellerman, "Daylight to go . . ."

33   **Ronnie Gilbert heard:** Gilbert, 48.

34   **Pete Seeger studied:** Pete Seeger, "Woody Guthrie: A Book Review," *People's Songs* (July & August, 1947), 18.

34   **People's Songs had sprouted:** Woody Guthrie, "People's Songs and Its People," in Ronald Cohen and James Capaldi, eds., *The Pete Seeger Reader* (Oxford: Oxford University Press, 2014), 79.

34   **"The spirit":** Mike Gold, "Change the World," *Daily Worker*, January 2, 1946.

34   **small beans:** Jeremy Brecher, *Strike!* (Oakland: PM Press, 2014), 216.

34   **Pittsburgh's city hall:** Dave Marsh, and Harold Leventhal, eds., *Pastures of Plenty: A Self-Portrait* (New York: HarperCollins, 1992), 174.

35   **"Oh. Well":** Ed Cray, *Ramblin' Man: The Life and Times of Woody Guthrie* (New York: W. W. Norton, 2006), 301.

35   **Back in New York:** Doris Willens, *Lonesome Traveler: The Life of Lee Hays* (New York: W. W. Norton & Company, 1988), 81.

35   **His half decade:** Ibid., 76–79.

35   **late nights with Lead Belly:** "Lee on Woody Guthrie, 1975," RR, Box 5, Folder 49.

35   **"I'm sure if I'd lived":** "Lee Hays Interview by Jim Capaldi, 10/27/79," RR, Box 5, Folder 48.

35   **back in his element:** Willens, 82.

35   **"What I saw":** Hellerman, "Daylight to go . . ."

35   **Francis Child:** Pete Seeger, *The Incompleat Folksinger* (New York: Fireside, 1972), 12.

36   **He was the one:** Willens, 82.

37   **Drinking together:** Fred Hellerman journal, ca. early 1950, FH.

37   **call for songs:** "Attention Songwriters," *People's Songs*, March 1946, 2, 8.

37   **"hundreds, thousands":** David King Dunaway, *How Can I Keep from Singing? The Ballad of Pete Seeger*, updated edition (New York: Villard, 2008), 133.

37   **a few days after:** Ibid., 134.

38   **That same year:** "Lee on Woody Guthrie, 1975," RR, Box 5, Folder 49.

38   **They're determined:** Beth McHenry, "Lee Hays and His Buddies Hit the Picket Line Again," *Daily Worker*, May 15, 1946, 13.

38   **Growing from the work:** Fred Turner, *The Democratic Surround: Multimedia & America Liberalism from World War II to the Psychedelic Sixties* (Chicago: University of Chicago Press, 2013), 4.

39   **Woody Guthrie encountered:** Marsh and Leventhal, 205.

39   **Buy Nothing Day:** Cunningham and Friesen, 343.

39   *FIGHT TO SAVE OPA:* "Fight to Save OPA," *People's Songs*, April 1946, 11.

39   **bitching about:** Willens, 84.

39   **"substantial singer":** *People's Songs*, September 1947, 2.

40   **"I saw these Peoples [*sic*] Songs":** Ronald D. Cohen, *Rainbow Quest: The Folk Music Revival & American Society* (Amherst: University of Massachusetts Press, 2002), 43.

40   **May 1946 at Town Hall:** "Two Hootenannies," *People's Songs*, April 1946, 14.

40   **"What has made":** Mike Gold, "Change the World," *Daily Worker*, February 24, 1946, 7.

40   **"all-purpose fuck-off ":** Willens, 82.

40   **"It struck me":** Lieberman, 82.

41   **"We recognize":** Pete Seeger, "People's Songs Workshop, The Jefferson School of Social Science," in Cohen and Capaldi, 85.

41   **Pete was called out:** Pete Seeger, *The Incompleat Folksinger* (New York: Fireside, 1972), 93.

41   **Popular Song Writers Committee:** "Popular Song Writers Committee Formed," *People's Songs*, March 1946, 1.

41   **"What Makes":** Paul Secon, "What Makes a Good Pop Song?" *People's Songs*, April 1946, 8.

41   **Lee Hays stepped in:** Lee Hays, "Let's Have More Common Sense About Folk Music," *People's Songs*, October 1946, 4.

41   **"You have to be":** B. R., Boise, Idaho, "Correspondence," *People's Songs*, December 1946, 12.

42   **Tin Pan Alley:** Elijah Wald, *How the Beatles Destroyed Rock 'n' Roll: An Alternative History of American Popular Music* (Oxford: Oxford University Press, 2009), 36.

42   **"We have set up":** Pete Seeger, "People's Songs and Singers," *New Masses*, July 16, 1946, 7.

42   **Independent jazz:** John Broven, *Record Makers and Breakers: Voices of the Independent Rock 'n' Roll Pioneers* (Urbana: University of Illinois Press, 2009), 59.

42   **Charter Records:** Ronald D. Cohen and Dave Samuelson, *Songs for Political Action, Folk Music, Topical Songs and the American Left, 1926–1953* (liner notes) (Holste, DE: Bear Family Records, 1996), 159.

42   **Josh White:** Elijah Wald, *Josh White: Society Blues* (Amherst: University of Massachusetts Press, 2000), 138.

42   **People's Radio Foundation:** "People's Songs on a People's Radio," *People's Songs*, June 1946, 3.

43   **filmstrips:** Felix Landau, "Film Strips in Action," *People's Songs*, September 1946, 3.

43   **wire recorders:** "Odds and Ends," *People's Songs*, November 1946, 12.

43   **regular sessions:** Charles Wolfe and Kip Lornell, *The Life and Legend of Leadbelly* (New York: HarperCollins, 1992), 55.

43   **Lee and Woody:** Willens, 88.

43   **policy discussions:** Ibid., 85.

43   **Confederate folk songs:** Ibid., 86.

44   **barely a year:** Ibid., 90.

44   **"A country needs":** George Sokolsky, "Stalin's Army," *Middletown Times Herald* (syndicated), June 24, 1946, 7.

44   **opening a file:** Dunaway, 135.

44   **"They play folksongs":** Ibid., 143.

44   **a few weeks after:** Navasky, 80.

45   **"It is important":** George Sokolsky, "Congress Is Target of Two Hostile U.S. Blocs," *Plain Speaker* (syndicated), September 13, 1946, 10.

45   **"the broadmindedness of the average liberal":** *Communist Infiltration in the United States: Its Nature and How to Fight It* (Washington, DC: United States Chamber of Commerce), 25.

45   **loyalty oaths:** Robert Justin Goldstein, "Prelude to McCarthyism: The Making of a Blacklist," *Prologue*, Fall 2006, https://www.archives.gov/publications /prologue/2006/fall/agloso.html.

45   **Taft-Hartley:** Lieberman, 97.

45   **unrepentantly anti-Semitic:** Navasky, 109.

45   **"one of the most dangerous":** Robert Vaughan, *Only Victims: A Study of Show Business Blacklisting* (New York: Putnam, 1972), 110.

46   **Walter Steele:** *Testimony of Walter S. Steele regarding Communist activities in the United States. Hearings before the Committee on Un-American Activities, House of Representatives, Eightieth Congress* (Washington, DC: Government Printing Office, 1947), 105.

46   **Alexander Bittelman:** Navasky, 26.

47   **Some nights:** Dunaway, 147.

47   **One hotel after another:** Ibid., 148.

47   **"The old books":** Ken Perlman, "Interview with Pete Seeger from 2000," *Banjo Newsletter*, March 2014, https://banjonews.com/2014-03/interview_with _pete_seeger_from_2000.html.

47   **"they weren't very funny":** Jeffrey Pepper Rodgers, "Pete Seeger: How Can I Keep from Singing?," *Acoustic Guitar*, July 2002, 58.

47   **In the spring:** "Cross-Country," *People's Songs*, February-March 1948, 12.

47   **Pete was in North Carolina:** Dunaway, 147.

47   **"Friendly Henry Wallace":** *Songs for Wallace* (New York: People's Songs, 1948), 3.

47   **"and his Communists":** "President Tells Wallace Party to Move to USSR," *Salem News*, March 30, 1948, 1.

48   **"artificially created crisis":** *Congressional Record: Proceedings and Debates of the 80th Congress, Volume 94, Part 3* (Washington, DC: Government Printing Office, 1948), 3173.

48   **ever-helpful Alan Lomax:** Cohen, 57.

48   **Paul Robeson took:** Joseph Haber, "Cleveland Sings for Wallace," *People's Songs*, February–March 1948, 3.

48   **paper records:** Cohen, 57.

48   **hitchhiked to Philadelphia:** Gilbert, 52.

48   **bass-baritone:** Anthony Tommasini, "Classical View: Of Basses, Baritones and Hedges," *New York Times*, April 19, 1998.

48   **"So much joy":** Gilbert, 52.

48   **"It wasn't terribly":** Willens, 104.

48   **Fred, too:** George Silk, photograph, 1948, Getty Images (see photo insert).

49   **dozen Communist leaders:** Navasky, 30.

49   **CIO had been moving:** Lieberman, 97.

49   **"in the middle of a long":** Lee Hays, "A Sermon to Songwriters," *People's Songs*, April 1948, 11.

49   **During the ill-fated:** Dunaway, 146.

50   **At an integrated rally:** Karl M. Schmidt, *Henry A. Wallace: Quixotic Crusade 1948* (Syracuse: Syracuse University Press, 1960), 205.

50   **"A number of people":** Dunaway, 146.

50   **Wallace's favorite song:** Pete Seeger, November 24, 1948, Irving Plaza, HAYS-RR-02 (audio recording), RR.

50   **another pitched battle:** "Prominent Americans Protest Quebec Songbook Ban," *People's Songs*, July 1948, 2.

50   **"I started learning":** Sylvie Simmons, *I'm Your Man: The Life of Leonard Cohen* (Toronto: McClelland & Stewart, 2012).

51   **"the end of the enthusiasm":** Willens, 106.

51   **Over brunch:** Gilbert, 53.

Chapter Three: Warp and Woof

53   **A leg of Lee Hays's chair:** Lee Hays, "Ten Years with the Weavers: A Personal Report," 1959, RR, Box 3, Folder 72.

53   **twenty blocks:** Sergey Kadinsky, *Hidden Waters of New York City: A History and Guide to 101 Forgotten Lakes, Ponds, Creeks, and Streams in the Five Boroughs* (New York: The Countryman Press, 2016).

53   **"A low ceiling":** Quoted in Ronald Cohen and James Capaldi, eds., *The Pete Seeger Reader* (Oxford: Oxford University Press, 2014), 79.

54   **Long thinking about:** Alec Wilkinson, *The Protest Singer: An Intimate Portrait of Pete Seeger* (New York: Alfred A. Knopf, 2009), 14.

54   **"Pete wanted"**: Kate Weigand, "Voices of Feminism Oral History Project: Ronnie Gilbert," Sophia Smith Collection, Smith College, 2004, https://www .smith.edu/libraries/libs/ssc/vof/transcripts/Gilbert.pdf, 10.

54   **"almost a random"**: Dave Samuelson, *The Weavers, 1949-1953* (Holste, DE: Bear Family Records, 2000), 9.

54   **He and Lee:** Ronald D. Cohen and Dave Samuelson, *Songs for Political Action, Folk Music, Topical Songs and the American Left, 1926–1953* (liner notes) (Holste, DE: Bear Family Records, 1996), 146.

54   **"You know"**: People's Songs postcard, November 1948, BJO.

54   **"as if the election"**: Ronnie Gilbert *Ronnie Gilbert: A Radical Life in Song*, (Oakland: University of California Press, 2015), 55.

54   **Both had yearned:** Dave Samuelson, *The Weavers, 1949-1953 (Goodnight Irene* liner notes) (Holste, DE: Bear Family Records, 2000), 7.

54   **"we can still be free"**: November 24, 1948, Irving Plaza, HAYS-RR-02 (audio recording), RR.

55   **"I can recall"**: Weigand, 10.

55   **"The Commonwealth of Toil"**: *People's Songs,* June 1948, 12.

55   **Pete's father, Charles:** David King Dunaway, *How Can I Keep from Singing? The Ballad of Pete Seeger*, updated edition (New York: Villard, 2008), 54.

55   **"Farther Along"**: Curtis Daniel MacDougall, *Gideon's Army: The Campaign and the Vote* (New York: Marzani & Munsell, 1965), 715.

55   **"We Will Overcome"**: Cohen and Samuleson, 191.

56   **Ronnie's girl-gang:** Samuelson, 9.

56   **Ronnie was working:** Gilbert, 49.

56   **"We have had"**: Lee Hays, "A Sermon to Songwriters," *People's Songs*, April 1948, 11.

56   **debuted by:** "Peoples Chorus Joins People Songs," *People's Songs*, December 1948, 5.

57   **"let its apparent irregularities"**: Ibid.

57   **"I had thought"**: "Lee Hays Interview by Jim Capaldi, 10/27/79," RR, Box 5, Folder 48.

57   **he'd kvetched:** Lee Hays to Pete Seeger, RR, Box 2, Folder 4.

57   ***Ellery Queen's:*** Doris Willens, *Lonesome Traveler: The Life of Lee Hays* (New York: W. W. Norton & Company, 1988), 108.

57   **Lee remained Southern:** Erik Darling, *"I'd Give My Life": From Washington Square to Carnegie Hall, A Journey by Folk Music* (Palo Alto: Science and Behavior Books, 2008), 133.

58   **early flash:** *Daily Worker,* January 11, 1949, 12.

58   **Lee who now provided:** Samuelson, 9.

58   **put out the call:** Oscar Brand, *The Ballad Mongers: Rise of the Modern Folk Song* (New York: Funk, 1962), 109.

58   **postcard went out:** People's Songs postcard, January 1949, BJO.

58   **"Out of somewhere":** January 23, 1949, appearance on *Folk Song Festival* on *Goodnight Irene: The Weavers, 1949-1953* (Holste, DE: Bear Family Records, 2000), disc 1.

58   **It was Freddie:** Samuelson, 11.

59   **People's Songs was broke:** Dunaway, 149.

59   **"This organization":** Sidney Finkelstein, *Worker Magazine*, March 6, 1949, 2.

59   **excitable kid:** Dunaway, 149.

59   **Lee was still:** Samuelson, 10.

59   **Now spread over:** People's Songs postcard, January 1949, BJO.

59   **But right now:** Willens, 88.

59   **In the Adirondacks:** Lee Hays, "Memoirs, Excerpts," ca. 1976, RR, Box 3, Folder 64.

60   **made its debut:** Bernard Rubin, "Broadway Beat," *Daily Worker*, June 1, 1949, 13.

60   **The organization had closed shop:** Dunaway, 150.

60   **"Let it out free":** "This Old World," *People's Songs*, February 1949, 3.

60   **professional informant:** Stephen J. Whitfield, *The Culture of the Cold War* (Baltimore: Johns Hopkins University Press, 1991), 47.

60   **"a hard driver":** Dunaway, 224.

60   *I Was a Communist*: Whitfield, 135.

61   **"tagging along":** Gilbert, 56.

61   **"Even people":** Mary Katherine Aldin, *Wasn't That a Time* (liner notes) (New York: Vanguard Records, 1993), 10.

61   **"He never acted":** Lee Hays to Jim Brown, RR, Box 2, Folder 47.

61   **"The Weavers are frankly":** "From Kentucky Mountain Ballads to Chinese People's Songs," *Daily Worker*, June 14, 1949.

62   **Lee was hardly confident:** Lee Hays to Jim Brown, RR, Box 2, Folder 47.

62   **"I didn't know":** "Ronnie Gilbert," *SongTalk*, Spring 1989, 18.

62   **At one especially:** Dunaway, 153.

62   **he and Toshi raised:** Wilkinson, 19.

62   **extolled the virtues:** "Use Your Library," *People's Songs*, December 1948, 2.

62   **Seeger returned:** Dunaway 158.

62   **As the weather:** Ibid.

63   **glorious green meadow:** Gilbert, 57.

63   **Allaben:** Ronnie Gilbert to Sarah Gilbert, September 1949, LW.

63   **Fred sent a third:** Willens, 111.

63   **Peekskill benefit:** Ronald D. Cohen, *Rainbow Quest: The Folk Music Revival & American Society* (Amherst: University of Massachusetts Press, 2002), 62.

63   **performed there the previous summers:** Joel Feingold, "Postwar Reaction and Popular Resistance: The Peekskill Songs and Riots of 1949," 2012,

http://www.academia.edu/25819578/Postwar_Reaction_and_Popular_Resistance_The_Peekskill_Songs_and_Riots_of_1949_2011-2012_, 1.

63   **"We shall not"**: Elijah Wald, *Josh White: Society Blues* (Amherst: University of Massachusetts Press, 2000), 188.

63   **"It is unthinkable"**: Feingold, 2.

63   **"Robeson Says"**: "Robeson Says U.S. Negros Won't Fight Russia," *Peekskill Evening Star*, April 21, 1949, 1.

64   **They were directed**: Ronnie Gilbert to Sarah Gilbert, September 1949, LW.

64   **Hootenanny Midsummer**: Cohen and Samuelson, 42.

64   **Pete arrived**: Dunaway, 5.

64   **advancing angry mob**: Howard Fast, "Howard Fast's Eyewitness Account of Fascist Mob's Attack," *Daily Worker*, August 30, 1949, 8.

65   **"I'll never forget"**: Robert Friedman, "Peekskill Victim Tells How She Was Beaten," *Daily Worker*, August 31, 1949, 3.

65   **initial anti-Robeson**: Feingold, 8.

65   **"time for tolerant silence"**: "The Discordant Note," *Peekskill Evening Star*, August 22, 1949.

65   **"Paul Robeson should have"**: Bill Mardo, "Investigate Mob, Jackie Says," *Daily Worker*, August 29, 1949, 1.

65   **"I'm going back"**: Arnold Sroog, "Robeson to Sing in Peekskill This Sunday," *Daily Worker*, September 2, 1949, 2.

65   **Lee and Woody got a ride**: Willens, 113.

65   **Wanting them to witness**: Dunaway, 10.

66   **BEHIND COMMUNISM**: Feingold, 13.

66   **Ronnie remembered**: Ronnie Gilbert to Sarah Gilbert, September 1949, LW.

66   **Even the police helicopter**: Ronnie Gilbert to Sarah Gilbert, September 1949, LW.

66   **By four p.m.**: Feingold, 12.

66   **"in a dark, leafy tunnel"**: Gilbert, 59.

67   **In Pete Seeger's Jeep**: Dunaway, 15.

67   **"One cop"**: "Second Battle of Peekskill," *Time*, September 19, 1949, 28.

67   **Lee and Woody experienced**: Lee Hays, "Simon McKeever at Peekskill," *The Sunday Worker*, September 13, 1949.

67   **"I was literally"**: "Lee on Woody Guthrie, 1975," RR, Box 5, Folder 49.

67   **"as if the air"**: Hays, "Simon McKeever at Peekskill."

68   **"imitation Storm Troopers"**: "They Fear the People," *Daily Worker*, September 6, 1949, 3.

68   **Pete Seeger quietly ceased**: Wilkinson, 73.

68   **When clearing**: Ibid., 29.

68   **"3,000,000 meetings"**: Ronnie Gilbert to Sarah Gilbert, September 1949, LW.

68   **Weavers' first proper:** Samuelson, 11. Later, thanks to an introduction by Lee Hays, "Peekskill Story" engineer Tony Schwartz would sign with Folkways and release a series of pioneering urban field-recording LPs.

69   **"A sort of political surrealism":** Arthur Miller, "The Year It Came Apart," *New York*, December 30, 1974, 30.

69   **Woody, as charged up:** Joe Klein, *Woody Guthrie: A Life* (New York: Delta, 1980), 363.

69   **Soviet Union's first successful:** David Halberstam, *The Fifties* (New York: Fawcett, 1993), 25.

69   **signed up to sing:** Cohen and Samuelson, 182, and accompanying recordings.

70   **Benjamin Davis Jr.:** Michael Denning, *The Cultural Front: The Laboring of American Culture in the Twentieth Century* (London: Verso, 1997), 335.

70   **"Be glad":** Dunaway, 164.

70   **Lee Hays had to be:** Lee Hays to Pete Seeger, March 18, 1977, RR, Box 2, Folder 4.

70   **(some think):** "Nighthawks: The Search for the Diner," 2010, http://shadeone .com/nighthawks/, accessed May 16, 2018.

71   **The group integrated:** Samuelson, 12.

71   **"female Paul Robeson":** Ron Cohen interview with Hope Foye, August 3, 1993, Ronald D. Cohen Collection, the Southern Folklife Collection, Louis Round Wilson Special Collections Library, University of North Carolina.

71   **"Always got sick":** Fred Hellerman journal, ca. early 1950, FH.

71   **fifteen-point Promotion and Publicity:** Lee Hays, "WEAVERS—Promotion and Publicity," c. October 1949, Ronnie Gilbert Collection, LW.

72   **"After a few":** Gilbert, 80.

72   **This idea of Fred:** Fred Hellerman journal, ca. early 1950, FH.

72   **missed Lead Belly's funeral:** Lee Hays, "Memoirs, Excerpts," ca. 1976, RR, Box 3, Folder 63.

73   **Ronnie sent queries:** Pete Seeger to Ronnie Gilbert, Ronnie Gilbert Collection, LW.

73   **single went nowhere:** Samuelson, 13.

73   **"I decided to stop":** Dunaway, 164.

73   **"poets' ghosts":** Gilbert, 63.

73   **"I don't know":** Lee Hays interview with David King Dunaway, 1977, RR, Box 2, Folder 44.

73   **Ronnie felt a twinge:** Gilbert, 64.

73   **"All those people":** Lee Hays, "from Lee's tapes," October 2, 1976, RR, Box 3, Folder 64.

74   **"Fred's look":** Gilbert, 66.

74   **"Can you imagine":** Lee Hays interview with David King Dunaway, 1977, RR, Box 2, Folder 44.

74   **At the very least:** Lee Hays, "from Lee's tapes," October 2, 1976, RR, Box 3, Folder 64.

74   **"We raced through":** Robert Shelton, "Former Weaver Threads Her Own Way," *New York Times*, February 29, 1964.

74   **Village Barn:** Rick Beard and Leslie Berlowitz, *Greenwich Village: Culture and Counterculture* (New York: Museum of the City of New York), 1993, 363.

74   **At Birdland:** Gordon Allison, "Dining and Dancing: Christmas at Birdland," *New York Herald Tribune*, December 21, 1949, 23.

75   **its own roots:** Robert Cantwell, *When We Were Good: The Folk Revival* (Cambridge, MA: Harvard University Press, 1996), 179.

75   **half-related answer song:** Elijah Wald, "Goodnight Irene (Lead Belly and Others)," April 3, 2016, http://www.elijahwald.com/songblog/goodnight-irene/.

75   **"anyone better":** Gilbert, 65.

75   **"internal rhythm":** Ibid., 66.

75   **"emulating [his] father":** "Lee on Woody Guthrie, 1975," RR, Box 5, Folder 49.

75   **"This number is called":** "Around the World," March 1950, on *Goodnight Irene: The Weavers, 1949–1953* (Holste, DE: Bear Family Records, 2000), disc 1.

75   **"In these days":** "Around the World," March 1950, Village Vanguard, New York, NY (recordings), FH.

75   **"It's a collection":** "Around the World," December 1951 or 1952, on *Kisses Sweeter Than Wine* (New York: Omega, 1994), disc 1.

76   **"There was no standard":** Gilbert, 66.

76   **"When we began working":** Aldin, 12.

76   **Clarence Williams:** March 1950, Village Vanguard, FH.

76   **Their old radical:** Lee Hays interview with David King Dunaway, 1977, RR, Box 2, Folder 44.

76   **"I remember":** Ibid.

76   **"We evolved":** Gilbert, 64.

77   **Pete Seeger helped himself:** Dunaway, 165.

77   **"Pete had":** Lee Hays, "Hays Memoirs," October 1976, RR, Box 3, Folder 63.

77   **"After a few weeks":** Lee Hays to Pete Seeger, March 18, 1977, RR, Box 2, Folder 4.

77   **"I was always hungry":** Lee Hays, "Hays Memoirs," October 1976, RR, Box 3, Folder 63.

77   **Toshi Seeger:** Gilbert, 66.

77   **"bilious":** Samuelson, 13.

77   **"they look as if":** Gordon Allison, "Dining and Dancing: Weavers in the Village," *New York Herald Tribune*, January 4, 1950, 19.

77   **"I leaned against":** *New Yorker*, February 4, 1950, 71.

78   **Pete Seeger discovered:** Rian Malan, "In the Jungle," *Rolling Stone*, May 14, 2000, 54.

78   **He transcribed the parts:** Fred Hellerman to Lee Hays, January 24, 1980, RR, Box 2, Folder 48.

78   **"Where was the song":** Gilbert, 68.

78   **"South Africa":** Ibid.

78   **At one performance:** Aldin, 12.

78   **Lee Hays discovered brandy:** Lee Hays, "Hays Memoirs," October 1976, RR, Box 3, Folder 63.

79   **sick days started:** Willens, 123.

79   **"We may have to take":** Dunaway, 168.

79   **"Not only was he":** Pete Seeger to Coyal McMahan, spring 1950, RR, Box 2, Folder 46.

79   **"alcohol and music":** Willens, 123.

79   **PS 50:** Parents Association to the Weavers, February 21, 1950, RR Box 2, Folder 46.

79   **funeral for Bob Reed:** Frederick Woltman, "Melody Weaves On, Along Party Lines," *New York World Telegram*, August 25, 1951, 15.

80   **Alan Lomax brought:** Stephen Petrus and Ronald D. Cohen, *Folk City: New York and the American Folk Music Revival* (Oxford: Oxford University Press, 2015), 73.

Chapter Four: Irene, Goodnight

81   **"a great hooting sound":** Bruce Jenkins, *Goodbye: In Search of Gordon Jenkins* (Berkeley: Frog, Ltd., 2005), 166.

81   **"pleasantly drunk":** Ibid., 130.

81   **"I had never":** Lee Hays to Pete Seeger, March 18, 1977, RR, Box 2, Folder 4.

81   **"This was coming":** Lee Hays, "Hays Memoirs," October 1976, RR, Box 3, Folder 63.

81   **Pete could still:** Mary Katherine Aldin, *Wasn't That a Time* (liner notes) (New York: Vanguard Records, 1993), 5.

82   **Ronnie loved it:** Ronnie Gilbert, *Ronnie Gilbert: A Radical Life in Song* (Oakland: University of California Press, 2015), 72.

82   **"That wasn't my New York":** Jenkins, 231.

82   **"Being a big-band guy":** Ibid.

82   **one-handed:** Ibid., 39.

82   **"I just flipped":** Ibid., 230.

82   **"I don't think he knew":** Ibid.

83   **"too-ready smile":** Gilbert, 72.

83   **Fred's memory amplified:** Aldin, 16.

83   "good *and* commercial": Fred Hellerman to Lee Hays, January 24, 1980, RR Box 2, Folder 48.

83   When they reconvened: Aldin, 16.

83   "A lot of Broadway": Ibid., 14.

83   Pete proposed that: Lee Hays to Pete Seeger, March 18, 1977, RR, Box 2, Folder 4.

84   solution presented itself: Doris Willens, *Lonesome Traveler: The Life of Lee Hays* (New York: W. W. Norton & Company, 1988), 125.

84   During the war: Margalit Fox, "Harold Leventhal, Promoter of Folk Music, Dies at 86," *New York Times*, October 6, 2005, https://www.nytimes.com/2005 /10/06/arts/music/harold-leventhal-promoter-of-folk-music-dies-at-86.html.

84   One of his first: Gilbert, 71.

84   In his version: Pete Kameron to Ronnie Gilbert, 2005, LW.

85   He went to Columbia: Dave Samuelson, *The Weavers, 1949-1953* (Holste, DE: Bear Family Records, 2000),16.

85   "We got ourselves": Pete Seeger to Coyal McMahan, spring 1950, RR, Box 2, Folder 46.

85   "You are a man": Coyal McMahan to Pete Seeger, spring 1950, RR, Box 2, Folder 46.

85   possibly drunken ramble: Lee Hays to Pete Seeger, "Pete's Birthday, 1950," RR, Box 2, Folder 4.

86   newest human face: David Halberstam, *The Fifties* (New York: Fawcett, 1993), 49.

86   first agent they encountered: David King Dunaway, *How Can I Keep from Singing? The Ballad of Pete Seeger*, updated edition (New York: Villard, 2008), 167.

87   Staring them down: Gilbert. 74.

87   "internationalist impulse": Ibid., 75.

88   Lee Hays stocked up: Lee Hays interview with David King Dunaway, 1977, RR, Box 2, Folder 44.

88   "We were about": Samuelson, 20.

88   making their television: Gilbert, 76.

88   very first late-night: Burt A. Folkart, "Jerry Lester; Comedian, Host of 1st Late-Night Show," *Los Angeles Times*, March 26, 1995.

88   "well known": *Counterattack*, June 9, 1950.

88   Ronnie especially loved: Gilbert, 76.

89   They weren't very good beans: Lee Hays interview with David King Dunaway, 1977, RR, Box 2, Folder 44.

89   "It is our belief": Lee Hays to Van Camp's, RR, Box 1, Folder 62.

89   Kameron's account: Pete Kameron to Ronnie Gilbert, 2005, LW.

89   "He had spoken": *Counterattack*, September 22, 1950.

89 **Vito Marcantonio:** Ronald D. Cohen and Dave Samuelson, *Songs for Political Action, Folk Music, Topical Songs and the American Left, 1926–1953* (liner notes) (Holste, DE: Bear Family Records, 1996), 182.

89 **Ronnie and her boyfriend:** Gilbert, 77.

89 *Sing Out!:* Stephen Petrus and Ronald D. Cohen, *Folk City: New York and the American Folk Music Revival* (Oxford: Oxford University Press, 2015), 70.

90 **homestead in Beacon:** Willens, 127.

90 **Pairing with a publisher:** Rian Malan, "In the Jungle," *Rolling Stone*, May 14, 2000, in Nick Hornby and Ben Schafer, eds., *Da Capo Best Music Writing 2001* (Cambridge: Da Capo Press, 2001), 74.

90 **By the time:** "Rights Fight Turns 'Tzena' Into a Dirge," *The Billboard*, July 1, 1950, 10.

90 **Following a system:** Dick Weissman, *Which Side Are You On? An Inside History of the Folk Music Revival in America* (New York: Continuum, 2005), 21.

90 **Released into the world:** "Advance Notice," *The Billboard*, June 24, 1950, 36.

91 **By mid-July:** "The Nation's Top Tunes," *The Billboard*, July 15, 1950, 32.

91 **Ronnie and Marty first heard:** Gilbert, 78.

91 **When the newlyweds stopped:** Jenny Wells Vincent, "Correspondence," *Sing Out!*, October 1950, 2.

91 **Another former People's Songster:** Robert M. Lichtman and Ronald D. Cohen, *Deadly Farce: Harvey Matusow and the Informer System in the McCarthy Era* (Urbana: University of Illinois Press, 2004), 35.

91 **Before he'd left:** Dunaway, 172.

91 **telegram from Weavers' management:** Gilbert, 78.

92 **At the Blue Angel:** Joe Klein, *Woody Guthrie: A Life* (New York: Delta, 1980), 376.

92 **"There were nights":** Michael Denning, *The Cultural Front: The Laboring of American Culture in the Twentieth Century* (London: Verso, 1997), 326.

92 **Blue Angel regulars:** Lorraine Gordon, *Alive at the Village Vanguard: My Life in and Out of Jazz Time* (Milwaukee: Hal Leonard, 2006), 112.

92 **up to Harold:** Klein, 376.

92 **"I'm a capitalist":** Pete Seeger, *The Incompleat Folksinger* (New York: Fireside, 1972), 43.

92 **"Long's I'm headin'":** Woody Guthrie, "Weaver Theme Song," in Willens, 117.

92 **Woody had a publisher:** Klein, 371.

93 **In its first three weeks:** Harry MacArthur, "After Dark," *The Evening Star*, August 15, 1950, B16.

93 **They made the cover:** *The Cash Box*, August 12, 1950, 1.

93 **When the Weavers played in Baltimore:** Lee Hays, "On Irene," 1980, RR, Box 2, Folder 50.

93   **"The folk song originally"**: "'Irene' Looms as Record Breaker," *The Billboard*, August 19, 1950, 13.

93   **alternate versions:** Elijah Wald, *How the Beatles Destroyed Rock 'n' Roll: An Alternative History of American Popular Music* (Oxford: Oxford University Press, 2009), 159; "Honor Roll of Hits," *The Billboard*, November 4, 1950, 26.

94   **global musical safari:** Wald (2009), 160.

94   **"three boys and a girl":** "Vaudeville Reviews," *The Billboard*, October 6, 1950, 20.

94   **They'd received their first:** Willens, 127.

94   **Many nights:** Gilbert, 78.

94   **"Is it the custom":** Ibid.

95   **"It's not so much fun":** "Out of the Corner," *Time*, September 25, 1950, 69.

95   **he discovered Woody:** "Lee on Woody Guthrie, 1975," RR, Box 5, Folder 49.

95   **sprawled on the floor:** Klein, 374.

95   **"They changed and twisted":** Agnes "Sis" Cunningham and Gordon Friesen, *Red Bust and Broadsides: A Joint Autobiography* (Amherst: University of Massachusetts Press, 1999), 251.

96   **"As he got sicker":** "Lee on Woody Guthrie, 1975," RR, Box 5, Folder 49.

96   **"You don't want":** Dunaway, 176.

96   **Josh White appeared:** Elijah Wald, *Josh White: Society Blues* (Amherst: University of Massachusetts Press, 2000), 192.

96   **"I Was a Sucker":** Josh White, "I Was a Sucker for the Communists," *Negro Digest*, December 1950, 6.

96   **"The Billboard does not":** "The Inside on Counterattack," *The Billboard*, September 9, 1950, 4.

97   **"repressive, alienating":** Gilbert, 80.

97   **"I'll go along":** Willens, 134.

97   **"Pete made us pay":** Ibid.

97   **"more professional":** Lee Hays, "Hays Memoirs," October 1976, RR, Box 3, Folder 63.

97   **But then Lee brought:** Gilbert, 83.

97   **Beginning and closing:** December 23, 1950, Town Hall, New York, NY (recording), FH.

98   **plaster blizzard:** Dunaway, 170.

98   **holiday cards:** Gilbert, 85.

98   **"He found laundries":** Robert S. Koppelman, ed., *"Sing Out, Warning! Sing Out, Love!": The Writings of Lee Hays* (Amherst: University of Massachusetts Press, 2003), 106.

98   **a tape of African drumming:** Lee Hays to Jim Brown, RR, Box 2, Folder 47.

98   **field-recording expedition:** Dunaway, 170.

98   **At the glitzy Ciro's:** Seeger, 443.

99   **"When we attempted":** Gilbert, 87.

99   **Lee adjusted instantly:** Willens, 138.

99   **"reading the kept press":** Lee Hays to Harold Leventhal, April 1951, Box 1, Folder 62. (RR)

99   **"Lee would appear":** Gilbert, 85

99   **occasionally reported:** "Hello, Patti; G'Nite, Irene; Or Let's Waltz," *The Billboard*, May 25, 1951, 1.

99   **Lee even made:** Willens, 138.

100   **"When you're poor":** "Lee Hays Interview by Jim Capaldi, 10/27/79," RR, Box 5, Folder 48.

100   **Ronnie adjusted:** Gilbert, 84.

100   **"All well here":** Ronnie Gilbert to Harold Leventhal, March 30, 1951, RR, Box 1, Folder 62.

100   **Fred noted in his journal:** Fred Hellerman Journal, spring 1951, BJO, source for much of the Weavers/Tiny Hill account.

101   **Confidential Informant T-18:** "FBI File on Pete Seeger," Section 2, 13.

102   **"a conspiracy on a scale":** Victor S. Navasky, *Naming Names* (New York: Viking Press, 1980), 24.

102   **Topping the bestseller:** Stephen J. Whitfield, *The Culture of the Cold War* (Baltimore: Johns Hopkins University Press, 1991), 34.

102   **turn down a tour with Paul Robeson:** Lee Hays interview with David King Dunaway, 1977, RR, Box 2, Folder 44.

102   **"<u>must</u> be doing good":** Ronnie Gilbert to Harold Leventhal, March 30, 1951, RR, Box 1, Folder 62.

102   **"They had already":** Samuelson, 24.

103   **Leading the song:** Wald (2000), 212.

103   **while musicians had recorded:** "Weavers Put Old Smoky on Sheet Map," *The Billboard*, March 31, 1951, 18.

103   **"I remember once":** Jenkins, 236.

103   **"I don't know about":** Pete Seeger to Pete Kameron, March 1951, Ronnie Gilbert Collection, LW.

103   **"usual male supremacy":** Irwin Silber, "The Weavers—New 'Find' of the Hit Parade," *Sing Out!*, February 1951, 6.

104   **In Minneapolis:** Jenkins, 245.

104   **Lee would likewise:** Lee Hays, "Hays Memoirs," October 1976, RR, Box 3, Folder 63.

104   **"opened up a lot of doors":** Jenkins, 244.

105   **"We didn't <u>work</u>":** Fred Hellerman to Lee Hays, January 24, 1980, RR, Box 2, Folder 48.

105   **At a band meeting:** Fred Hellerman journal, spring 1951, BJO.

106   **"that the Weavers had busted up":** Woody Guthrie, letter to Jolly Robinson, January 1951, BJO. Excerpt of letter from Woody Guthrie to Jolly Robinson

dated January 1951. © Woody Guthrie Publications, Inc. (BMI) All rights reserved. Used by permission.

106   **Adjacent to Planet Pete:** Fred Hellerman journal, spring 1951, BJO.

106   **about to embark:** "Hill Does Phenomenal 249 One-Nighters in 270 Days," *The Billboard*, December 22, 1951, 17.

107   **"I don't like to":** Dunaway, 172.

107   **"For in the eyes":** Ronnie Gilbert to Weavers and Harold Leventhal, March 31, 1951 (unsent), Ronnie Gilbert Collection, LW.

108   **"Sometimes I feel like":** Erik Darling, *"I'd Give My Life": From Washington Square to Carnegie Hall, A Journey by Folk Music* (Palo Alto: Science and Behavior Books, 2008), 132.

108   **"how much we meant":** Lee Hays to Harold Leventhal, April 1951, RR, Box 1, Folder 62.

108   **"This is a discussion":** Pete Seeger to Pete Kameron, spring 1951, RR, Box 2, Folder 46.

108   **"why we four people":** Ronnie Gilbert to Weavers, spring 1951 (unsent), Ronnie Gilbert Collection, LW.

109   **"conflicting schedules":** Willens, 142.

109   **"Damn it":** Gilbert, 93.

109   **When Pete and Toshi:** Wilkinson, 71.

109   **"There is a certain":** Lee Hays to Harold Leventhal, spring 1951, RR, Box 1, Folder 62.

109   **Lee had spoken:** Frederick Woltman, "Melody Weaves On, Along Party Lines," *New York World Telegram*, August 25, 1951, 15.

109   **"Bob Reed was":** "Weavers Show Up at O. State Fair But Are Nixed; Heidt Puts $ With AFM," *The Billboard*, August 29, 1951, 49.

110   **"If I know anything":** Jenkins, 243.

110   **"We don't know who":** "Weavers Show Up," 49.

110   **and for good reason:** *The Billboard*, August 18, 1951.

110   **"the diskery hasn't":** "Decca Six-Month Net $362,204; Gain Shown," *The Billboard*, August 11, 1951, 14.

110   **citizen of Middletown:** "Non-Controversial Fair," *Akron Beacon Journal*, August 14, 1951, 6.

110   **the governor contacted:** Dunaway, 180.

111   **"First instance":** "Night Club Cancels Show by 'Weavers,'" *New York Journal American*, October 3, 1951.

111   **Lena Horne canceled:** Navasky, 192.

111   **"undesirable characters":** John K. Dungey to Gordon Jenkins, October 14, 1951, Ronnie Gilbert Collection. LW.

111   **"We never met":** Jenkins, 244.

112   **At one session:** Lee Hays, "Hays Memoirs," October 1976, RR, Box 3, Folder 63.

112 **"on the sheet music":** Ibid.

112 **When Decca's promo:** Ibid.

112 **Richmond claimed "Wimoweh":** Malan, 75 .

113 **"Your record of it":** Seeger, 129.

113 **rare live appearance:** "Many Dinners Held at Halloween Ball on Starlight Roof," *New York Herald Tribune*, November 1, 1951, 29.

113 **Two more Town Hall:** December 21 and 22, 1951, Town Hall, New York, NY (recordings), FH.

Chapter Five: Ballad for Un-American Blues

115 **"Witness Tells":** "Witness Tells of Sex Orgies By Red Recruiters," *Chicago Tribune* (via Associated Press), February 8, 1952, 43.

115 **By the end of the tour:** Robert M. Lichtman and Ronald D. Cohen, *Deadly Farce: Harvey Matusow and the Informer System in the McCarthy Era* (Urbana: University of Illinois Press, 2004), 53.

116 **"I think I remember":** David King Dunaway, *How Can I Keep from Singing? The Ballad of Pete Seeger*, updated edition (New York: Villard, 2008), 185.

116 **"You could feel":** Bruce Jenkins. *Goodbye: In Search of Gordon Jenkins* (Berkeley: Frog, Ltd., 2005), 242.

116 **"It's just music":** Dunaway, 188.

116 **"Do you want":** Ibid., 180.

116 **letter to Ronnie:** Pete Kameron to Ronnie Gilbert, June 8, 2005, Ronnie Gilbert Collection, LW.

116 **two telegrams:** Ibid., Xeroxes included in correspondence.

117 **"The public seems":** "Akron Stay Cut Short by Weavers," *Akron Beacon Journal*, February 7, 1952, 1.

117 **"feeling like we":** Jenkins, 242.

117 **In Philadelphia:** Doris Willens, *Lonesome Traveler: The Life of Lee Hays* (New York: W. W. Norton & Company, 1988), 150.

117 **"Rustics Penetrate":** "Rustics Penetrate Major Nightclubs," *The Billboard*, February 9, 1952, 22.

117 **"for a while":** "There'll Always Be a Ballad," *The Cash Box*, March 1, 1952, 4.

118 **"Because they are":** "A Discussion: Can an All-White Group Sing Songs from Negro Culture?," *Sing Out!*, January 1952, 2.

118 **"The idea was":** Author interview with Ernie Lieberman, November 2017.

118 **Freedom Festival:** Ronald D. Cohen, *Rainbow Quest: The Folk Music Revival & American Society* (Amherst: University of Massachusetts Press, 2002), 86.

118 **who'd once presided:** Ronald D. Cohen and Dave Samuelson, *Songs for Political Action, Folk Music, Topical Songs and the American Left, 1926–1953* (liner notes) (Holste, DE: Bear Family Records, 1996), 194.

118   "colossal presumptuousness": Irwin Silber, "Weavers Issue Folk-Song Folio," *Sing Out!*, March 1952, 5.

118   "Joel Newman": Dick Weissman, *Which Side Are You On? An Inside History of the Folk Music Revival in America* (New York: Continuum, 2005), 69.

119   "If the Weavers didn't": Earl Robinson, "Correspondence," *Sing Out!*, April 1952, 14.

119   "the Weavers themselves": Irwin Silber, 16.

119   Both he and Betty Sanders: "The Un-Americans Retreat," *Sing Out!*, April 1952, 2.

119   Alan Lomax: Andrew J. Bottomley, "The Ballad of Alan and Auntie Beeb: Alan Lomax's Radio Programmes for the BBC, 1943–1960," *Historical Journal of Film, Radio and Television*, 2016, 604.

119   "pernicious influence": "Folk-Singer Oscar Brand Joins Witch-Hunt Hysteria," *Sing Out!*, November 1951, 2.

119   In May 1952: Cohen, 80.

120   "The future of Burl": "Burl Ives Sings a Different Song," *Sing Out!*, October 1952, 2.

120   "stool pigeon": Dunaway, 235.

120   There were 76: Lichtman and Cohen, 69, 71.

120   "They could integrate": "3 of the Weavers Called Communists," *New York Herald Tribune* (via Associated Press), February 26, 1952, 6.

120   "I sat in closed": "Communist Youth Chief Is Named," *Newark Advocate* (via Associated Press), February 25, 1952, 1.

120   "Agent Calls": "Agent Calls Singer Reds," *New York Times*, February 26, 1952, 14.

120   "My reaction": "Singers Accused of Communist Ties," *Philadelphia Inquirer*, February 27, 1952, 12.

120   "extraordinary possibilities": Pete Seeger to Weavers, ca. 1951–1952, RR, Box 2, Folder 46.

121   DOWN WITH: FPG/Fulton Archive/Getty Archive, "Down with Scumunists" (photograph), May 7, 1952, Getty Images.

121   In a photograph: "Lee Exhibit No. 1," in "Testimony of Miss Madeline Lee," *Investigation of Communist Activities in New York Area—Part VI (Entertainment)* (Washington, DC: Government Printing Office, 1955), 2397.

121   "to set a concert": "Weavers to Get Europe Dates," *The Billboard*, June 28, 1952, 24.

121   Rotary International gala: Dave Samuelson, *The Weavers, 1949-1953* (Holste, DE: Bear Family Records, 2000), 35.

121   steel company: Willens, 150.

121   Of the thirty-four songs: December 27, 1952, Town Hall, New York, NY (recording), FH.

122   **"used to bring":** "Die Gadanken Sind Frei," December 1952, on *Kisses Sweeter Than Wine* (New York: Omega, 1994), disc 1.

122   **"We took a sabbatical":** Willens, 150.

122   **When Pete Seeger reported:** Dunaway, 193.

122   **recording console:** Joe Klein, *Woody Guthrie: A Life* (New York: Delta, 1980), 285.

122   **"It's much easier":** Moses Asch interview by Chris Strachwitz, KPFA, 1981, http://arhoolie.org/moses-asch-folkways-records/.

122   **starting in 1939:** Cohen, 37.

122   **"Unlike most record companies":** "Offbeat," *Time*, February 25, 1946, 65.

123   **Sam Goody pushed:** Asch interview, 1981.

123   **eighty-four songs collected:** Greil Marcus, *Invisible Republic: Bob Dylan's Basement Tapes* (New York: Henry Holt and Company, 1997), 87.

124   **Asch became a patron:** Dunaway, 193.

124   **over two dozen:** David King Dunaway, *A Pete Seeger Discography: Seventy Years of Recordings* (Lanham, MD: The Scarecrow Press, 2011).

124   **"I always believed":** Robert Cantwell, *When We Were Good: The Folk Revival* (Cambridge, MA: Harvard University Press, 1996), 82.

124   **Pete would speak fondly:** Jenkins, 243.

124   **label's main source:** Stephen Petrus and Ronald D. Cohen, *Folk City: New York and the American Folk Music Revival* (Oxford: Oxford University Press, 2015), 86.

125   **"Guerrilla cultural tactics":** Alec Wilkinson, *The Protest Singer: An Intimate Portrait of Pete Seeger* (New York: Alfred A. Knopf, 2009), 4.

125   **Harold Leventhal secured:** Willens, 157.

125   **"I detest":** Lee Hays to Harold Leventhal, ca. 1953, RR, Box 1, Folder 64.

125   **He got some beer:** Willens, 153.

125   **"Why not join":** Ronnie Gilbert *Ronnie Gilbert: A Radical Life in Song* (Oakland: University of California Press, 2015), 99.

126   **changing his name:** Ibid., 100.

126   **"blight of guilt":** Lee Hays to Harold Leventhal, ca. 1953, RR, Box 1, Folder 64.

126   **"I just made":** Lee Hays, "lee's tapes," October 2, 1976, RR, Box 3, Folder 64.

126   **only given Walter:** Lee Hays to Pete Seeger, March 18, 1977, RR, Box 2, Folder 4.

126   **"I was flushed":** Willens, 158.

126   **Since returning from:** Ibid., 148.

126   **started writing again:** Ibid., 160-161.

127   **whole erotic novel:** Ibid., 112.

127   **"Banquet and a Half":** Lee Hays, "Banquet and a Half," *Ellery Queen's Mystery Magazine*, October 1954; and Robert S. Koppelman, ed., *"Sing Out, Warning!*

Sing Out, Love!": The Writings of Lee Hays (Amherst: University of Massachusetts Press, 2003), 178.

127   **"A little gem":** Ronnie Gilbert to Lee Hays, ca. 1955, Ronnie Gilbert Collection, LW.

127   **Pregnant during:** Gilbert, 101.

127   **Belafonte's success:** Elijah Wald, *How the Beatles Destroyed Rock 'n' Roll: An Alternative History of American Popular Music* (Oxford: Oxford University Press, 2009), 93.

128   **Befriending Robert De Cormier:** Michael A. Ciavaglia, "The Choral Music of Robert De Cormier" (doctoral thesis) (University of Cincinnati, 2013); Author interviews with Caleb Hellerman, 2017.

128   **"workshop for myself":** "Fred Hellerman: In His Own Words," The Weston Forum, September 10, 2016, https://archive.thewestonforum.com/68715/fred -hellerman-in-his-own-words/.

128   **Fred helped arrange:** Ed Cray, *Ramblin' Man: The Life and Times of Woody Guthrie* (New York: W. W. Norton, 2006), 368.

128   **"housewifery":** Ronnie Gilbert to Lee Hays, ca. 1955, Ronnie Gilbert Collection, LW.

129   **"When the purpose":** "FBI File on Pete Seeger," Section 3, 32.

129   **deployed to track:** David Wise, *Cassidy's Run: The Secret Spy War over Nerve Gas* (New York: Random House, 2000), 12.

130   **passport revoked:** Dunaway, 201.

130   **half sister Peggy:** Ibid., 266.

130   **A contemporary survey:** Whitfield, 14.

130   **"Unquestioning party members":** Ibid., 33.

131   **director Elia Kazan:** Victor S. Navasky, *Naming Names* (New York: Viking Press, 1980), 199.

131   **"public exposure":** Arthur Miller, *Time Bends: A Life* (New York: Harper & Row, 1988), 329.

131   **landmark case:** *Dennis v. United States*, 341 U.S. 494 (1951).

131   **"What a clever trick":** Whitfield, 103.

132   **"Bill of Rights":** *Investigation of Communist Activities in the New York Area, Committee on Un-American Activities* (Washington, DC: Government Printing Office, 1953), 1370.

132   **"I haven't been":** Dunaway, 189.

132   **The week before:** All solo Seeger dates, "FBI File on Pete Seeger," Section 3, 18–29.

133   **"Only Pete knows":** Cantwell, 242.

133   **"Maybe I've got":** Dunaway, 140.

134   **"We didn't see him":** Elijah Wald, *Dylan Goes Electric! Newport, Seeger, Dylan, and the Night That Split the Sixties* (New York: Dey Street, 2015), 266.

134   **In a metric:** Dunaway, 232.

134   **the wrong Lee Hays:** Willens, 162.

134   **"Greeting":** subpoena, August 16, 1955, RR, Box 2, Folder 55.

134   **"Are you Pete":** *Landmark cases left out of your textbooks: herein restored by the original lawyers & litigants and by Meiklejohn legal interns* (Berkeley: Meiklejohn Civil Liberties Institute, 2006), 38.

135   **Paul Ross:** Ronald Cohen and James Capaldi, eds., *The Pete Seeger Reader* (Oxford: Oxford University Press, 2014), 130.

135   **"contrary to Senatorial traditions":** "The Censure Case of Joseph McCarthy of Wisconsin (1954)," https://www.senate.gov/artandhistory/history/common/censure_cases/133Joseph_McCarthy.htm.

135   **"unprecedented mudslinging":** James Cross Giblin, *The Rise and Fall of Senator Joe McCarthy* (Boston: Clarion Books, 2009), 200.

135   **"but may require":** "Red Probe Opens Here Tomorrow," *New York Herald Tribune*, August 14, 1955, 21.

136   **"Another Fifth Amendment":** Edward R. Murrow, "A Report on Senator Joseph R. McCarthy," *See It Now* (news report), CBS TV, March 9, 1954. http://www.lib.berkeley.edu/MRC/murrowmccarthy.html.

136   **"Using the Fifth":** Willens, 163.

136   **"I want to get up":** Dunaway, 207.

136   **"If it wasn't":** Koppelman, 17.

137   **"I wanted to":** Dunaway, 203.

137   **"When I walked":** Lee Hays, "The Era of McCarthyism," May 18, 1981, RR, Box 2, Folder 54.

137   **"I consider it":** "Robeson's Court Plea for Passport Rejected," *Washington Post*, August 17, 1955, 16.

138   **"Do you recall":** Elliott Sullivan, July 29, 1955, *Investigation of Communist Activities, New York Area—Part 5 (Summer Camps)* (Washington, DC: Government Printing Office, 1955), 1391.

138   **"I believe that I am":** Elliot Sullivan, August 16, 1955, *Investigation of Communist Activities in New York Area—Part VI,* (Washington, DC: Government Printing Office, 1955), 2346.

139   **"I had a good":** Lee Hays, "The Era of McCarthyism," May 18, 1981, RR, Box 2, Folder 54.

139   **"I have before me":** Lee Hays, August 16, 1955, *Investigation of Communist Activities in New York Area—Part VI,* (Washington, DC: Government Printing Office, 1955), 2348.

140   **night watchman:** Willens, 77.

140   **"We have hopes":** "4 More Defy Probe of Theater Reds," *New York Herald Tribune*, August 17, 1955, 10.

140   **small donation:** Matthew C. Roudane, ed., *Conversations with Arthur Miller* (Jackson: University Press of Mississippi), 200.

140   "a burly sandy-haired": "Folk Singer Is Heard," *New York Times*, August 17, 1955.

141   "When I got home": Hays, "The Era of McCarthyism."

141   "watched until": Willens, 166.

141   "Sir, I refuse": Pete Seeger, August 18, 1955, *Investigation of Communist Activities in New York Area—Part VII (Entertainment)* (Washington, DC: United States Government Printing Office, 1955), 2447.

141   "There was a job": Dunaway, 214.

143   "I'd always been amused": Wilkinson, 80.

143   "a member of the Marxist": Warren R. Ross, "Singing for Humanity: The Pete Seeger Saga," *UU World*, July/August 1996, https://www.uuworld.org/articles /pete-seeger-saga.

143   "Jack Sprat": Lichtman and Cohen, 53.

144   children's set: Dunaway, 204.

144   Outside the courtroom: Willens, 164.

Chapter Six: This Land Is Your Land

145   None of the Weavers wanted: Mary Katherine Aldin, *Wasn't That a Time* (liner notes) (New York: Vanguard Records, 1993), 23.

145   "Not us radicals!": Ibid.

146   "It was all due": Ibid.

146   "I was still mourning": Ronnie Gilbert *Ronnie Gilbert: A Radical Life in Song* (Oakland: University of California Press, 2015), 101.

146   Ronnie couldn't fail: Ibid., 100.

146   "Folkish waltz-tempo": "Review of New Pop Records," *The Billboard*, April 17, 1954, 22.

146   He and Lee: Dave Samuelson, *The Weavers, 1949-1953* (Holste, DE: Bear Family Records, 2000), 28.

147   *It's a hell*: Doris Willens, *Lonesome Traveler: The Life of Lee Hays* (New York: W. W. Norton & Company, 1988), 164.

147   "I have sung in": Pete Seeger, August 18, 1955, *Investigation of Communist Activities in New York Area—Part VII (Entertainment)* (Washington, DC: United States Government Printing Office, 1955), 2452.

147   *Billboard* noted: "Weavers' Carnegie Already Sold Out," *The Billboard*, December 17, 1955, 42.

147   Over the course of the autumn: "FBI File on Pete Seeger," Section 3, 18–29.

147   In Louisiana: David King Dunaway, *How Can I Keep from Singing? The Ballad of Pete Seeger*, updated edition (New York: Villard, 2008), 227.

148   few weeks early: Gilbert, 101.

148   "I will never forget": Aldin, 24.

148 **"breathless feeling":** David King Dunaway and Molly Beer, *Singing Out: An Oral History of America's Folk Music Revivals* (Oxford: Oxford University Press, 2010), 105.

148 **they opened with:** Master tape reels, Ronnie Gilbert Collection, LW.

148 **as much as a full LP's side:** The Weavers, *The Weavers at Carnegie Hall* (New York: Vanguard Recording Society, 1957).

148 **"on intimate terms":** R. B., "The Weavers Sing at Carnegie Hall," *New York Herald Tribune*, December 26, 1955, 13.

149 **noted as a turning point:** Susan Montgomery, "The Folk Furor," *Mademoiselle*, December 1960, 177.

149 **"voice of a strong":** Aldin, 26.

149 **"contemporary inquisition":** Irwin Silber, "Carnegie Hall Rocks as the Weavers Return," *Sing Out!*, Winter 1956, 31.

149 **"Frankly I had":** Harold Leventhal, "Report on the Concert," January 6, 1955, RR, Box 2, Folder 64.

150 **"Lee was always an old man":** Willens, 21.

150 **"Young musicians":** Ibid., 170.

150 **"was tottering":** Ed Cray, *Ramblin' Man: The Life and Times of Woody Guthrie* (New York: W. W. Norton, 2006), 268.

150 **meeting was convened:** Joe Klein, *Woody Guthrie: A Life* (New York: Delta, 1980), 430.

150 **Lee served as narrator:** Pete Seeger, *The Incompleat Folksinger* (New York: Fireside, 1972), 172.

151 **nearly burned down:** Klein, 432.

151 **staggered to Lee's:** "Lee on Woody Guthrie, 1975," RR, Box 5, Folder 49.

152 **opened and closed:** May 18, 1956, Orchestra Hall, Chicago, IL (recording), FH.

152 **stink bomb:** Willens, 172.

152 **They demonstrated Pete's:** May 18, 1956, Orchestra Hall, Chicago, IL (recording), FH.

152 **"My dear":** Gilbert, 102.

152 **"Everything will be":** Dunaway and Beer, 94.

152 **"entertainment specialist":** Chris Drake, *The Life and High Times of John Henry Faulk* (Newcastle: Cambridge Scholars Printing, 2007),144.

152 **"Co-operate":** "A Picasso on the Wall and You Lose Your Job," *New Age*, September 8, 1955, 4.

152 **deployed to leak news:** Arthur Miller, *Time Bends: A Life* (New York: Harper & Row, 1988), 251.

153 **"Everybody knows Pete":** Seymour Raven, "Folk Singers Are Cheered by Audience," *Chicago Tribune*, May 19, 1956, A4.

153   **when they lived nearby:** Robert Cantwell, *When We Were Good: The Folk Revival* (Cambridge, MA: Harvard University Press, 1996), 287.

153   **scene that resulted might be observed:** Stephen Petrus and Ronald D. Cohen, *Folk City: New York and the American Folk Music Revival* (Oxford: Oxford University Press, 2015), 108.

154   **"to tell [him] what they knew":** "Lee on Woody Guthrie, 1975," RR, Box 5, Folder 49.

154   **occasional park visitor:** Ronald D. Cohen, *Rainbow Quest: The Folk Music Revival & American Society* (Amherst: University of Massachusetts Press, 2002), 107.

154   **"essentially summer camp":** Dave Van Ronk and Elijah Wald, *The Mayor of MacDougal Street* (Boston: Da Capo Press, 2005), 22.

155   **"if there was one thing":** Ibid.

155   **bowled over:** "Blind Rafferty" in Ronald Cohen and James Capaldi, eds., *The Pete Seeger Reader* (Oxford: Oxford University Press, 2014), 136.

155   **Highly disciplined:** Erik Darling, *"I'd Give My Life": From Washington Square to Carnegie Hall, A Journey by Folk Music* (Palo Alto: Science and Behavior Books, 2008), 16.

156   **"I needed a song":** Ibid., 76.

156   **Tarriers were first paired:** Ibid., 88.

156   **"felt quite complimented":** Pete Seeger, "Summary of Government Charges, 1955–1957," in Cohen and Capaldi, 128.

156   **even night terrors:** Dunaway, 224.

157   **cast recording:** Elijah Wald, *How the Beatles Destroyed Rock 'n' Roll: An Alternative History of American Popular Music* (Oxford: Oxford University Press, 2009), 186.

157   **Harry Belafonte:** Ibid., 195.

157   **$128.11:** Harold Leventhal, "Report on the Concert," January 6, 1955, RR, Box 2, Folder 64.

158   **prevented the band:** Milt Gabler to Pete Kameron, November 2, 1953, BJO.

158   **Lee wanted to include:** Lee Hays to Harold Leventhal, May 1956, RR, Box 2, Folder 35.

158   **"cutting, blending and fading":** Lee Hays to Fred Hellerman, ca. 1980–1981, RR, Box 2, Folder 40.

158   **deal with Vanguard Records:** Cohen, 103.

159   **They came for Fred:** Fred Hellerman, *Investigation of Communism in the Metropolitan Music School, Inc., and Related Fields—Part 2* (Washington, DC: Government Printing Office, 1957), 871.

159   **"has the same right":** Stephen J. Whitfield, *The Culture of the Cold War* (Baltimore: The Johns Hopkins University Press, 1991), 11.

160   **Scotti was partially:** Drake, 144.

160   **"You are the nonpatriots":** Paul Robeson, *Investigation of the Unauthorized Use of United States Passports—Part 1* (Washington, DC: Government Printing Office, 1956), 4509.

161   **"the happiest time":** "Fred Hellerman: In His Own Words," The Weston Forum, September 10, 2016, https://archive.thewestonforum.com/68715/fred -hellerman-in-his-own-words/.

161   **at one of these Neighbors gigs:** Michael A. Ciavaglia, "The Choral Music of Robert De Cormier" (doctoral thesis) (University of Cincinnati, 2013).

161   **peculiar international truce:** Billy Bragg, *Roots, Radicals and Rockers: How Skiffle Changed the World* (London: Faber & Faber, 2017), 209.

162   **"Rock Island Line" had deep roots:** Ibid., 3.

162   **during the Village Vanguard:** March 1950, Village Vanguard, New York, NY (recordings), FH.

163   **"He had little sense":** Bragg, 212. *Roots, Radicals and Rockers* is an infectious history of the British skiffle craze.

163   **"For years":** John Halstead, "Don't Scoff at Skiffle," *Sing Out!*, Spring 1957, 29.

164   **"A must for any":** "Packaged Records: Folk," *The Billboard*, April 27, 1957, 36.

164   **the same week that Pete pled:** Seeger in Cohen and Capaldi, 129.

165   **discovering at the last moment:** undated clip, ca. March 1957, Ronnie Gilbert Collection, LW.

165   **Shadow Pete:** "FBI File on Pete Seeger," Section 4, 130.

165   **checked *The Cash Box*:** "Weavers tp Tour," *The Cash Box*, March 23, 1957, 31.

165   **"My recurring nightmare":** Willens, 173.

165   **Paul Endicott:** Cohen, 149; Statement from Harold Leventhal to Lee Hays, RR, Box 2, Folder 64.

165   **increasingly specific demands:** Willens, 173.

165   **"As a fellow worker":** Gilbert, 105.

166   **a $1,200 advance:** Statement from Harold Leventhal to Lee Hays, RR, Box 2, Folder 64.

166   **non-album Weavers singles:** Untitled item, *The Billboard*, June 24, 1957, 26.

167   **Vox announced:** "Hour-Long Sides: 16 2/3 Speed Poses Program Challenge," *The Billboard*, November 25, 1957, 26.

167   **fired up with ideas:** Lee Hays to Harold Leventhal, ca. spring 1957, RR, Box 2, Folder 35.

167   **a Weavers summit:** Lee Hays to Harold Leventhal, ca. spring 1957, RR, Box 2, Folder 42.

167   **pre-organization meeting:** Lee Hays to Toshi Seeger, ca. June 1957, RR, Box 2, Folder 4.

167   **"the Weavers are not":** Harold Leventhal to Lee Hays, June 1, 1957, RR, Box 2, Folder 42.

167   **patiently cataloged:** Harold Leventhal to Lee Hays, June 20, 1957, RR, Box 2, Folder 42.

168   **"I think I can understand":** Ronnie Gilbert to Weavers, June 22, 1957, RR, Box 2, Folder 42.

168   **"If I demanded":** Kate Weigand, "Voices of Feminism Oral History Project: Ronnie Gilbert," Sophia Smith Collection, Smith College, 2004, https://www.smith.edu/libraries/libs/ssc/vof/transcripts/Gilbert.pdf, 17.

169   **"If at all possible":** Ronnie Gilbert to Weavers, June 22, 1957, RR, Box 2, Folder 42.

169   **supremely passive-aggressive:** Lee Hays to Toshi Seeger, ca. June 1957, RR, Box 2, Folder 4.

169   **"Let the other three":** Lee Hays to Harold Leventhal, ca. spring 1957, RR, Box 2, Folder 42.

169   **"rural, laid-back atmosphere":** Gilbert, 107.

169   **"But I've had":** Ronnie Gilbert to Weavers, June 22, 1957, RR, Box 2, Folder 42.

170   **summer of 1957:** Dave Samuelson, "The Vanguard Studio Sessions: A Preliminary Exploratory Discography" (unpublished, courtesy of Dave Samuelson).

170   **Vanguard Records had contracted:** Dunstan Prial, *The Producer: John Hammond and the Soul of American Music* (New York: Macmillan, 2007), 202.

170   ***Downbeat* even reported:** Thomas P. Hustad, *Born to Play: The Ruby Braff Discography and Directory of Performances* (Lanham: Scarecrow Press, 2011), 118.

171   **"most commercial singer":** "Lee Hays Interview by Jim Capaldi, 10/27/79," RR, Box 5, Folder 48.

172   **"Red Monday":** Landon R. Y. Storrs, "McCarthyism and the Second Red Scare," *American History*, 2015, http://americanhistory.oxfordre.com/view/10.1093/acrefore/9780199329175.001.0001/acrefore-9780199329175-e-6.

172   **"Age of the C.I.O.":** Michael Denning, *The Cultural Front: The Laboring of American Culture in the Twentieth Century* (London: Verso, 1997), 21.

173   **Pete had first visited:** Klein, 167.

173   **Seeger met two:** Dunaway, 273.

173   **Red-baiting headline:** Elijah Wald, *Dylan Goes Electric! Newport, Seeger, Dylan, and the Night That Split the Sixties* (New York: Dey Street, 2015), 84.

174   **up to 20,000 copies:** Harold Leventhal to the Weavers, "Re: THE WEAVERS," November 18, 1957, RR, Box 2, Folder 64.

174   **sold 15,000 copies:** Vanguard Recording Society statement, February 28, 1958, RR, Box 2, Folder 64.

174   **singles would wait:** "Vanguard Aims to Break into Singles Field," *The Billboard*, November 25, 1957, 26.

174   **With a royalty statement:** Leventhal to the Weavers, "Re: THE WEAVERS."

Chapter Seven: Twelve Gates to the City

175 **first television appearance:** "Hour of Music Plans Variety of Folk Songs," *Chicago Tribune*, January 12, 1958, N12.

175 **jam session:** "Series 2: Old Town School of Folk Music" (photographs), Robert C. Malone Photographs, 1957-1961, RR.

175 **Old Town School of Folk Music:** Dick Weissman, *Which Side Are You On? An Inside History of the Folk Music Revival in America* (New York: Continuum, 2005), 124.

175 **Two days later:** Dave Samuelson, "The Vanguard Studio Sessions: A Preliminary Exploratory Discography" (unpublished, courtesy of Dave Samuelson).

176 **they were handed arrangements:** Lee Hays to Harold Leventhal, ca. early 1958, RR, Box 2, Folder 35.

176 **Fred had been named:** "Elektra Skeds 45 12-Inchers During 1958," *The Billboard*, January 13, 1958, 18.

177 **"rated 70 or less":** "Reviews of New Records," *The Billboard*, March 3, 1958, 52.

177 **"A rockin' item":** "Record Reviews," *The Cash Box*, March 1, 1958, 8.

177 **"every last one":** Lee Hays to Harold Leventhal, October 1958, RR, Box 2, Folder 42.

178 **this was considered:** Ronnie Gilbert *Ronnie Gilbert: A Radical Life in Song* (Oakland: University of California Press, 2015), 107.

178 **Toshi's mother:** Doris Willens, *Lonesome Traveler: The Life of Lee Hays* (New York: W. W. Norton & Company, 1988), 181.

178 **"Why couldn't it be":** David King Dunaway, *How Can I Keep from Singing? The Ballad of Pete Seeger*, updated edition (New York: Villard, 2008), 238.

178 **"Lee argued":** Gilbert, 107.

179 **"would have nothing more":** "Lee Hays with Don McLean (transcript)," RR, Box 5, Folder 48.

179 **"Fred and I":** Gilbert, 108.

179 **"that dreadful night":** Lee Hays, "Lee's tapes," September 26, 1976, RR, Box 3, Folder 64.

179 **"It came out":** Willens, 182.

179 **"If you get your way":** Mary Katherine Aldin, *Wasn't That a Time* (liner notes) (New York: Vanguard Records, 1993), 27.

180 ***Variety*'s top 15:** "Goody's Album Bestsellers," *Variety*, April 2, 1958.

180 **Pete assigned half:** Irwin Silber to Harold Leventhal, January 23, 1958, RR, Box 2, Folder 37.

180 **"a real understatement":** Pete Seeger to Weavers, March 1958, RR, Box 3, Folder 50.

180 **didn't immediately know:** Lee Hays to Harold Leventhal, ca. early 1958, RR, Box 2, Folder 35.

180   **end of a path:** Erik Darling, *"I'd Give My Life": From Washington Square to Carnegie Hall, A Journey by Folk Music* (Palo Alto: Science and Behavior Books, 2008), 118.

181   **"performance shifted":** Ibid., 64.

182   **"I can't remember us":** Aldin, 29.

182   **Pete Seeger departed:** Dunaway, 237.

182   **"Weavers' rehearsals consist":** *At Home* (liner notes) (New York: Vanguard Recording Society, 1958).

182   **"Another wonderful album":** "Review Spotlight on Albums," *The Billboard*, June 16, 1958, 18.

182   **almost 8,500 copies:** Harold Leventhal, "Financial Statement to the Weavers," October 6, 1958, RR, Box 2, Folder 65.

182   **group officially informed their label:** Maynard Solomon to Harold Leventhal, October 22, 1958, RR, Box 2, Folder 37.

182   **"No one was boss":** Darling, 129.

182   **"I was treated":** Ibid., 130.

182   **"Ronnie was eager":** Ibid., 134.

183   **"male competition":** Kate Weigand, "Voices of Feminism Oral History Project: Ronnie Gilbert," Sophia Smith Collection, Smith College, 2004, https://www.smith.edu/libraries/libs/ssc/vof/transcripts/Gilbert.pdf, 17

183   **"I loved singing":** Gilbert, 109.

183   **"qualities that were":** Aldin, 29.

183   **"couldn't help but":** Darling, 129.

183   **"I must say":** "Lee Hays with Don McLean (transcript)," RR, Box 5, Folder 48.

184   **"In my father's house":** Darling, 127.

184   **"Lee's nature":** Willens, 173.

184   **"I was working":** Aldin, 27.

185   **"I could feel":** Darling, 130.

185   **"If you want better biscuits":** Lee Hays and Erik Darling, ca. 1958, RR, Box 3, Folder 45.

185   **"It is obvious":** Lee Hays to Harold Leventhal, October 1958, RR, Box 2, Folder 42.

186   **"Greenland Whale Fisheries":** Ronnie Gilbert to Weavers, June 22, 1957, RR, Box 2, Folder 42.

186   **"mostly unpleasant":** Darling, 128.

186   **"spectacular yodeling":** Bernie Hodes, "Weavers Score in Carnegie Date," *Billboard*, May 25, 1959, 42.

187   **A pair of ghosts:** Ronald D. Cohen, *Rainbow Quest: The Folk Music Revival & American Society* (Amherst: University of Massachusetts Press, 2002), 131.

187   **"We were all in tears":** William J. Bush, *Greenback Dollar: The Incredible Rise of the Kingston Trio* (Lanham, MD: The Scarecrow Press, 2013), 61.

187   **"We were sort of "**: Bruce Pollock, *When Rock Was Young: A Nostalgic View of the Top 40 Era* (New York: Holt, Rinehart and Winston, 1981), 132.

188   **Gateway Singers:** Cohen, 95.

188   **the Re-Weavers:** Frank Fried, "Lou and the Gateway Singers," From Lenin to Lennon, September 10, 2011. http://www.showbizred.com/?p=96.

188   **"When I joined":** Author interview with Ernie Lieberman, November 2017.

188   **form the Limeliters:** Cohen, 176.

189   **"good folk music":** Ron Radosh, "Commercialism and the Folk Song Revival," *Sing Out!*, Spring 1959, 27.

189   **entrepreneur named Izzy Young:** Stephen Petrus and Ronald D. Cohen, *Folk City: New York and the American Folk Music Revival* (Oxford: Oxford University Press, 2015), 94.

190   **"I'd especially like":** "Free Plug: Richmond Thanks Roulette," *The Billboard*, December 16, 1957, 28.

191   **He knew much more:** Theodore Bikel, *Theo: An Autobiography* (Madison: University of Wisconsin Press, 1994), 164.

191   **"She sounds more":** "Memories of Bessie," *HiFI & Music Review*, July 1958, 10.

191   **singularly shitty:** Gilbert, 109.

192   **Lee had befriended:** Willens, 178.

192   **"I don't think Earl":** Author interview with Alan Arkin, December 2017.

193   **"possibly the only children's":** Willens, 167.

193   **"Breathes there not":** Lee Hays, *Folk Songs for Babies, Small Children, Parents and Baby Sitters* (liner notes) (New York: Vanguard Recording Society, 1959).

193   **Dr. Benjamin Spock, too:** Michael Denning, *The Cultural Front: The Laboring of American Culture in the Twentieth Century* (London: Verso, 1997), 95.

194   **"This is easily":** Willens, 179.

194   ***The Bosses' Songbook*:** Dave Van Ronk and Richard Ellington, *The Bosses' Songbook: Songs to Stifle the Flames of Discontent* (Richard Ellington: New York, 1959).

195   **"He was just *gooder*":** Elijah Wald, *Dylan Goes Electric! Newport, Seeger, Dylan, and the Night That Split the Sixties* (New York: Dey Street, 2015), 30.

195   **"work ten times":** Willens, 182.

195   **first installment:** Wald (2015), 115.

196   **At Pete's recommendation:** Petrus and Cohen, 205.

196   **placed controversially:** Christopher Mele, "'We Shall Overcome' Is Put in Public Domain in a Copyright Settlement," *New York Times*, January 26, 2018, https://www.nytimes.com/2018/01/26/business/media/we-shall-overcome-copyright.html.

196   **"Had he drank [*sic*] less":** Darling, 133.

197   **Fighting the case:** *Kent v. Dulles*, 357 U.S. 116, 1958.

197   **Robeson departed:** The Editors of Freedom Ways, *Paul Robeson: The Great Forerunner* (New York: International Publishers, 1998), 149.

197   **"names out of books":** Gilbert, 110.

197   **"We have been here":** Lee Hays to Harold Leventhal, May 1959, RR, Box 2, Folder 36.

197   **"London is drab":** Ibid.

198   **"whom should I meet":** Gilbert, 110.

198   **"There was not a soul":** Lee Hays to Harold Leventhal, May 28, 1959, RR, Box 2, Folder 36.

198   **"There was a hauntedness":** Darling, 151.

198   **"There was a sense":** Author interview with Alan Arkin, December 2017.

198   **out carousing:** Lee Hays to Harold Leventhal, May 29, 1959, RR, Box 2, Folder 36.

198   **gained a political consciousness:** Billy Bragg, *Roots, Radicals and Rockers: How Skiffle Changed the World* (London: Faber & Faber, 2017), 351.

199   **Kameron went to work:** Lee Hays to Harold Leventhal, June 4, 1959, RR, Box 2, Folder 36.

199   **tracking sixty-three songs:** Ibid.; Radio Luxembourg (recordings), FH.

199   **Erik especially loved:** Darling, 128.

200   **"When we stepped":** Ibid., 137.

200   **"Nobody gave a damn":** Gilbert, 111.

200   **"As everywhere":** Lee Hays, *A Newsletter from Lee Hays*, July 11, 1959, RR, Box 2, Folder 51.

200   **absorbing local slang:** Lee Hays to Harold Leventhal, June 23, 1959, RR, Box 2, Folder 35.

200   **promoters had manifested:** Darling, 138.

201   **"It seems America":** Lee Hays to Harold Leventhal, July 4, 1959, RR, Box 2, Folder 36.

201   **few shared road stories:** Gilbert, 112.

201   **Lee's deterioration:** Darling, 142.

201   **"I thought I was going":** Lee Hays to Harold Leventhal, July 1959, RR, Box 2, Folder 36.

201   **"It's a little difficult":** Fred Hellerman to Harold Leventhal, July 1959, RR, Box 2, Folder 36.

202   **"Beautiful fields":** Lee Hays to Harold Leventhal, July 1959, RR, Box 2, Folder 36.

202   **roadside picnic:** Hays, *A Newsletter*.

202   **Erik and Joan dreamt:** Darling, 148.

202   **come across a book:** Ibid.

Chapter Eight: Hammer Songs

203   **bypass the blacklist:** Doris Willens, *Lonesome Traveler: The Life of Lee Hays* (New York: W. W. Norton & Company, 1988), 185.

203   **"We resent":** "Quartet Barred from Paar Show for Refusing to Sign Loyalty Oaths," *Austin American-Statesman* (via Associated Press), January 3, 1962, 18.

203   **Harold Leventhal filed:** Len Chaimowitz, "Loyalty Oath Issue Bars Weavers at NBC," *Newsday*, January 4, 1962, 3C.

203   **the station balked:** Theodore Bikel, *Theo: An Autobiography* (Madison: University of Wisconsin Press, 1994), 173.

204   **"It seemed so ridiculous":** Willens, 185.

204   **"weeping, guffawing":** Ronnie Gilbert *Ronnie Gilbert: A Radical Life in Song* (Oakland: University of California Press, 2015), 114.

204   **"worst kind of fatalism":** Ronnie Gilbert to Lee Hays (draft), ca. 1963, LW.

205   **Maynard Solomon's request:** David Hadju, *Positively 4th Street: The Lives and Times of Joan Baez, Bob Dylan, Mimi Baez Fariña, and Richard Fariña* (New York: Picador, 2001), 59.

205   **"How on earth":** Robert Shelton, *No Direction Home: The Life and Music of Bob Dylan* (New York: Ballantine, 1986), 123.

205   **"heavy people going by":** Bob Dylan. *Chronicles, Volume One* (New York: Simon & Schuster, 2004), 47.

205   **in the People's Songs days:** Ed Cray, *Ramblin' Man: The Life and Times of Woody Guthrie* (New York: W. W. Norton, 2006), 295.

205   **Ronnie, on the other hand:** Gilbert, 114.

206   **"that no good songs":** Agnes "Sis" Cunningham and Gordon Friesen, *Red Bust and Broadsides: A Joint Autobiography* (Amherst: University of Massachusetts Press, 1999), 283.

206   **He signed to Columbia:** David King Dunaway, *How Can I Keep from Singing? The Ballad of Pete Seeger*, updated edition (New York: Villard, 2008), 249.

206   **judge had once seen:** Ibid., 246.

206   **"Some of my ancestors":** Seeger in Ronald Cohen and James Capaldi, eds., *The Pete Seeger Reader* (Oxford: Oxford University Press, 2014), 155.

206   **"I have a rendezvous":** Dunaway, 25.

207   **"Lacking a legislative":** Paul L. Ross and Samuel M. Koenigsberg, *Defendant-Appellant's Brief, United State Court of Appeals For the Second Circuit, No. 27,101,* BJO.

207   **won his lawsuit:** Victor S. Navasky, *Naming Names* (New York: Viking Press, 1980), 327.

207   **seemed like a matter:** Erik Darling, *"I'd Give My Life": From Washington Square to Carnegie Hall, A Journey by Folk Music* (Palo Alto: Science and Behavior Books, 2008), 168.

207   **period flashed by:** Gilbert, 115.

208   **"I had to affirm":** Darling, 162.
208   **"I don't recall":** Author interview with Alan Arkin, December 2017.
208   **"I still didn't":** Darling, 251.
209   **"Another career":** Ibid., 168.
209   **"never give up":** Willens, 98.
209   **"When I talked":** Erik Darling to Lee Hays, June 12, 1962, RR, Box 2, Folder 48.
209   **"I want to believe":** Robbie Lieberman, *"My Song Is My Weapon": People's Songs, American Communism, and the Politics of Culture, 1930–1950* (Urbana: University of Illinois Press, 1989), 23.
209   **traveled into the South:** Ronald D. Cohen, *Rainbow Quest: The Folk Music Revival & American Society* (Amherst: University of Massachusetts Press, 2002), 3.
209   **"This booming voice":** Ibid., 5.
210   **formal press release:** Harold Leventhal Management, Inc., "The Weavers Announce Change in Personnel, Erik Darling Resigns and Is Replaced by Frank Hamilton," May 9, 1962, RR, Box 2, Folder 50.
210   **luncheon at Al and Dick's:** "Record Ramblings," *The Cash Box*, June 2, 1962, 21.
210   **"California!":** Cray, 387.
210   ***Billboard* cover story:** June Bundy, "Disk Dates in Clubs, Concert Hall Show Strong as LP Sellers," *Billboard Music Week*, October 30, 1961, 1.
211   **likely from the same:** "Music As Written," *The Billboard*, August 29, 1960, 22; "Record Ramblings," *The Cash Box*, September 10, 1960, 16.
211   **only Weaver that *didn't*:** Lee Hays to Harold Leventhal, May 24, 1966, RR, Box 2, Folder 37.
211   **Tokens turned the title:** Rian Malan, "In the Jungle," *Rolling Stone*, May 14, 2000, in Nick Hornby and Ben Schafer, eds., *Da Capo Best Music Writing 2001* (Cambridge: Da Capo Press, 2001), 68.
212   **"They are able to play":** *Little Sandy Review* 6, 1960, 9.
212   **Peter, Paul & Mary:** Cohen, 191.
212   **new ABC show:** Ibid., 178.
214   **"serious record player":** Gilbert, 116.
214   **"I danced, really danced":** Ronnie Gilbert to James Watt, ca. 1962, LW.
214   **She watched Fred struggle:** Ronnie Gilbert to James Watt, ca. 1963, LW.
214   **"It was very calm":** Fred Hellerman to James Watt, May 1963, FH.
215   **"The other night I walked into":** Fred Hellerman to James Watt, ca. 1964, FH.
215   **"I think I preferred":** Undated note, Ronnie Gilbert Collection, LW.
215   **"puerile":** Author interview with Bernie Krause, July 2017.
216   **"I left":** Mary Katherine Aldin, *Wasn't That a Time* (liner notes) (New York: Vanguard Records, 1993), 31.
216   **night's main act:** "Club 47 Schedule," *Broadside* (Boston), October 5, 1962, 9.

216   **made a demo:** Bernie Krause to Lee Hays, February 26, 1963, RR, Box 1, Folder 59.

217   **"That was a time":** Aldin, 32.

217   **"Pete Seeger and Erik Darling will":** "Weavers at Kresge Auditorium," *Broadside* (Boston), April 5, 1953, 3.

217   **"fussed like an old lady":** Ronnie Gilbert journal, ca. spring 1963, LW.

218   **own experience with LSD:** Darling, 209.

218   **"Walk Right In":** Ibid., 201.

219   **"horn parts":** Ibid, 212.

219   **Frank Hamilton finished out:** Harold Leventhal Management, Inc., "The Weavers Announce New Member, Bernie Krause, to Replace Frank Hamilton," May 3, 1963, RR, Box 2, Folder 50.

221   **"final Final FINAL":** Lee Hays to Weavers, ca. late 1963, Ronnie Gilbert Collection, LW.

221   **Leventhal performed calculations:** Willens, 204.

221   **"I'm doing my damnedest":** Pete Seeger, *The Incompleat Folksinger* (New York: Fireside, 1972), 306.

221   *Rainbow Quest:* Dunaway, 311.

221   **Smothers Brothers:** Ibid., 326.

Chapter Nine: This Too Shall Pass

223   **Pete Seeger probably didn't:** Elijah Wald's *Dylan Goes Electric* is a definitive treatment of this myth.

223   **California band may have even tried:** Keith Badman, *The Beach Boys: The Definitive Diary of America's Greatest Band, On Stage and in the Studio* (San Francisco: Backbeat Books, 2004), 16.

223   **"I was interested":** Author interview with Al Jardine, January 2018.

224   **"idea of people":** Mike Greenhaus, "Paul Kantner Locates Jefferson's Tree of Liberty," JamBands.com, October 25, 2008, http://www.jambands.com /features/2008/10/25/paul-kantner-locates-jefferson-s-tree-of-liberty.

224   **"Most importantly":** Nick Hasted, "Jefferson Airplane," *Uncut*, March 2014.

224   **"The Weavers are back in town":** On Jerry Garcia, *Before the Dead,* disc 1, track 2, recorded May 26, 1961 (San Rafael, CA: Round Records, 2018). Robert Hunter's version of "Oh Mary Don't You Weep" can be heard on this set, though versions of "Wasn't That a Time" and "Follow the Drinking Gourd" remain unreleased.

224   **"The Weavers songs weren't":** Author interview with Brigid Meier, May 2018.

225   **"They were a really good":** Author interview with David Crosby, December 2017.

225   **"He made it sound":** Author interview with Roger McGuinn, January 2018.

226   **When Arlo starred:** Doris Willens, *Lonesome Traveler: The Life of Lee Hays* (New York: W. W. Norton & Company, 1988), 227.

226   **taped endless interviews:** Ibid., 206.

226   *The Russians Are Coming*: Lee Hays, *A Newsletter from Lee Hays*, 1966, RR, Box 1, Folder 34.

227   **middlebrow pop-poet:** Rod McKuen to Lee Hays, December 28, 1965, RR, Box 1, Folder 68.

227   **onstage at the Newport:** Jim Rooney to Lee Hays, August 2, 1968, RR, Box 2, Folder 30.

227   **street called Memory Lane:** Willens, 219.

227   **"I remember him showing up":** Author interview with Jim Brown, November 2017.

227   **Lee often insisted:** Lee Hays to Pete Seeger, March 18, 1977, RR, Box 2, Folder 4.

228   **"Life is fairly simple":** Lee Hays to Harold Leventhal, March 14, 1973, RR, Box 1, Folder 64.

228   **"I think what is needed":** Pete Seeger to Lee Hays, October 29, 1969, RR, Box 2, Folder 3.

228   **Ronnie rolled her eyes:** Ronnie Gilbert *Ronnie Gilbert: A Radical Life in Song* (Oakland: University of California Press, 2015), 173.

228   *To Ronnie Gilbert*: Holly Near, *A Live Album* (liner notes) (Ukiah: Redwood Records, 1974).

228   **"you and Pete":** Ronnie Gilbert to Lee Hays, ca. mid-1970s, RR, Box 1, Folder 23.

229   **theater called:** Gilbert, 133.

229   **Arthur Janov's experimental:** Ibid., 161.

229   **"Music interested me":** Ibid., 173.

230   **Detroit's Trans-Love Commune:** Jeff A. Hale, "The White Panthers' 'Total Assault on the Culture'" in *Imagine Nation: The American Counterculture of the 1960s & '70s* (New York: Routledge, 2002), 143.

230   **often be seen a-sail:** David King Dunaway, *How Can I Keep from Singing? The Ballad of Pete Seeger*, updated edition (New York: Villard, 2008), 352.

230   **"It was wonderful":** Ronnie Gilbert to Lee Hays, 1979, RR, Box 1, Folder 23.

231   **"dignified silence":** Willens, 238.

231   **"I'm Lee Hays":** Ibid., 232.

231   **"suicidal almost":** Author interview with Jim Brown, November 2017.

231   **"Harold has heard":** Lee Hays to Pete Seeger, December 1, 1979, RR, Box 1, Folder 64.

232   **"good marriage":** Fred Hellerman to Lee Hays, January 24, 1980, RR, Box 2, Folder 48.

232   **"I hate to say it":** Ronnie Gilbert to Weavers, ca. early 1980, RR, Box 2, Folder 47.

232   **"I sure as hell":** Lee Hays to Pete Seeger, early 1980, RR, Box 1, Folder 64.

233   **ordered an Esperanto dictionary:** Lee Hays to Pete Seeger, early 1980, RR, Box 1, Folder 47.

233   **brought up Erik Darling:** Ronnie Gilbert to Weavers, ca. early 1980, RR, Box 2, Folder 47.

233   **"We simply couldn't":** Gilbert, 211.

234   **nearly two hours of material:** Willens, 243.

234   **"It has often been said":** Lee Hays, Carnegie Hall scripts, ca. 1980, RR, Box 3, Folder 48.

234   **"His mind was":** Author interview with Jim Brown, November 2017.

235   **public rehearsal:** Willens, 253.

235   **heated discussion:** Fred Hellerman to Harold Leventhal, May 20, 1981, RR, Box 2, Folder 49.

235   **"I might have a few":** Eleanor Blau, "Weavers to Be Reunited at Hudson River Revival," *New York Times*, June 19, 1981, C00003.

235   **Hudson River got appreciably:** Dunaway, 412.

236   **"It starts out":** Kate Weigand, "Voices of Feminism Oral History Project: Ronnie Gilbert," Sophia Smith Collection, Smith College, 2004, https://www.smith.edu/libraries/libs/ssc/vof/transcripts/Gilbert.pdf, 19.

236   **"I love that":** Ronnie Gilbert to Pete Seeger, August 9, 1998, Ronnie Gilbert Collection, LW.

236   **band bombed:** Erik Darling, *"I'd Give My Life": From Washington Square to Carnegie Hall, A Journey by Folk Music* (Palo Alto: Science and Behavior Books, 2008), 269.

237   **"It was like reaching":** Ibid., 273.

237   **"Bruce blew my cover":** Edward Halmore, "Bruce Blew My Cover," *Guardian*, February 1, 2007, https://www.theguardian.com/music/2007/feb/01/folk.features11.

237   **Ronnie had to virtually ask:** Ronnie Gilbert to Pete Seeger, January 8, 2005, Ronnie Gilbert Collection, LW.

238   **joined the Women in Black:** Ronnie Gilbert, "The FBI Knocks Again," *The Progressive*, November 2001, 59.

238   **"We Shall Overcome" returned:** Christopher Mele, "'We Shall Overcome' Is Put in Public Domain in a Copyright Settlement," *New York Times*, January 26, 2018, https://www.nytimes.com/2018/01/26/business/media/we-shall-overcome-copyright.html.

INDEX